NAZI
GERMANY

History *Examined*

NAZI
GERMANY

History *Examined*

by Robert Smith Thompson, PhD with Alan Axelrod, PhD

ALPHA

A member of Penguin Random House LLC

Publisher: Mike Sanders
Associate Publisher: Billy Fields
Development Editor: Phil Kitchel
Cover Designer: Rebecca Batchelor
Book Designer: Ayanna Lacey
Indexer: Brad Herriman
Layout: Ayanna Lacey
Proofreader: Jamie Fields

Published by Penguin Random House LLC
001-308594-February2018
Copyright © 2018 by Robert Smith Thompson

International Standard Book Number: 978-1-465-47021-8
Library of Congress Catalog Card Number: 2017948327

20 19 18   10 9 8 7 6 5 4 3 2 1

Interpretation of the printing code: The rightmost number of the first series of numbers is the year of the book's printing; the rightmost number of the second series of numbers is the number of the book's printing. For example, a printing code of 18-1 shows that the first printing occurred in 2018.

Printed in the United States of America

Note: This publication contains the opinions and ideas of its author. It is intended to provide helpful and informative material on the subject matter covered. It is sold with the understanding that the author and publisher are not engaged in rendering professional services in the book. If the reader requires personal assistance or advice, a competent professional should be consulted. The author and publisher specifically disclaim any responsibility for any liability, loss, or risk, personal or otherwise, which is incurred as a consequence, directly or indirectly, of the use and application of any of the contents of this book.

Most Alpha books are available at special quantity discounts for bulk purchases for sales promotions, premiums, fund-raising, or educational use. Special books, or book excerpts, can also be created to fit specific needs. For details, write: Special Markets, Alpha Books, 345 Hudson Street, New York, NY 10014.

Trademarks: All terms mentioned in this book that are known to be or are suspected of being trademarks or service marks have been appropriately capitalized. Alpha Books and Penguin Random House LLC cannot attest to the accuracy of this information. Use of a term in this book should not be regarded as affecting the validity of any trademark or service mark.

Reprinted from *The Complete Idiot's Guide to Nazi Germany*

Again, as always and forever, to Judy.

Contents

APPENDIXES

Introduction

What happens when an educated and cultured people, famed not only for their industrial prowess and military might but also their traditions in philosophy, science, and the arts, put aside their critical faculties to follow what the English essayist and novelist George Orwell called the tom-tom beat of modern tribalism? What happens when such a people abandon the ordinary politics of barter and compromise for the extraordinary politics of faith, hope, and hatred? What happens when, instead of facing problems rationally and working out reasonable and moral solutions, such a people become seduced by visions of a utopia with no problems at all and solutions based on the extermination of their enemies, actual or perceived? And what happens when, poisoned by the prejudices of the past and the propaganda of the present, such a people turn to warfare and mass murder? In 1923-1945, Nazi Germany happened.

This isn't to say that all Germans of the era became Nazis. From the very moment of Hitler's illegal seizure of power in 1933, some—but never the majority—raised their voices in protest. Most of those who did protest ended up in flight and exile, were imprisoned, or were killed. Those who took flight, such as the physicist Albert Einstein, the novelist Thomas Mann, and the symphonic conductor Erich Leinsdorf, often found refuge in the United States, which became a haven for many "ordinary" German refugees as well. Among those who remained in Germany, a significant minority resisted the Nazi regime by covert anti-Hitler activism. Others, doubtless, silently withheld their own hearts and minds from the regime.

The hard truth, however, is that the majority of Germans heartily approved of and supported the Nazis. Although many of his provocative and even inflammatory conclusions have been called into question by some historians, Daniel Goldhagen, in *Hitler's Willing Executioners* (1996), presented chilling evidence that the vast majority of the German people did not merely tolerate, but applauded, the mass murder of Jews known as the Holocaust.

So we come to the question of this book: Why were the Germans, apparently as civilized as any people on earth, consumed by a movement of mayhem, murder, and military aggression?

There's no single answer to this question. But *Nazi Germany: History Explained* provides the historical perspective that allows readers to find their own answers. For what history reveals is that, in key ways, Germany was unlike other European countries. Except for Russia, it had a bigger population than any other European country, and no other country on the continent could match its industrial base and capacity for wealth and power.

Yet, compared to England, France, and Spain, Germany was a Johnny-come-lately as a unified nation. Until the middle of the nineteenth century, Germany did not even exist as a state. Once it came into that existence, its leaders, beginning with the brilliant Otto von Bismarck, began to demand a place in the sun. The tragedy that befell all who lived in Germany was that most of the German people eventually succumbed to the delusion that they could find that glorious place by following Adolf Hitler.

How to Use This Book

For your ease of use, this book is organized into five different parts, plus three appendixes:

Part 1, The German Colossus, traces out the rise of Germany under Bismarck and its defeat in the First World War under Kaiser Wilhelm II.

Part 2, The Ascendancy of Evil, takes us through Hitler's rise to power in 1933.

Part 3, The Nazi State, shows how Hitler consolidated his power at home and started on his course of aggression abroad.

Part 4, The Rising Tide, goes from Hitler's first conquests to the turning point at Stalingrad.

Part 5, The Decline and Fall of Nazi Germany, portrays Germany's defeat and Hitler's death.

Additional Features

You'll notice notes that I've inserted in the margins and throughout the pages of this book. These extras take the following forms:

MEMORABLE PLACES

Germany was full of beautiful cities and famous locales. As you encounter them, you'll see that they formed the stage-setting of the drama that was the story of the Third Reich.

TERMS AND TRANSLATIONS

These bits of text define terms or provide translations to explain German words you might not be familiar with.

SUPPORTING ACTORS

If Hitler was the greatest villain in the drama of the Third Reich, he did not lack for an eager supporting cast. You'll meet them—Himmler, Goebbels, and others.

MODERN DAY PARALLELS

Was the phenomenon of Nazi Germany completely different from anything that exists in the world today? No. And this feature points out the parallels.

BET YOU DIDN'T KNOW

You're probably familiar, at least generally, with the story of Nazi Germany. Still, its history included a great many unfamiliar details, most relating to the economic and political background of the rise and fall of the Nazi state.

Acknowledgments

The staff at the reference desk of the Thomas Cooper Library at the University of South Carolina has been kind, patient, and most helpful. So have two colleagues, Richard Mandell and Robert Herzstein, both experts on Nazi Germany; their assistance has been far greater than they realize. My thanks above all, for her kind and ever-patient help with the author's computer problems, as well as her support, to Polly Thompson.

Trademarks

All terms mentioned in this book that are known to be or are suspected of being trademarks or service marks have been appropriately capitalized. Alpha Books and Penguin Random House cannot attest to the accuracy of this information. Use of a term in this book should not be regarded as affecting the validity of any trademark or service mark.

PART 1

The German Colossus

After World War I, many people (and not just Germans) believed that Germany had been victimized by the punitive terms of the Treaty of Versailles. Others, however, believed that the Germans had gotten precisely what they deserved. After all, didn't they start the war?

Well, not exactly, and certainly not alone. Yet it was true that Germany had developed into a colossus astride the continent of Europe. It was also true that Kaiser Wilhelm II ordered his forces into what he believed was a preemptive war. His objective was to hit Germany's enemies before they hit Germany. Did this make his nation the sole aggressor in 1914?

The chapters in this part present the facts and let you be the judge. In light of your verdict, you will also have the materials to assess whether the Treaty of Versailles, the peace settlement of 1919, was or was not fair to a defeated Germany.

The Making of the German Empire: 1815–1871

On April 30, 1945, Adolf Hitler, the *Führer* (leader, guide) of Nazi Germany, climbed the stairs to the top of his ferroconcrete bunker dug into the center of Berlin. With him was Eva Braun, who had been his mistress and only days before became his wife. As they stepped into the sunlight, they heard the detonation of Red Army artillery shells all around them. Overhead was the drone of Soviet bombers. Around them as far as they could see, the once-magnificent buildings of the German capital were smoldering ruins. The German armies, bled out, were no longer sufficient to turn back the invaders. The fall of Berlin was inevitable, only hours away. Before the day ended, Hitler and Eva Braun would be dead, a double suicide.

The Nazi radio network was still functioning, barely, and it reported that the *Führer* had died heroically on the field of battle. With that news, Germany's resistance to the Allies—primarily Russia, Great Britain, and the United States—collapsed altogether. After 12 years, Nazi Germany (the Third Reich that Hitler had boasted would last a thousand years) came to an end. The greatest horror of modern times had passed into history.

But why had that horror arisen? What were its roots? Its origins?

After World War I, Nazism and political movements like it had great appeal in Spain, France, Italy, and several of the countries of Eastern Europe. But it reached its most virulent form in Germany. Why?

Nazi Germany was more than the creation of the warped political genius of Adolf Hitler. To understand how it came to be, we have to go far back in German history. For what we call Germany was never a typical European nation. Its unique evolution helps explain the rise of the Nazi regime.

The Land

Germany lies in the center of Europe. When the country was in its military prime, from the middle of the nineteenth century to the end of World War II, its location was a source of strategic strength. But before that, it was a source of weakness, because Germany had no well-defined natural boundaries. The British became identified with a large island, the Italians with a peninsula, and the French with sharp seacoast boundaries. But from the Middle Ages onward, German borders expanded and contracted like an accordion, depending on wars, treaties, and royal marriages. Unlike the British and the French, the Germans had little sense of *national identity*. Split up by mountain ranges, valleys, plateaus, ridges, lakes, and rivers, what we today call Germany was comprised of hundreds of kingdoms, duchies, principalities, bishoprics, archbishoprics, and free cities even in the late eighteenth century.

TERMS AND TRANSLATIONS

Whatever our ethnic origins, we Americans share a **national identity.** Most of us speak the same language and share a common history, and we know that if born or naturalized within the 50 states we are legally Americans. But suppose our regional dialects—the way people speak in Maine versus South Carolina versus Oregon, etc.—were so different that we could not understand each other. What if people in Michigan and Texas knew nothing of the American Revolution? And imagine, as once was the case, that Florida was still Spanish, Louisiana and most of the land up the Mississippi and the Missouri Rivers was French, and California was Mexican. Could we then say that we were all Americans—as opposed to New Yorkers, Virginians, or Hawaiians? Old Germany was something like this.

The Culture

Still, the German-speaking peoples were unsurpassed in poetry, drama, music, and philosophy. In the late eighteenth and early nineteenth centuries, the Germans reveled in the age of the *Aufklärung*, the Enlightenment.

TERMS AND TRANSLATIONS

Believe it or not, German is not a difficult language. It has long words, but so does English. So let's take a look at the word **Aufklärung.** The first part is *Auf*, like the English *up*. The second part, *klärung*, is the same as *clearing*. Take a look. *Klär* is pronounced like the name Clare and means "clear." The *ung* in German is *ing* in English. So Aufklärung means "clearing up"—or "enlightenment."

The greatest writers of the German Enlightenment—Gotthold Lessing, Friedrich von Schiller, and Johann Wolfgang von Goethe—advocated the liberation of the human spirit. At least one carried the idea to an extreme. The Lutheran theologian J. G. Herder wrote of a German *Volksgeist,* or spirit of the people. He believed that the various peoples of Europe should develop their own spirit in their own ways. He did *not* espouse the idea of the superiority of the Germans over other peoples, but he did voice the notion of *nationalism* and in particular German nationalism: the right to be free of oppression.

Were the Germans an oppressed people? Some came to think they were. The years 1789 to 1815 saw the French under Napoleon Bonaparte coming to reign supreme over them.

TERMS AND TRANSLATIONS

Let's break down the word **Volksgeist.** In German, the letter *v* is pronounced *f.* So *Volks* means "folk." Ghost and *geist* are cognate words. You've heard of a poltergeist? It's a kind of ghost. And a ghost is a spirit. So Volksgeist means "spirit of the people." **Nationalism** means more than national identity. Nationalism suggests that a nation—a people with a common past, a common heritage, and a common sense of being oppressed—has a common right to be freed from that oppression. The American Revolutionary War was an example of nationalism in action.

The Birth of German Nationalism Under Napoleon's Oppression

We all know of Napoleon—Napoleon I, Emperor of the French, King of Italy, and Protector of the Confederation of the Rhine—who conquered nearly all of Europe. Napoleon's impact on conquered peoples reshaped institutions. This was true of the Poles, the Dutch, the Italians, and especially the Germans. In the German-speaking regions to the east of France, Napoleonic conquest introduced a common legal code and the beginnings of political unity.

An example was the Duchy of Württemberg in southern Germany. Take a look at the following two maps. In 1800, the duchy possessed islands of territory well separated from its main mass. Only 50 miles wide, Württemberg was surrounded by a mosaic of tiny, independent political units ruled, nominally, by something called the Holy Roman Empire (which some wit once said was neither holy nor Roman nor an empire). But in 1810, after Napoleon had overrun central Europe, what was now the Kingdom of Württemberg was consolidated and enlarged, sticking down across the Danube, touching the border of Switzerland, and in the west extending almost to the Rhine. Similar consolidations under Napoleon all over Germany reduced the number of states to about 40 and added to the efficiency of law and government.

BET YOU DIDN'T KNOW

Napoleon defeated Prussia in the field of battle, a loss Prussia resented, and yet well-to-do Germans adored French culture.

Rise of Nationalism

If Napoleon got thanks from some, he got resistance from others. Across Europe, nationalism (the longing for freedom from French oppression) became the big idea.

Nowhere was the idea bigger than in Germany. After 1800, nationalism there was directed not only against Napoleon and the French, but also against the Frenchified upper classes. Nationalism in Germany was felt most acutely by the middle and lower classes; Hitler later would pitch his appeals to the descendants of these same elements. German nationalism, as it arose in the time of Napoleon, set the stage for Hitler.

A pastor named Friedrich Ludwig Jahn (1778–1852) put together a youth movement in which young men engaged in physical exercise for the Fatherland. He led them on long hikes in the countryside and staged rallies in which they screamed denunciations of German-speaking, pro-French aristocrats. In fact, he taught them to be suspicious of foreigners, Jews, and others who would supposedly corrupt the purity of the German *Volk* (folk).

The organization was a forerunner of the *Hitlerjugend,* or Hitler Youth. But the Hitler Youth organization was a long-term effect of the German revolt against the French. In the short term, the major effect was the political transformation of Prussia and its rulers, the Hohenzollerns. An ancient, German-speaking family, the Zollerns boasted an ancestral home in a castle on the Danube. During the Middle Ages they migrated northward, and they added "Hohen"—high—to their name, establishing themselves as rulers of Prussia.

Map of Europe in 1815.

Kingdom of Prussia

By the time of Napoleon, Prussia was the biggest kingdom in northeastern Germany. It spread out along the Baltic roughly from Berlin, its capital, in the west, to Lithuania in the east. Prussia was an agricultural land, ruled by the Hohenzollerns and their aristocratic allies. The king and his nobles were a rigid caste, authoritarian in view, despising the merchant classes of western Germany, keeping their peasants in a state of serfdom, and worshipping all things military.

There was only one catch. Prussia had lost to Napoleon during the Napoleon Wars. So how was the kingdom to strengthen itself enough to get revenge against the French? During the late eighteenth and early nineteenth centuries, one Prussian statesman came up with an answer. Give the people a stake in preserving Prussia. Heinrich Friedrich Karl vom und zum Stein, called Baron vom Stein, liberated the peasants from serfdom and introduced reforms that permitted Prussia's small merchant class to buy land and to serve as army officers. Many of the merchants were bankers, and thus Prussia's financiers began funding Prussia's rulers, a pattern to be repeated when Hitler rose to power.

Militarily, however, Prussia remained weak. Victory over France came about only when Napoleon retreated from his ill-conceived invasion of Russia in 1812 and Prussia joined a coalition of other European nations. Still, the peace settlement produced at Vienna in 1814 and 1815 left the German territories almost as divided as ever.

BET YOU DIDN'T KNOW

Did you know that the last of the Zollerns was still ruling during the first four decades of the twentieth century, and then died in exile in Holland in 1941? The ruler was Kaiser Wilhelm II.

The Congress of Vienna

In October 1814, Prince Klement von Metternich, the foreign minister of Austria, Tsar Alexander I of Russia, Lord Castlereagh, the foreign secretary of Great Britain, Charles Talleyrand, the French foreign minister, and Prince Karl August von Hardenberg, the chancellor of Prussia, gathered in Vienna to redraw the map of Europe. They shared an all-important conviction: Nothing like the Napoleonic wars should ever be allowed to happen again.

To achieve an enduring *balance of power,* the Congress redistributed the territory of Europe. Great Britain, with the mightiest fleet in the world, needed no land on the continent, although Lord Castlereagh reserved the right to intervene militarily if another power upset the balance. France had to withdraw from Holland, the Rhineland, and Belgium to within its prerevolutionary borders; Russia expanded into Poland; Austria got control of Lombardy and Venetia, the two provinces of northern Italy; and Prussia got the right to rule a patch of western Germany that bordered on Luxembourg, Belgium, and Holland.

To prevent militaristic Prussia from ever gaining too much territory, the Congress created the *German Confederation* between Prussia proper and its new western acquisition.

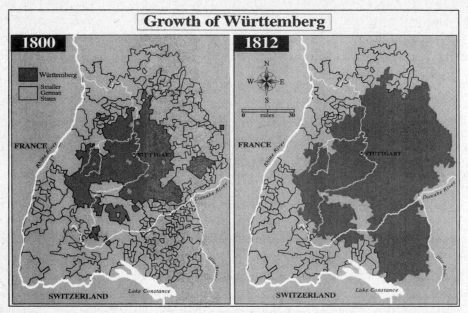

The Congress of Vienna.

TERMS AND TRANSLATIONS

Absolutism is the idea that the monarch (or his equivalent, such as Stalin or Hitler) rules with an iron fist, tolerating no opposition and regarding himself as above the law. So the ruler's authority is absolute. But a warning: If you aspire to be such a dictator, you had better be good at it. Any display of weakness invites your enemies to try to overthrow you. This almost happened to Hitler.

The German Confederation

The membership of the German Confederation included the kingdoms of Bavaria, Saxony, Württemberg, and Hanover, and numerous grand duchies, duchies, an electorate, four "free cities" (Lübeck, Bremen, Hamburg, and Frankfurt-am-Main), and numerous smaller principalities. No member of the confederation could declare war on any other member—and no member could form an alliance with a foreign country that would hurt any other member. The Confederation was forbidden to create its own army.

The limitations imposed on the Confederation made the nationalist dream of a united German nation seem impossible. The fragmented Germanies after 1815 were economically backward. Three quarters of the people lived in villages or small towns, most roads were paths through forests, and there were no modern factories.

TERMS AND TRANSLATIONS

The idea of **balance of power** is this: If all the European great powers—Britain, France, Austria, Russia, and Prussia—were equal in military strength, then no one could get away with Napoleon-style aggression. What made up military strength? Largely, the number of soldiers. So a great power's population base and its territorial extent were important.

Economic and Social Change, 1815–1848

Today's Germany is renowned for its industrial prowess. Yet in the two decades or so after the end of the Napoleonic wars, Germany was the least advanced of all the big European countries (except Russia). Nevertheless, ambitious German investors began to copy Great Britain's manufacturing cornucopia. In 1835, the first German railroad was laid between Nürnberg and Fürth. By 1860, more than 6,600 miles of rail had been put down, and locomotive factories were constructed in Essen, steel plants in Solingen, and textile sheds in Silesia. In 1850, the Germanies produced only 208,000 tons of iron; by 1860, the output had risen to 1,391,555 tons. Using mechanized equipment, German farmers increased their food output. The German postal system became the most efficient in the world.

MEMORABLE PLACES

Having been built and added to over many centuries, the palace was full of contrasts. A dark fifteenth-century courtyard opened through an archway into a wide expanse of wall. Inside the huge windows, the chambers were done in gilt and white paneling and hung with glittering chandeliers. At green baize–covered tables under those chandeliers, the statesmen of Europe decided their continent's future.

These remarkable economic developments were accompanied by shifts in the German social order. In line with medieval practice, the various monarchies and dukedoms of the German Confederation had excluded the middle classes from any role in public life. The newly rich business families, however, saw no reason why they should not share in political decisions. They would soon make their voices heard.

The Zollverein (Customs Unions)

Another innovation was also underway. The divisions among the Germanies of the confederation presented barriers to further economic growth. Trade in the region was impeded by a bewildering variety of water, inland, and provincial tolls. Gradually, between 1818 and 1834, merchants and manufacturers in the various Germanies consulted, demanded, and finally got a customs union called the *Zollverein*.

The idea of a Zollverein was to provide freedom from internal tariffs. Only with a free market inside, List held, could the Germanies become as efficient and productive as possible. Announced on January 1, 1834, the Zollverein included 18 German states and a population of more than 23 million people, all under Prussian leadership. Economically speaking, the Germanies at last were on the way to becoming a united Germany.

But what kind of Germany? The Revolution of 1848 provided a tragic answer to that question.

TERMS AND TRANSLATIONS

Zollverein is easy to translate as well. The German *Zoll* (pronounced *tsoll*) is the English "toll," what you pay when you drive across many of our bridges. The German prefix *ver* often conveys the sense of bringing something about, or moving toward something. *Ein* means "one" or "un," as in "unity." So the Zollverein was a customs union, meaning an agreement among the various entities of the German Confederation to move toward the elimination of duties, tariffs, and quotas on goods that crossed their mutual borders. The European Community today is, among other things, a customs union or a Zollverein.

The Revolution of 1848

For the aristocratic classes all over Europe, the year 1848 was a nightmare. Popular revolutions against Europe's autocrats spread from Copenhagen to Palermo and from Paris to Budapest, lasting from the early spring to late in the summertime. But the revolutionaries in various countries had little contact with each other and, poorly armed, were soon defeated, including the Revolution of 1848 in the Germanies.

As the tide of revolution receded, liberalism was submerged in the stronger sentiment of nationalism. Throughout the Germanies people were left with a legacy of Prussian discipline, efficiency, and authoritarianism. The revolutionaries of 1848 had hoped that German unity could lead to freedom. But after 1848, the prevailing view was that unity could come only through force. As the political liberalism of 1848 faded away, the idea of German unification through *Eisen und Blut* (iron and blood) became the prevailing doctrine.

So, by the early 1860s, the Germanies were ready for the advent of the political and diplomatic genius who would forge just such a unification. He was Otto von Bismarck.

The Rise of Bismarck

Of all the European great powers, Prussia had always been the smallest and weakest. Although the Congress of Vienna had allowed Prussia to expand westward, leaders in Berlin after the Revolution of 1848 were frightened. The state had survived the uprisings, but who knew what lay ahead? Then, in the middle of the 1850s, the British and French on the one side and the Russians on the other had gone to war (the Crimean War) over Russia's desire to expand into the Mediterranean. Britain and France had won, without bothering to seek Prussian help. And by 1861, Italy had unified, driving the Austrians from most of the area north of the peninsula, without any Prussian input. High-ranking Prussians saw their country becoming irrelevant in European affairs.

The Prussian king, Wilhelm I, believed that he had to double the size of his army and wanted a new *Diet,* or parliament, to fork over the money. The Prussian Diet was dominated by men of great wealth. Unfortunately for the king, the wealthiest men in his domains were the new capitalists from along the Rhineland. They all professed patriotism, naturally, but they also despised standing armies and all the militarist traditions of the Prussian *Junkers* (the land-owning class), from whom the officer corps was almost entirely recruited and whom they despised as antiquated agriculturalists. So the Diet refused to put up the money to increase military numbers.

Desperate to strengthen the military, the king cast about for help. The person he turned to was Otto von Bismarck. Born in 1815, Bismarck was a tall, bulky man of aristocratic Junker background but with a reputation for utter rebelliousness. As a youth, he had been a playboy, an indifferent student, a classic devotee of wine, women, and song—and of duels (supposedly 25 in all). A wastrel, who had indifferently occupied minor governmental posts, he had abandoned one position to run off to Switzerland in the hopes of marrying a young woman who rejected him. He then returned, bankrupt, to his ancestral manor house in East Prussia; there he had made a pretense of being a stolid, unimaginative, dull Junker landlord.

As a manager of his estates, he had been an utter failure. Yet he was an aristocrat, so he came to the attention of the king. Bismarck was no German nationalist and he did not look upon Germany as the Fatherland. He was a Prussian who regarded the members of the Diet as unwelcome free-thinkers and liberals. When the king chose him as chancellor in 1862, he had but one goal: buttressing the might of Prussia. And if Prussia became strengthened at the expense of the liberals, too bad for them.

By Blood and Iron

So, Bismarck did have a principle: Prussian supremacy. But no other principle bound him for long; he accepted no formal ideology or any conventional morality. Once in high office, he became the classic practitioner of *Realpolitik.*

TERMS AND TRANSLATIONS

When the Spanish conquered the New World, they used the word *real* to mean the wishes of the king. In time, the French picked up the word, and then the Germans under Bismarck. Because the king was supposed to be above the law, **Realpolitik,** the German version of the term, meant a foreign policy uninhibited by considerations of morality, religion, or ethics, but rather one based on what the king—or his first minister—considered to be the Prussian national interest.

For Bismarck, the only thing that mattered was Prussia's national interest, at least as he saw it. Nothing else made any difference. The king would fear him, the Junkers would consider him a traitor to his class, and the liberals of the West would think him their friend, only to later consider him their enemy. To Bismarck, enemies and friends were about the same: The friend of today might be the opponent of tomorrow. He loathed making long-range plans. Instead, he was practical and opportunistic. When he saw his opportunities, he took them.

When Bismarck became chancellor in 1862, he set out to get the capitalists in the Diet to appropriate money to enhance the army. The struggle went on for four years. The members of the body simply refused to raise taxes. But under Bismarck, government officials collected the revenues anyway. He did not care what the Diet thought. The people of Prussia were docile, respectful of uniforms, and readily intimidated. Military needs won out over any doctrine of government by consent.

There was another reason people paid up: Nationalism was strong enough to lead them to believe that a reorganized, retrained, and re-equipped army was the key to the unification of Germany.

Members of the Diet argued that Bismarck's tax policy was unconstitutional. The constitution, he replied, was hardly intended to weaken the state. Bismarck was undermining freedom, and the liberals fought back. What Germans admired in Prussia, Bismarck retorted coldly, was its power.

Bismarck went even further. The borders of Prussia, he declared, as established by the Congress of Vienna in 1815, had to be changed; Prussia must be ready and willing to seize any and all chances for expansion. To this, he added his most memorable utterance: "Not by speeches and majority votes are the great questions of the day decided—that was the great error of 1848—but by blood and iron!"

Something Is Rotten in the State of Denmark

One of Bismarck's opportunities arose in 1867, only a year after his victory over the parliamentarians. The northernmost provinces of the German Federation were Holstein and, just south of Denmark, Schleswig. The population of Schleswig was about half German and half Danish. Like Bismarck, the king of Denmark wanted to expand, so he set his sights on the acquisition of Schleswig. Germans of all stripes could agree on one thing: Denmark was not going to have Schleswig. So, the legislative body of the German Confederation called for an all-German war against Denmark.

Did Bismarck, the man of "iron and blood," go along with this? Absolutely not! He didn't want the confederation strengthened, and he did not want German unity unless Prussia was the unifier. At the same time, he didn't want to frighten the Germans outside of Prussia into forming an alliance against him. He formed his own alliance with Austria.

TERMS AND TRANSLATIONS

An **alliance** is a formal pact between nations in a common cause. Are alliances enduring? The answer to this depends on what the partners want.

In 1864, Prussia and Austria allied in war against Denmark and easily won. Schleswig was now safe from Danish control, but Bismarck wanted more. He wanted to annex both Schleswig and Holstein to Prussia. He chose to act by stealth. He persuaded the Austrians to agree to a Prussian occupation of Schleswig while they, the Austrians, marched into Holstein. The Austrians thought it was a fair deal. We come back, though, to the old business of tariffs and other rights of transit. Despite the *Zollverein*, Bismarck made it difficult for farmers in Holstein to sell their goods across the border in Schleswig. This began a dispute that would soon provide him with a pretext for another war, this one against Austria.

In the meantime, Bismarck worked to isolate Austria diplomatically. Adhering to a policy of "splendid isolation," the British deliberately stayed out of continental conflicts. In 1863, Bismarck had taken care to join Russia in suppressing a Polish rebellion, so St. Petersburg was well disposed toward Prussia and Bismarck. Italy had just become unified, driving the Austrians out of Lombardy; to win over the new Italian king, Bismarck held out the lure of Venetia, the Austrian-held province around Venice.

What about France? France had a new emperor, Napoleon III, nephew of Napoleon I. Having committed himself to trying (unsuccessfully) to create an empire in Mexico, he was not paying much attention to what was going on in the Rhineland. Besides, Bismarck met with Napoleon III at Biarritz, a popular resort on the southwestern coast of France. Usually gruff and forbidding, Bismarck was charm itself. In his meeting with the French monarch, Bismarck hinted vaguely that he would allow France to expand somewhere. He did not specify just where. But the tactic worked; Napoleon III agreed to condone a Prussian war against Austria.

Bismarck was still not finished. He wanted widespread German support against Austria, so he presented himself as a democrat. He said that he was all for reform in the German Confederation: It could have a real legislature elected by universal male suffrage. He figured that most Germans were not supporters of either the capitalists or the various governmental entities of the confederation. Like Hitler later, Bismarck used mass support to undermine all established interests that stood in his way. He was now ready for his war with Austria.

Bismarck Coaxes Austria into War

Bismarck had made sure that Prussia and Austria would keep on squabbling over transit rights between Schleswig and Holstsein. Things got so bad that Austria went before the German Confederation to ask for help. Convinced of the justice of the Austrian cause, the ambassadors to the confederation demanded that Bismarck end the border disputes. Rather than give way, Bismarck sneered at the confederation as having no authority, accused Austria of aggression, and ordered Prussian troops to march into Holstein, which had earlier been occupied by Austria. Austria in turn declared war on Prussia and persuaded the confederation to send an all-German force against Prussia. So, now, in 1866, Bismarck was at war not only with Austria but also with most of the other German states along the Rhine.

His enemies didn't have a chance. The Prussian army was the best-trained in Europe. Its troops were also equipped with the new needle-gun, a modern breach-loading rifle with which infantrymen could fire off an impressive five rounds per minute. Commanded by the brilliant General Helmuth von Moltke, the Prussian troops rode off to battle most of the way aboard trains that by the mid-1860s steamed along the most sophisticated railroad network in Europe.

The opposition was no match for Prussia's troops. The decisive battle took place at a town called Königsgrätz near Prague. The Austrian defeat was humiliating, and Moltke soon defeated the other German states, picking them off one by one.

The Austro–Prussian War lasted just seven weeks. Bismarck brought it to a triumphant close before the other European great powers even realized what had happened.

Bismarck Forms the North German Confederation

Bismarck annexed both Schleswig and Holstein, along with Hanover (a big state just south of Holstein), the Duchies of Nassau and Hesse-Cassel, and the free city of Frankfurt. These acquisitions joined Prussia proper with the western territories gained at the Congress of Vienna. In those captured territories, old governments simply disappeared.

So did the German Confederation. In its place, Bismarck created a North German Confederation in 1867. It included the newly expanded Prussia and 21 other German states.

South of the Main River, in the middle of Germany, Bavaria, Baden, Württemberg, Hesse-Darmstadt, and Austria were outside Bismarck's new group, with no kind of union among themselves. Italy had taken advantage of Austria's defeat to take over Venetia, just as Bismarck had promised it could do.

Bismarck next busied himself with organizing the North German Confederation. He made it much stronger than the older German Confederation. The Prussian king became its hereditary monarch. Bismarck set up a parliament with two chambers. In the upper house, as in the United States, the states were represented. Members of the lower house, again as in the United States, were elected by universal male suffrage.

Recall that Bismarck had made the Prussian king monarch of the new confederation. However, Wilhelm I was weak. So, while the constitution made the ministers of the various states responsible to him, in practice they reported to Bismarck. He was, in effect, a dictator, backed by secret police and the potent Prussian army.

Why did Bismarck implement the parliament (a democratic style of government)? Because he wanted allies against the wealthy industrialists whose factories lined the banks of the Rhine and its tributaries. What allies? The socialists and the labor unions, which had arisen in protest during the 1850s and 1860s against the excesses of the capitalists.

The socialist leader in Germany at this time was Ferdinand Lassalle. Unlike Karl Marx, the architect of communism, Lassalle believed it possible to improve the conditions of the working class through the existing political system rather than by overthrowing it. So, Bismarck, the archconservative from East Prussia, formed an alliance with Lassalle. In so doing, Bismarck linked nationalism and socialism to support his empire. This concept of "national socialism," developed by Bismarck, became ingrained in German thinking and would surface years later under Hitler.

SUPPORTING ACTORS

We usually associate "socialism" with Karl Marx. Ironically, however, the heart of his doctrine—that a revolution by the workers in the industrialized countries was inevitable—has never come true. The major socialist or communist revolutions have taken place in Russia and China, two countries that until well into the twentieth century were agricultural lands. Marx underestimated the power, wealth, and simple survivability of the capitalist classes in Western and Central Europe. But the socialism of Lassalle was not revolutionary: It called for the use of *political* power.

The French Are Next to Fall

The situation on both sides of the Rhine was unstable. The remaining states in southern Germany were adrift and, sooner or later, would likely be caught up in a larger orbit—Austrian, Prussian, or French. France, however, was having troubles. Napoleon III's intervention in Mexico was a fiasco; a united Italy was rising on France's southeastern frontier. And in violation of the cardinal principle of French foreign policy for centuries—the disunion of Germany—most of the German people were now citizens of a single and powerful state.

In Paris, the administration of Napoleon III began to mutter of war against the east. If only France could seize the moment and defeat Germany, the debacle in Mexico would be forgotten! Italy would no longer be a factor! And the old divisions of Germany could be restored.

In Berlin, Bismarck heard the war rumors. He must have been pleased. At a minimum, he could use them to frighten the southern German states into an alignment with Prussia and the North German Confederation.

Luck played into Bismarck's hands. A revolution in Spain brought to power a provisional government in Madrid that invited Prince Leopold of Hohenzollern, a cousin of Prussia's Wilhelm I, to be Spain's constitutional monarch. As it turned out, Prince Leopold had no interest in going to Spain and three times refused the offer. Enter Bismarck: He persuaded the Spanish to try again, and on July 2, 1870, news of Leopold's acceptance reached Paris. Outraged, Paris instructed Vincente Benedetti, its ambassador to Prussia, to protest. Benedetti met Wilhelm I at the spa of Ems, officially demanding that the acceptance be withdrawn. The king complied, and on July 12, Leopold stated definitively that he would not be the Spanish king. This disappointed Bismarck. But then the French government cabled Benedetti to see the Prussian king again at Ems and to demand that never again should a Hohenzollern be named king of Spain. Refusing to make that commitment, Wilhelm I wired a report of the conversation to Bismarck in Berlin. Bismarck saw another opportunity. He doctored the Ems telegram so that when it was published, Prussian readers would think their king had been insulted and the French would think their ambassador had been treated rudely.

Bismarck's editing produced the results he wanted. In both France and Prussia, people demanded war. The issue of the Spanish throne had already been settled. However, on July 19, 1870, the government of Napoleon III made the fatal mistake of declaring war on Prussia.

Bismarck had done the work to isolate France. The British frowned upon Napoleon's adventure in Mexico. Italy had not yet taken Rome, because French troops were there; but with the outbreak of war between France and Prussia, Paris withdrew those troops and the Italians waltzed right into the Eternal City. The Russians also had no love for France: According to the peace treaty of 1856, which ended the Crimean War, Russia had been forbidden to keep naval ships on the Black Sea. With Prussia and France on the brink of war, Russia gleefully broke the treaty.

BET YOU DIDN'T KNOW

You might have the idea that countries disregard treaties at will. Usually they don't, or if they do, there are good reasons. In tearing up the 1856 treaty, Russia took advantage of France's weakness. However, as you'll soon learn, Russia later entered into a treaty *with* France. There's an old expression: The enemy of my enemy is my friend. After Bismarck's invasion of France, who do you think Paris and St. Petersburg saw as their enemy? Germany, of course.

Without allies, France didn't have a chance. What's more, the French were not as militarily and economically advanced as Prussia. The Franco–Prussian War began on July 19, 1870. Prussia now had the support of the southern German states (with the exception of Austria). Crossing Luxembourg, Bismarck's army simply crashed into France. As the troops marched in their spiked helmets, "Prussian blue" uniforms, and jackboots across the pleasant countryside of northeastern France, huge columns of dust rose against the late summer sky. Moving as fast as they could, thousands of French peasants and refugees clogged the roadways; their numbers were more effective than the French army in slowing the German advance.

Then came the Battle of Sedan in a frontier fortress town. When the principal French general was seriously wounded and had to be evacuated, Napoleon III himself showed up on the scene. The Germans captured Napoleon III and made him a prisoner. Later they released him and, along with the Empress Eugénie, he hightailed it to England.

But Bismarck wasn't finished. He ordered General von Moltke to proceed into Paris. For four months in the winter of 1870 to 1871, the Germans besieged the French capital. Paris did not surrender, but people in the city were reduced to eating rats and sparrows.

At the palace of Versailles, outside Paris, on January 18, 1871, Bismarck proclaimed the creation of the German Empire, the Second *Reich*. He also staged a ceremony whereby his king, Wilhelm I, received the hereditary title of Emperor of Germany. The rulers of the lesser German states (except, of course, Austria) accepted Wilhelm's imperial authority.

Ten days later, the people of Paris, shivering and starving, at last opened the gates to the Teutonic troops. Entering the city, Bismarck imposed harsh terms of peace. France had to pay Germany an indemnity of five billion gold francs, an enormous sum and without precedent in European history. They also had to forfeit most of two provinces along their eastern border, Alsace and Lorraine.

The Alsatians spoke German, but they considered themselves to be French, and they protested vigorously over being moved around like cattle. They protested in vain. In Frankfurt on May 10, 1871, Bismarck dictated the peace treaty. Alsace and Lorraine were now part of the German Empire—an amputation that the French were not about to forget.

TERMS AND TRANSLATIONS

The German word **reich** is a cognate of the English *rich*. An empire is supposed to be rich, so the Germans called their empire a Reich. The First Reich was buried in the mystical mists of medieval history. Bismarck's was the Second Reich. Hitler's was the Third Reich.

Germany Unites at Last

The consolidation of Germany (except for Austria) under Bismarck changed the face of Europe, creating a geographical, political, and economic German colossus astride the center of Europe. The new empire was by far the strongest state on the continent and, industrializing rapidly after 1871, it became even stronger.

In bringing the German Empire into existence, Bismarck outfoxed many, including the Germans themselves. He allowed each of the German states to keep its own laws, government, and constitution. On paper, the German Empire looked like a federation, but Bismarck's new Germany was based on the coupling of authoritarianism with nationalism and socialism.

Otto von Bismarck died in 1898, when Adolf Hitler was a glum nine-year-old boy. Many in Europe believed Bismarck's masterful diplomatic manipulations brought stability to Europe. Indeed, Western Europe was generally peaceful for the forty-three years separating the Franc-Prussian War from World War I. Beneath the stability and the rationality of the "Iron Chancellor's" German-dominated Europe, however, were the institutions, the culture, and the sentiments Bismarck had fostered and Adolf Hitler would exploit to the fullest.

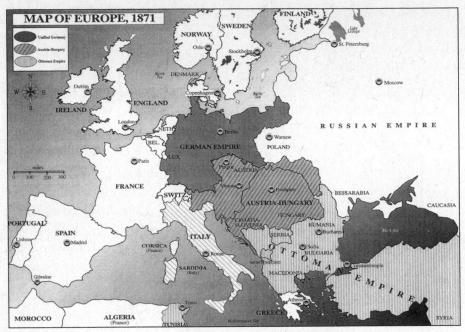

Map of Europe, 1871.

The Least You Need to Know

- As late as the mid-nineteenth century, what we call Germany was not even a country at all.

- Although revolutionaries had hoped the unification of Germany would result in freedom, German nationalism continued to be marked by stressed authority and military power.

- After Napoleon, Bismarck was the great political genius of the nineteenth century.

- Blood, iron, and superb diplomatic skills where the tools Bismarck used to bring about the unification of the German Empire.

- The methods by which Bismarck expanded Prussia into that German Empire laid the groundwork for Hitler's Third Reich: an authoritarian state supported by the ideas of nationalism and socialism.

Wilhelm's Germany: 1871–1914

Bismarck has been called a "white revolutionary"—as opposed to a "red revolutionary"; conservative as opposed to a Communist—who overturned the existing order in Europe. But after he dismissed Bismarck, could Kaiser Wilhelm II maintain the new international order? Sadly for the future of Germany, Europe, and the world, the answer was no, he could not.

Bismarck's Final Years of Power

After Bismarck's unification of Germany, the sense of safety that had marked international relations since the Congress of Vienna began to turn into fear. The statesmen at Vienna had pinned their hopes for peace on the disunity of Germany; an effective union of Germany, they believed, would revolutionize European affairs. Events proved them right. Once united (or almost united, because it still lacked Austria), Germany embarked on a period of unprecedented industrial expansion. Manufacturing, finance, and shipping grew phenomenally. In 1865, for example, Germany had produced less steel than France; by 1900 it was outproducing France and Great Britain combined. Not surprisingly, German nationalists craved Europe-wide recognition of Germany's superpower status.

Bismarck saw the dangers of such a position. Germany, he realized, was powerful but fragile. Its divisions were deep: peasants versus landowners; workers versus capitalists; northerners versus southerners; Protestants versus Catholics; and just about everybody, overtly or covertly, against Slavs, Jews, and other "foreigners." Any one of these divisions, Bismarck feared, could tear his creation apart.

So, having overturned the balance of power, he scrambled to restore it. He forged alliances with both Russia and Austria-Hungary (as Austria was renamed after its loss of most of northern Italy), even though those two empires were competitors with one another in the Balkans. And in 1878, he staged a new European convocation, the Congress of Berlin. At issue was control of the Balkans. The Ottoman Empire (modern Turkey), ruler of the region for centuries, was now reviled as the "sick man of Europe," its power receding fast. Russia had big ambitions in the region, and so did the French and the Austrians. Although desiring no Balkan colonies, Great Britain wanted to keep the Russians out of the Mediterranean and hence out of the Balkans. At the Congress of Berlin, Bismarck brought about a solution. Russia could make advances down the Black Sea into Romania, but no farther; France could trade with the locals; and Austria-Hungary got control of Croatia and Slovenia in the north, and influence in the provinces of Bosnia and Herzegovina, right in the middle of what one day became (and then ceased to be) Yugoslavia. Bismarck came out of the Congress with the reputation of being an honest broker.

MODERN DAY PARALLELS

A diplomatic term: honest broker. A modern parallel: In 1978, President Jimmy Carter led the Egyptian president and the Israeli prime minister to enter into full diplomatic relations. Under Carter, the United States sought no territory, only peace. What did Carter have to gain from his work? A reputation as a peacemaker. So it was with Bismarck. He didn't want any land in the Balkans. But he did want to show the leaders of the other European great powers that he could be trusted to keep the peace. That was his way of ensuring Germany's safety abroad.

The Kulturkampf

Bismarck-the-honest-broker, however, had not become a liberal at home. In the last two decades of his chancellorship (from 1871 to 1890), he restricted the power of the parliament, crushed press freedoms, and drove many socialists underground. Ironically, he himself became a quasi-socialist, using the resources of the German state to insure workers against sickness, accident, and incapacity in old age. In this way, he cracked the lid on the pressure cooker of social discontent. *Imperial* Germany under Bismarck was years ahead of "democratic" France, Great Britain, and the United States when it came to social welfare. Bismarck pioneered the welfare state, albeit merely to keep the masses content, using what the ancient Roman satirist Juvenal called "bread and circuses." In this case, the bread was welfare, the circuses public displays of military might.

To further control the masses, Bismarck initiated the Kulturkampf in 1871. It was an anti-Catholic campaign designed to consolidate the loyalty of the Protestant liberals of western Germany. New laws imposed restrictions on Catholic worship and education, the Jesuits were expelled from Germany, and many Catholic bishops were arrested or exiled.

TERMS AND TRANSLATIONS

Kulturkampf. *Kultur,* obviously, means "culture." What about *kampf?* Look at the first four letters of the English word *campaign. Kampf* and *camp* are almost the same. So *kampf* means a "campaign" or "struggle." Hitler's later infamous autobiography, *Mein Kampf,* meant, simply, *My Struggle.*

Bismarck Is Fired

Many of the Catholics living within the borders of the German Empire were Poles, and so the Kulturkampf took on an anti-foreign aspect. Like other Slavs, the Poles were supposed to be "racially inferior" to those of *pure* Germanic stock. Later, it would be an easy step for those "pure Germans" to target another foreign group, the Jews.

In time, Bismarck came to believe that his anti-Catholic efforts had been fruitless; Catholicism was deeply ingrained in southern Germany. Besides, he wanted the political support of Catholics for his social reform programs. In his later years, Bismarck focused less on Catholics than on socialists, Poles, and Jews, groups that he came to believe would try to destroy his empire from within. He even contemplated military action through which he could overthrow civilian rule altogether.

He never quite got to that point, however. In 1890, when Bismarck was 75 years old, Wilhelm II forced him to retire. Enraged and disheartened, the Iron Chancellor nevertheless acted the part of the good Prussian royalist and meekly accepted his monarch's decision.

The Kaiser and His Character

Kaiser Wilhelm I died in 1888. His son, Kaiser Friedrich III, ill with cancer, passed away after only three months on the throne. So began the reign (1888–1918) of Wilhelm's grandson and Friedrich's son, Kaiser Wilhelm II. From the outset, he was determined to be what his grandfather had not been: Bismarck's true superior. Unfortunately, he lacked both Bismarck's strength of will and sheer intellect.

Born in 1859 of then-Prince Friedrich and Princess Victoria (a daughter of England's Queen Victoria), Wilhelm had been an energetic child, albeit physically marred by a withered left arm and hand, a condition called Erb's palsy, which was the result of a birth injury. Even as an adult, he could not use a knife and fork, and at state dinners he had to rely on a partner or footman to cut his meat. The left sleeves of his coats and uniforms were cut short, and his formal photographs almost always showed his miniature left hand holding a pair of gloves, an optical illusion intended to elongate the appearance of the arm.

Some historians have claimed the handicap distorted his character. Perhaps. He was not shy, however. Of middling height at 5'9", he carried himself as if he were much taller, strutting into a room with the stiff stride of a Prussian officer. "If he laughs," a British observer commented, "which he is sure to do a good many times, he will laugh with absolute abandonment, throwing back his head, opening his mouth to the fullest extent possible, and often stamping with one foot to show his excessive enjoyment of any joke …" He blustered, both in German and in English, which he spoke fluently and idiomatically. Indeed, he worshipped his grandmother, Queen Victoria, and all other people and things English.

The world outside Germany saw the kaiser as a caricature, with the upturned moustaches, the metallic, snarling voice, the spiked Prussian helmet, the uniforms, and the parade-ground manner that itself looked like a declaration of war. Behind the image was a surprisingly vulnerable man. His barber visited him every morning to wax the facial hair into position; his grating voice was the result of a throat operation; and his bellicosity was a public show that in private turned timid. Like his father and grandfather before him, he was most fearful of Otto von Bismarck. And it was out fear that he fired him. All across Europe, stunned people referred to Wilhelm's action as "dropping the pilot." They feared the continent had lost its guide.

TERMS AND TRANSLATIONS

Dropping the pilot came from an 1890 political cartoon published in the British humor magazine *Punch*, showing Bismarck, dressed as a harbor pilot (the mariner who maneuvers a ship in hazardous waters, as in a crowded port) being sent ("dropped") off the German ship of state.

After March 1890, Wilhelm II personally dominated policy. Domestically, his new course was only partly new. True, there was no Kulturkampf, the anti-socialist laws were abandoned, the social-welfare programs were expanded, elections were permitted, and a few political parties were allowed to exist.

But Wilhelm II inaugurated no truly serious moves toward democracy. He was obsessed with what he believed to be the divinely ordained rights and privileges of the House of Hohenzollern. And the German Empire still rested on the power of the various local princes, the arms, the industrialists, and the ancient landowning class, the Junkers.

Nevertheless, a democratic spirit was growing. A new party, the Social Democrats, called for political reforms, especially by allowing majority rule in the Reichstag, or federal parliament. In the election of 1912, they got four and a quarter million votes, about one third of all votes cast, and they were the largest single party in the assembly. Yet the kaiser excluded the Social Democrats from the highest posts in the government. The German Empire, as created by Bismarck, was moving toward a political crisis over the choice between democracy and autocracy. And Germany under Wilhelm II was also moving toward something else: outright domination of Europe.

Germany's Place in the Sun

In the late nineteenth century, all the major European powers were engaged in imperialism. Great Britain led the way, with colonies or dominions (such as Canada) stretching all around the world; India was considered the jewel in the British imperial crown. The French acquired colonies in North and sub-Saharan Africa and in Vietnam. Belgium got the Congo. Russia had expanded across Manchuria to Vladivostok, the port city on the North Pacific. Japan, too, got into the act, defeating China in a war fought in 1894 to 1895 and taking Taiwan and Korea as colonies.

Germany got what was left over: Tanganyika (now Tanzania) on the East African coast, a scattering of Pacific islands spread out above New Guinea, and Shandong, a Chinese peninsula that jutted up toward Korea. This wasn't much of an overseas empire, and to German imperialists its small size was an embarrassment.

Building a Strong Navy

As Bismarck had stirred German nationalism, so Wilhelm II and his ministers sought to infuse the German population with imperialism. Why did they have to preach? Because building an empire overseas meant the construction of a powerful new German navy, and navies are expensive. Many throughout Germany wanted the government to spend more on social welfare. So, in speech after speech, the kaiser proclaimed that "our future lies on the seas" and "the trident must pass into our hands." "Our navy," he went as far as to say, "will grow and flourish, during peaceful times to promote the peaceable interests of the Fatherland, and in war times to destroy the enemy, if God helps us."

TERMS AND TRANSLATIONS

Obviously, **imperialism** is related to empire. But an empire, such as Germany's under Bismarck, does not necessarily try to expand. Imperialism thus is a doctrine that says the empire has a *right* to expand. So imperialism is nationalism taken a step further: Nationalism talks about a people's common destiny and imperialism says that such a destiny lies in taking over other people's lands.

Wilhelm did not name the enemy. But he did repeatedly raise the possibility of a general war.

Once Bismarck had consolidated the German Empire, he presented a peaceful face to the rest of Europe. Not so with Wilhelm II. Jealous of his personal rule, he followed Bismarck with a string of weak chancellors: General von Caprivi (1890–1894), an old soldier; Prince Hohenlohe (1894–1900), aged uncle of the emperor; Prince Bernhard von Bülow (1900–1909), a courtier whose principal quality was his ability to flatter; and Theobald von Bethmann Hollweg (1909–1917), an inexperienced administrator. Thus Wilhelm kept German diplomacy in his own hands.

BET YOU DIDN'T KNOW

If you go to a Chinese restaurant or supermarket, you might encounter Tsingtao Beer. The name is Chinese and it is imported from China. But from its strong taste, you might think it must be a German beer. That's because it is. Tsingtao (now spelled Qingdao) is the capital of Shandong Province, and the Chinese have preserved a brewery that was commissioned by Kaiser Wilhelm II.

Wilhelm's Political Faux Pas

Unlike Bismarck, the kaiser was a deplorably inept diplomat. In January 1896, when a British raid against the Boers in South Africa failed, Wilhelm II sent a telegram of congratulations to Paul Kruger, president of the Transvaal Republic. "I express to you my sincere congratulations that, supported by your people and without appealing from help to friendly powers, you have succeeded by your energetic action against armed bands that invaded your country as disturbers of the peace, and have therefore been able to restore peace and safeguard the independence of the country against outside attacks." When the message was published in England, it aroused a storm of protest. Three years later, Lord Salisbury, the prime minister, said: "The raid was folly, but the telegram was even more foolish."

It was foolish because it made the kaiser look as if he were trying to stir up trouble with London. The ham-handed telegram was nevertheless wildly popular throughout Germany and even much of the European continent. The continentals loathed the British Empire, including its aggression in South Africa. Yet now the British had an excuse to portray Wilhelm as the aggressor.

More diplomatic clashes followed. In March 1905, Wilhelm II disembarked from a German warship at the port of Tangier in Morocco, a French colony. Riding ashore on a white horse, he gave a strongly worded speech in favor of Moroccan independence. After the speech, Germany demanded and got an international conference in 1906 at Algeciras, Spain, to resolve the French–Moroccan issue. Representatives of all the European great powers and the United States attended. To Wilhelm's consternation, the conference supported France's claims in Morocco. Only Austria-Hungary voted with Germany. Most other heads of state thought the kaiser was trying to push the French out of the way so that he could grab more colonies for Germany. As a diplomat, Wilhelm was his own worst enemy. In October 1908, the *Daily Telegraph,* a British newspaper, published an account of an interview between the kaiser and an unnamed British subject. In the interview, Wilhelm presented himself as a lover of peace:

> What more can I do than I have done? I declared with all the emphasis at my command, in my speech at Guildhall [in London] that my heart is set upon peace, and that it is one of my clearest wishes to live on the best of terms with England ... I have said time after time that I am a friend of England, and your press—or, at least, a considerable section of it—bids the people of England refuse my proffered hand and insinuates that the other holds a dagger ...

A Chip off the Old Block

The next move Wilhelm made showed him to be more of a disciple of the man he had dismissed, Bismarck, who wielded sheer force in international relations.

A second Moroccan crisis came in 1911. A German gunboat, the *Panzer*, steamed into the port of Agadir to "protect German interests." Berlin promised no further such incidents in Morocco if Germany could take over the French Congo. In the end, Germany obtained only trifling concessions in sub-Saharan Africa. But the damage was done. All three of Germany's major enemies were convinced that the kaiser was on the march toward world domination—or, more precisely, colonial dominion competing with their own.

A Ring of Enemies

Once he had created the German behemoth, Bismarck tried through diplomacy to present his empire as peace-loving. But keeping all Germany's potential enemies at bay required all the Iron Chancellor's diplomatic skill. Had he remained in office after 1890, no one knows what might have happened. But none of Bismarck's successors, neither Kaiser Wilhelm II nor the subsequent weak chancellors, came close to possessing Bismarck's acumen. By the end of the nineteenth century and the beginning of the twentieth, the leaders of France, Russia, and Great Britain were intent on restoring a balance of power—this time against Germany.

The first to become allies, in 1896, were France and Russia. Now, remember this: France, once the great revolutionary power, was still a hotbed of democracy, and Russia, headed by the tsar, the Orthodox church, and the secret police, was an *autarchy*. So, what did France and Russia have in common? Nothing, except the principle that the enemy of my enemy is my friend. Russia feared the new Germany, and France wanted revenge for its defeat in the Franco-Prussian War of 1870-1871. Thus, Paris and St. Petersburg signed the Dual Alliance in 1896.

TERMS AND TRANSLATIONS

An **autarchy** refers to a country under absolute rule, complete control from the top. Old Prussia and then Germany had come close to being autarchies, but they didn't come close to the Russian model. Russia allowed hardly even a whiff of liberalism.

The third great power, Great Britain, was not far behind Russia and France. Ever since the Napoleonic Wars, London had maintained its policy of "splendid isolation," concentrating on affairs of the empire and remaining neutral in the Franco–Prussian War. Faced with the rise of German commercial and naval competition, however, the sea lords of Britannia began to reassess isolation when it came to Germany. In 1904, British and French generals and admirals got together in Paris and agreed to coordinate their military planning. This was not exactly an alliance, but it was close. The agreement was called an *entente cordiale,* French for a "cordial understanding," And it was aimed against Germany—as Berlin well knew.

Then, as if to tighten the noose, Britain and Russia signed a treaty. In the nineteenth century, during the Crimean War (1853-1856), the British had seen the Russians as their main enemy. No more. In 1907, Britain agreed that Russia could have a *sphere of influence* in northern Persia (now Iran).

· TERMS AND TRANSLATIONS

A **sphere of influence** is not quite a colony, but a region that certain countries, such as country A, B, and C, agree that another country (for this example, country D) can pretty much run as it sees fit.

Why Persia? Britain and Russia had been contesting the country for a century, the British to protect India and Russia to gain access to warm-water ports. London wanted an alignment with Russia against Germany: hence the Persian concession.

Finally, in 1912—as German intelligence strongly suspected—Great Britain and France entered into a secret alliance. If Germany invaded France, the agreement was that the British navy would defend the French ports along the English Channel.

The governments of France, Russia, and Great Britain, now called the Triple Entente, saw this network of ties as defensive. The German government saw it as offensive, and was accordingly determined to hang on to its one ally, Austria-Hungary.

An Inferior Ally (but the Only One They've Got)

Having lost to Bismarck and having been thrown out of northern Italy, the Austrian Empire was in sharp decline. Stretched out over a multitude of linguistic and ethnic groups in Eastern Europe, it was like an old cracked jar held together by wire—a wire called the Compromise of 1867. In theory, the Austrian emperor, Franz Josef, ruled; but in practice, Hungary had acquired an equal share of the government: hence Austria-Hungary. That was the substance of the compromise.

Austrian troubles did not end with the creation of this so-called Dual Monarchy. Numerous groups— Czechs, Poles, Slovaks, Jews, Romanians, Croats, and, most significant for what was to come in the Balkans, the Serbs—clamored for various degrees of independence. To stifle these demands, especially in the Balkans, Austria-Hungary in 1908 effectively annexed Bosnia and Herzegovina, which had been placed under its administrative control by Bismarck at the Congress of Berlin. (Soon after that meeting, a grateful Vienna accepted an alliance with Germany.)

This next point is crucial: Germany approved the occupation and then annexation of Bosnia and Herzegovina. This would have world-shattering consequences. More immediately, however, the approval served to cement the German-Austrian alliance. Austria-Hungary fielded a poor army, but, to Germany, the alliance appeared to be better than nothing. Now the kaiser could turn his attention to his naval rivalry with Great Britain.

Tirpitz's Navy

Alfred Thayer Mahan, an American naval officer and maritime historian who taught at the Naval War College in Rhode Island, had written extensively on the importance of sea power in international relations. He contended that sea power was the foundation of imperial greatness and concluded that a powerful navy could always choke off and through attrition destroy a land power. He cited the example of Napoleon's ultimate defeat as the effect of British naval supremacy.

Nowhere were Mahan's books read with more interest than in Germany. Led by Admiral Alfred von Tirpitz, chief of staff of the German fleet, Germany began a crash shipbuilding program in 1898.

Interservice rivalry was rife in the Germany of Wilhelm II. Tirpitz's naval program cost money, and the German army, proud of its traditions and successes, was hostile to the upstart navy. As for the socialists, they clamored for increased welfare funding. Although the kaiser was emperor, he still had to mediate among these competing claims. So, the Tirpitz naval expansion, though ambitious, never produced a fleet that could outmatch the British fleet.

In international relations, perception is often as important as reality. Facts aside, the British government persuaded itself that Germany's naval growth was a threat. Berlin insisted that a high-seas fleet was essential to secure its colonies, protect its trade, and safeguard its home waters. London held with equal resolution that, because Great Britain was almost wholly dependent on imports for food, it must at all costs maintain control of the sea lanes.

Berlin and London saw each other from the point of view of a zero-sum game: Your gain is my loss.

The Road to War

The crisis that triggered World War I seemed to have little to do with British–German relations and much to do with nationalism. By the beginning of the twentieth century, Serbian nationalists down in the Balkans had begun to work for the breakup of the Austro–Hungarian Empire. Right next to Bosnia and Herzegovina, Serbia was the center of anti-Austrian agitation; Serbia looked forward to the expulsion of the Austrians from Bosnia and Herzegovina, as well as from the northern Balkan provinces of Croatia and Slovenia. With Austria out of the picture, these territories could be unified under the monarchy in Belgrade. So, after Austria-Hungary's annexation of Bosnia-Herzegovina in 1908, Serb nationalists swore revenge against Vienna.

In the three years after 1908, Balkan tensions subsided. Then, in 1911, the Balkans suddenly erupted in warfare. Serbia, Bulgaria, and Greece ganged up against Turkey, expelling the "sick man of Europe" from the Balkans altogether. But Bulgaria and Serbia squabbled over Macedonia and, in two wars fought in 1912 and 1913, Serbia, Greece, and Romania defeated Bulgaria. Serbia and Greece then nearly went to war over control of Albania. To keep the peace, the great powers of Europe intervened to create Albania as an independent kingdom.

Despite verbal support from Russia, landlocked Serbia failed to gain access to the sea. Frustrated and inflamed, factions among the Serbian nationalists vowed to try again.

The result of their resolution was the great international explosion of World War I. The fuse was lit in Sarajevo, the provincial capital of Bosnia. Years earlier, Otto von Bismarck, pleased with the handiwork of his diplomacy, remarked that if war ever did come again to Europe, "it will be some damn foolish thing in the Balkans that sets it off." No nation would be more profoundly impacted by World War I than the German nation. The rise of Nazi Germany was the direct product of that conflict and its conclusion at Versailles.

The Least You Need to Know

- ✪ Bismarck, the genius of nineteenth-century international relations, followed his forcible unification of Germany with sustained efforts to preserve the general peace. However, he was fired by Kaiser Wilhelm II.

- ✪ Wilhelm was not necessarily a warmonger, but he certainly gave a good impression of one. Under his leadership, Germany sought, or seemed to seek, its place in the international sun, and thus became a rival to Great Britain and its preeminent world position.

- ✪ In response to German expansionism, France, Russia, and Great Britain formed an interlocking series of understandings and alliances, which Germany took to be a hostile, encircling ring.

- ✪ Germany had only one ally, the decrepit Austro–Hungarian Empire. But Kaiser Wilhelm II believed in the need to preserve that alliance; as we'll see, that belief led to disaster for Germany; the catalyst of that disaster lay down in the obscurity of the Balkans.

CHAPTER 3

The Coming of the First World War: June 28, 1914–August 4, 1914

Sarajevo, the provincial capital of Bosnia, was shaped like a bowl. The mountains that surrounded it sloped down past farmlands and orchards, then whitewashed houses, scatterings of churches, mosques, and synagogues, and at last the shops and bazaars of the central town. At the bottom of the bowl ran the major thoroughfare, the Appel Quay, which lay alongside the Miljacka River, a stream that divides Sarajevo in two.

Landlocked amid all those mountains, Bosnia had become an Austrian territory. For some years before 1914, however, elements in Serbia next door (Serbia lay between Bosnia and the Danube River; Austria-Hungary stretched north from the Danube) had been fomenting revolution. They were Serb nationalists who dreamed of unifying all the Slavs of the Balkans (Yugoslavia means "southern Slav") as Italy and Germany before them had been unified. But unification meant expelling the Austrians from the region, just as earlier the Austrians had been expelled from Italy. So, the Serbian nationalists had been using the classic techniques of insurgents: propaganda, boycotts, and, on occasion, murder. Whenever they could, they targeted Austro–Hungarian officials for assassination.

Not wanting to lose Bosnia as it had earlier lost Lombardy and Venetia, Austria increased its military presence in the province and, late in June 1914, the Crown sent Archduke Franz Ferdinand, heir presumptive to the throne of the Austro–Hungarian Empire, to inspect local troop maneuvers. His observations completed, Franz Ferdinand and his wife, the Grand Duchess Sophie, paid an official visit to Sarajevo. Provocatively, the archduke scheduled the visit for Vidovan (St. Vitus Day), a Serbian nationalist-religious holiday.

On the morning of June 28, 1914, in a display of Austro–Hungarian rule, a royal motorcade drove down the Appel Quay. In the third car, which was open, rode the archduke and his wife. After he gave a speech at the town hall, the procession returned toward the river, heading up into the hills for a visit to the Bosnian museum.

Just as the archduke's automobile slowed to make the turn up a side street, however, a young Bosnian Serb named Gavrilo Princip stepped forward from the crowd that was lining the curb. Trained and financed by a secret society in the Serbian capital of Belgrade called the Black Hand, , Princip was armed with a revolver. When he neared the imperial car, he fired three times. One shot went wild, one killed the archduke, and one killed the grand duchess. Six weeks later—incredibly—Europe was at war.

MODERN DAY PARALLELS

Were the Serb assassins patriots or terrorists? It depended on your point of view. For the Austrians, they were clearly terrorists. To many Serbs, they were patriots. Are there any parallels to this in the world today?

Austria-Hungary Devises a Final Solution

In Vienna, Franz Josef, the Austro–Hungarian emperor, and his foreign minister, Count Leopold Berchtold von und zu Unargschitz, Frättling und Püllütz, saw an opportunity in the murder of the Austrian heir presumptive. It was a reason to punish Serbia and to crush its insurgent activities. Princip had been apprehended within seconds of firing the fatal shots, and half a dozen co-conspirators were quickly arrested as well. Interrogation soon uncovered the connection to the Serbian Black Hand. Berchtold was determined to do one of two things. Either he would subjugate Serbia itself to Austria, or he would find an excuse to destroy the small nation in a war. Either way, it would be a "final solution" to Serbian opposition to the empire.

TERMS AND TRANSLATIONS

The Austro–Hungarian use of the phrase **final solution** eerily foreshadows the Nazis' use of the same phrase as a code word for the policy of Jewish extermination. Vienna's target, however, was Serbian nationalism. And the Austro–Hungarian authorities were not trying to eradicate an entire population. Their attitude, nonetheless, was that the time had come to deal decisively with a people they regarded as subhuman and therefore worthy of any kind of abuse. The Austrian-born Adolf Hitler would transfer that attitude to the Jews.

Spoiling for war, Berchtold dispatched an emissary to Germany, Austria-Hungary's ally, to assure itself of Berlin's support. Kaiser Wilhelm II seemed not to take the possibility of war very seriously. Over lunch with the emissary, he almost casually guaranteed Germany's absolute support, issuing what has been called a "blank check" that acknowledged Austria-Hungary's need to stop the agitation in the Balkans.

Soon—and throughout World War I—Kaiser Wilhelm II would be blamed as the aggressor who started the war. In fact, he wanted no war, at least not until his navy was larger. But he could not bring himself to say no to his Austrian ally, and he did not want to look weak. He effectively endorsed Austria-Hungary's imperialist and racist policy in the Balkans. He did not seriously weight the consequences. Perhaps he assumed, as Berchtold did, that war would be limited to Austria and Serbia, that the little nation would be crushed, and that the war would be short and sharp. Encouraged, in the last week of July 1914, Vienna presented Belgrade with a multipart ultimatum. Surprisingly, Serbia agreed to every demand, including an end to Serbia's anti-Austrian propaganda and its boycotts of Austrian trade. The Serbian government stopped short, however, of allowing Austrian police to operate with total authority inside Serbia. To permit this would breach the country's sovereignty and independence. Serbia would, in effect, cease to exist.

Vienna seized on that single objection as a reason to declare war. On July 28, 1914, Austro–Hungarian artillery began to shell Belgrade, just across the Danube River.

The Kaiser's Misjudgment Leads to a Fatal Delusion

As he had done for years, Kaiser Wilhelm II devoted the month of July to a North Sea excursion aboard the royal steam yacht *Hohenzollern*. The cruise along the Norwegian fjords was peaceful, the meals aboard were excellent, and during the "white nights" so near the Arctic Circle, the kaiser and his closest ministers gathered in the smoking lounge for cards. On July 25, the *Hohenzollern's* radio picked up the text of the Austro–Hungarian ultimatum to Serbia. Admiral George Müller, chief of the naval cabinet, handed a copy to Wilhelm after breakfast as he strolled the deck.

> Reading the document, Wilhelm commented, *"Was, das ist doch einmal eine forsche Note."* ("Well, for once that's a strong note.")

> Müller replied: *"Ja, forsche ist die Note, aber sie bedeutet Krieg!"* ("Yes, the note is strong, but it signifies war!")

The kaiser countered that Serbia would surely capitulate and that no war would ensue. A short time later, another message was received. This one stated that Austria-Hungary was on the verge of war—*and* Russia was preparing to mobilize in aid of Serbia. At that moment, 6 P.M. on the afternoon of July 25, Wilhelm ordered the ship back to Germany.

"It was a beautiful summer evening," Admiral Müller wrote. "The kaiser stood for a long time on the bridge enjoying the peaceful picture of forests, mountains, and farmhouses as we sailed out of Sognefjord. I said to him: 'In times of political tension such as these, one could almost look with envy upon this land which lies outside the great conflicts of world history ….' His Majesty agreed and maintained that at the last moment the leaders of the states involved would shrink from the appalling responsibility of starting a war."

He was wrong.

The kaiser lacked Bismarck's uncanny ability to read reality. True, Slavic Russia was allied to Slavic Serbia, but, surely, Wilhelm believed, all he had to do was talk to his first cousin, Tsar Nicholas II. How could Nicholas resist his extraordinary powers of persuasion? Surely, the Russian autocrat would see the folly of going to war.

Here was Wilhelm's fatal delusion. He had a choice. He could disown Austria-Hungary, refusing to sanction Vienna's final solution. Or he could accept the coming of war. Reasoning that the fighting would be "localized"—his term—in the Balkans, he chose war.

On July 29, at 8:20 P.M., the Tsar Nicholas II sent this message to the kaiser:

> In this serious moment, I appeal to you to help me. An ignoble war has been declared to a weak country. The indignation in Russia shared fully by me is enormous. I foresee that very soon I shall be overwhelmed by the pressure forced upon me and be forced to take extreme measures which will lead to war. To try and avoid such a calamity as a European war I beg you in the name of our old friendship to do what you can to stop your allies from going too far.

Wilhelm wanted no war. He just didn't want to stop Austria-Hungary from going too far. He responded to his cousin immediately:

> … I think a direct understanding between your government and Vienna possible and desirable, and as I already telegraphed to you, my government is continuing its exercises to promote it. Of course military measures on the part of Russia would be looked upon by Austria as a calamity we both wish to avoid and jeopardize my position as mediator which I readily accepted on your appeal to my friendship and help.

At the Congress of Berlin in 1878, Bismarck also had been the mediator. Wilhelm, however, forgot—or refused to recognize—that you cannot be a mediator if you favor one side. The tsar wrote to the kaiser on July 30:

> Thank you heartily for your quick answer. The military measures, which have now come into force were decided five days ago for reasons of defense on account of Austria's preparations. I hope from all my heart that these measures won't in any way interfere with your part as mediator, which I greatly value. We need your strong pressure on Austria to come to an understanding with us.

That pressure the tsar desired was not forthcoming from the kaiser.

The Allies Close In

So here were the issues:

- ✪ Austria-Hungary was determined to crush Serbian nationalism once and for all.
- ✪ Refusing to recognize any merit in Serbia's position, Kaiser Wilhelm II sympathized wholly with Vienna; his claim to being a mediator was a gross exaggeration.
- ✪ Russia was allied to Serbia and was determined to go to that small state's defense.

Still, nothing had occurred that should have driven Germany into a war. Kaiser Wilhelm II almost certainly intended to go to war against France and perhaps Britain as well. He wanted to expand Germany as a colonial power. But he believed that his military was not yet ready. Events, not monarchs, were taking the lead. The technical word for Russia's military preparations was "mobilization," which meant that Russia was calling up its reserves and putting them aboard troop trains headed for Austria. Those trains ran on tracks along the German border. Even so, the kaiser could have overlooked the Russian troop movement—had it not been for France.

Archduke Franz Ferdinand.
(Culver Pictures)

Russian–French Alliance

Recall that, from 1896 onward, Russia and France had been leagued in an alliance aimed against Germany. In the middle of July 1914, after the Sarajevo murders, the French president and premier paid an official state visit to Nicholas II for the purpose of reinforcing the treaty of alliance. The visit ended with the French president publicly assuring Nicholas that in case of war, France would march against Germany.

In fact, most of the French public and the Chamber of Deputies (equivalent to a parliament) favored war with Germany. They wanted to avenge the loss of Alsace and Lorraine to Bismarck. The dissenting voices, favoring peace, were outnumbered. Jean Jaurès, the head of the French Socialist Party, believed that for the working classes of Europe war would be a calamity. He was eloquent and persuasive. On the night of July 31, as he was eating dinner in a Paris café, an assassin gunned him down. Was the assassin an agent of the French government? Possibly. In any case, with this latest assassination, just about all calls in France for peace fell silent. So, as Austria-Hungary went to war against Serbia, France began to mobilize against Germany.

The kaiser's premature drift toward war was very nearly thoughtless. France, however, marched toward it boldly, eagerly, purposefully.

The German high command had long foreseen a two-front war with Russia and France, and it had drawn up a plan accordingly. Named for General Alfred von Schlieffen, Berlin's turn-of-the-century chief of staff, the Schlieffen Plan accurately assumed that the Russian army, though the largest in Europe, was poorly led and poorly equipped. It would be slow to mobilize. Therefore, Germany would devote most of its army to immediately invading France while deploying a smaller portion to defend its eastern borders against Russia.

The most modern land force in Europe, the German army would advance quickly through Belgium (ignoring Belgium's neutrality) in a gigantic, scythe-like sweep through the country and down into France. Schlieffen instructed commanders that the right sleeve of the last soldier on the right should brush against the English Channel. Thus the German army would not attack the French army head-on, but on its left flank and rear. This would pin the French back against the Argonne Forest (just above Switzerland) and the Swiss Alps.

Victorious, the Germans would take Paris, much as they had done under Bismarck in 1870. Then the German army could turn back toward the east and overwhelm the slow-moving Russians.

The German high command was confident that the Schlieffen Plan would bring about the defeat of Germany's enemies and do so quickly. Yet, in the last days of July 1914, Kaiser Wilhelm II was reluctant to unleash it. Perhaps he did not want to be blamed for starting a continental war; perhaps he had inherited Bismarck's fear that a continental war would tear Germany apart (which it did). Whatever the reason, even as Russia and France mobilized, Wilhelm withheld his final approval for war.

The British Arrive

It was the action of the British that may have moved Wilhelm's reluctant hand. In July 1914, much of the British Royal Navy had been staging annual maneuvers off the Isle of Wight in the English Channel. Normally, at the conclusion of maneuvers, the fleet returned to its battle stations at Gibraltar, Malta, Cyprus, Suez, and beyond. At the end of July 1914, however, after obtaining the approval of Prime Minister H. H. Asquith, the first lord of the admiralty ordered most of the ships to proceed to Scapa Flow, a huge naval base in the Orkney Islands, high above Scotland.

From Scapa Flow, the British fleet had a straight shot down the North Sea at the northwestern coast of Germany and at the Kiel Canal, Germany's lifeline between the North Sea and the Baltic.

In Berlin, the kaiser and his top officials had long feared such a strike. They called it *die englische Gefahr* (the English danger). So, by the morning of July 31, 1914, the kaiser knew that the time for a decision had come.

BET YOU DIDN'T KNOW

Guess the name of the first lord of the admiralty who ordered the ships to proceed to Scapa Flow. It was Winston S. Churchill.

Wilhelm Decides on War

That morning, a huge crowd gathered in the center of Berlin, hoping for news. Good news or bad news, it almost didn't matter. People wanted to hear anything that would ease their uncertainty.

The people were gathered in the *Lustgarten*, a park in front of the kaiser's *schloss* (castle). Over the turrets floated the yellow imperial standard, the sign of the presence of His Majesty.

TERMS AND TRANSLATIONS

In English, *lust* suggests sexual desire. It does in German, too. To Germans, it also means pleasure or delight, and so the *Lustgarten* was an amusement park where ordinary Berliners could go for enjoyment.

As the morning progressed, the air became warm, even sultry. The huge crowd grew restless. A month had gone by since the Sarajevo assassinations, a month of endless negotiations, threats, and assurances of peace.

At about 10:30 A.M., the crowd suddenly went silent. People stared up at the windows of the castle. They thought they had seen movement on a balcony. There was nothing. They tried to peer up through the panes, but the glass only reflected the sunshine. In the park below, people could glean nothing of what was taking place behind the heavy yellow draperies of the palace windows.

Noon came, and there still was no news. More and more people, husbands and wives and their children, joined the multitude. In the tower over the castle the clock struck five.

Then, ever so slowly, a door opened. The people could see a policeman emerge. He walked out onto the balcony and, moving to one side, slowly took off his helmet. He held it in front of his chest. The policeman opened his mouth and the crowd leaned forward. Then they could hear his words: "His Majesty Kaiser Wilhelm II."

In that moment, Wilhelm himself, in full uniform, with spiked helmet, tunic covered with medals and medallions, high, polished boots, and a sword at his side, strode into view. There, on the balcony of the Berlin Castle, he made his declaration of war:

> A momentous hour has struck for Germany. Envious rivals everywhere force us to legitimate defense. The sword has been forced into our hands. I hope that in the event that my efforts to the very last moment do not succeed in bringing our opponents to reason and in preserving peace, we may use the sword, with the help of God, so that we may sheath it again with honor. War will demand enormous sacrifices by the German people, but we shall show the enemy what it means to attack Germany. Go forth into the churches, kneel down before God, and implore his help for our brave army.

After telling his people that Germany had declared war on Russia and France, the kaiser disappeared again into the castle.

As Wilhelm withdrew, a few voices below, then hundreds and thousands, joined together in singing the German chorale of thanksgiving, written in the seventeenth century and eventually harmonized by the composer Felix Mendelssohn, *"Nun danket alle Gott"* ("Now Thank We All Our God"):

> Now thank we all our God,
> With heart, and hands, and voices,
> Who wondrous things hath done,
> In whom the world rejoices;
> Who from our mother's arms
> Hath blessed us on our way
> With countless gifts of love,
> And still is ours today.

On August 1, another crowd gathered, this one in Munich. A photograph of that demonstration shows at least 100,000 people jammed together. The faces are blurred and are almost indistinguishable. But a magnifying glass brings one of those faces to startling life. The hair is dark, plastered down over the left side of the forehead; a brush moustache adorns the upper lip. The man is small and young, but unmistakable. He is Adolf Hitler.

Big Ben Sounds Doom, Doom, Doom

The morning of August 4, 1914, brought gloomy weather to London. Dark clouds scudded up from the Channel, spitting down flurries of rain and brushing in patches of fog. The English capital was shrouded in gray, the atmosphere being, in the word of *The Westminster Gazette*, "unsettled." The term described the sky above as well as the mood below.

German troops, British intelligence had reported the day before, had crossed the border into Belgium. In 1839, by the Treaty of London, Britain had pledged to defend Belgian neutrality. Now, 75 years later, the House of Commons authorized Prime Minister Asquith and his foreign secretary, Sir Edward Grey, to send an ultimatum to Berlin. If Germany did not withdraw from Belgium by 11 P.M. that night (midnight Berlin time), Great Britain, treaty-bound, would declare war.

Shortly before 3 P.M., Asquith went to the House to announce that the ultimatum had been sent. The announcement was greeted with cheers.

Shortly after the House adjourned, Walter Hines Page, the American ambassador, called on Grey. Tall, worn, and pallid, Grey was standing against the mantelpiece in his ornate room in the Foreign Office, right across the street from Ten Downing Street. "England would be forever contemptible," Grey said, "if it should sit by and see this treaty [with Belgium] violated. Its position would be gone if Germany were thus permitted to dominate Europe. … We have told Germany that, if this assault on Belgium's neutrality is not reversed, England will declare war."

"Do you expect Germany to accept it?" Page asked.

Grey shook his head. "No," he said. "Of course everybody knows that there will be war."

That evening, as the rain stopped, a huge crowd filled the center of London. After dark, a multitude surged around the Victoria Memorial and toward Buckingham Palace. On one of the balconies appeared King George V, a first cousin of Kaiser Wilhelm II. As one, a million voices sang, "God Save the King!"

After dinner at 10 Downing Street that night, Asquith, Grey, and a few others from the ministry gathered in the Cabinet Room. David Lloyd George, serving then as chancellor of the exchequer, joined them.

By 9 o'clock they had heard nothing from Berlin. Ten o'clock came. Only an hour remained until the ultimatum to Berlin would expire; still nothing from Berlin. The clock on the mantelpiece showed 10:55 P.M. Every one seated around the green baize–covered table in the Cabinet Room was watching that clock, encased in the most private of thoughts. The room, dimly lit, was still.

Then, from down the Whitehall and across Parliament Square and high in the tower beside the Houses of Parliament resounded the bells of the most famous clock in the world, the deep sonorities of Big Ben. The time was 11 P.M.

In the Cabinet Room, Lloyd George later wrote, "Every face was suddenly contracted in a painful intensity. 'Doom!' 'Doom!' 'Doom!' down to the last stroke." Great Britain and Imperial Germany were at war.

In that same moment, out of the harbor at Portsmouth, on the Channel coast, a ship called the *Telconia* slipped out to sea. *Telconia* was a cable tender, unarmed, equipped with a crane for laying the underwater cables of trans-Atlantic communication. On this night, its mission was different. Under the cover of fog, it chugged to the German coastline, between Holland and Denmark. There the crane dipped down to lower a huge shears to the seabed below. There lay five cables, intended to transmit messages from Germany to South America, Mexico, and the United States. In a single swift motion, the *Telconia* cut those cables, hauled the severed parts aboard, and returned to Portsmouth.

No single mission, on land or sea, could have done more harm to the German cause. Whatever the rights or wrongs of their cause, in going to war the leaders of Wilhelm's Germany had forgotten an overwhelmingly crucial fact: If they could not get their side of the story to the United States—and with their trans-Atlantic cables cut, then British propagandists would control the "truth." And if the United States were ever to enter the war on the side of Britain and France, Germany would be doomed.

The Least You Need to Know

- Two murders in Sarajevo, an obscure town in the faraway Balkans, triggered the First World War.

- Austria-Hungary's response to the murders in Sarajevo, with its imperialist and racist overtones, foreshadowed Hitler's "final solution" for the Jews.

- Contrary to legend, Kaiser Wilhelm II may not have been seeking an aggressive war. Nevertheless, he succumbed to the fatal delusion that he could have his strudel and eat it too: He could support Austria-Hungary and not face a general war.

- Britain's entry into the war, and in support of Britain, the probability of America's entry, practically guaranteed that Germany would face disaster.

The Great War: 1914–1918

World War I began in a burst of optimism. The cheering crowds in the capitals of all the great powers believed that the war would be over soon. "You will be home before the leaves fall from the trees," Wilhelm II told his soldiers as they marched to the French frontier.

It was not to be. The stalemate of war was to drag Europe—and Germany in particular—ever deeper into ruin.

War Breaks Out

Let's start with something often overlooked but crucial. Hitler, by birth, was an Austrian. By attacking Serbia, Austria-Hungary had done more than any of the other belligerents to start the war. Germany and Austria-Hungary were allies (although their high commands never really coordinated with each other). And in time, Hitler would unite Germany and Austria. So, as we look at World War I, it seems reasonable to treat Germany and Austria-Hungary together; certainly, the war brought them tumbling down together.

When war came, the Viennese were as excited as the citizens of Berlin and Munich. Throngs in the *Ringstrasse* (the Ring Street, Vienna's central avenue) waved flags and sang anthems. The city's Friedrich Cardinal Piffl called upon the imperial forces to strike down "the enemies of God," meaning the Serbs. As they did in Germany, the Austrian socialists, as nationalist as they were socialist, wholeheartedly endorsed the war.

For Austria-Hungary as well as Germany, the war got off to a glorious start. Crossing the Danube in gunboats, ferries, and barges, the forces of Austria-Hungary marched into Belgrade with ease. Transporting an army of almost 4,000,000 men, Germany's trains thundered across the Rhine bridges and poured across Belgium into northeastern France. Born in England and no lover of Prussia, a princess named Evelyn Blücher wrote in her diary that the Germans "take to war as a duck takes to water."

MEMORABLE PLACES

Like his English cousin, George V, Wilhelm had a lot of castles. His favorite was at Potsdam, then a medieval town about 10 miles from Berlin. Because it had been his principal residence, at the end of World War II the victorious Big Three, Marshal Josef Stalin, Prime Minister Winston S. Churchill, and President Harry S. Truman, chose the Potsdam palace as the site for their summer, 1945, so-called peacemaking conference.

On August 18, Kaiser Wilhelm spoke to troops from a balcony in his castle at Potsdam, just outside Berlin. The "entire German nation to the last man has grasped the sword," he declared. "And so I draw the sword which with the help of God I have kept in its scabbard for decades." At this point he drew his sword and held it high above his head. "The sword is drawn, and I cannot sheathe it again without victory and honor. All of you shall and will see to it that only in honor is it returned to the scabbard. You are my guarantee that I can dictate peace to my enemies. Up and at the enemy … Three cheers for our army!"

Soon afterward, the kaiser took the royal train to still another castle, this one at Coblenz high on a bluff where the Mosel and Rhine Rivers flowed together. During Bismarck's war with France, Wilhelm's grandfather, Wilhelm I, had ensconced himself in the same *schloss* (castle). Wilhelm II was determined to stay there until Germany once again defeated France.

He had every reason to believe that his wait would not be long. In East Prussia, a region of hills, lakes, and scrub pines, near a town called Tannenberg, the Germans destroyed an advancing Russian force, inflicting some 170,000 casualties—killed, wounded, and captured. Along the western front, the German armies in August 1914 wheeled in a wide arc toward Paris, precisely according to the Schlieffen Plan. The Schlieffen Plan was brilliant—on paper. But what the German high command neglected was the human element. A war plan is no better than the people who carry it out.

Gloomy Gus

The German commander on the western front was General Helmuth von Moltke, known as "the Younger" to distinguish him from his uncle of the same name and surname, victorious architect of Bismarck's wars. Tall and heavy, with a perpetual air of distress, the younger von Moltke had received from the kaiser the nickname of *der traurige Julius,* or in American slang, Gloomy Gus. His given name, *Helmuth,* meant "bright courage." But he turned out to be neither bright nor courageous. Shortly before the German victory at Tannenberg, von Moltke learned that the Russians had pushed two armies into Germany, penetrating East Prussia. Panicking, he withdrew troops from the German right wing, the one that was supposed to sweep along the English Channel, and sent them to the eastern front. There they brought about the victory over the Russians.

But at such a cost! General von Moltke threw a monkeywrench into the clockwork of the Schlieffen Plan in the west. After a month of defeat, with the German armies virtually at the doorstep of Paris, the French commander in chief, General Joseph Joffre learned that the German attacking force was diminished. He regrouped the reeling French army. With support from the British contingent, which was still quite small, he ordered a counterattack at the Marne River. Between September 5 and 12, 1914, this tranquil stream suddenly flowed red. The German advance was stopped at the Marne, and what had been a seemingly unstoppable Teutonic juggernaut was forced to assume the defensive. The war on the Western Front settled into a static bloodletting as Berlin's hope of felling France in a single blow vanished.

The Military Stalemate

By the end of 1914 and on into 1915, Germany's initial victories over the Russians in the east were of little help. The Germans pushed on into the tsarist empire, inflicting huge losses—in 1915 alone, the Russians lost more than 2 million men—but the spaces to be covered were enormous, and the Russians kept fighting.

The Austro–Hungarians had taken Belgrade with ease. But Serbia is a mountainous country, ideal for guerrilla warfare. Heading for the hills and then staging ambushes, Serb peasants stopped the Austrian advance and inflicted huge casualties.

Most important, on the western front what had promised to be a war of movement had become one of position. In August 1914, the German cavalry had pranced off to war in high spirits. By the end of the year the horses were gone. Instead there were the trenches, hundreds of miles of interconnected ditches filled with mud, lice, and rats, sometimes as big as cats. Between the two lines of trenches, which stretched all the way from the English Channel to the Swiss border, was a no-man's-land. The weapons technology of the early twentieth century gave all the advantage to defenders. An entrenched two-man machine-gun team could kill a hundred attackers.

Having failed to complete the Schlieffen Plan, the Germans faced two armies in the west, the French and the British, and were outnumbered. Because the Germans were dug in within French territory, however, they enjoyed the advantages of defending their position with plenty of room to retreat, counterattack, and retreat again, if necessary. The French and British could not break through, and stalemate prevailed all along the western front.

Map of battlegrounds in World War I.
(Eric Stevens)

The Diplomatic Stalemate

Stalemate prevailed on the diplomatic front as well. For a couple of decades, Italy had been allied with Germany and Austria-Hungary (the three together were called the Central Powers). But once the war broke out, Rome cut the tie, holding out for a better offer. Central and Allied officials alike rushed to the Italian capital, offering what they didn't have to offer, money and land. At last the Allies won out, promising that once the war was over, Italy could have an empire in North and East Africa. So, in May 1915, Italy went to war on the Allied side, attacked Austria-Hungary, and created a new stalemate, this one in the mountains between Italy and Austria.

In the meantime, Bulgaria and Turkey had allied themselves with the Central Powers. The Bulgarians hated the Russians, and Turkey had been receiving military aid from Berlin. Bulgaria and Turkey clearly could not do much for Germany on the western front, but they *could* block access by the British and the French to Russia. London and Paris could send no aid to St. Petersburg.

Hoping to open up communications with Russia (the German navy had closed the Baltic), Great Britain in the spring of 1915 launched an attack on Turkey. Their objective was to take Constantinople (now Istanbul), which lay at the entrance to the Black Sea. But to get to Constantinople, the British had to get up through a strait called the Dardanelles, a narrow body of water formed by the Asiatic part of Turkey along the southeast and, along the northwest, a peninsula called Gallipoli.

On its western flank Gallipoli had a long beach, backed by cliffs. Atop the cliffs was a row of fortresses. The idea was that British ships could steam up the strait, blast away at the forts, then land troops on the beach. But the Germans had strewn the strait with mines. That stopped the ships. The Turks stopped the troops. Armed and trained by the Germans, Turkish forces in the forts let loose murderous gunfire upon the British (mostly Australians and New Zealanders, known as the "ANZAC") who were caught on the beaches, trapped between sea and cliff. Within a few days after the start of the assault, the ANZAC had lost nearly 150,000 men and abandoned the mission.

The Paralysis of the Fronts

In 1916, both sides tried to break the deadlock in northern France. In February, the Germans hurled a million men at Verdun, a French fortress complex near the southern end of the front. French general-in-chief Joffre put General Philippe Pétain in charge of holding Verdun and its environs. For more than six months, he and his troops took on much of the German army. Despite more than 300,000 casualties on both sides, the Germans could not break through. To some, Verdun symbolized French heroism. To others, it was the most horrific example of the war's bloody futility.

The British and the French in the meantime had been planning their own offensive at the Somme River.

Factories in Great Britain had finally began cranking out artillery in unprecedented volume, and, through military conscription, London had raised a huge new army. British high command proposed to break through at the Somme by dint of brute force. It didn't work. In the first day of the attack, the British lost 60,000 men. After a week, the Tommies (as British troops were called) had advanced no more than a mile; after a month, two and a half miles. The Battle of the Somme, lasting from July to October 1916, cost Britain 400,000 men and the Germans 500,000. And no one gained anything.

With the armies locked together on the land, both sides looked to the sea. Here the Germans were at a disadvantage from the very beginning of the war. The *englische Gefahr* (English danger) that the British fleet would attack the Kiel Canal never materialized. But an even greater danger to Germany was that of a British naval blockade.

As an industrialized country, Germany was heavily dependent on imports for food; Germany also had no oil reserves to speak of, except in the Austro–Hungarian Empire, and its war production could not function without shipments of iron ore from northern Sweden. So, the British used their much larger fleet, based in Scapa Flow, to control the English Channel and the North Sea, and thus to grip Germany in a stranglehold.

Early in the war, Germany's admirals tried to break the encircling ring. At the Battle of Jutland (May 31-June 1, 1916), off the Danish coast, the German High Seas Fleet took on the Royal Navy. After several hours of combat, during which Germany sank more British ships than they themselves lost, the kaiser's vessels withdrew into the mined waters around Kiel. The Germans had not lost the battle, but neither had they won. The High Seas fleet never again came out of home waters to challenge the British dominance at sea.

The British blockade endured. A desperate Berlin turned from surface ships to submarines—U-boats (*Unterseeboote*). With these vessels, Germany imposed a counterblockade. In February 1915, Berlin declared all the waters around the British Isles to be a war zone. Within this area, any Allied vessel, military or civilian, were subject to torpedo attack. Even neutral vessels traversing these waters were targeted.

At first, Allied shipping was helpless against the submarine threat. Then the Germans made a fateful strategic and diplomatic error. Early in May 1915, the British-owned *Lusitania,* the largest and fastest passenger ship in the world, set sail from New York, heading for Liverpool. Before the ship left the United States, the German embassy placed notices in the New York papers, warning people not to take passage; indeed, the *Lusitania* was carrying munitions manufactured in America and purchased for Allied use. The *Lusitania* was torpedoed and sunk off the Irish coast. About 1,200 persons were drowned, 128 of them U.S. nationals.

The American public was shocked, and President Woodrow Wilson sternly warned Berlin. Fearful of U.S. entry into the war on the side of the Allies, Germany refrained from making full ("unrestricted") use of its submarine fleet for nearly two years. Yet it was the one weapon that might have brought Great Britain to its knees. In the meantime, the British blockade continued to strangle the German economy and starve the German people.

BET YOU DIDN'T KNOW

The Somme, Marne, and Meuse rivers in northeastern France took on the reputations as being sites of some of the most horrific battles in history. But the important thing to remember is that, as they meandered through the fields of Flanders, they were very close together. Once the Germans were stopped at the Marne in 1914, the front lines did not move more than about 10 miles in either direction. Such was the nature of the paralysis of the war.

The Domestic Scene in Germany

From the very beginning of the war, Germany had engaged in a total mobilization of the home front. All able-bodied men were forced into the military, and huge numbers of women were drafted to work in the factories. Women were liberated from their traditional roles of cooking and cleaning. But their new income contributed to an unforeseen consequence: *inflation*.

Christmas 1915, illustrated the mounting shortages on the home front. Most people could no longer afford Christmas trees. In Stuttgart, bakers produced only two modest forms of Christmas cake. In Berlin, pancakes and fritters fell victims to the shortage of fat. Even traditionally festive Christmas markets looked sad: The usual chocolates, wooden toys, and tree ornaments were missing.

Other kinds of shortages were felt. Throughout Germany and Austria-Hungary in 1916, consumer-related industries were closed down altogether. Workers went through old slag heaps in hope of recovering anything metal. Chemical industries had to turn over their supplies for war production. Barns were scraped to recover (from animal waste) nitrates, used in explosives. Church bells came down to be melted and recast as guns. The governments of Germany and Austria-Hungary alike appealed to their citizens to turn in doorknobs and brass ornaments. Princess Evelyn Blücher wrote of this war effort: "It is an interesting sight … to see cartloads of old pots and kettles and candlesticks, door handles, chandeliers, etc., being driven along the street, and a poor woman or schoolboy carrying a copper kettle or brass lamp to the collecting offices to be weighed and paid for." Yet all the while came official claims of no metal shortage. Propagandists struggled to maintain morale at all costs.

No propagandist could explain away the growing hunger. In both Germany and Austria-Hungary, staples such as flour and potatoes were in short supply. "I noticed strings of poorly dressed women and children held in line by police, waiting for milk, vessel in hand," wrote an official at the American embassy in Vienna late in 1916. "Latecomers went home empty handed, while lucky ones obtained only half as much as they expected. Similar lines … can be observed standing in the morning hours in front of the bakers' shops and stores where coffee, tea, and sugar are being sold."

Economic Conditions: From Bad to Worse

Economic conditions were turning from bad to worse. Shortages of corn and oats for horses and cattle led to their widespread slaughter—just as the governments in Berlin and Vienna were demanding more meat for the troops on the fronts. Austria-Hungary itself was starting to break apart. Hungary banned food exports to Austria, which gave rise to cries of treason. And remember Bismarck's *Zollverein* (Custom Union)? It broke down barriers to trade. Now, in Austria in 1916, provinces, districts, and villages *raised* trade barriers against each other.

On into 1917, Germany and Austria-Hungary were turning to *Ersatz* (substitutes) to meet food shortages. Roasted acorns and beechnuts replaced coffee beans. Tea was made of grasses and wild flowers. Plant fats took the place of animal fats.

A black market arose, meaning that given the shortages, some persons sold food products above the state-set price. Some were caught doing so. Princess Evelyn Blücher at the Breslau train station said, "A well-dressed, dignified-looking lady appeared at the luggage-room with the object of checking her trunk. Her flurried mien, and the obvious nervousness with which she hurried on the porter to weigh her trunk, aroused the suspicion of the stationmaster. The trunk was promptly opened, and to the surprise of the amused onlookers a whole pig was discovered in it. It was confiscated and sold in the town at the official price, to the great discomfiture of the stately lady."

TERMS AND TRANSLATIONS

Inflation is a complicated topic, but here a simple point will do. Germans had more money to spend than ever before. Yet because industry was producing almost wholly for the war, there were fewer consumer goods than ever before. More money chasing fewer goods is a classic formula for inflation.

The Russian Revolution and the Berlin Blunders

In the spring of 1917, an event took place that promised to alleviate all the privations. A combination of military reverses, incompetent leadership, and popular disaffection led in March to a revolution in Russia. All indications were that Russia would soon leave the war. That meant the German high command could withdraw forces from the eastern front to launch a great, perhaps decisive, offensive in France. For the people of Germany and Austria-Hungary, victory flickered into sight.

However, in early 1917, Berlin committed two world-class blunders. First, it announced the resumption of unrestricted submarine warfare. Second, on January 19, 1917, Alfred Zimmermann, the German foreign secretary, sent over the radio a note to the German ambassador in Mexico City proposing to Mexico an alliance in a joint war against the United States, promising Mexico recovery of the American Southwest, which it had lost in U.S.-Mexican War (1846-1848). British intelligence intercepted and decoded the message and passed it along to President Wilson.

These two blunders were the tipping point that ended American neutrality. On April 2, 1917, Woodrow Wilson, who had narrowly won a second presidential term on the campaign slogan "He Kept Us Out of War," asked Congress for a declaration of war on Germany. Four days later, on April 6, Congress voted for the declaration. With this, the vast manpower and economic resources of the United States were thrown against Germany and the other Central Powers.

The German general staff put everything it could into a series of offensives intended to defeat the Britain and France before the Americans could arrive in significant numbers. These took a terrible toll—on both sides—and while Germany won some victories, it could not break through decisively. In the middle of July 1918, the British and the French, now reinforced by American divisions, launched a counterattack. The new push from the west so weakened the German positions that Berlin initiated inquiries about the possibility of an armistice.

TERMS AND TRANSLATIONS

In German the noun *Satz* has several meanings; the most common are "part" or "ingredient." *Ersatz* means "equivalent" or "substitute."

Peace Ploys

On July 15, 1918, the Germans reached their farthest advance along the Marne River, putting them essentially where they had been at the end of August 1914. This time, however, nine American divisions were waiting for them; the new French commander in chief, the extremely aggressive Ferdinand Foch, used the Yanks as the advance guard of his July 18 counterattack. Badly overstrained, the Germans faltered. The ensuing American assault through and beyond the zone of the trenches proved more than the Germans could withstand. With its forces in retreat, the German high command informed the government in Berlin that Germany could not win the war. By this time, the foreign office had already made overtures of peace to Wilson through neutral embassies.

BET YOU DIDN'T KNOW

Bismarck once remarked that there are two things you don't want to see being made: laws and sausages. By 1917, German sausages were being stuffed with sawdust and, get this, pigeon droppings.

Early in 1918, Wilson had gone to Congress to promulgate the "Fourteen Points" he deemed to be the American objectives in the war. In his address, Wilson made it clear that he wanted not only to end the war but also to end colonial empires. Since Britain and France had the biggest empires, Berlin concluded that Wilson wanted a balanced peace, with Germany to be kept intact.

Wilson did want a balanced peace. But he also laid down a condition for an armistice: Kaiser Wilhelm II must go. And that was the deal. On November 10, an unwilling and embittered Wilhelm, this time taking orders from his general staff, fled Germany to exile in neutral Holland. Then, at the eleventh hour of the eleventh day, November 11, 1918, the World War I came to an end.

Germany? "Intact" it would not be. Created by Otto von Bismarck and taken to war by Kaiser Wilhelm II, the Second Reich was set to implode in revolution.

BET YOU DIDN'T KNOW

"On the first of February we intend to begin submarine warfare unrestricted. In spite of this, it is our intention to endeavor to keep neutral the United States of America. If this attempt is not successful, we propose an alliance on the following basis with Mexico: That we shall make war together and together make peace. We shall give general financial support, and it is understood that Mexico is to reconquer the lost territory in New Mexico, Texas, and Arizona …"

Just how Mexico was to retake the territories lost in the 1840s war with the United States, Zimmermann failed to make clear; nor did he explain how Germany was to cross the Atlantic Ocean when its fleet was bottled up in Kiel.

Germany's Revolution

When the war broke out, the German government succeeded in gaining the support of the Socialists, the largest opposition party in the country. Remember that Bismarck had forged a coalition of nationalists and socialists, and working-class patriotism carried over into the war itself.

But as the British blockade took its toll, as inflation set in and *real incomes* fell, as the maimed emerged from the hospitals and the dead were lowered into graves, the costs of the war were apparent. It became increasingly clear that the support of the Socialists was eroding. As early as December 1915, a group of 20 Social Democrats in the parliament refused to approve the government's request for war credits.

Next came a series of labor strikes. But the most violent center of unrest was not on the home front but in the German navy itself, where disparities in privileges between officers and enlisted personnel created a genuinely revolutionary situation. When the officers tried to launch a last suicidal attack on the British Royal Navy, which still maintained the blockade in the North Sea, open revolt broke out at the naval base at Kiel on October 30, 1918.

It touched off a revolution. The sailors at Kiel called upon sympathetic groups in the army and throughout the country to assume political power. The call was answered, particularly in the large cities.

Before this revolt, the government in Berlin had been keenly aware of Germany's political instability. Along with the defeat on the western front, that awareness led the authorities to make their approach to President Wilson. But they hardly realized the consequences of their dealings with the American president. As Wilson had demanded, the kaiser abdicated. With his abrupt departure, Germany no longer had a government.

TERMS AND TRANSLATIONS

Real income is a fairly straightforward concept. If I pay one dollar for a bushel of potatoes today but because of inflation I have to pay a dollar and a half tomorrow, my actual purchasing power has declined. My real income has gone down.

Collapse

With Wilhelm gone, the revolutionaries struggled among themselves for power in the ruins of the German Empire.

In ruins as well was the Austro–Hungarian Empire. With Vienna's armies having suffered humiliating defeat on the Italian and Serbian fronts, the various subject nationalities (Czech, Slovak, Hungarian, Romanian, Croatian, and so on) obtained recognition from the Allies.

Austria's Emperor Franz Josef had died during the war, on November 21, 1916, at a decrepit 87. His successor, Charles I, a distant relative, abdicated on November 12, 1918, and on the next day Austria was proclaimed a *republic*, and the tie with Hungary was dissolved. Within a week, Hungary, Czechoslovakia, Romania, and Yugoslavia (centered around Serbia) had proclaimed independence.

TERMS AND TRANSLATIONS

"… And to the republic for which it stands," we say in the Pledge of Allegiance. But what are we saying? The word *republic* emerged from the French Revolution and traced back to ancient Rome. It means simply a country that is not a monarchy.

We are now at a crucial junction on the road to Nazi Germany. Just about everything that German nationalists (from the days of Napoleon Bonaparte onward) had longed for was gone. Both major German states, Germany itself and Austria, had suffered defeat on the fields of battle. Yet rather than accept responsibility for those defeats—Austria's grievance against Serbia and Germany's blind support of Austria when the German economy would not support a sustained war—the inclination in German and Austrian nationalist circles was to blame someone else.

Who? The answer would emerge from the 1919 Treaty of Versailles, signed in the Hall of Mirrors at that fabled palace, the very place where Otto von Bismarck had proclaimed the founding of the German Empire.

The Least You Need to Know

- ✪ Despite Germany's high hopes, the movement of its troops into France in the autumn of 1914 ended in a stalemate.

- ✪ Despite Germany's vaunted industrial and military strength, the British Royal Navy played a major part in reducing Germany to surrender: Germany could never counter the naval embargo.

- ✪ Not surprisingly, given the embargo of food and raw materials, the German and Austrian populations became increasingly restive. Late in 1918, that restiveness turned into outright revolution.

- ✪ The First World War led to the collapse of the German and Austrian Empires. Nationalists began looking for scapegoats.

CHAPTER 5

The Peace to End All Peace:
January 18, 1919–June 28, 1919

IN THIS CHAPTER

⭐ The Palace of Versailles is the site for the signing of the new peace treaty

⭐ The negotiation process and its major players—although Germany is shut out from these proceedings

⭐ The major changes brought about by the Versailles Treaty

⭐ A new German government, called the Weimar Republic, is formed after the Versailles Treaty

In November and December 1918, the leaders of France, Great Britain, and the United States agreed to hold peace talks the following spring. The last great peace talks had taken place at the Congress of Vienna in 1814 and 1815. This time, however, the victors had no intention of establishing a balance of power. Quite the contrary.

How the Paris Peace Talks Opened

The peace talks opened in Paris on January 18, 1919. It was a historically significant date. Forty-eight years earlier, to the day, Otto von Bismarck had proclaimed the creation of the German Empire. The ghost of the Iron Chancellor still loomed over Europe.

BET YOU DIDN'T KNOW

At the Congress of Vienna in 1814-1815, the victors brought the defeated French into their councils, allowing France a say in its own future. That what we might call the "Vienna system" lasted for a century might be due to the fairness and legitimacy of this meeting: All the great powers (not necessarily the lesser ones and certainly not the various nationalists) had a stake in keeping international relations pretty much as they were. They had their squabbles, as with the Crimean War; however, until the coming of Bismarck, none of the great powers was willing to risk a continental war; and even he, after creating the German Empire, tried to make Germany look as if it respected the rights and privileges of the other great powers. But the victors at Paris excluded the Germans; therefore, Germany would have no reason to see any arrangements made at Paris as legitimate.

Should Germany have been included in the peace talks? Would the world possibly have been spared its future horrors?

Europe, however, looked different than it had in Bismarck's time. The Russian Empire was no more, and the Bolsheviks had moved its capital from Petrograd (up to 1914 called St. Petersburg) to Moscow. The Russian and Bolshevik revolutions had given way to a brutal civil war raging all across Russia. The German and Austro–Hungarian Empires were also defunct, with revolutionary regimes struggling to establish themselves in Berlin and Vienna. In Estonia, Latvia, and Lithuania down the Baltic coast, as well as in Poland and along the basin of the Danube, new republics sprang into being, but these were without strong leaders or even borders on which everyone could agree. East of the Rhine and in Italy, Europe was anarchic, with criminal gangs and warlords terrorizing the people and looting at will. France and Great Britain, although victorious, had lost a million men each and their treasuries were empty. Artillery had transformed northeastern France into a barren moonscape. In France, 4.39 percent of the population died as a result of the war. In Germany, perhaps as much as 4.32 percent. But the highest fatality rate occurred where the war began, in Serbia: as high as 27.78 percent.

Germany had been spared an invasion and physical destruction, but it was devastated nonetheless. Everywhere people were gaunt from hunger; for even as the peace got under way, the British maintained their naval blockade. Inflation was steadily mounting and soon would become hyperinflation, German money rushing toward worthlessness. Kaiser Wilhelm II, whom the German people had been taught to revere as a god, was gone, disgraced. His empire, once so seemingly stable, was riddled with social and moral disintegration.

Worst of all, the victors in Paris barred the Germans from taking part in the peace talks. The French, the British, and the Americans had also excluded the Bolsheviks. To be excluded from a voice in the future of Germany? To the Germans, it seemed precisely what it was: outrageous. The people and the politicians of Germany rejected the Allied thesis that the Central Powers alone bore the guilt for the coming of the war. (Today, almost all historians agree that England, Italy, Russia, and especially France share some of the responsibility.) Even before the Paris talks were under way, Germany was aggrieved.

The Big Four

Twenty-seven countries—but none of the Central Powers—were represented at the Paris peace talks. Even far-off China had sent a contingent to fight on the side of the Allies and believed it was entitled to a share of the spoils. The full sessions, however, were unimportant. All that really mattered were the talks among the Big Four—Premier Vittorio Orlando of Italy, Prime Minister David Lloyd George of Great Britain, Premier Georges Clemenceau of France, and President Woodrow Wilson of the United States.

SUPPORTING ACTORS

Wilson might have been the closest thing to the hero of the Paris peace talks, but he was also a very sick man, the war and the presidency having worn him down. He didn't have the strength to insist on a truly just treaty for Germany.

Italy had sided with the Allies only after being bribed to do so. And Italy's military contribution to the Allied cause, by comparison to the British and French efforts, had been minimal—though its losses (thanks to the incompetence of its generals) had been grievous. A small man with a bushy mustache, Prime Minister Vittorio Orlando carried the least weight among the Big Four.

David Lloyd George had taken over the British premiership at the end of 1916. A fiery and mercurial politician with an impressive mane of white hair, his primary interests before the war were in domestic reforms. He cared little about international relations; finely tuned to the nuances of British public opinion, he wanted Germany to acknowledge defeat, but he was not obsessed with a desire for revenge.

Georges Clemenceau, in contrast, lived for vengeance against "the Boche." As the premier of France, with a drooping mustache and sweeping white hair, he was known as the "le tigre"—the tiger. Born in 1841, he was an aged patriot who well remembered the humiliation of the Franco–Prussian War. Clemenceau would have been quite content to see Germany pulverized, reduced to its pre-Bismarckian disunity. Even better would have been seeing the entire nation turned into a pasture.

Woodrow Wilson wanted a just peace—by which he meant peace on *his* terms. Just as he believed his duty was to serve as the "brain" of the American people, so he was confident that only he could draw the outlines of a lasting peace, one that would truly make the Great War (as the combatants called it) the "war to end all war" (as Wilson called it).

It's hard now to imagine the hopes that just about everyone in Europe, including the Germans, placed on the narrow shoulders and frail frame of bespectacled President Wilson. A college professor who had become president of Princeton University, governor of New Jersey, and then, in the election of 1912,

President of the United States, Wilson commanded both awe and great expectations. He was welcomed to Paris in January 1919 as if he were Christ in His Second Coming. As he entered the French capital in an open carriage, people threw roses, violets, and holly from their windows. As he stood in the carriage, raising his silk top hat, French citizens screamed in holy fervor. He rode under red, white, and blue bunting and draped flags. Military bands beat drums and sounded bugles. Their blare was lost in the tumultuous cheers for the man who would save France from another 1870 and another 1914. A huge banner stretched across the width of the Champs Élysées: "Wilson the Just."

The Germans, too, looked to Wilson for justice. His "Fourteen Points" had seemed so promising: "open covenants openly arrived at"; freedom of the seas "alike in peace and in war"; worldwide free trade; arms limitations; readjustments of colonies; the self-determination of peoples and the redrawing of the map of Europe along national lines; and, above all, a League of Nations, an international organization created to allow nations to resolve their differences with negotiation rather than arms. Wilson's principles were democratic, liberal, and progressive, apparently in tune with the prevailing ideas in the Germany of 1919.

Germany looked to Woodrow Wilson to create a new era, even in peace talks from which the nation was excluded.

Negotiations Without the Germans

In the first week of the peace conference, the Allies and Wilson agreed to establish the League of Nations. Then they got down to shaping the peace.

Almost immediately, the Allies began to fight among themselves. Just how great a victory should they claim? Clemenceau wanted a lot. He wanted France to occupy not only the Saarland, the industrialized region in southwestern Germany that bordered on Luxembourg and eastern France, but also the entire left bank of the Rhine. Wilson and Lloyd George objected: They considered Clemenceau's territorial demands excessive and injurious to peace.

Lloyd George and Clemenceau did agree that Germany should pay all their war costs. Wilson disputed the demand: He thought that an enduring peace required a prosperous Germany, not one saddled with crushing reparations.

Orlando threatened to walk out of the conference if Italy's claims along the eastern Adriatic coast were rejected. Two cities there, Trieste and Fiume, were Italian-speaking, although they had been part of the Austro–Hungarian Empire. The Italians wanted still another poke at the Austrians.

The principals at Paris did agree that Germany should be punished, and the most important decisions at Paris did indeed punish Germany. Germany lost all its colonies. Actually, they were already gone, overrun by the British and the Japanese. Under the Covenant of the League of Nations, the Allies agreed to call the former colonies of Germany and other Central Powers "mandates." The word was a way of pretending that those colonies were not simply being shifted to new colonial masters. So, Turkey's domains to the south, Syria and Lebanon, became French mandates. "Palestine" (the present-day Israel, Jordan, Kuwait, and Iraq) became a British mandate. The Union of South Africa (part of the British Commonwealth) took over German Southwest Africa (now Namibia). Australia got German New Guinea and the Solomon Islands; New Zealand took over German Samoa. Japan got other once-German islands in the Pacific, most notably the Marshalls and the Carolines, as well as China's Shandong Peninsula.

Then came the German war machine. The British and the French asserted their authority over the German fleet at Kiel; rather than surrender their vessels, German crews scuttled them. The Allies also decided to limit the German military to 100,000 men; because they also forbade conscription, the reduced German army became exclusively professional. The German navy was allowed up to six warships, but no aircraft or submarines. Germany was to place no troops on the left bank of the Rhine or within 30 miles of the river's right bank. All German rivers, including the Rhine, were to be open to international shipping.

Next were the territorial provisions. Alsace and Lorraine went back to France. Three cities along the border became Belgian. Out in the east, two provinces, Posen and West Prussia, were made part of the newly created Poland. Poland got a corridor of land to the Baltic; the German city of Danzig (now Gdansk) was put under the control of the League of Nations. Memel, a German-speaking port on the Baltic, was handed over to Lithuania. And all along the borders of France, Denmark, Belgium, and Poland, areas that were ethnically mixed, residents could vote on which country to join.

Last but not least was the matter of money. Deeply in debt to the United States, the British and the French were determined to restore their own finances from German pockets. So, they insisted that Germany accept total responsibility for starting the war and therefore total payment for all the costs; those payments were called *reparations*.

TERMS AND TRANSLATIONS

The word **reparation** implies giving compensation to satisfy someone who has suffered injury, loss, or wrong at the hands of another. Thus, it assumes that one party or another is exclusively guilty of wrongdoing. And that was precisely what the vast majority of the German people denied: They insisted that the Russian and French mobilizations and the British move of the fleet to Scapa Flow had been precipitative acts that had forced Germany to launch a preemptive war; that Germany had struck first for reasons of self-defense.

Germany was supposed to pay the Allies for both military and civilian losses. Germany was to start payments immediately, and the bill eventually was figured at nearly $32 billion (roughly $452 billon today). But that wasn't all. Germany had to hand over most of its merchant and fishing boats, hand over most of its coal, and give up all property owned by German private citizens in other countries. This last bit meant that Germany could no longer invest abroad, as it had done before the war.

Understanding the Treaty of Versailles

The Paris peace negotiations produced separate treaties dealing with Germany's alliance partners, Austria, Hungary, Bulgaria, and Turkey (the "Central Powers"). The most famous of the treaties was signed at Versailles. Here (as they exactly appeared) were its major provisions:

ARTICLE 31: "Germany, recognizing that the Treaties of 1839, which established the status of Belgium before the war, no longer conform to the requirements of the situation, consents to the abrogation of said treaties. …"

Translation: In 1839, the great powers of Europe had agreed that Belgium should be independent of Holland and neutral. Now Germany was to consent to Belgium being aided by the Allies.

ARTICLE 42: "Germany is forbidden to maintain or construct any fortifications either on the left bank of the Rhine or on the right bank to the west of a line drawn 50 km [30 miles] to the east of the Rhine. …"

Translation: The Rhineland was to be a demilitarized zone.

ARTICLE 45: "As compensation for the destruction of the coal mines in the north of France and as part payment toward the total reparation due from Germany for the damage resulting from the war, Germany cedes to France in full and absolute possession, with exclusive rights of exploitation, unencumbered and free from all debts and charges of any kind, the coal mines situated in the Saar Basin. …"

Translation: Coal had been the fuel of the mighty German economy. Now that fuel was to be turned over to France.

ARTICLE 51: "The territories which were ceded to Germany [in 1871] are restored to French sovereignty. …"

Translation: Alsace and Lorraine were to be returned to France.

MEMORABLE PLACES

Back in the seventeenth century, France's King Louis XIV had built a whole new town at the old village of Versailles about 10 miles from Paris. Fitted out with polished mirrors, glittering chandeliers, and tall windows that looked out on formal gardens, the palace was a monument to wealth and power.

ARTICLE 80: "Germany acknowledges and will respect strictly the independence of Austria. …"

Translation: Germany could not force German-speaking Austrians to join its country.

ARTICLE 81: "Germany … recognizes the complete independence of the Czecho–Slovak state. …"

Translation: A newly created country, Czechoslovakia contained a sizable German-speaking population, mainly in an area called the Sudetenland. This article meant that Germany was to leave those German-speaking people alone.

ARTICLE 87: "Germany … recognizes the complete independence of Poland. …"

Translation: Germany was to accept the transfer of some of its pre-war territories to the new Polish state.

ARTICLE 119: "Germany renounces in favor of the principal Allied and associated powers all her rights and titles over her overseas possessions. …"

Translation: Germany's colonies were forfeited.

ARTICLE 160: "By a date which must not be later than March 31, 1920, the German army must not comprise more than seven divisions of infantry and three divisions of cavalry. After that date the total number of effectives in the army of the states constituting Germany must not exceed 100,000 men, including officers and establishments of depots. The army shall be devoted exclusively to the maintenance of order within the territory and to the control of the frontiers. The total effective strength of officers, including the personnel of staffs, whatever their composition, must not exceed 4,000. … The German general staff and all similar organizations shall be dissolved and may not be reconstituted in any form."

Translation: Except for police and border functions, Germany was disarmed.

ARTICLE 180: "All fortified works, fortresses, and field works situated in German territory to the west of a line drawn 50 km to the east of the Rhine shall be disarmed and dismantled."

Translation: Germany was shorn of all defenses along its frontier with France.

ARTICLE 181: "After the expiration of a period of two months from the coming into force of the present treaty the German naval forces in commission must not exceed: 6 battleships, 6 light cruisers, 12 destroyers, 12 torpedo boats, or an equal number of ships constructed to replace them. … No submarines are to be included. All other warships, except where there is a provision to the contrary in the present treaty, must be placed in reserve or devoted to commercial purposes. …"

Translation: The kaiser's high seas fleet was reduced to the status of a coast guard.

ARTICLE 198: "The armed forces of Germany must not include any military or naval air forces."

Translation: Toward the end of the First World War, the airplane had come into play over the battlefields. Because it could bomb the trenches, its use may have given Germany a decided advantage. Under this article, Germany was prevented from taking advantage of her airplanes.

ARTICLE 231: "The Allied and Associated governments affirm and Germany accepts the responsibility of Germany and her allies for causing all the loss and damage to which the Allied and Associated governments and their nationals have been subjected as a consequence of the war imposed on them by the aggression of Germany and her allies. …"

Translation: First of all, the major "Associated" government was the United States: President Wilson resolutely refused to consider the United States technically an ally of Great Britain and France. This on his part was a sop to American isolationists. More broadly, this was the war guilt clause: The Versailles treaty pinned all the blame for the war on Germany, which justified the requirement for Germany to pay up.

ARTICLE 245: "Within six months after the coming into force of the present treaty, the German government must restore to the French government the trophies, archives, historical souvenirs or works of art carried away from France by the German authorities in the course of the war of 1870 to 1871 and during this last war. …"

Translation: Germany had to return the spoils of war, past and present.

ARTICLE 428: "As a guarantee for the execution of the present treaty by Germany, the German territory situated to the west of the Rhine, together with the bridgeheads, will be occupied by Allied and Associated troops for a period of 15 years from the coming into force of the present treaty. …"

Translation: The French especially were likely to occupy the western part of Germany for 15 years to come.

ARTICLE 431: "If before the expiration of the period of 15 years Germany complies with all the undertakings resulting from the present treaty, the occupying forces will be withdrawn immediately."

Translation: Germany might get time off for good behavior.

The Versailles Treaty was unquestionably harsh, and almost everyone in Germany was outraged. Its government had made a deal with President Wilson—the departure of the kaiser in return for the nation's being kept intact and sovereign—and Berlin had lived up to its side of the bargain. When news of the treaty got around, people in Germany felt betrayed, and they saw Wilson as the betrayer. To almost all Germans, the war guilt and reparations clauses were utterly repugnant. No one wanted to sign a treaty damning himself, his party, and his principles in the eyes of fellow Germans.

But the Germans had no choice. With their country in political turmoil, starved by the British blockade, and faced with the threat of an actual invasion, the Germans had no choice but to sign the treaty. So, leaders of the Catholic and Social Democratic Parties agreed to shoulder the hateful burden: They would regretfully provide the signers.

Two virtually unknown and deeply embarrassed German representatives showed up at the Hall of Mirrors at Versailles and, in the presence of a huge number of European and American dignitaries, signed the treaty. The date was June 28, 1919, five years to the day after the assassination of Archduke Franz Ferdinand in that obscure town so far away in the Balkans, Sarajevo.

Ever since that day, diplomats, journalists, historians, and others have debated the wisdom of the Treaty of Versailles. Most have pronounced it too punitive. But this much is clear: From the very beginning, well before Hitler and the Nazis rose to power, Germany had no real intention of abiding by the treaty.

Map of Germany after the Treaty of Versailles.
(Eric Stevens)

The Weimar Republic

Some elements in Germany, to be sure, wanted to fashion a western-style democracy. Indeed, after several months of discussions in Weimar, a town about 50 miles southwest of Berlin, a group of political moderates in July 1919 drew up a constitution remarkably similar to the United States Constitution. Adopted on August 11, 1919, the Weimar Constitution preserved the word *Reich* but declared that Germany was a republic; no more kaiser. It went on to create a *Reichstag,* which acted much like the American Congress.

The members of the Reichstag were to be elected by the people, as in the American House of Representatives. There was also to be a *Reichsrat,* in which each of the German *Länder* (states) were to be represented: Think of the U.S. Senate.

TERMS AND TRANSLATIONS

The first part of **Reichstag** is easy: **Reich** means "rich" or "realm," hence a country. **Tag** seems obscure, but isn't really. It is a cognate of the English *day*. *T* and *d* are both pronounced at the tip of the tongue. We also usually consider *y* to be a consonant, as in "yes." *G* is also a consonant. Indeed, *Tag* means "day." And who sits in deliberation every day, or nearly every day? Congress, or the Reichstag. The Reichstag became very important in Hitler's rise to power.

No, **Reichsrat** does not mean a rich German rodent. When you be*rate* somebody, you are telling that person off, saying that he or should not have done such and such. So you're giving a kind of advice. **Rat** in German means advice. The Reichsrat was supposed to supply counsel, as the American Senate supposedly does. A **Ratskeller** is a town hall cellar that doubles as a restaurant or beer hall. Now, **Länder.** When we say land, we can mean the soil or an area. The old areas or states of Germany persisted into the Weimar period. The umlaut and the -**er** ending make the word plural. It's pronounced almost like the English word *lender.* So the German Senate was composed of the states. Sound familiar?

The Weimar Constitution was also strong on the rights of free expression, as in the American First Amendment, and it made a lengthy provision for the "general welfare," a phrase found twice in the U.S. Constitution.

So far, so good. The Weimar Republic looked like a democracy, on paper. But its major supporters were confined to the parties in the center of the political spectrum, the Catholics and the Social Democrats, precisely the groups associated with the signing of the hated Treaty of Versailles.

Still, even the U.S. Constitution was no guarantee of democracy. In the version originally ratified in 1788, only white, male property owners could vote. And under the Alien and Sedition Acts, passed by Congress in the time of President John Adams, the Bill of Rights was virtually overthrown. So, no document is perfect. That said, democracy in America has been the product of a long, slow evolution. In contrast, the Weimar Republicans were trying to establish a German democracy overnight.

It was a noble effort, but the German people had had virtually no experience with democracy. Before Bismarck, a few of the free cities did respect individual rights. But most of the kingdoms and duchies had been authoritarian—as had Prussia. True, in the nineteenth century, a lot of Germans did seek freedom, but by and large they were the ones who emigrated to the United States. To those who remained behind, democracy was an alien phenomenon.

So, right from the start of the Weimar Republic, most Germans still adhered to the traditional authoritarianism. Yes, Germany was again deeply divided.

On the left were the so-called Spartacists, named for a Roman slave who fomented a slave revolt in southern Italy in 72 B.C.E.; they were led by two out-and-out Communists, Karl Liebknecht and Rosa Luxemburg, who, in January 1919, took over Berlin and tried to make it a Bolshevik city. Their revolution failed. Liebknecht and Luxemburg were arrested and subsequently shot to death while "trying to escape." Even in failure, however, their revolt signaled the contempt of the German left for the Weimar democracy.

And then there was the right. In 1920, a cabal of army officers staged a *Putsch,* or armed revolt, in Berlin. (*Putsch* is a cognate of the English word "push," as when you push someone out of power.) They put the republican government to flight and tried to put in place a new government of their own, headed by a figure named Dr. Wolfgang Kapp. Shutting down the public utilities, it was workers in Berlin who managed to halt the takeover.

Many historians scorn the Weimar Republic as feckless and inept. In fact, between 1924 and 1929, the Republic presided over a period known as the *Goldene Zwanziger,* the Golden Twenties. It was a time of surprising stability, a decrease in civil unrest, and a measurable increase in economic growth. The U.S. "Dawes Plan" (named for the U.S. banker and politician Charles G. Dawes) facilitated loans that helped Germany pay some of its reparations, and the liberal constitution nurtured a brief but exciting cultural renaissance of art, architecture, literature, music, and film—centered in Berlin.

Thanks to the earnest leadership of Foreign Minister Gustav Stresemann (a more dynamic figure than President Friedrich Ebert), the Weimar Republic showed real promise. Yet three events doomed it. First, 51-year-old Stresemann died of a heart attack on October 3, 1929, leaving the Republic in the hands of the uninspired Ebert. Second, on October 29, the Wall Street Crash brought down the U.S. banks that had financed the Dawes Plan. The Weimar Republic found itself cash-strapped. Third, despite its promise, the Weimar Republic failed to build enduringly broad support. It was too weak to suppress the armed gangs, led by anti-democratic, authoritarian agitators, that made life in Germany violent and anarchic. As early as 1923, one of these very agitators had led what at first seemed an abortive, run-of-the-mill revolt, this one in Munich. The name of its instigator and leader was Adolf Hitler.

The Least You Need to Know

○ Probably the most significant decision made at the Paris peace talks of 1919 was that of excluding the Germans from the deliberations. This meant that whatever treaty the conversations produced was bound to be illegitimate in the eyes of the German people.

○ Of all the world leaders who met in Paris, starting in January 1919, the most important was Woodrow Wilson. He put forth a vision of peace based on justice. To the German people, though, he seemed to betray his own principles, leaving Germany to the mercy of the French and others who wanted to take chunks of the German Empire.

○ The Treaty of Versailles was based on the assertion that Germany was solely responsible for the advent of the war. The treaty therefore left Germany geographically shrunken, militarily weakened, and financially ruined.

○ The German government that emerged after the signing of the Versailles Treaty was called the Weimar Republic, named for the town where the new German constitution had been drafted. Although it showed real promise, the Weimar Republic was a weak government, unable to withstand the buffetings from the Communists on the left and the forces led by Hitler and others on the right.

PART 2

The Ascendancy of Evil

Defeated in World War I, Germany was a dissatisfied and aggrieved country. But why did it fall under the spell of Adolf Hitler, turn to Nazism, and become a machine of war? The answers, as detailed in the next five chapters, lie in the organizational and communication tactics Hitler learned as a young man, his exploitation of the sense of crisis in Germany during the 1920s and the Great Depression, his successful political appeals to a suffering nation, and, finally, his bold seizure of power in 1933.

CHAPTER 6

Hitler's Youth: 1889–1923

IN THIS CHAPTER

- ⭐ Hitler's dysfunctional childhood
- ⭐ Down and out in Vienna and Munich
- ⭐ Hitler's military career
- ⭐ The formation of the Nazi Party
- ⭐ How membership in the Nazi Party slowly grows, through passionate speeches in beer halls

We saw Germany evolve from an almost feudal land of political divisions—with various kings and dukes in their independent castles—to an ostensibly unified and certainly economically powerful giant of a country. We also saw Germany enter into a war of unprecedented mass destruction, a war its leaders should have known it could not win. We saw Germany defeated, humiliated, and scorned. And we saw the beginnings of the spirit that was to overwhelm Germany and indeed much of the world— the widespread desire to recapture the mythical glories of the German past.

After the signing of the Treaty of Versailles, Germany was swept by an obsessive desire for the resurrection and redemption of the country socially, politically, and internationally. Germany had to be a great power once again, even a greater power than before. And that brings us to Adolf Hitler.

A Look at Hitler's Character

Before we trace the rise of Hitler, we need to assess his character to answer the questions most often asked about him.

Was Hitler mad? Many have thought so. In the end, he was certainly out of touch with reality. But we've got to be careful to avoid the trap of branding our enemies as crazy. His childhood was dysfunctional, to be sure. But did that make him crazy? In the beginning of his career, at least, Adolf Hitler was "crazy like a fox." By the early 1920s, he was clearly in touch with what multitudes of Germans believed.

MODERN DAY PARALLELS

Many studies of abused children show that when they grow up, they often become abusers themselves. Some people, of course, break the chain of abuse. Without question, though, Hitler grew up in an atmosphere of domestic violence that foreshadowed his role in bringing greater violence.

Was Hitler anti-Semitic? Of course he was. From the perspective of today, his anti-Semitism was not only immoral and obscene, but also unhinged. Yet in the Germany—in the Europe—of Hitler's birth, childhood, and youth, anti-Semitism was common as dirt. It was also organized. In 1879, 10 years before Hitler was born, the influential League of Anti-Semites was founded by Wilhelm Marr. A masterful agitator and publicist, Marr is widely credited with coining the very term anti-Semite. Hitler grew up in a Germany in which politicians could rise to office almost exclusively on the basis of anti-Semitic platforms. Jews represented only about 1 percent of the German population in the late nineteenth century, yet they loomed large as a target of hatred and persecution.

Was Hitler a born leader? Probably not. By all accounts, he was a dull child, abused by his father and doted on by his mother. He showed no early promise. To put it cruelly, he started life as a nobody. Only later did he discover a kind of actor's gift for mesmerizing crowds. Only later did he find that espousing extreme right-wing, anti-Semitic, anti-foreign positions appealed to ever-larger audiences.

This raises another question. Did Hitler passionately believe the doctrines he proclaimed? This is difficult to answer. Most who have studied the man believe he was at bottom a cynical manipulator of public opinion who used his skill on the platform to elevate himself to a position of power. It was the power and prestige he craved, as if desperate to fill some inner void. Perhaps he had no real ideas and no true patriotism, however twisted. Perhaps his objective, first and last, was the acquisition of power.

Some have seen Hitler as a lower-class, "populist" incarnation of Bismarck. Yet if Bismarck craved power, he did wield that power in the service of Germany. He built an empire, made necessary compromises, and, at least for a time, brought a certain stability to Europe. Hitler's promised "thousand-year Reich" lasted but a dozen bloody years.

Speculative interpretation is important, but it is the known facts that are indispensable. Here they are.

Hitler's Birth and Boyhood

Hitler's parents grew up in the Waldviertel (the Wood Quarter), an Austrian farming region northwest of Vienna and not far from the current border of Czechoslovakia. Hitler's father, Alois Hitler (born illegitimate as Alois Schicklgruber and legitimized by a priest as Hitler—a name that over the generations had undergone several spelling changes), rose above the status of local peasant by becoming a minor bureaucrat in the Austro–Hungarian customs bureau. He was, however, a brutal drunk who routinely beat his wife and their two children who lived to adulthood; four died in infancy. Adolf Hitler, born in 1889, came to hate his father.

Born in Braunau am Inn, the largest town of the Wood Quarter, Hitler grew up speaking the local dialect. Indeed, for many years, he could not speak standard German (Hochdeutsch), and all his life stumbled over the niceties of correct grammar. In describing where some people come from, the Germans have an expression: "Aus Buxtehude," which means "from the back of beyond." This was Hitler—a hick.

Early on, he also exhibited the makings of a drifter. He went off to school at the nearby city of Linz, but was an indifferent student and dropped out at 16. This was not unusual for his time and place, but it hardly suggested a future of bright promise. He did have one stroke of luck, however. The year he left school, his despised father died, and he inherited a small sum of money. With it, he took up a Bohemian existence. With another aimless youth, August Kubizek, he rented a small apartment and whiled away his time reading, filling sketchbooks with drawings, and going to the opera. Wagner especially enchanted him. He dreamed vaguely of becoming an architect, and he even enrolled in a Realschule (secondary school) at Steyr, passing his certificate exam on his second try in 1905, but emerging without any definite plans for life and career.

In the spring of 1906, his mother let him visit Vienna. For a month he roamed the glorious old city, staying with his godparents and gawking at the baroque buildings of the Austrian capital.

When he returned to Linz, he was already an architect—in his imagination. His friend Kubizek recalled many years later how Hitler would stand in front of the Linz cathedral, praising some features and in his sketchpads showing how he would redesign others. In fact, on paper he redesigned almost all of Linz, planning a new railroad station and a public park. For the first time in his life, he showed an urge to make or to remake the reality around him. He had yet to discover politics, but, in these sketches, he showed a degree of vision and a politician's desire to take control.

Late in December 1907, Hitler's mother died of cancer. As much as he hated his father, Hitler had loved his mother, and her death deepened his growing sense of emptiness. The next year, Hitler and Kubizek headed to Vienna, where Hitler believed he would at last make his mark.

Once in the metropolis, Kubizek won admission to the Academy of Music. Hitler's application to the Academy of Art, however, was rejected twice. The architectural drawings he submitted were accurate but without the spark of life. Nor could he qualify for the Academy of Architecture, which demanded a serious educational background for admission. Kubizek's success, contrasted with his own failure, led Hitler to break off the friendship. Now he was in Vienna alone, the meager funds from his inheritance dwindling.

Down and Out in Vienna and Munich

By late summer 1909, his money all but gone, Hitler had been living in a series of rooms, each meaner than the last and each farther out into the slums surrounding Vienna. Each time he moved, he registered his changes of address with the police, as required by Imperial law. His last registration was dated August 22. Within a month of that, he dropped from sight into the underworld of poverty. Unable or unwilling to work, he spent the autumn as a tramp. For a while his "home" was a bench in the Prater, Vienna's famed amusement park, complete with Ferris wheel. Selling a few small watercolors and most of his clothing, Hitler met the coming of winter without a coat. He resigned himself to lining up for dinners and a bed at a Viennese homeless shelter.

For Hitler, this asylum turned out to be a significant place. Along with the other down-and-outers—and for the first time in his life, apparently—he began talking politics. Like his fellow derelicts, Hitler blamed his plight on the upper classes of Vienna, and, above all, on "the Jews." This was routine. His anti-Semitism at this point was far from the all-consuming obsession of his mature years. Nevertheless, there, in that shelter, he began to harbor political ambitions. In Hitler's celebrated political memoir, Mein Kampf, he wrote:

> You know—without exaggeration—I always believe that the world has lost a great deal in that I could not attend the Academy [of Art] and learn the technical end of the art of painting. Or has fate chosen me for something else?

In time, Hitler was able to sell a few more of his paintings and move into another cheap room of his own. But after five years of a love-hate relationship with Vienna, he was ready to move on. When he left, he hung a placard over his bed that read:

> We look free and open
> We look steadfastly,
> We look joyously across
> To the German Fatherland!
> Heil!

On May 25, 1913, Hitler got off the train from Vienna and made his way through the lobby of Munich's Hauptbahnhof, the main railroad station. Full of hope, he found a room and immediately began to paint his pictures. But the art market in Munich was small and Hitler made few sales. The winter of 1913 to 1914 found him again on the brink of starvation.

TERMS AND TRANSLATIONS

Hauptbahnhof. *Haupt* means "head," or "main." You've heard of the famous German *Autobahns*. **Bahn** means "road," as in "railroad." *Hof* doesn't seem to have any cognates in English, but it suggests a court or palace.

Then a peculiar incident took place. On the afternoon of January 18, Hitler heard a knock on his door. When he opened it, he was confronted by a Munich police officer, who served him with a summons from Vienna. It ordered Hitler to report to Linz for military duty within two days. Failure to do so would result in a charge of leaving Austria-Hungary "with the object of evading military service." He would be subject to imprisonment and a heavy fine.

The officer took Hitler to a Munich police station, and the next morning he was escorted to the Austro-Hungarian consulate general. What happened next reveals another of Hitler's talents: an ability to win sympathy. Seeing his ragged clothes and skinny frame, the consul-general took pity on this young man, especially after hearing his tale of woe. Back in 1911, Hitler claimed, he had tried to register for military service in Vienna but had heard nothing since. The summons had taken him by surprise and gave him no time to return to Linz by the deadline. Besides, he had no money for the trip. Relenting, the official let him go to Salzburg at government expense, arriving there on February 5. Here is how Hitler described his sorrowful story in *Mein Kampf*:

> I was a young, inexperienced person, without financial help and also too proud to seek assistance from anyone or beg. Without any support, depending only on myself, the kronen and heller received for my work were often only enough to provide a place to sleep. For two years my only girl friend was Sorrow and Need, and I had no other companion except constant unsatisfied hunger. I never learned to know the beautiful word "youth." Today, after five years, my memories are still in the form of frostbitten fingers, hands, and feet. … I kept my name clean, and am not guilty in the face of the law and have a clear conscience. …

Back in Austria, Hitler was found physically unqualified for military service— "unfit for combat and auxiliary duties. Unable to bear arms." Returning to Munich, he resumed his efforts to sell his paintings and took up again his dream of a career as an architect.

On the afternoon of June 28, 1914, there came another knock on the door. It was his landlady—with news: "The Austrian heir, Archduke Franz Ferdinand, has been assassinated!"

War followed a month later. Swept up in sudden patriotic fervor, Hitler volunteered for service—not in Austria, but in Germany. He enlisted in Munich and, this time, was accepted. On August 16, he reported for duty at the barracks of the First Bavarian Infantry Regiment.

His most immediate problems were solved. He would have food, clothing, and shelter. He would have companionship. Most of all, he would have a purpose in life.

Hitler the Soldier

Hitler's basic training, on the grounds of a public school, was short but intensive. Soon, he was transferred to the Sixteenth Bavarian Reserve Infantry Regiment. Still in Munich, the training there was tougher. Lots of the men groaned under the strain. Not Hitler. He loved every minute of it. One of his fellow soldiers later recalled that when Hitler held his rifle, he "looked at it with a delight that a woman looks at her jewelry."

On October 17, Hitler's unit marched out of Munich, heading for yet more training at a military camp 40 miles to the west. The drilling was even more strenuous, with extensive rifle practice and long night marches. At last, on October 20, Hitler's unit was ready to move out. He wrote to his Munich landlady: "I'm so happy."

At daybreak, Hitler's train was puffing along above the Rhine. As the river mists cleared, the rising sun burst upon an immense statue. Germania, it was called, and it stood high on the river bank. Throughout the train, the soldiers burst into "Wacht am Rhein," or "Watch on the Rhine," a patriotic song from the days of Bismarck. Eight days later, Hitler and his comrades were in battle at the front lines.

"Now the first shrapnel hisses over us and explodes at the edge of the forest, splintering trees as if they were straws," Hitler wrote to an acquaintance back in Munich. "We watch with curiosity. We have no idea as yet of the danger. None of us is afraid. Everyone is waiting impatiently for the command, 'Forward!' … We crawl on our stomachs to the edge of the forest. Above us are howls and hisses, splintered branches and trees surround us. Then again shells explode at the edge of the forest and hurl clouds of stones, earth and sand into the air, tear the heaviest trees out by their roots, and choke everything in a yellow-green, terribly stinking steam. We cannot lie here forever, and if we have to fall, it's better to be killed outside [the trenches]."

Finally, Hitler and his comrades heard the order to go over the top. "Four times we advance and have to go back; from my whole batch only one remains beside me; finally, he also falls. A shot tears off my right coat sleeve, but like a miracle I remain safe and alive. At two o'clock we finally go forward for the fifth time, and this time we occupy the edge of the forest and the farms."

BET YOU DIDN'T KNOW

On both sides of the fighting, the Allies on the west and the Germans on the east, soldiers had little idea of what was happening even as close as a mile away. We have many accounts of the trench warfare, and they all seem to focus, as did Hitler's, on what was close by, the trees, the trenches, and the deaths of people all around. Although Hitler could not see it, the difficulties of his unit's advance were part of the overall German slowdown.

Clearly, Hitler had a way with words. Poorly educated, he nevertheless possessed an innate expressive flair that would later underlie the hypnotic quality of his speeches. He also seemed to be getting a sense of invulnerability. In stark contrast to his days as a tramp in Vienna and Munich, he was beginning to feel that destiny was saving him for some mission.

"I was eating my dinner in a trench with several comrades," he said years later to a British journalist. "Suddenly a voice seemed to be saying to me, 'Get up and go over there [through no-man's land].' It was so clear and insistent that I obeyed mechanically, as if it had been a military order. I rose at once to my feet and walked 20 yards along the trench, carrying my dinner in its tin-can with me. Then I sat down to go on eating, my mind being once more at rest. Hardly had I done so when a flash and deafening report came from the part of the trench I had just left. A stray shell had burst over the group in which I had been sitting, and every member of it was killed."

Was Hitler making this up? Who knows? But we do know that a few weeks later he told fellow soldiers, "You will hear much about me. Just wait until my time comes."

Maybe it was in the trenches that Hitler acquired his sense of destiny. The fact is that he volunteered for hazardous duty as a "runner," or messenger, a job that continually exposed him to enemy fire. He never rose above the rank of corporal, and although toward the end of the war he was badly gassed and had to be hospitalized, he not only recovered, but was decorated with the Iron Cross, a medal awarded for valor and only rarely bestowed on lowly enlisted men.

Germany's surrender in November 1918 came as a bitter blow to many Germans, but none were harder hit than Hitler. To him, surrender seemed a betrayal by an illegitimate government under the influence of Communists and Jews.

The Right-Wing Revolutionary

Demobilized in 1919, Hitler, embittered over Germany's defeat, returned to Munich. Once again, he was dirt poor, hungry, and living in a squalid room. This time, however, at least he had the consolation of being not much different from everyone else. "1919 in Munich was a sad time," he wrote. "Little light, lots of dirt, poorly dressed people, impoverished soldiers, in short, the picture resulting from four years of war and the scandal of revolution."

In *Mein Kampf*, Hitler undoubtedly lied frequently and exaggerated much. This particular passage, though, rings true. We know from many sources that life in postwar Germany was grim.

Corporal Hitler, in uniform and wearing the Iron Cross.
(Found in John Toland's Adolph Hitler; U.S. Army)

The discontent was also real, as Hitler quickly found out. He became involved with a small circle of men, only half a dozen or so, who called themselves the *Deutsche Arbeiterpartei*. Later, Hitler expanded the name to the *National Sozialistische Deutsche Arbeiterpartie* (NSDAP, the National Socialist German Workers' Party, or, simply, the Nazis). *National* and *Socialist*—the two words had been significant among the German masses since before the rise of Bismarck.

TERMS AND TRANSLATIONS

Nazi is simply the abbreviation made up of the first syllables of "National" and "Socialist." **Deutsche** is German, as in "Pennsylvania Dutch." **Arbeit** means "work."

The group's appearance was most unimpressive. Hitler described them as clothed in "military pants, dyed coats, hats of indefinable shapes but shiny from wear, our feet in remodeled war boots ..." The little band was hardly a party and certainly not a political movement. It was just a ragtag collection of veterans who met in the back room of a clubhouse to cry into their beer.

But Hitler had ideas for these men. He persuaded one of them, who had access to a mimeograph machine, to run off invitations for membership. Slowly, the ranks swelled. A dozen become about 35.

At the larger meetings, Hitler passed the hat. With the collection in hand, he bought advertising space in the *Münchener Beobachter* (the Munich Observer), a *völkisch*, anti-Semitic newspaper. Hitler was calling for a mass meeting in Munich's *Hofbräuhaus*, a beer hall, to be held on the evening of October 16, 1919.

TERMS AND TRANSLATIONS

Here, the use of the German word *Völkisch* seems appropriate. *Völkisch* obviously can be translated as "folkish." But we don't use that word in English. In German, it takes on the meaning of folk tradition, folklore, some kind of mythic past. More exactly, it implies the so-called Aryan "race" as distinct from the Jews.

That evening marked the start of Hitler's rise. About 70 people showed up. After some preliminaries, Hitler walked to a lectern that someone had placed on the head table. At first, he spoke quietly, so quietly that the audience had to strain to hear his words. Then his voice grew stronger and his message became violent. For half an hour he ranted, spewing out denunciations of the English and the French, Communists, the people who supposedly had stabbed Germany in the back by arranging the surrender (actually, it had been instigated by the German high command), and, above all, the Jews. He spoke without restraint, grimacing, scowling, waving his arms, calling for revenge against all of Germany's enemies. The crowd loved it. He finished to deafening applause.

Hitler built on his success. More meetings followed, larger crowds assembled, and ever more vociferous speeches were delivered. Hitler's appeal was especially great to the army veterans who, like him, had survived the trenches only to be rejected by their own country when they marched home. These former troops, anti-Marxist and anti-Semite alike, formed the nucleus of a private army.

He went further. Toward the end of 1919, Hitler sat down in his room with some of these former troops and worked out a series of 25 points to be delivered at a mass meeting. He called them "theses," an allusion to the "95 theses" Martin Luther nailed to the door of the Wittenberg Cathedral in 1517, launching the Protestant Reformation. On one point, Luther's theses agreed with the Catholic Church from which he was otherwise breaking away: "the Jews" had killed Jesus.

The meeting at which Hitler was going to proclaim his theses was scheduled for 7:30 p.m., February 24, 1920. All over Munich posters printed in bright red were plastered on walls and doors. Red would figure prominently in Hitler's propaganda. It symbolized blood.

The publicity worked. When the meeting opened in the large room of the *Hofbräuhaus*, more than 2,000 persons were in attendance. The audience was quiet, even when Hitler got to his feet. Wearing a shiny old blue suit, he hardly looked like the demagogue he was. He began, as usual, in a low voice. Almost like a professor, he traced out the recent history of Germany. So far, no histrionics. Then he came to the revolutions that had swept Germany in 1918 and 1919. Now he showed some emotion, especially as he denounced the leftists.

At that point, trouble broke out. Some of those in the audience were socialists. They shouted back at Hitler. Soon beer mugs were flying through the air, many of them aimed at Hitler's head. That's when Hitler's army buddies went into action. Armed with whips and billy clubs, they beat up on the troublemakers, driving most of them outside.

Hitler continued his speech. He spelled out all his theses. They were the foundation of what would become his official ideology: the restoration of the colonies; the overturning of the Treaty of Versailles; the creation of a new army; social welfare for the workers; the union of all German-speakers in a new Reich; a ruthless battle against the socialists; and the *Entfernung* of the Jews. Right there in the Munich *Hofbräuhaus* on the night of February 24, 1920, Hitler was calling for the Holocaust.

TERMS AND TRANSLATIONS

In German, the prefix *ent* conveys the sense of "away." *fernung*, related to the English word far, means "distance." So *Entfernung* meant "removal." But it also has an extended meaning: "elimination."

Those who had not been expelled from the audience reacted with rapturous joy. Hitler's theses had something for everyone—he was emerging as a shrewd politician—except, of course, the Jews. So great was Hitler's popularity that, 11 months later, on January 22, 1921, Munich hosted the first national congress of the Nazi Party. Hitler's magnetism on stage, together with his message of anti-Semitism, made him a respected force—at least in Bavaria.

Respected—and feared. The brawl at the *Hofbräuhaus* told him that he could attain eventual victory through violence. By 1922, he began to win disciples who were clearly attracted to the use of force. One of these was Hermann Göring, an extroverted, flamboyant military pilot who had been a flying ace in World War I. Another early follower was also a pilot, though a far more reserved presence than Göring: Rudolf Hess. Another unquestioning follower, Julius Streicher, joined the ranks. Stocky, bald, and vulgar, Streicher was, if anything, even more virulently anti-Semitic than Hitler. He soon founded an anti-Semitic newspaper called *Der Stürmer*. It meant *The Stormer*, a reference to the Storm Troopers, or *Sturmabteilung* (SA, literally "Storm Detachment"), the paramilitary wing of the Nazi Party created in 1920.

On the Brink of the Beer Hall *Putsch*

The emerging Nazi Party was a paramilitary organization. And an army costs money. Hitler had another ally, the German-born, Harvard-graduated, handsome and cultured Ernst Hanfstängl. Suave and persuasive, Hanfstängl knew how to ingratiate himself with the very people who had the money, the industrialists of the Rhineland. Their fortunes, to be sure, had been much diminished. Before and during the war, however, those fortunes had been based largely on sales of munitions to the German military. The industrialists therefore had every reason to finance someone who convincingly promised to restore the German state. Hanfstängl presented that someone as Adolf Hitler.

Hitler's ability to appeal to workers and big businessmen alike speaks volumes. Whatever else he was, he was as good as Bismarck at forging unlikely political coalitions.

By 1923, he was even beginning to see himself as the *new* Bismarck, the man who had conquered all Germany. And why not? Only the year before, Benito Mussolini, another working-class "nobody," had marched a private army into Rome and seized the Italian government. If Mussolini could do it, why not Hitler?

Hanfstängl's wife, Helene, would recall that "absolutely no one could ever persuade [Hitler] to change his mind. On a number of occasions … I noticed the faraway expression in his eyes; it was as though he had closed his mind to all ideas but his own."

In the summer of 1923, Hitler's idea was that, in emulation of Mussolini, he would lead his Nazis to Berlin. But first they would take over Munich. And the starting point there would be the *Hofbräuhaus*, the beer hall.

The Least You Need to Know

- Adolf Hitler was born into a backwoods family in rural Austria. His schooling was desultory, for he was in constant rebellion against all forms of authority—his father, his teachers, and his Austro–Hungarian overlords. But he did not turn out to be a left-winger. Like Bismarck, he would be a "white revolutionary," white as opposed to red, or Communist.

- As an adolescent and a young adult, Hitler the life of a Bohemian—and, often, an outright tramp. He manifested artistic yearnings, but he by no means found himself as an artist.

- Vienna was crucial for Hitler's development. It was almost two cities: One put on display the glitter of imperial pomp; the other was a vast slum of poverty and disease. From the former, Hitler learned how to stage political theater; from the latter, he imbibed a radicalism that he later linked with German nationalism.

- Hitler's formative experience was as a soldier in the trenches of northeastern France. There he came to worship the German state and to see himself eventually as a politician.

- Hitler would aspire to be no ordinary politician. Once decommissioned, he discovered that he had a gift as a rabble-rouser, indeed one with an undoubted talent for political dramaturgy. Thus, as early as 1923, he decided to make a stab at seizing power in Germany.

The Beer Hall *Putsch*: 1919–1923

Germany in the early 1920s was in chaos: Hitler's was not the only right-wing revolutionary society. Conspirators murdered Matthias Erzberger, a political moderate who had signed the Versailles Treaty, and Walter Rathenau, a financier who had organized the German economy during the war. Rathenau's sins were that he supported international conciliation and that he was Jewish.

Everywhere leftists battled rightists in the streets. Criminal gangs robbed banks almost unimpeded and with impunity. Jews lived in a state of increasing fear. The police barely functioned, at least as protectors of the public safety. And while the government, seated at Weimar, showed flashes of real promise, it too functioned as a government in name only.

Weaknesses of the Weimar Republic

The Weimar government brought with it the promise of democracy. Under it, as we saw in Chapter 5, there was even a brief rebirth of the arts, both fine and popular. Yet the Weimar government was not fully legitimate because it was not fully accepted by the people, most of whom simply felt that they had no stake in the new government.

As it turned out, the glue that had held the German political system together since the creation of the empire in 1871 was the German monarch. Now he was gone. Despite the existence of the Reichstag, imperial Germany had been an absolutist state with only a very weak tradition of political parties. After the World War I, a host of parties suddenly sprang up, but none of them could build a clear majority. Between 1920 and the end of 1923, the Weimar Republic consequently went through seven different cabinets. The German people failed to come together around democracy as they had around the Hohenzollerns.

The weakness of the republican government was hardly surprising. Its single greatest flaw was an inability to levy and collect taxes efficiently. Bismarck and the kaiser had no trouble bringing in revenue. The public deferred to their authority because German political culture had always been authoritarian. But when you have an authoritarian culture without a source of authority, you are doomed to fail. Each group or political party grabs what it can, with no interest in compromise. No one has a stake in the system.

Hitler's was not the only paramilitary group that sprang up in the Weimar power vacuum. By the time he was organizing the Nazis, a *putsch,* or revolt, led by Gustav von Kahr, had already turned the state of Bavaria into a haven for right-wing extremists. In fact, a map of western and central Germany between 1918 and 1923 showed nearly 30 different cities to be centers of revolutionary and counter-revolutionary activity.

During the early years of the Weimar Republic, effective power lay almost wholly in the hands of the states and cities. It was as if the old French dream of a pulverized Germany had come true. Indeed, even after agreeing to the onerous terms of the Treaty of Versailles, the Germans could not get the French off their backs. In 1919 came the Ruhr crisis.

TERMS AND TRANSLATIONS

Political culture simply represents the fundamental political values of a country.

The Ruhr Crisis

In the bend where the Rhine River winds its way down through the foothills of the Alps and turns upward on its course toward Holland lies the valley of the Ruhr. (The Germans called it the *Ruhrgebiet,* the Ruhr territory.) The area is small, no larger than metropolitan New York, really just a dot on the continent of Europe. But its significance in the early twentieth century was immense. Its mines yielded more coal than all the rest of Europe combined. It also produced fine steel. For coal could be converted to coke—pure carbon, acquired by cooking coal to draw off its gases—and coke was indispensable for the conversion of iron into steel. The Ruhr was Europe's main source of coke.

In short, the valley of the Ruhr had been the engine of Germany's economic prowess. "The German Empire," John Maynard Keynes, the British economist, noted, "has been built more truly on coal and iron than on blood and iron."

No wonder that the French gazed upon the valley of the Ruhr, right across the border, with greedy eyes. Early in 1923, claiming that Germany had defaulted on reparations payments, France sent an army into the Ruhr to seize the coal and iron industries. Wilhelm Cuno, head of the German government at the time, reacted by canceling all reparations, period. He also asked businessmen, workers, and public officials in the region not to cooperate in any way with the French.

For once, the Weimar government had done a strong and a popular thing. Germans cheered this act of defiance, and the workers of the Ruhr went on strike.

But this meant that the engine of the German economy ceased to function. The production of all goods came to a grinding halt. With fewer goods being chased by a constant stream of money, the stage was set for inflation to rise to hyperinflation.

Prior to the Ruhr crisis, the value of the German currency, the deutsche mark, had already fallen from 8.9 to over 190 to the U.S. dollar. Internally, German inflation was already profound. Then came the peace settlement. Two years after Versailles, the Allies presented Germany with a reparations bill set at 132 billion gold marks. All the major countries had reserves of gold, and they now demanded payment in that metal rather than in paper money. John Maynard Keynes calculated that the sum was three times more than Germany could afford to pay.

BET YOU DIDN'T KNOW

In America we buy things with the dollar and in Europe now with the euro. So, when a European comes to the U.S. or an American goes to Europe, that person must obtain dollars or euros. This means you buy the other side's currency, pretty much as you buy a loaf of bread at the store. Pretty much. But usually the price of the loaf of bread doesn't change much, at least in the short run. Sometimes, currencies change in value dramatically and quickly. This happened with the deutsche mark before the Ruhr crisis. Americans could buy a lot more of the German currency than before. Now imagine: Suppose that today a loaf of bread costs $1 and tomorrow, say 20¢; so you can buy a lot of bread. That's what happened in Germany in the early 1920s. Americans could buy a lot of the German currency.

Hyperinflation

During World War I, increased German arms production came about at the expense of consumer manufacturing. But Wilhelm II and his ministers lacked the will to impose a progressive taxation system. So, instead of extracting funds from the rich, the government in Berlin covered its mountain of debt by borrowing money through the issue of war bonds. As the war progressed, the purchase of such bonds by the German public became less "voluntary" and ultimately amounted to an unofficial tax. Yet even coercion failed to raise enough cash to pay for the billions of marks' worth of munitions *consumed* by the German army. (If you build a lathe, you can use it over and over; if you fire an artillery shell, it's gone.) The government's solution was to print more money. In the short term, this pays the bills, but it also creates inflation. By the end of the war, the amount of paper money in circulation in Germany was six times that available in 1913.

During the war, the government had introduced rationing and closed currency exchanges with the Allies. Those steps hid the alarming degree of inflation from the public. Nevertheless, by November 1918, the German currency had fallen by half in the neutral countries. Inflation exploded into hyperinflation, which is inflation at an unusually high and accelerating rate.

For most Germans, hyperinflation was devastating. By September 1929, the average factory worker had lost 30 percent of his 1913 income. A pensioner who in 1913 had been able to invest 100,000 marks found that his account was worth about 100 marks 10 years later.

By the autumn of 1923, hyperinflation hung over Germany like a thick, dark cloud. Especially with the government supporting the striking Ruhr workers, the shaky German economy disintegrated so rapidly that in November 1923, the dollar was quoted at 4.2 trillion marks. Internally, the currency was so worthless that people would go to grocery stores with wheelbarrows full of paper currency, only to find that they did not have enough to buy the needed food. Germans collected their wages in paper money and stuffed the bills into sacks and washing baskets. Citizens even sold bills as waste paper to be recycled into paper. Paper money, however, was not as valuable to paper makers as old rags. Thus, an old rag was literally worth more than a paper mark.

BET YOU DIDN'T KNOW

A widow who just before the war had rented out rooms in her house found that a decade later the cost of replacing a pane of broken glass was more than all the rent being received: The government had stabilized the level of rents.

The Working and Middle Classes Suffer Most

Hyperinflation was tough on the working class, but it was actually even tougher on the middle class, whose members found their savings wiped out. At least the workers had not expected much from life, so had very little to lose. Throughout the middle class, however—in the families of doctors, lawyers, professors, editors, stockbrokers, insurance executives, and the like—the sudden loss of status was humiliating, and debts (such as mortgages) could no longer be serviced. Abandoning the money economy, city dwellers began to barter, exchanging prized possessions for the necessities of life.

Stories were rife of peasant huts resplendent with grand pianos and elegant furniture, handed over by impoverished professionals from the cities for a chicken or a dozen eggs. It seems little wonder that the hitherto "respectable" members of the urban middle classes began to look for saviors—and scapegoats.

Hyperinflation Spells Profit for a Select Few

Under hyperinflation, not everyone was a loser. Exporters experienced a boom of unprecedented proportions: With the German currency valued so low, and hence with their prices at rock-bottom, they could undercut competitors abroad with ease. Those who owned physical assets, such as land, which rose fiercely in value, found themselves newly rich. Instantly wealthy as well were those who held foreign currencies. Speculators with dollars, pounds, francs, and so on swooped in, buying up great tracts of land, apartment blocks, and individual houses, all in the expectation (quite true, as things turned out) that when the German economy returned to sanity these properties would be worth many times their purchase prices.

Who were these speculators? They were a mixed bag of foreigners and Germans. Some of those Germans were Jews. None of this speculation was going to endear those who became wealthy to those who had had to sell their properties at a loss. Nazi propaganda would portray the speculation as engineered exclusively by Jews. It was the grossest of gross exaggerations, but it worked. Hyperinflation, which lasted through 1923, caused bitter resentment. In a Germany already profoundly anti-Semitic, the bitterness focused on Jews.

By curtailing industrial production, the Ruhr crisis worsened the inflation that was already besetting the German economy. The aggravated inflation in turn destroyed the fabric of Weimar society and prepared the way for the rise of Nazi Germany.

The Role of the Army

Although the Treaty of Versailles had reduced the German army to a shadow of its former self, its postwar commander, General Hans von Seeckt, had done his best to adapt to circumstances. Recognizing that a 100,000-man force could not defend Germany from *any* of its neighbors, he turned it into a *Führerheer,* or an "army of leaders." It would serve as the professional core around which a larger army could be quickly conscripted—in violation of the Treaty of Versailles, of course—in case Germany decided to go to war.

TERMS AND TRANSLATIONS

Let's take the last part of *Führerheer* first. *Heer,* like the English *horde,* means a "multitude," a "host," hence an "army." Now, you think of *Führer* in the context of Hitler. But it's a noun, derived from the verb *führen,* which means "to drive, guide, or lead." So its use is much broader than Hitler.

All soldiers were required to serve long terms and to feel a strong sense of dedication, as if the army were a religious order. Because the treaty had abolished the pre-war military schools, the army itself became one large military training organization. Each service branch (infantry, cavalry, artillery, and engineers) prepared officer candidates for commission. Noncommissioned personnel received training within the normal activities of troop units. The effectiveness of von Seeckt's efforts would become clear during Germany's rearmament in the 1930s and its string of victories in the first years of World War II.

What held the *Führerheer* together was its ideology. The officer corps was devoted to the monarchy. In 1918, they had been released from their oath to the kaiser and had sworn oaths to the Weimar Republic. But they still believed that a monarchy was the best form of government for Germany and they never gave their complete loyalty to the republic.

The officers were looking for a leader. Adolf Hitler was emerging as precisely that.

The Attempted Putsch

By early 1923, Hitler had come to see the virtue of an alliance with the army. The Ruhr crisis and hyperinflation were tearing Germany apart. Hitler also had reason to believe that in Saxony and Thuringia, provinces to the north of Bavaria, Communists were on the verge of insurrection. Hitler's hope, therefore, was that, by pulling off a daring deed—as Mussolini had done in Italy by marching on Rome—he could get the support of army groups in central and northern Germany and establish a national military dictatorship.

Action would require the services of the paramilitary segment of the Nazi Party, known as the *Sturmabteilung* (or SA), Storm Troopers, or just plain "Brownshirts."

TERMS AND TRANSLATIONS

Let's break down the term *Sturmabteilung.* *Sturm,* obviously, is "storm." **Ab** conveys the sense of "down" or "away from." *Teil* means "a part" or "a portion"; *teilung* becomes "division" or "separation." So *abteilung* is a "compartment" or a "department." The Sturmabteilung, abbreviated to "SA," was the department of the Nazi Party that would storm a citadel. In imitation of Mussolini's Blackshirts, they donned uniforms—albeit brown rather than black.

Who were these Storm Troopers? Almost to a person they were not members of the regular army. Most were youths from lower-class, impoverished backgrounds. They had grown up in violent families and they themselves were violent. Frequently, as adolescents, they were gang members. Who were the Storm Troopers? They were thugs.

But they were thugs of a distinct sort. They loved to swagger around in their uniforms, uniforms with German imperial symbols on the collars and swastikas and death skulls on the caps. Born followers, they craved strong leadership. They readily fell under Hitler's spell and they were the backbone of Hitler's attempt to overthrow the Bavarian government.

When the Nazi Party held its annual congress in Munich in 1923, Hitler put his Storm Troopers on display. They marched about holding up swastika flags and showing off their martial discipline. They greatly bolstered Hitler's confidence.

So did support from General von Seeckt and Hugo Stinnes, leader of right-wing industrialists. At the height of the hyperinflation, Stinnes made the notorious statement: "We [the industrialists] must have the courage to say to the people, for the present and for some time to come, you will have to work overtime without any payment." When von Seeckt and Stinnes engineered Hitler's appointment as political leader of the *Kampfbund* (*Bund* is a cognate of the English word "bound," so *Kampfbund* meant people "bound together" or "organized for struggle," a confederation of Bavarian veterans and paramilitary units), Hitler thought himself on the threshold of major success.

But Hitler was going to have to wait. Somehow or other the Weimar government managed to take effective action. It sent forces into Saxony and Thuringia to stop the Communists from taking over. Then the Allies pressured the government to do something about the right-wingers in Bavaria. Even the top brass in the army, despite their own right-wing leanings, got nervous. Apparently, they were afraid of French intervention. In any case, von Seeckt warned Hitler against taking illegal action.

Now the plot really thickened. Ritter von Kahr, head of the Bavarian provincial government and a right-winger himself, told Hitler that if the *kampfbund* tried to seize control in Munich, he would use the provincial army to stop them. Von Kahr also informed Hitler that any march on Berlin was forbidden.

All this was too much for Hitler. On the night of November 8, 1923, von Kahr was scheduled to speak at a Munich beer hall called the *Bürgerbräuhaus;* several of the provincial ministers were going to be present. When night fell, SA troopers surrounded the beer hall while Hitler strode inside. When he reached the speaker's platform, he pulled out a pistol, fired it toward the ceiling, and proclaimed: "The national revolution has begun!"

Pointing the pistol at von Kahr, Hitler demanded permission for the march on Berlin. To save his life, von Kahr gave his approval. Hitler and his followers were overjoyed.

In the morning, however, Hitler's fortunes took a turn for the worse. The police were dispatched to guard the city hall. Von Kahr then rescinded his approval for the Berlin march.

When Hitler, staying in the eastern suburbs of Munich, heard the news, he was dismayed. But with him was General Erich Ludendorff, architect of those costly German offensives at the end of World War I. Hitler let Ludendorff convince him that all was not lost. So, with Hitler and Ludendorff in the lead, a column of 3,000 Storm Troopers and other Nazis formed a parade, crossed the Isar River, and marched to the *Feldherrnhalle,* Soldiers' Hall, Munich's major monument to German military might.

When the marchers reached the building, they found a row of policemen guarding the entryway. The column froze. But then Ludendorff strode forward, and those behind him followed in his steps.

At that moment, the police opened fire. The shooting lasted a full minute and left 14 Nazis dead and many more wounded. Those still on their feet fled the scene. Diving for cover, Hitler painfully dislocated his shoulder. An automobile spirited him away.

SUPPORTING ACTORS

Hermann Göring, the ace aviator, was with the group. He sustained a bullet wound in the thigh. Carried into a nearby bank, he received first aid from the manager—who happened to be Jewish.

Hitler in Jail

A few hours after the shooting, during the evening, three Munich police officers knocked at the door of the Hanfstängl residence in the eastern suburbs. Asking permission to search the house, they found Hitler in a sitting room, wearing pajamas and a bathrobe. Upon seeing the officers, he broke into a tirade against the Bavarian government and all its officials. Then, abruptly, he shut his mouth and submitted to arrest.

After arraignment, a police automobile drove Hitler to the Landsberg prison, some 40 miles west of Munich. Throughout the trip, Hitler was silent, except to inquire after the fate of Ludendorff (because of the general's prestige, the authorities had let him go). Before midnight, Hitler was in a cell at Landsberg.

Learning of Hitler's failure at Munich, Arthur Möller van den Bruck, a political writer, commented: "There are many things that can be said against Hitler. But one thing one we will always be able to say: He was a fanatic for Germany. … Hitler was wrecked by his proletarian primitivism. He did not understand how to give his National Socialism any intellectual basis. He was passion incarnate, but entirely without measure or sense of proportion."

Others, too, started speaking of Hitler in the past tense. His career seemed to be at an end, almost before it had started. Within days of Hitler's arrest, however, in the Munich underground, a certain announcement was being passed from hand to hand:

> The first period of the national revolution is over. Our highly revered *Führer,* has again bled for the German people. The most shameful treachery that the world has ever seen has victimized him and the German people. Through Hitler's blood and the steel directed against our comrades in Munich by the hands of traitors the patriotic Battle Leagues are welded together for better or worse.

The Least You Need to Know

- ✪ The Weimar Republic may have looked like a legitimate government, but it was shaky from the start, lacking almost all public support.

- ✪ Germans of all political persuasions saw the French occupation of the Ruhr valley as humiliating. Even worse than that humiliation, the hyperinflation of the early 1920s ripped German society apart, leading the usually conservative middle classes looking for radical solutions.

- ✪ Although the army looked with disfavor on illegal coup attempts against governmental units, its deeply patriotic officers saw in Hitler the savior they believed Germany desperately needed.

- ✪ The failure of Hitler's Putsch of 1923 and his subsequent imprisonment gave him the opportunity to rethink the next phase of his revolution.

Hitler's Years of Struggle: 1923–1929

In September 1923, the Weimar government appointed a committee to find a way out of the financial chaos produced by hyperinflation. Its recommendation was currency reform, and on November 15, 1923, a new *Mark* was established, called the *Rentenmark*. *Rente* means income or profit, and the Rentenmark was backed by land values. One Rentenmark was equal to 4.2 trillion old Marks. This stabilization of the German currency introduced a period of political consolidation and relative prosperity. At this time, Germany joined the League of Nations. And, as foreign minister, Gustav Stresemann (1878–1929) slowly regained confidence for Germany at the international conference table.

But in 1929 the Great Depression set in. A global phenomenon, it severely jeopardized the economic life of all the European nations as well as of Japan, Canada, and the United States. In a country like Germany, where the economy was already so shaky, the collapse assumed catastrophic proportions. A widespread wave of unemployment quickly wiped out the recovery made between 1924 and 1929.

As mentioned, many Germans believed that the failure of Hitler's beer hall *Putsch* in Munich spelled the end of any Nazi hopes for power. The Great Depression put the Nazi star back on the rise. Those who had written Hitler off grossly underestimated his strength of will and—what many to this day still deny—the magnitude of his political skills.

Hitler's Trial and Imprisonment

In 1923, the town of Landsberg looked much as it had in medieval times. Steep woods surrounded it, and its ancient fortress walls still stood. An old wooden bridge across the Lech River led to the prison, a group of gray-white buildings encircled by tall stone walls. Hitler's cell, in the section reserved for political prisoners, was actually more spacious than the tiny rooms in which he had lived much of his impoverished youth. The narrow iron bed had a comfortable mattress, and the double-barred window afforded a view of trees and shrubbery outside. The cell also came equipped with a writing desk and chair—indispensable tools of Hitler's trade.

After suffering from depression for several days after his arrest, Hitler used the chair and desk to put down some thoughts. He had made a mistake, he realized. He had tried to copy Mussolini. If his movement were to succeed, he had to find a uniquely German way to move forward. This could only be based on his own unique connection with the German people and what he had reason to believe was the magic of his oratory.

Finally tried for treason, Hitler put his oratorical skills to good use. He commandeered the courtroom in Munich as a political platform. On his final day before the jury, he proclaimed:

> The army which we have formed grows from day to day; from hour to hour it grows more rapidly. Even now I have the proud hope that one day the hour is coming when these raw recruits will become battalions, when the battalions will become regiments and the regiments divisions, when the old cockade will be raised from the mire, when the old banners will once again wave before us; and then reconciliation will come in that eternal last Court of Judgment—the Court of God—before which we are ready to take our stand. Then from our bones, from our graves will sound the voice of that tribunal which alone has the right to sit in judgment upon us. For gentlemen [Hitler was addressing himself to the jury], it is not you who pronounce judgment upon us, it is the eternal court of history which will make its pronouncement upon the charge which is brought against us.

The court found Hitler guilty as charged, yet handed down a lenient sentence. Hitler could have been deported to Austria, but the judge refused to take that step. "Hitler is German-Austrian," his judgment read. "In the opinion of the court a man who thinks and feels as German as Hitler, a man who voluntarily served four and a half years in the German army during the war, who earned high war decorations for bravery in the face of the enemy, who was wounded and whose health was impaired … should not be subjected to the Republic Protection Law [and thus deported]."

The court acknowledged Hitler's crime, but valued his patriotism more highly and therefore sentenced him to a year in the relative comfort of the Landsberg prison. In confinement, Hitler and other political prisoners had plenty of time to exercise in the prison garden, have dinner (usually a one-pot meal served at noon) together in the common room, tea or coffee at four, and easy access to beer or wine. Lights went out at 10 P.M.

Hitler put on weight in prison as nationalist organizations and admirers throughout Bavaria inundated him with food packages. He also read books in the prison library, received the Munich newspapers, and heard thorough reports of politics within the Nazi Party.

The news from his party was not good. In Hitler's absence, the Nazis disintegrated into warring factions, each claiming to uphold the "true values of the Hitler movement." Some of the Nazis saw themselves as out-and-out left-wing socialists, while those in the ultra-right-wing focused narrowly on anti-Semitism.

In his prison cell, Hitler refused to mediate or give his approval to any faction. This neutrality let him maintain his image as the Nazis' natural leader. By staying out of the squabbles, he also had time to compose his propagandistic and political autobiography, *Mein Kampf.*

Mein Kampf

Mein Kampf (*My Struggle*) is a mix of Nazi history, political theory, and street-smarts. Its style is almost illiterate. (Hitler, after all, was largely unschooled.) It rambles and drones and makes for hard reading.

Hitler, however, was a shrewd author. Public opinion, he asserted, could be readily swayed. He wrote that crowds were like blank pieces of paper, on which the artistic orator could draw whatever he wished. Hitler went on to describe the proper use of gestures, symbols, and stage-effects, which he learned on the streets of Vienna. He was describing the very methods by which he would motivate the masses.

Many pages of *Mein Kampf* are devoted to tirades against the Jews. Jewish influence in Germany, Hitler proclaimed, had led directly to the defeat of November 1918. The Jews, he wrote, were the source of all degeneracy, with their own special link to Marxism. Hitler stood for the purification of the German race, the purging of alien elements from its bloodstream. He called for the expropriation and banishment of the Jews as parasites and the seducers of honest German working people. Anyone who thinks that anti-Semitism was a byproduct of Nazism needs to read *Mein Kampf* with care. In its pages, Hitler explains that he founded the Nazi Party to take German property back from the Jews and then to force the Jews out of Germany.

Although anti-Semitism was at the heart of *Mein Kampf,* there was more. Hitler also wrote that, once under Nazi leadership, the German people would have to reestablish their supremacy in western Europe and then acquire much-needed *Lebensraum* (living space) in the east. As to exactly where in the east, Hitler wasn't entirely clear. But he seemed to have in mind the vast territories of Poland, Russia, and Ukraine. Of course, there were Slavic people living there already, but this didn't matter. The land to the east, he insisted, was rightfully German. It was Germany's birthright.

TERMS AND TRANSLATIONS

The word Hitler used for living space was *Lebensraum. Raum* means "room." *Leben* is "life."

How to claim that birthright? By force, of course. But a military drive toward the east required the support of the German people. Here's where propaganda came in. As Hitler pointed out, he had made himself a master of propaganda. It had to appeal to emotion, not to reason. It aimed to woo the stupid and unthinking masses, to hypnotize them into fulfilling their own destiny in the east.

As a veteran of the fighting in the fields of Flanders, Hitler had come out of the war thinking of France as Germany's main enemy. But reflection in his prison cell had changed his mind. He was very explicit. "We must take up where we broke off 600 years ago," Hitler wrote. "We must stop the endless German movement to the south and west and turn our gaze upward toward the land to the east."

Who, besides the Slavic people, lived to the east of Germany? Jews.

Russia, Hitler wrote, had fallen "under the yoke of the Jew." God had chosen Germany to bring about the conquest of that vast, Jew-controlled territory. Right there, in *Mein Kampf,* was the awful aim of the war that would begin in 1939. Germany would extend the Holocaust as far as it could into Poland and the Soviet Union.

Hitler's time in prison served him well. Had he just gone on making speeches, he might have worn himself out. But in prison, he rested, ate well, and became something of a martyr. Most important, he had time to write his manifesto. Released late in 1924, he immediately set about rebuilding the Nazi Party.

BET YOU DIDN'T KNOW

Once out of prison, Hitler wrote a second volume of *Mein Kampf, The National Socialist Movement.* It largely reiterated the themes of the first. Before 1930, sales of *Mein Kampf* were modest: 23,000 of Volume I and 13,000 of Volume II. By the end of 1933, the year Hitler became chancellor, however, 1.5 million copies had been sold, and during Hitler's lifetime, total sales were somewhere between 8 and 9 million copies. Hitler became a rich author.

Rebuilding the Party

Without question, Hitler had good (albeit evil) political instincts. When he was released from prison on December 19, 1924 (the Bavarian Supreme Court had demanded that he be set free), he was met at the gate by Adolph Müller, his printer, and Heinrich Hoffmann, a Nazi photographer. They were driving a big touring car. Because the day was raw and gray, the canvas top was locked shut. As they sped toward Munich, Hoffmann asked what Hitler intended to do now. The answer was, "I shall start again, from the beginning."

That was not quite true. Although his influence had not reached much beyond Bavaria, Hitler still enjoyed a large coterie of followers in southern Germany. What he probably meant in his reply to Hoffmann was that he had to strengthen the Bavarian base before moving ahead.

So, back in Munich, Hitler refused to take sides with any of the Nazi factions. He would be the leader, holding himself above the fray. And, of course, he would dramatize himself as that leader.

He's Back Again!

Hitler's first major speech after his release was set for February 27, 1925. Significantly, it took place in the *Bürgerbräuhaus*, the site of his failed coup.

He had not lost his touch. Delivered amid a frenzy of excitement, his speech expertly rallied all groups within the party around his leadership. He stated again his faith in the "inviolable principles of National Socialism," and he denounced Marxism and the Jews. But, this time, he also made a demand. He demanded that the party membership vote him dictatorial powers.

By late March 1925, Hitler had received oaths of loyalty from almost all the Bavarian Nazis. Now he was truly the Führer, at least on the provincial level. As tokens of his new power and prestige, in the spring of 1925 Hitler acquired two possessions, the sorts of things dear to the hearts of Germans. First, he somehow got hold of a new red Mercedes; he spent many hours touring the Bavarian country-side with selected aides. And second, he set up personal headquarters in the mountain village of Berchtesgaden. The mountain house was rustic, but its windows afforded spectacular views. Hitler spent still more hours wearing *lederhosen* (leather shorts)—the traditional Bavarian costume emblematic of a nationalist—and hiking through the hills.

While at Berchtesgaden, Hitler also acquired the services of a new secretary, Josef Goebbels. Son of a middle-class Catholic family from the valley of the Rhine, Goebbels had earned a doctorate from Heidelberg University. His fields had been literature and drama. Sharp-faced and dark of complexion, Goebbels was a small man, just over five feet tall and weighing not much more than 100 pounds. As a child he had been wracked by polio, a disease that had left him with a twisted foot. Because of his deformity, he had not been able to perform military service.

SUPPORTING ACTORS

Why did Goebbels, a cultured Catholic, hook up with the loutish Nazis, who would attack the Catholic Church? We can only speculate.

But Goebbels's special talents more than made up for his physical shortcomings. He was a gifted writer, and on the lecture platform his dark eyes, expressive hands, and resonant baritone made him an appealing figure.

He was also careful never to upstage Hitler. But as an educated man from the middle class of Germany, he did have an advantage over Hitler: He could speak *Hochdeutch,* High German, the language of the northern plains, and he could speak it masterfully.

Even so, Hitler and Goebbels were in for a tough time in northern Germany. This largely Protestant region had a long history of antagonism to the largely Catholic south. Furthermore, in the northern stretches of the Rhine and over into Prussia, even where people had some sympathy for National Socialism, many were attracted to the fighting qualities of the leftists. Northern Germany was the land of cities, where inflation had left the middle classes feeling uprooted. There urbanites had little use for Hitler, a peasant guttersnipe from Austria.

Hitler Sets the Stage for Power

Hitler, however, could bide his time. Prison had given him patience. In the presidential election of 1925, instead of going for a Karl Jarres, a compromise candidate between northern and southern Nazis, Hitler endorsed General Ludendorff. To the northerners, this step made Hitler seem even more reactionary than before. But, as he had suspected and hoped, the general ran a hopeless campaign and lost dismally. With Ludendorff humiliated, Hitler's claim to leadership of the far right in Bavaria was strengthened.

But he was far from strong enough to seize national power. From the mid-1920s onward, the German economy gradually stabilized. Thanks mainly to loans from the United States, Germany enjoyed a period of economic growth. Real wages (as opposed to inflationary ones) went up, and unemployment went down. With the election in 1925 to the presidency of the other famed general from the war, Paul von Hindenburg, the Weimar Republic at last took steps toward becoming a genuinely legitimate government.

So, what appeared to be the tide of history was moving against Hitler. Undaunted, he used this period to perfect his oratory. He rehearsed his speeches before a full-length mirror and practiced hand movements by the hour. Once on stage he appealed to audiences with vivid language. An actor of brilliance, he could switch from humor to sentiment to invective at will. He was the consummate showman.

An actor, of course, needs a stage, and through contributions to the party, Hitler had bought, or rented, a most impressive political theater: the party's official residence on an elegant Munich street. Visitors had no trouble spotting the building. A huge red banner billowed from the rooftop. Beneath a lintel, a horizontal beam emblazoned with Gothic—"Germany Awake"—were two heavy bronze doors. A pair of young sentries in black breeches and brown shirts stood guard. Inside, a third sentry gave a Nazi salute and checked all papers. From the lobby, a magnificent staircase rose to the showpiece of the edifice, the Party Senate Chamber. There, two dozen red leather chairs set in a semicircle faced the Führer's throne. On every wall hung commemorative tablets, which bore the names of those who had died in the Beer Hall *Putsch.* They were the first Nazi martyrs. Invoking their names, Hitler would enter the room, handing down his dictates from on high. The throne was Hitler's pulpit, and the chamber was the auditorium of the Hitler theater.

But Hitler's mastery of the theater was never an end in itself. He wanted power, national power, and to get it he adopted a new strategy. He sent Goebbels into Berlin to sell the "Führer Principle" in the old Prussian capital.

TERMS AND TRANSLATIONS

The term **Sturmabteilung,** or Storm Division, suggests elite military discipline. In fact, the division was staffed by uniformed thugs.

Into the Cities

On October 1926, Josef Goebbels took over leadership of the Berlin branch of the Nazi Party. The Berlin group was thoroughly reactionary, but its structure was loose, and it had little support among members of the working class. So, Goebbels organized a united front with two other right-wing paramilitary groups in Berlin, the *Stahlhelm* (Steel Helmet) and the *Wehrwolf* (a play on words: the German word for werewolf is *Werwolf*; *Wehr* means "defense").

Goebbels's efforts came to nothing. The Berliners simply did not wish to cooperate with these hinterland hicks.

Hitler, however, still wanted to take Berlin; he never gave up that dream. In November 1926, he placed Franz von Pfeffer in charge of the SA. Pfeffer's job was to turn the thugs and street brawlers into a disciplined and therefore useful paramilitary force. Pfeffer tried, and Pfeffer failed. The Storm Troopers resisted all efforts to reduce their independence—Hitler had feared that they might even turn against him—and the Führer had to make a personal appeal for the group's loyalty.

That done, in the spring of 1927, Hitler ordered SA units to attack his opponents in Berlin. By May, however, he stood defeated. After weeks of provocations and bloody street fights, the Berlin police succeeded in evicting the whole of the Nazi Berlin apparatus.

Hitler and the Nazi Party were heading down a dead-end road. The Führer found himself in the worse of two worlds. He had opposed working class socialists and neglected his support within the dispossessed middle class. Like many a politician elsewhere, after the failure in Berlin he began to hear the usual question: "What have you done for us lately?"

In Bavaria, the original loyalists were drifting away. Revenues were dropping. And when Hitler approached businessmen for renewed financial support, he was told bluntly that the socialist aspect of national socialism would have to go.

By 1927, Hitler's movement faced extinction. He had brilliantly forged a coalition of Bavarian workers, professionals, and businessmen. He had spoken to their needs and desires. And he had projected the image of a political winner.

Then he lost. And we probably would never have heard of him again had it not been for the plight of farmers in Schleswig-Holstein.

The Farmers of Schleswig-Holstein

Yes, the original black-and-white Holstein cows came from Holstein. That northern region, fighting over which Bismarck had won his first military victory, was dairy country. There Hitler calculated that he, too, could enjoy his first victory.

Even before the onset of the Great Depression in 1929, the agricultural sectors of all the western economies had suffered from their own depressions. These were relatively minor, but they were real. In general, post-World War I agriculture had become so efficient that the supplies of food exceeded the demand. So, market prices for farmers hit new lows. In Schleswig-Holstein, conditions were especially dire. The collapse of farmers' incomes coincided with the outbreak of foot-and-mouth disease. Dairy farmers were unable to sell their milk. Worse, hyperinflation had already wiped out most of the rural banks, leaving most of the farmers deeply in debt.

Where could the farmers turn? They could go to the large commercial banks, but these institutions charged prohibitively high rates of interest. By the late 1920s, the farmers of Schleswig-Holstein were at the end of their rope. They and their families faced poverty and eviction.

To whom could they turn? The Nazi Party.

MODERN DAY PARALLELS

Most professional economists argue the virtues of free trade. Some contend that with free trade everyone everywhere becomes as prosperous as is possible. Perhaps. But free trade also means that someone loses out in the economic competition. In this case, those who lost were the farmers of Schleswig-Holstein. Embittered at losing their jobs, they were ripe for conversion to the Nazi cause.

Does Hitler's strategy of helping the "little man" sound familiar? It should. Faced with their own economic woes, many American farmers of the late nineteenth and early twentieth centuries—many of them members of a third party known as the Populists—looking for scapegoats, blamed what they saw as the doings of Jews on Wall Street.

Earlier, the peasants of the region had placed their faith in a group called the Farmer's League. The League had pretended to be the farmers' friend, but it really was a tool of big business, which was all for free trade. "Free trade," in this case, meant cheap food imports from Poland and Denmark. These commodities flooded the German market, deepening the problems of the farmers of Schleswig-Holstein.

In the plight of those northern farmers, Hitler saw an opening. Rushing into the region, Nazis made appeals to the "little man," persuading the farmers that their problems lay in the machinations of Germany's Jewish financiers.

In a way, the Nazis were getting it "right" at last. Their talk of doom and destruction, their offer of simplistic solutions to complicated problems, and their anti-Semitism all proved irresistible to rural audiences. Schleswig-Holstein proved once and for all that the Nazis could appeal to people beyond Bavaria.

The Way Forward

Hitler and his colleagues were indeed looking beyond Munich. Offsetting the Nazi Party's still dismal showing in the cities, in the Reichstag election of May 1928, it made substantial gains in Schleswig-Holstein, and in the rural areas of Hannover, Upper Franconia, and Nuremberg. As they analyzed the voting patterns, the Nazi leaders all but abandoned the workers in the cities, directing their appeals to farmers and small shopkeepers—people who were already anti-Semitic. By and large, these were the most conservative-minded people in Germany. So, Nazi propaganda conjured up a mythical golden age of the past, which was music to these people's ears

A New Respectability

In Hitler's judgment, the party's electoral base was still too narrow to gain him national power. He especially wanted to broaden his appeal to those who were most likely to vote, the middle-class suburbanites.

In 1929, therefore, the fifteenth anniversary of the outbreak of the World War I, Adolf Hitler staged a huge Nazi rally in a stadium at Nuremberg. The stadium was decorated with the usual swastikas and red, white, and black bunting. And Hitler engaged in his usual anti-Semitic ranting.

But this time there was a key difference. Hitler shared the platform with leaders of veterans' associations and, much to the horror of lower-class Nazis, with prominent businessmen as well. Finally, he also put on display Alfred Hugenberg, a media mogul who controlled some 500 newspapers.

Hitler built additional support by opposing the so-called Young Plan. Germany had been paying its reparations on schedule. But officials in Washington and financiers in New York believed that Germany could be a rich market for American goods only if the burden of reparations were lessened. Under the Young Plan, named for the American banker Owen D. Young, the U.S. government offered to scale down reparations. Most Germans, however, believed that they should not have to pay anything at all. In espousing *their* view, Hitler aligned himself for the first time with mainstream opinion.

SUPPORTING ACTORS

Paradoxically, Hitler, Goebbels, and others combined backward views with modern techniques. In an era before television and even widespread use of radio, propagandists in the Munich headquarters drew sophisticated graphs of Germany, correlating relationships among economic problems, membership growth, and patterns of political loyalty. When elections were in the offing, they would then select promising regions, blanketing them with rallies, flags, and speeches.

All this seemed so reasonable. Those people who showed up at the mass meetings would be invited for discussions in the village pubs and invited to join the party. The Nazis actually began to appear respectable.

The Breakthrough

By 1929, the Nazi Party had scored a series of successes in local and regional elections. All the same, Hitler's party was still stubbornly rooted in the small towns and villages and was unable to build sufficient momentum to make it on the national scene.

Then an event occurred that made all the difference. In October 1929, the New York Stock Exchange collapsed. The effect on Germany was almost immediate. On October 31, the *Beamtenbank* (the Official Bank), one of Germany's biggest financial firms, failed. Unemployment, which in August had dropped to 1.4 million, by December skyrocketed to 3 million.

The Great Depression was underway in Germany. For Hitler and the Nazi Party, it made all the difference. What was misery to most was a bonanza for them.

The Least You Need to Know

- ✪ Hitler's time in Landsberg Prison gave him an opportunity to rethink his line of propaganda and to pose as a martyr.
- ✪ Upon his release, Hitler worked to stop the factional warfare in party ranks and establish his dictatorial control over it.
- ✪ Throughout the 1920s, the Nazi Party was a distinctly minor political party, appealing largely to conservatives in the villages and small towns.
- ✪ Hitler tried to broaden his base of support by affecting an air of respectability. This step helped fill the party coffers, but by 1929 the Nazis had yet to make it to the national stage.

The Great Depression: 1929–1932

Early in 1930, a 21-year-old law student and son of a Lutheran pastor, a young man who had rebelled against his middle-class upbringing, become a Storm Trooper, and fought bloody street battles in Berlin against the Communists, wrote a poem. He titled it, "Raise High the Flag!" He had the swastika in mind.

Around the time he penned the verse, he met and fell in love with a former prostitute and moved into her apartment. Trying to eject the couple, who in her eyes were living in sin, the landlady sought help from the Communists. At her request, a gang of Reds burst into the flat and shot the young man dead.

When Goebbels learned about the incident, he saw an opportunity to transform the young man into a working-class Jesus. "Leaving home and mother," Goebbels wrote, "he took to living among those who scorned and spit on him. Out there, in a proletarian section [of Berlin], in a tenement attic he proceeded to build his young, modest life. A socialist Christ! One who appealed to others through his deeds!"

Goebbels soon saw to it that the young man's poem was set to music. Sung first by a huge chorus at a Nazi rally in the Berlin *Sportpalast,* the words went:

> Hold high the banner! Close the hard ranks serried!
> SA marches on with sturdy stride.
> Comrades, by the Red Front and Reaction killed, are buried,
> But march with us in image at our side.
> Gangway! Gangway now for the Brown Battalions!
> For the Storm Trooper clear roads over the land!
> The Swastika gives hope to our millions,
> The day for freedom and bread is at hand.
> The trumpet blows its shrill and final blast!
> Prepared for war and battle here we stand.
> Soon Hitler's banners will wave unchecked at last,
> The end of German slavery in our land!

The young man's name was Horst Wessel. The "Horst Wessel *Lied* [Song]" became the marching music of the Nazi Party. The way Goebbels made the youth a martyr to the Nazi cause was typical of his skill with propaganda. With the coming of the Great Depression, Hitler and Goebbels saw their main chance to identify themselves as the saviors of the German nation.

Unemployment

The German people unquestionably were looking for salvation—anything to free them from the scourge of joblessness. With the coming of the Great Depression, millions of Germans were out of work. Without income, their meager savings exhausted, their only recourse were weekly visits to government offices to pick up compensation cards.

They were the equivalent of modern food stamps, but they barely staved off starvation. Nothing was left over to buy goods, and, unable to sell their wares, businesses threw even more people out of work. Unemployment was a vicious cycle.

As in the United States at the time, unemployment produced hopelessness and hate. Unlike America, Germany became an out-and-out battlefield. Shop owners who had lost their businesses railed against the big department stores. The jobless loathed the bosses. University graduates with thwarted hopes of employment in the civil service turned their wrath against the government. Forced to sell their produce at bottom prices yet required to pay high taxes, peasants turned against city-dwellers, even as the urban jobless hatefully envied the peasants their crops.

Of a total population of roughly 50 million, eventually 6 million Germans were registered as being without work. The number was deceptive; millions of other Germans had part-time work insufficient to make a living, and more were simply too proud to register as jobless. Whatever the exact numbers, the Great Depression hit Germany harder than any other country.

BET YOU DIDN'T KNOW

Are you familiar with the musical *Cabaret?* It was based on a book called *Berlin Stories: I Am a Camera,* by the English author Christopher Isherwood (Random House, 1952). He lived in Berlin during the early 1930s. The city, he wrote, "was in a state of civil war. Hate exploded without warning, out of nowhere, at street corners, in restaurants, cinemas, dance halls, swimming baths; at midnight, after breakfast, in the middle of the afternoon. Knives were whipped out, blows were dealt with spiked rings, beer mugs, chair legs or leaded clubs; bullets slashed the advertisements on the poster columns, rebounded from the iron roofs of latrines."

For Freedom and Bread and a New Election

To those hit by the economic collapse, one thing seemed clear: The Weimar Republic could not solve the problem. Hitler offered an alternative. In his speeches, he continued his anti-Communist, anti-Semitic tirades, as well as his denunciations of the Treaty of Versailles. But in 1930 what mattered most was his new campaign slogan: "For Freedom and Bread."

The first test of Hitler's slogan came in September 1930. That month, Heinrich Brüning, the German chancellor, called a general election. It is not clear why he chose to call the election at this time. We can speculate that, since Paul von Hindenburg had appointed him to the chancellorship, he may have thought that only by winning in a popular election could he legitimize and solidify his power.

BET YOU DIDN'T KNOW

In the American political system, a presidential election takes place every four years, no matter what. But in Britain, which has a parliamentary system, the prime minister may call for an election at any time (within five years). In this regard, the Weimar Republic resembled the British model: There was a president (General von Hindenburg), who like the British monarch was head of state, and there was the chancellor, who like the British prime minister headed the legislature. So, the chancellor could call an election.

Brüning's standing was tenuous. Like U.S. President Herbert Hoover, he had followed a policy of deflation. This was orthodox economic thinking at the time. If you're faced with a recession or a depression, cut government spending. But that meant cutting government jobs, and laying off public employees only deepened unemployment. Reducing government spending may have lowered prices—that's deflation—but when prices fell, businesses had to lower their costs, which resulted in yet more layoffs. Unemployed people cannot buy very much. This made the deflationary cycle more vicious.

Not surprisingly, the election reflected the widespread animosity toward Brüning. The numbers told the tale. In the election of May 1928, the Nazis had polled a mere 3.6 percent of the total votes cast. Now, in September 1931, they racked up 18.3 percent and gained 107 seats in the *Reichstag,* making their party the second largest in that legislative body.

But what was stunning about the Nazi victory was just who gave it to them. In Wedding, a working-class neighborhood in Berlin, the Nazis won just 9 percent of the vote. In solidly middle-class Steglitz, however, they received 26 percent, and in Zehlendorf, a wealthy quarter, they polled nearly 18 percent. The Nazis had improved their standing in all social classes. They were no longer a party of the countryside.

Clearly, the Nazi Party had built a much more diverse constituency than before. The Nazis couldn't pitch their propaganda exclusively to conservative farmers. In fact, while party officials in rural Saxony expressed opposition to labor strikes, Nazis in Berlin sided with striking metal workers. So, despite the impressive showing at the polls, the Nazi Party seemed on the verge of breaking apart into feuding factions.

BET YOU DIDN'T KNOW

Totalitarian countries, such as Nazi Germany, the Soviet Union, and Communist China under Chairman Mao Zedong, rest on a foundation of violence. But violence begets violence. To stay in power, the leaders often hurl new groups of supporters against old ones. But trust is rare. So, the purges start all over again.

The Storm Trooper Rebellion

The threat of disintegration became real. Soon after the general election, the Berlin Storm Troopers (SA) announced that they were no longer going to protect party meetings. The reasons for their rebellion ran deep. Rank-and-file Storm Troopers had come to resent the lifestyles of the Nazi rich and famous. They also distrusted the way Hitler and other leaders had been courting big business and the old Prussian aristocracy. They had come to feel like outsiders in their own party.

In response, in the autumn of 1931, Hitler went to Berlin. There he removed Franz von Pfeffer as head of the SA, and he put himself in command of the organization. Moreover, Hitler continued to live as he always had, modestly, which served to defuse complaints about lavish living among the Nazi elite.

Because Hitler was always busy, he could not devote all his time to Storm Trooper issues. He turned over day-to-day management to Ernst Röhm. A former officer, Röhm had played a leading part in the Beer Hall *Putsch*. His current assignment was to assure the SA rank-and-file that when the Nazis finally rose to national power, they would get their share of the spoils.

Some SA members were mollified, but overall satisfaction plummeted when, to show German voters that his party would act legally, Hitler ordered SA units to stop their street fighting. But these were thugs, and street fighting was their stock in trade. The ban on violence triggered a major revolt. Some Storm Troopers even broke with the Nazis to join the Communist Party.

For Hitler, it was the last straw. After directing Hermann Göring to purge the SA of dissidents, Hitler temporarily dissolved the organization. He cut the SA budget and refused permission for it to recruit new members. At the same time, he began to replace it with a new organization, the *Schutzstaffel* (Defense Echelon), or SS.

The SS had actually come into existence in 1925 as a small unit of the SA. It was a kind of body-guard that provided Hitler and other party officials protection at rallies. It was a distinctly minor organization.

TERMS AND TRANSLATIONS

Schutzstaffel. Schutz means "shelter" or "refuge"; *staffel* is "step," "stage," "degree," and by extension, "echelon"; so, the SS was the Protection Detachment.

The Roles of Heinrich Himmler and Reinhard Heydrich

In 1929, the lowly status of the SS began to change. Hitler turned over leadership of the organization to Heinrich Himmler. He was a man with a receding hairline, eyeglasses, tiny clipped mustache, and a weak chin. He looked like a meek clerk or a harried schoolteacher. In fact, he came from a respect-able academic family. His father held a professorship at the University of Munich. Heinrich had been a studious child—not brilliant, but capable. His chief interests were mathematics, Latin, and Greek—subjects that followed clear sets of rules. He went on to study at his father's university, specializing in biology and chemistry—sciences with well-developed rules.

Appropriately enough, in the chaos following World War I, Heinrich found work as a filing clerk. Once he hooked up with the Nazis and then took over the SS, he became a master of the dossier. He kept dossiers on everyone—probably even Hitler. To maintain his files, he took on as his assistant one Reinhard Heydrich, a blond, long-faced, blue-eyed spy and accomplished classical violinist.

Heydrich's own agents found out that Röhm, head of the now rival SA, was a homosexual. Himmler filed the information away for future use.

Goebbels's Propaganda

But Himmler's dossiers were only one part of Hitler's program to bring the Nazi movement under his personal and exclusive control. While he was replacing the SA with the SS (which, was by and large a middle-class organization, reflecting Himmler's own background), he made Goebbels the party's undisputed head propagandist. Under Goebbels, Nazi propaganda became highly centralized. The party would speak with one voice. No Nazi group was allowed to produce its own propaganda. From party headquarters, now in Berlin, Goebbels directed every detail, down to the size and color of posters and leaflets.

No one says that you can't borrow from the enemy. In the Soviet Union, the font of Communism Hitler so hated, Vladimir Lenin had developed the principle of democratic centralism. The idea was that there could be discussion before a decision was reached, but, once the decision had been made, there could be no more dissent. Hitler took the principle a step further. There was to be no discussion before *or* after a decision. Führer's word was law.

MODERN DAY PARALLELS

The Nazi Party wasn't an ordinary political party, as we know parties in America to be—big, loose-knit, with lots of differing voices and opinions. Hitler was building an organization that was much more like an elite army corps than a conventional political party.

Nazi Attacks on the Weimar Republic

In the 1931 election, Hitler campaigned as if he were an ordinary politician, intent on working within the normal political system. That was the image he projected. He pretended that, once in power, he would maintain the Weimar constitution.

In reality, he was getting ready to overthrow that constitution. The German word for what he was really up to was *Gleichschaltung*, usually translated as "coordination." He talked about "coordination," but what he was really engaged in was the elimination of political opponents, including trade unions, religious organizations, universities—all groups likely to organize against a Nazi regime.

TERMS AND TRANSLATIONS

Gleichschaltung is one of those German words that drive English-speaking people crazy. It looks so pompous, so abstract, so Teutonic. But let's break it down. The first part of the word is *Gleich.* For a moment, forget the *G.* What does *leich* sound like in English? Get it? *Ei* in German is pronounced like the *i* in *like.* So *gleich* means "like," "alike," or "same." The other part of our word is not so obvious. The verb *schalten* means "govern" or "rule." So *Gleichschaltung* means "political coordination," bringing into line (and even eliminating) political opponents.

Hitler's political acumen was acute. At that time in Germany, poorer people didn't play a role in politics. In Germany, it was the middle class that voted. So, Hitler set out to penetrate the interest groups that represented the German middle class. The Nazis began to flood the membership of such groups with party members and to replace independent spokesmen with dedicated Nazis.

The most effective campaign of Gleichshaltung was organized by a Nazi official named Walter Darré. He headed a so-called Agricultural Office, whose agents infiltrated the *Landbund* (Country Union). In a short time, they turned it into an instrument of Nazi propaganda. The Nazis even organized their own interest groups. On behalf of mom-and-pop establishments, the Militant Association of Retailers mounted a campaign against the large department stores, accusing them of being run exclusively by Jews. Nazis worked with foresters, demanding that they be given higher wages.

MODERN DAY PARALLELS

An *interest group* is an organization of people who share certain attitudes and goals and who work to shape public opinion, support sympathetic candidates for office, and influence the decisions of governmental officials. Washington is full of such groups: the Sierra Club, the National Rifle Association, the Teamsters, and so on. Germany was similar. It had interest groups representing doctors, various industries, public employees, and so on. As in America now, in Germany then, you could join such groups at will. You paid your dues and you were in. The Nazis took full advantage of that openness.

By the second half of 1931, Nazi cell groups had slipped into every institution of the Weimar Republic, including the civil service, the schools, and the military. Himmler the file-collector even reached into the police forces of Bavaria and Berlin.

The middle of October 1931, produced an overwhelming display of Nazi might. On the eleventh of the month, at Harzburg in central Germany, Hitler joined with other nationalistic right-wingers in a protest against the Brüning ministry. Hindenburg was present. A towering man from the old Prussian aristocracy, he looked down on Hitler with disdain. Insulted, Hitler left the parade reviewing stand. A week later, in nearby Braunschweig (Brunswick), the Nazis staged an immense rally. One hundred thousand party members marched. These numbers alone made it seem likely that Hitler commanded enough force to topple the Weimar Republic.

As the Nazis continued to do well in local elections, their membership rolls exploded. In December, Hitler told another huge rally: "The movement is approaching the last hour of the march!" He predicted that 1932 would be "the first year of the Third Reich."

The Last Hour of the March

Now we are coming to the all-important question of how Hitler finally rose to power. Consider his position at the end of 1931. The Nazi Party had made considerable gains at the polls but was still a minority party. Hitler had no assurance that he could rise to the top through further elections. Nor did he dare to attempt a *coup d'état*. He had learned from his time in Landsberg that if he acted in blatantly unconstitutional ways, the army would turn against him. The old officers corps still regarded him as a guttersnipe.

So he resorted to back-room intrigue. Here Hitler proved himself a master tactician.

Hitler Uses Hindenburg

The back-room gamesmanship began in January, 1932. Remember: General Paul von Hindenburg, the most revered German commander of World War I, was the duly elected president of the Weimar Republic. As such, he had the authority to appoint the chancellor. But Hindenburg was an aged figure, verging on senility—and susceptible to bribery.

Already an honored officer, Hindenburg was now part of the nobility. In a presidential office in Berlin that had come to look like a royal court, he saw himself as the proper successor to Kaiser Wilhelm II. Hindenburg surrounded himself with fawning courtiers from the Junker class and the officer corps. Among the latter was the new commander of the army, General Kurt von Schleicher.

In 1930, Schleicher had gone to Hindenburg and recommended Brüning as chancellor. The idea had appealed to Hindenburg. Although not a clever politician, Brüning was an honest civil servant, who cherished the ancient conservative values of old Germany and who loathed the upstart demagoguery of Hitler and the Nazis. Like Hindenburg, Brüning feared the Nazis and tried to suppress them. Among other things, he forbade the Storm Troopers to march in their iconic brown shirts.

At the same time, and without Brüning's knowledge, General Schleicher was urging Hindenburg and the defense minister to refrain from taking steps against the Nazis. They were, after all, anti-Communist, and they could provide the army, still restricted in size by the Versailles Treaty, with a useful reserve militia. Schleicher wanted to integrate the Nazis into the traditional German institutions. He figured that it was better to have the Nazis inside the tent glaring out than outside the tent glaring in.

General Schleicher Conspires Against Brüning

In January 1932, Hitler, in Munich, received a telegram inviting him to Berlin to participate with Brüning and Schleicher maneuvering to extend Hindenburg's seven-year presidential term. Upon receiving the invitation, Hitler gloated to his subordinates: "Now I have them in my pocket. They have recognized me as a partner in their negotiations."

Brüning offered Hitler a deal. If he would go along with the extension of Hindenburg's term, Brüning promised to step down as chancellor, and he would urge Hindenburg to appoint Hitler in this place. When Hitler, surprisingly, turned the offer down cold, most thought that he had made a terrible decision. He had rebuffed an opportunity for high political office. Without the extension of his term, the elderly Hindenburg ran again and, on April 10, 1932, won reelection by a solid margin. Three days later, Brüning announced a ban on all SA and SS activities. He would enforce the ban by turning the police and the army against Hitler's legions.

Alas, Brüning was not aware of what was going on around him. Behind his back again, General Schleicher was conspiring against him. Not long before, Chancellor Brüning had proposed letting unemployed farm workers live on a deserted estate in Prussia. Schleicher's trick was to get a group of Prussian landlords to visit Hindenburg on his own estate and to denounce Brüning as an "agrarian bolshevist." This was too much for the old field marshal. On May 29, 1932, Hindenburg announced that he had fired Brüning.

Now the chancellorship was open, and General Schleicher knew who he wanted to fill it: Franz von Papen. Descended from the Prussian aristocracy, von Papen had family ties to big business, and he was a smooth flatterer—just the kind to appeal to Hindenburg.

General Schleicher and Hitler Strike a Deal

The palace intrigues continued. On the very day of Brüning's dismissal, Schleicher and Hitler struck a deal. Hitler would go along with von Papen as chancellor on the condition that the government lift its ban on the SA and the SS. The deal was done; Hindenburg accepted von Papen and, at the end of June, von Papen in turn lifted the ban.

At that very point, as Hitler had planned, violence erupted, especially in and around Berlin. Throughout the capital, Communists and Nazis, each provoking the other, engaged in pitched battles. The streets ran red with blood, and in July alone 86 people died in the fighting.

All that was bad enough. But remember: the German Empire under Bismarck had been a federation, in which the various *Länder,* or states had their own spheres of authority. Such was also the case in the Weimar Republic, and, despite all the conservative landowners, Prussia had been using its powers to give a measure of protection to workers and their left-wing organizations. This came to a crashing end on July 29, 1932, when von Papen used the emergency powers of the chancellor's office to abolish the Prussian government. For all practical purposes, the Weimar Republic was dead.

Hitler's Setback

In July, nonetheless, Germany held elections to the Reichstag. This time, although they did not win a majority, the Nazis emerged with more seats than any other party. Hitler accordingly took a hard line with Schleicher and Hindenburg by offering them a take-it-or-leave-it proposal: He would accept Schleicher as defense minister, but he wanted the chancellorship for himself, with Nazis in the most important cabinet positions. Having made his demands, Hitler retired to the mountain air at Berchtesgaden to await the response.

When he was subsequently summoned to the presidential palace in Berlin, he was in for a shock. Refusing to dismiss von Papen, Hindenburg offered Hitler only the vice chancellorship. Indignant, Hitler turned him down.

Just as Hitler had hoped, no party in the Reichstag made up a majority, and the rift between the right-wing and left-wing members in that body was so deep and wide that no one could form a coalition government. Von Papen was left with no choice but to call for a new election.

This time, the Nazis suffered a setback. In the November 1932 general election, their percentage of the vote fell from 37.3 percent to 33.1 percent. Many observers thought that the Nazi appeal to the voters had peaked.

But the election also brought forth another set of numbers. While the Nazis lost two million votes, the Communists gained almost six million. And the combined Social Democratic and Communist votes came to 13,228,000 versus the Nazi sum of 14,696,000. So, while the Nazis remained the largest party in the Reichstag, the existence of several minor parties kept them from having a majority. The working-class parties were therefore still in a strong position.

Within a year, however, the trade unions and other organizations built by three generations of German workers were smashed to pieces. As for the leftist intellectuals, most were either behind the barbed-wire of concentration camps or out of Germany in exile. Hitler and his Nazi Party held the country in their grip, already well on their way to creating the totalitarian state. As the Depression wore on, the Nazis gained electoral strength. That strength, however, was still not sufficient to give them the commanding control they craved. The next chapter explains how Hitler finally emerged in power.

The Least You Need to Know

- In the background of Hitler's rise to power was the Great Depression and the ensuing unemployment in Germany. The rate of joblessness in the Weimar Republic was probably higher than anywhere else in the world. Desperate, many people looked to the Communists for a solution; others longed for Nazi rule.

- Hitler's Storm Troopers often resented the privileges of high-ranking Nazis and thus reflected the mood of the country at large. Hitler could deal with them only by enlarging the powers of the SS, which emerged as a rival to the SA.

- Hitler demonstrated his organizational genius by infiltrating Nazis into the institutions of the state, ostensibly coordinating them, but in reality undermining their function under the Weimar Republic.

- The Weimar Republic, moribund, was dead even before Hitler assumed power.

The Nazis Seize Power: 1933

On March 9, 1933, Storm Troopers broke into the Munich offices of a newspaper called *Der Gerade Weg (The Right Way)* and arrested the editor, Fritz Gerlich. Born a Protestant in the north but raised in heavily Catholic Bavaria, Gerlich was something of an outsider. He earned a doctorate in history and then turned to journalism. During the early 1920s, he covered Hitler and soon become the future Führer's bitter enemy.

By 1933, convinced that Hitler was about to seize ultimate power and lead Germany down the road to hell, Gerlich let it be known that he was going to stop his enemy. He was going to publish the exposé of exposés.

What was going into that exposé we can never know. Maybe Gerlich was going to accuse Hitler of having had an affair with his (Hitler's) underage half-niece, Geli Raubal, and then ordering her murder. Maybe Gerlich was going to reveal that Hitler and the Nazis had received funding from foreign sources, including the American automobile manufacturer Henry Ford. Or maybe the editor had uncovered information about a mysterious fire that burned down the Reichstag— proof that the Nazis had torched the building and put the blame for the blaze on the Communists.

We don't know the content of the story because when the Nazis crashed into Gerlich's office, they ripped the story from the presses, smashed the type, and destroyed every shred of the exposé.

But this we do know. Gerlich was arrested and shipped to the Nazi concentration camp at Dachau, just north of

Munich. There, a year later, during what was called the "Night of the Long Knives," Nazis dragged him from his cell and shot him through the head. By way of notifying his widow, they sent her Gerlich's steel-rimmed eyeglasses, spattered with blood.

Hitler's Appointment to Chancellor

Nazi Germany was born in blood. This fact was not unusual in history. Think of the French Revolution and the American Civil War: Heads rolled onto the streets of Paris, and the Battle of Gettysburg still holds the record as the bloodiest fight on North American soil. But France and the United States were nations long-formed. This was not the case with Nazi Germany.

Remember that the German Empire had been built on the military triumphs of Prussia, and the Weimar Republic had been imposed on Germany by the Allies after the World War I. Thus the two regimes that preceded the Nazis, the first forged by Bismarck, the second by the Allies of 1914-1918, were likewise founded in violence. Nazi Germany was just one more.

Sometimes we wonder why Nazi Germany wasn't more like the West. After all, German culture was identified with that of Western Europe, and the Germans themselves identified with the West, scorning the "Slavic" East. Yet the Nazi rise to power has more in common with the Russian and Chinese Revolutions of 1917 and 1949 than with, say, the English Civil War or the American or French Revolutions. The difference between the earlier revolutions of the West and Hitler's rise was that it was a revolution not from the left but from the right.

Think back to Bismarck. He has often been called the White Revolutionary, as opposed to a Red Revolutionary. He was a conservative who revolted against the established European international order. As blood-soaked as he was, Hitler fell into Bismarck's tradition. His aim was to establish a new world order, but one that was backward-looking, conservative, and aligned with the moneyed class of financiers and industrialists.

Only two weeks after the November 1932 general elections, leading industrialists such as Fritz Thyssen, the steel magnate, and Alfried Krupp, the munitions-maker, wrote a letter to President von Hindenburg. They laid down the law, demanding that he create an authoritarian nationalist regime based on mass support. Even before Hitler completed his rise to power, they wanted what was, in effect, a Nazi state.

They had a model in the fascism of Benito Mussolini's Italy. His March on Rome had made him prime minister of Italy, but his partnership with Italian industry and arms manufacturers had made him *Duce* (leader), with absolute authority. In contrast to Communism, which nationalized industry, fascism formed a partnership with business. Whereas Communism is founded on "statism"—in which the state controls economic policy—fascism included business and industry as partners in a "corporatist" state. In effect, state and industry controlled each other. This is what the German industrialists wanted from the Nazis—and Hitler was eager to comply. He had looked on with admiration at the rise of Mussolini. A corporatist partnership between state and industry seemed to Hitler highly desirable, especially since German industry was far more extensive and advanced than that in Italy.

SUPPORTING ACTORS

The industrialists' letter to President von Hindenburg read: "We recognize in the national movement which has penetrated our people the beginning of an era, which through the overcoming of class contrasts, creates the essential basis for a rebirth of the German economy."

This letter was introduced as evidence at the Nuremberg trials.

In the short run, what the big industrialists wanted from the German government was to crush the labor movement. Weimar was not about to do that. The tycoons believed that Hitler *would* do it—and with gusto. They wanted Hindenburg to get rid of Schleicher and von Papen and to make Hitler chancellor.

Neither Schleicher nor von Papen wanted to step aside, however. And so, the backstage maneuvering went on. Then, on December 1, 1932, Schleicher got old Hindenburg to appoint him chancellor. He did it through blackmail, threatening to make public a government report about how land-owning Prussian aristocrats had been bilking the state for funds. Schleicher showed that Hindenburg himself would be implicated in the scandal.

The Schleicher appointment gave Hitler the opening he needed. He met secretly with the resentful von Papen in the home of a Berlin banker. A few of the top industrialists were also present. Just who said what to whom is unclear, but, by the end of the meeting, the Nazi Party's debts were mysteriously paid off. On January 5, Goebbels noted in his diary, "The present government knows that this is the end for them."

Goebbels was right. As chancellor, Schleicher suddenly began working with the labor movement. The big business interests were outraged. Pressured by the industrialists, who may have promised to bury any charge against the aged general, Hindenburg summoned Hitler to the presidential palace on January 30, 1933. When he emerged from Hindenburg's office, Adolf Hitler was the chancellor of Germany.

Hitler was elated, even though he recognized that he by no means held all the power—all the power he needed and all the power that was. He was chancellor by the grace of Hindenburg. Most of the cabinet members had been appointed under von Papen and Schleicher. They made up a cabinet of barons, who saw no reason why they should not be able to control Hitler. Their strategy was simple: If they made themselves look sufficiently populist, they could make an alliance with the left.

Hitler, however, was not to be managed or manipulated so easily. He had plans to use the government itself to suppress the left.

The Position of the Left

It is worth repeating: In the elections of 1932, the combined vote of the Communist and Social Democratic parties was almost equal to that of the Nazis plus another, much smaller right-wing party, the German Nationalists. In terms of numbers, the working-class parties were almost as strong as their rivals on the right. Given the organizational know-how of the trade unions, in existence for decades, it would seem likely that the German left could have successfully defended itself against the right. But this was not what happened. By the end of 1933, the left was not just defeated, it was crushed.

In Weimar Germany, the left consisted primarily of the Social Democrats and the Communists. As the name suggests, the Social Democratic Party was an avid supporter (just about the only supporter in Germany) of democracy. It was also the party of the trade unions. True to their Leninist heritage, however, the Communists despised the unions. Vladimir Lenin, the founder of the Soviet Union, had argued that organized labor was just a big sell-out. As soon as union members got wage increases and better working and living conditions, Lenin argued, they would abandon the cause of the Russian Revolution. In Germany, Ernst Thälmann, leader of the German Communists, held that "There is no difference between a fascist dictatorship and a bourgeois dictatorship." Indeed, he even preferred the Nazis to the Social Democrats. Under Nazi rule, the Reds would at least *know* who the enemy was. We speak of "right" and "left" as if they were monolithic political parties. They were no such thing, and the leftist parties of Weimar Germany were fragmented and fractious.

In the background of Hitler's electoral victory was this rift on the left. Don't forget that, despite previous financial difficulties, the Nazis got financing from big business. And the Communists appealed mainly to those hardest hit by the Great Depression—the unemployed, those without funds.

While election figures showed a rough balance between the forces of the left and the right, they hid profound imbalances. The left was divided and poor; the right was united and rich. And Hitler had a special advantage: Once he was chancellor, he could use the power of the state against his opponents.

Hitler's Big Moves

No sooner had Hitler received his appointment as chancellor, on January 30, 1933, than the jackboots of the Storm Troopers and Himmler's SS units were heard assembling in Berlin's parks and gardens. The Nazis were preparing for a triumphal march through the Brandenburg Gate and down the Wilhelmstrasse. Confident of Hitler's ultimate victory, the marchers appeared first in huge numbers in front of the Communist Party headquarters. The Nazis were gloating.

They had good reason to gloat. Hitler had completely outmaneuvered President Hindenburg. The old field marshal had made Hitler chancellor on condition that he could put together a majority in the Reichstag. Taken together, the Nazis and the Nationalists did not make up that majority. Hitler might have got his majority by forming an alliance with the Catholic Center Party, but he didn't want them and they didn't want him. So, Hitler asked Hindenburg to dissolve the Reichstag and call a new election. Hindenburg, by this point senile and pliant in Hitler's hands, signed the necessary decree. The new elections were scheduled for March 5, 1933.

Goebbels was overjoyed. "Now it will be easy," he wrote in his diary on February 3, "to carry on the fight, for we can call on all the resources of the state. Radio and press are at our disposal. We shall stage a masterpiece of propaganda. And this time, naturally, there is no lack of money!"

The New Regime's Financial Resources

The money was indeed plentiful. With the new regime committed to crushing the labor unions, prominent business people were funding generously. To make sure the money continued to flow, Hitler called them into Göring's office—Göring having been made president of the Reichstag. Hitler harangued them with a long speech. "Private enterprise," he declaimed, "cannot be maintained in the age of democracy; it is conceivable only if the people have a sound idea of authority and personality. ... All the worldly goods we possess we owe to the struggle of the chosen. ... We must not forget that all the benefits of culture must be introduced more or less with the iron fist."

Hitler went on to pledge the "elimination" of the Socialist and Communist "menace." Then he wrapped up: "We stand before the last election," he told the gathered businessmen. It would be Germany's last election in a decade, maybe even in a century. And no matter how the election turned out, "there will be no retreat." If he lost the election, Hitler warned ominously, he would remain in power "by other means."

Göring added a practical point. "Those circles not taking part in the political battle should at least," he stated, "make the financial sacrifices necessary at this time."

The businessmen present coughed up three million marks.

Justifying the Regime

Despite the "by other means" remark, Hitler and his associates wanted their takeover to seem legitimate. On January 31, 1933, the day after Hitler became chancellor, Goebbels had confided to his diary:

> In a conference with the Führer we lay down the line for the fight against the Reds. For the moment we shall abstain from direct counter-measures. The Bolshevik attempt at revolution must first burst into flame. At the proper moment we shall strike.

Goebbels wanted a clear justification for taking action against the left, and Hitler was prepared to provoke the left into the necessary violence. He persuaded Hindenburg to issue a decree suppressing all civil liberties. The order restricted freedom of speech and the press and outlawed assembly in public places except by permission. It allowed the police to read private letters and other papers, and it expressly permitted what the U.S. Bill of Rights took pains to forbid: "unreasonable searches and seizures."

MODERN DAY PARALLELS

The First Amendment to the U.S. Constitution reads: "Congress shall make no law respecting an establishment of religion, or prohibiting the free exercise thereof; or abridging the freedom of speech, or of the press; of the right of the people peaceably to assemble, and to petition the government for a redress of grievances."

The Fourth Amendment reads: "The right of the people to be secure in their persons, houses, papers, and effects, against unreasonable searches and seizures, shall not be violated, and no warrants shall issue, but upon probable cause …"

As we have seen, the constitution of the Weimar Republic had been largely modeled on that of the United States. With Hindenburg's Hitler-induced edict, the Weimar constitution was effectively nullified.

Pursuant to Hindenburg's edict, German authorities under Hitler censored the Communist press and broke up Communist meetings. Cooperating with officials, Nazi thugs disbanded Social Democratic rallies and smashed their printing presses. Even the Catholic Center Party came in for bad times. Nazis beat up a Catholic leader when he tried to speak to his followers. Heinrich Brüning, the former chancellor who belonged to the Center Party, was obliged to seek protection.

BET YOU DIDN'T KNOW

On February 22, Göring put together an auxiliary police unit to help suppress all organizations hostile to the state. Four-fifths of its membership came directly from SA and SS forces. These Nazi paramilitaries killed at least 51 people and injured hundreds, perhaps thousands, more.

Though the Nazi Party was literally beating down the other parties, the left had not erupted into counter-violence as Hitler had hoped it would. Well, if a leftist uprising did not arise on its own, could one be invented? Might there not be something sensational that would get the electorate to vote for the Nazis in March? A fire, say?

The Reichstag Fire

On the night of February 27, von Papen, now reduced to the office of vice chancellor, was dining with President von Hindenburg at a downtown Berlin club. "Suddenly," von Papen later wrote, "we noticed a red glow through the windows and heard sounds of shouting in the street. One of the servants came hurrying up to me and whispered: 'The Reichstag is on fire!' which I repeated to the president. He got up and from the window we could see the dome of the Reichstag looking as though it were illuminated by searchlights. Every now and again a burst of flame and a swirl of smoke blurred the outline."

Asking a driver to take Hindenburg home, von Papen left the club to view the burning edifice up close for himself. In the meantime, Hitler and Goebbels, who also had been having dinner together, were in an automobile, hurtling "at 60 miles an hour toward the scene of the crime," as Goebbels later said. He did not refer to the fire as accidental because he fully intended to blame the blaze on the Communists.

The Reichstag fire.
(Culver Pictures)

When Hitler and Goebbels reached the scene, Göring was already there. Having put on much weight since his days as a dashing military pilot, he was sweating and out of breath. His lack of physical conditioning, though, didn't stop him from yelling, "This is the beginning of the Communist revolution! We must not wait a minute! We must show no mercy! Every Communist official must be shot, wherever he is found! Every Communist deputy must this very night be strung up!"

Moments later, Nazi agents were breaking down the front doors of known Communist leaders and trucking them off to concentration camps. And the next day, Nazi newspapers were blaming the fire specifically on a Dutch Communist, Marinus van der Lubbe, who happened to be living in Berlin.

Van der Lubbe was indeed an arsonist, who had even somehow made his way into the Reichstag building and set off a few small fires. Yet he was desperately poor and could not possibly have afforded the equipment and fuel necessary to ignite the catastrophic blaze that was now burning down the building. Besides, he was mentally disabled and could not even defend himself in a court of law.

For the Nazis, Van der Lubbe was the perfect fall guy. Quickly arrested, he was just as quickly tried for arson and found guilty.

To this day, it is not known for certain what actually happened. The fire may have been set by Communists. Just as likely, it could have been the work of the Nazis themselves. They had the stronger motive, which was the need for a pretext to persecute the Reds.

It didn't matter. Hitler moved fast to make maximum use of the fire. On the next day, he prevailed on Hindenburg not only to abolish civil liberties *but also* to take over all authority from the federal states *and* to decree the death penalty for anyone guilty of "serious disturbances of the peace."

Thus Hitler hoped to frighten the German people into casting their ballots for the Nazi Party. By way of reinforcing Hitler's threat, Göring, on March 3, just two days before the elections, spoke at Frankfurt:

> Fellow Germans, my measures will not be crippled by any judicial thinking … I don't have to worry about justice; my mission is only to destroy and exterminate, nothing more! … Certainly, I shall use the power of the state and the police to the utmost … [This is] a struggle to the death, in which my fist will grasp [Communist] necks; I shall lead with the Brownshirts.

The Last Election

Remarkably, despite the intimidation, the March election failed to give Hitler the total support he wanted. With 17,277,180 votes, the Nazi Party secured just 44 percent of the total. When combined with the Nationalist Party votes, this figure translated into a slight majority of seats in the Reichstag.

With a majority so slender, Hitler could now carry out the routine operations of government. But he wanted much more, and he knew just what to do. Nazi thugs rounded up and threw most of the Communist and Social Democratic deputies in jail. This act gave the Führer an overwhelming majority.

MODERN DAY PARALLELS

Imagine this: One party or the other, Republican or Democratic, gains a slight majority in the American Congress and then bumps off the opposition. It's never happened here, but it's exactly what Hitler did.

What to do with that majority? On March 24, when the remaining members of the Reichstag gathered in their temporary home, the Kroll Opera House, Hitler gave the opening speech, introducing the "Enabling Act." The measure was the ultimate *Gleichshaltung* (coordination). It provided that the Reichstag would turn over all its functions to Hitler.

With SS and SA men ringing the opera house outside and thronging the corridors inside, any remaining opposition evaporated in a cold sweat of terror. The Catholic Center Party voted for the legislation and then passed out of existence.

Germany was no longer a parliamentary democracy. It was a dictatorship.

SUPPORTING ACTORS

The last German election before the end of World War II took place on March 5, 1933. Only the day before, Franklin D. Roosevelt had taken the oath of office of President of the United States. Although probably no one realized it at the time, FDR would be Hitler's chief nemesis on the global stage.

The Potsdam Ceremony

Always the dramatist, Hitler wanted to seal his triumph with a grand ceremony of investiture. Goebbels arranged for Hindenburg to go to Potsdam and give his blessing to the new Nazi regime. Göring and Goebbels sat in the front row of the spectators; a few World War I military chiefs were in the background.

The spectacle took place at Potsdam, site of the principal palace of Kaiser Wilhelm II. More particularly, it took place in the Garrison Church at Potsdam. The bones of Frederick the Great, the most celebrated Prussian monarch of the eighteenth century, were buried here; the Hohenzollern kings had worshipped their Lutheran God here; and Hindenburg, as a young officer in 1866, when Bismarck defeated Austria, had come here to celebrate the beginning of Germany's unification. Hitler wanted to legitimize his new regime by linking it to the memories of the triumphs of the German past.

Even the date of the ceremony, March 21, 1933, had its symbolic significance. It was the date on which Bismarck, in 1871, had first opened the all-German Reichstag.

At the start of the ceremony, Hindenburg marched down the nave of the church, Hitler beside him. Hitler was wearing a morning coat and striped trousers—a far cry from the time in Vienna when he had had to sell his threadbare clothes to eat. Hindenburg was decked out in his Feldgrau field marshal's uniform, his spiked helmet in one hand. The old field marshal paused below the imperial gallery and the empty pew of Kaiser Wilhelm II. He snapped off a salute, and then reached the altar. Turning to the audience, he delivered a brief homily, consecrating the Nazi regime:

> May the old spirit of this celebrated shrine permeate the generation of today, may it liberate us from selfishness and party strife and bring us together in national self-consciousness to bless a proud and free Germany, united in herself.

Hitler responded in kind:

> Neither the kaiser nor the government nor the nation wanted the war. It was only the collapse of the nation which compelled a weakened race to take upon itself, against its most sacred convictions, the guilt for this war.

Having gone to the altar himself, Hitler looked down on Hindenburg, who had taken a seat in the front pew. He addressed the old man directly:

> By a unique upheaval in the last few weeks our national honor has been restored and, thanks to your understanding, *Herr Generalfeldmarschall*, the union between the symbols of the old greatness and the new strength has been celebrated. We pay you homage. A protective providence places you over the new forces of our nation.

After uttering these words, Hitler stepped down from the altar, bowed to Hindenburg, and shook his hand. Hitler was trembling with emotion.

During the ceremony, in a church filled with Nazi banners and swastikas, movie cameras whirred. Goebbels had put them in place along with microphones, so that he could bring to German movie theaters moving images of Hitler uniting the old and the new.

But the show inside the Garrison Church at Potsdam was more than a cinematic event. It was the moment in which Hitler proclaimed the creation of the Third Reich, supposed to endure for a thousand years. It was the moment in which Nazi Germany was born.

Hindenburg's death on August 2, 1934, came almost as a footnote to the historic event of March 21, 1933. But it was a crucial footnote nonetheless. On that day, Hitler passed a law merging the offices of chancellor and president. Because the president of Germany was legally the commander in chief of the armed forces, Hitler was now total master of Germany, civilian and military. Thus Germany was now a totalitarian state.

In the next part of this book, we look at precisely what that meant.

The Least You Need to Know

- ✪ Hitler's rise to the chancellorship of Germany was by no means accidental. He enjoyed the support of his own paramilitary units as well as the financial and political help of Germany's most prominent industrialists, who thought he would be their tool. (How wrong they were!)

- ✪ Once chancellor, Hitler moved quickly against the Social Democrats and Communists. A deep ideological rift separated those two groups. Hitler took full advantage of the split to weaken them both. His was an old strategy that Bismarck had used against his various enemies: Divide and conquer.

- ✪ The most dramatic episode of Hitler's rise to power in 1933 was the Reichstag fire. Who set the blaze remains unknown, but it is likely that the perpetrators were the Nazis themselves. In any event, the Nazis used the conflagration as a pretext to use the organs of the German state to persecute the parties of the left.

- ✪ In Germany's "last election," held in early March 1933, the Nazis blatantly used terror and intimidation against the parties on the left. The election nonetheless failed to give Hitler the parliamentary majority he needed to set up his absolute rule. Therefore, he ordered his Nazi minions to arrest and even murder enough of the opposition deputies in the Reichstag to give him what he wanted: an overwhelming majority.

- ✪ Hitler's Enabling Act enabled him to transform Germany into a totalitarian state, with all power and authority, state and federal, gathered into the hands of Hitler, the Dictator.

- ✪ Hitler sought to legitimize the totalitarian state with a ceremony at Kaiser Wilhelm's chapel at Potsdam. Through that ceremony, Hitler tried to persuade the German people that he was merely the inheritor of the policies of old. But there was no mistake about it: He had inaugurated the Third Reich, the new totalitarian state called Nazi Germany.

Consolidation of Power: 1933-1934

As we've seen, Germany before the Weimar Republic had no experience with democracy. Those who came of age during and just after World War I knew only the Prussian–German monarchy. In contrast to modern constitutional monarchies like the United Kingdom, the German kaisers enjoyed something close to absolute political power. The very title, *kaiser,* was the Latin pronunciation of *caesar* (with a hard *c* and the *ae* sounded out like a long *i*), the Roman title that signified absolute imperial authority. Indeed, the German word had the same origin of the Russian *tsar,* a contraction of *caesar.* True, some constitutional monarchs had significant political power even during the early twentieth century. Increasingly, however, the role of European monarchs was mainly ceremonial. In some cases, as in Britain, the monarch had no political authority.

The situation was very different in Germany. Kaiser Wilhelm II may have been rather a weak character, but he wielded enormous political power, and the Germans revered him not as a figurehead but as a real person who ruled over them. Once he was forced into exile at the end of the war, there was no one to replace him. Certainly, no leader in the Weimar government could fill that void. Post-World War I Germany, therefore, was a political vacuum.

BET YOU DIDN'T KNOW

Does the fact that Hitler was able to create so much support mean that all Germans were killers? In 1996, Daniel Jonah Goldhagen, a young professor at Harvard, published a highly provocative book called *Hitler's Willing Executioners* (Knopf, 1996). In it he concluded that German culture was "pregnant with murder." Germans followed Hitler in perpetrating the Holocaust because "they wanted to." Since its appearance, the book has been criticized by historians—include prominent Holocaust specialists—as an "ahistorical" distortion. Nevertheless, Hitler's rise began with a popular election, and, despite some heroic voices that rose (at great peril) against the Holocaust, the Holocaust swept every place the Nazis reached. This could not have happened without the complicity of Germans in every walk of life.

Why Hitler?

Why Hitler? The short answer is simple. He filled the power vacuum.

Although Adolf Hitler started life as a nobody and lived much of his young adulthood as a drifter and a derelict, he was an Austrian, and his native dialect was similar to that spoken in Munich. He sounded like one of the people. As noted previously, he was gradually able to pull together a coterie of supporters during bad times in Germany. He did this by appealing to the lowest instincts of increasingly desperate Germans.

Although hatred and scapegoating of Jews were at the very core of Hitler's campaign for power, his appeal was certainly broader than his anti-Semitic platform. He presented himself as an artist, a working man, a soldier, and a kind of German everyman. The one thing he denied being was a politician.

Denying that they are politicians is a disclaimer nearly universal among politicians, including Americans, who frequently deny being "Washington insiders." They have good reason for this, since, traditionally, Americans have distrusted politicians. An even more intense distrust characterized popular opinion in Weimar Germany. It was, after all, "the politicians" who "betrayed the people" by signing the hated Versailles Treaty.

Take this point to its next logical step. Question: What other prominent German leader had not been a politician? Answer: Kaiser Wilhelm II.

Historian Robert G. L. Waite, in his 1998 book *Kaiser and Führer,* shows that Wilhelm and Hitler were, at bottom, startlingly similar. Both had miserable childhoods. Both suffered intense self-doubt, yet called themselves all-powerful. Both considered themselves honest, yet lied constantly in matters great and small. Both were narcissistic, numbing those around them with endless talk about themselves. Both were racists and anti-Semites. Both considered themselves artists. Most important of all, both had visions of a Germany destined to occupy its "rightful" place in the world.

In effect, Adolf Hitler presented himself to Germany as a version of the kaiser, restyled for the modern world. While the Allies who wrote the Treaty of Versailles believed that German autocracy would be replaced across Europe by liberal democracy, Hitler admired the sudden rise of Benito Mussolini as dictator of Italy. In this, Hitler saw a model for his own rise—not into an era of democracy in Europe or even of monarchy, but into an age of great dictators. He would be the caesar—the kaiser—not as an emperor, but as the Führer: absolute dictator. This, he believed, is what the age demanded.

Once he was in power, Hitler behaved much in the tradition of Bismarck and Wilhelm, at home and abroad. Soon, however, he went much further than either of them would have ever dared go. Unlike Bismarck, Wilhelm, or even Frederick the Great (his personal idol), Adolf Hitler had no sense of self-restraint or of practical limitations.

The Collapse of Previous Institutions

To understand the rise of Hitler, we must peer beyond our own generally democratic way of looking at things. The outcome of the U.S. Civil War (1861-1865) brought the seceded states of the Confederacy back into the Union, yet modern Americans do not think it strange that, to this day, many in the southern states, the former Confederacy, still jealously guard what they call their states' rights— a significant degree of autonomy from the federal government. This may make it difficult for many Americans to accept the almost casual ease with which the quasi-autonomous German states (*Länder*) caved in to the central German government as soon as Hitler ascended to power. They simply gave up all claims to independence.

Two weeks before the Enabling Act took effect, Bavaria accepted Nazi leadership. All the other states soon received Nazi governors. These officials had the authority to dissolve the old local governments and to replace them with administrations favored by Hitler. The same was true of lower state officials and, even more important, of judges. Under Hitler, the administration of justice was not independent, but, rather, a tool of the Führer and his central government. Courts and state governments alike became mere administrative bodies of the Third Reich. The *federalism* of old Germany simply disappeared.

TERMS AND TRANSLATIONS

Federalism is a political system in which the legal power of government is divided between a central or national government and smaller units of state or provincial government, usually under the authority of a written constitution. The United States and Canada are, to some degree, federations.

The centralization did not stop with the states. Through a combination of laws and government-sanctioned terrorism, non-Nazi political parties also soon disappeared. The regime quickly suppressed its main rivals, the Communists. The Nazis did this with the help of the Social Democrats, who were, under normal circumstances, allies of the Communists. Now, however, in a vain hope of appeasing and mollifying Hitler, the Social Democrats denounced "the Reds," often even volunteering to the authorities the names and addresses of those to be arrested.

After the Social Democrats served their purpose in helping to purge the Communists, the Nazi regime turned on them, denouncing them as traitorous subversives. The Catholic Center Party suffered a similar fate. The Catholics had once been Bismarck's most formidable enemies, and if any party supported the Weimar Republic it was the Catholic Center Party. Accordingly, on July 4, 1933, the party was summarily outlawed. This did not, however, stop Cardinal Eugenio Pacelli, secretary of state to Pope Pius XI and himself destined to become Pope Pius XII, from negotiating with Hitler the Concordat of 1933, which defined relations between the Catholic Church and the Reich.

BET YOU DIDN'T KNOW

Inside Germany, the Catholic Church itself soon became a victim of persecution; many Catholics developed an almost instinctive empathy with the plight of the Jews. Yet the Vatican was notoriously complicit in preventing Jews from getting out of Germany.

Then there was Germany's other right-wing party, the German Nationalists. Although this was a minor party, it had had close ties to Hindenburg, the army, and the land-owning class. The German Nationalists had even helped Hitler in his rise to power. But Hitler felt no loyalty to that party when, on June 21, 1933, he sent police agents and SA troops to raid Nationalist Party offices all over Germany. The German Nationalists came to an abrupt end as a political party.

SUPPORTING ACTORS

The purge didn't stop with political parties or private organizations. Government bureaucrats who showed the slightest taint of disloyalty to Hitler were ousted from their posts and replaced by Nazi Party members, whether qualified or not. A case in point: The *Reichsbank* was Germany's central bank, roughly the equivalent of America's Federal Reserve; its president, Dr. Hans Luther, a cautious and highly respected economist, had stayed out of politics. His enthusiasm in question, he was removed from the bank and named ambassador to the United States. In his place, Dr. Hjalmar Schacht was appointed to head the Reichsbank. Although he was an economist, his far more prominent credential was an invariably groveling obeisance before Hitler.

By the middle of July of 1933, only one political party existed in the Third Reich. "The National Socialist German Workers' Party"—the Nazi Party—an edict proclaimed, "constitutes the only political party in Germany."

The trade unions were also crushed. Back in the early 1920s, as we have seen, a strike by the workers prevented a right-wing takeover of the government in Berlin. With Hitler now in power, however, there was no such resistance. On May 2, 1933, police agents and SA troops moved in on trade union headquarters, destroyed their papers, stole their money, and packed their leaders off to jail.

By the middle of 1934, Hitler had gone a long way toward establishing a *totalitarian state*.

MODERN DAY PARALLELS

A **totalitarian state** or dictatorship consists of an ideology, a single party typically led by one man, a terroristic police force, a monopoly of communications and weapons, and a centrally directed economy. Besides Nazi Germany, other examples include the former Soviet Union and the People's Republic of China under Mao Zedong.

But not all the way. Hitler and his comrades had smashed the left. But there was still the right. Allied with big business, the old Prussian powers—the generals and the aristocrats—were still a formidable force, by no means under Hitler's control. In fact, he still needed them as much as they needed him. A political pragmatist despite the uncompromising belligerence of his speeches, Hitler's inclination was to maintain his alliance with the right. It was, after all, the source of much of his power.

The Night of the Long Knives

Ernst Röhm, head of the SA, saw things differently than Hitler. The SA, remember, was made up of toughs from the lower classes—people Hitler now considered riff-raff—who thought that the Nazi revolution was aimed against their social superiors. The conflict between Hitler, who knew where the power was and how to cozy up to it, and Röhm, who saw himself as a kind of vanguard of the proletariat, was building to a climax.

The Röhm–Hitler Conflict

Röhm presided over roughly two million Storm Troopers by June 1934, when he made his position public:

> One victory on the road of German revolution has been won. … The SA, however, who bear the great responsibility of having set the German revolution rolling, will not allow it to be betrayed at the halfway mark. … If the Philistines believe that the national revolution has lasted too long … it is indeed high time that the national revolution should end and become a National Socialist one. … We shall continue our fight—with them or without them. We are the incorruptible guarantors of the fulfillment of the German revolution.

In his remarks, Röhm practically accused the Führer of betraying the cause, selling out to the moneyed right. It was opposition Hitler could not let stand, and, with this, the conflict between the two men took on an aspect of personal tragedy.

They had been very close. Of all the Nazi entourage, Röhm alone had the privilege of addressing Hitler with the familiar *du*. Their former closeness made their estrangement even more bitter. Yet 1933 came and went without a public rupture. Hitler even wrote to Röhm:

> At the close of the year of the National Socialist Revolution, I feel compelled to thank you, my dear Ernst Röhm, for the imperishable services which you have rendered to the National Socialist movement and the German people, and to assure you how very grateful I am to fate that I am able to call on such men as you my friends and fellow combatants.
>
> In true friendship and grateful regard,
>
> Your Adolf Hitler

Published in the Nazi daily newspaper, the *Völkischer Beobachter (The People's Observer)*, the letter used the *du* form of address. It would prove the kiss of death.

Röhm Seals His Fate

Perhaps Röhm truly did not see what was coming when he took the step that sealed his fate. In February 1934, he presented the Nazi cabinet with a memorandum proposing that the SA be renamed the "People's Army"—a term that sounded suspiciously Communist—and that he be named minister of defense. In effect, he was asking to be put in charge of the regular army and that it be merged with the SA.

If Röhm thought that the officer corps would accept this, he was deceiving himself. The military brass had sworn allegiance to the Weimar Republic only with the greatest reluctance. Now they were supposed to be loyal to a bunch of street thugs—thugs led by a man with suspiciously leftist leanings?

And there was something else. As Himmler had earlier discovered, Röhm was a homosexual, and the generals learned (Himmler made sure of it) that most of the top SA officials were also gay. As one general put it later in the war crimes trials held in Nuremberg after World War II, "Rearmament was too difficult a business to permit the participation of peculators, drunkards, and homosexuals."

Did the generals think any more highly of Hitler than they did of Röhm? Most likely not. (Indeed, rumors circulated that Röhm and Hitler had engaged in a sexual relationship.) But Hitler gave them no choice other than to accept his leadership. It was now the army that prodded Hitler into action. Likely, little prodding was required.

The Purge on the Night of the Long Knives

The action came at the end of June 1934. Himmler's agents tracked Röhm and other SA leaders to a hotel by a lake outside Munich. Shortly after dawn on June 30, Hitler and a group of loyal Nazis barged into the establishment. They discovered two SA men in bed together. Hitler summarily ordered them taken outside to the courtyard and shot. Next, he woke up Röhm, gave him a dressing gown, and packed him off to Stadelheim prison in Munich. He was escorted to a cell that had been furnished with a table on which a pistol had been placed. When Röhm refused to use it, two police officers entered the cell and shot him dead with their own service revolvers.

In the meantime, in Berlin, Göring and Himmler were carrying out other aspects of the purge. They lined up some 150 SA officers against the wall of a military school. A firing squad gunned them all down.

Early the same morning, a squadron of SS men in civilian clothes rang the doorbell at the villa of General Kurt von Schleicher on the outskirts of the capital. Von Schleicher had served as Reich Minister of Defense under Chancellor Franz von Papen and then briefly as chancellor. During his tenure in the Weimar government, he maneuvered against Hitler. Now Hitler "maneuvered" against him. The general answered the door—and was shot dead. Gregor Strasser, with whom von Schleicher had schemed against Hitler, also lost his life. Placed under house arrest, von Papen alone among Hitler's rivals survived the Night of the Long Knives.

The purge lasted more than a single night, commencing on June 30 and ending on July 2, 1934. In the aftermath, the army almost unanimously applauded Hitler's action, and President Hindenburg even sent his chancellor a telegram expressing "gratitude" for his having "nipped treason in the bud."

Kaiser Wilhelm II, living in Dutch exile, was, however, nothing less than horrified. He advised all Germans to "be prepared for the possibility that the Nazis will push their way in and put them up against the wall."

BET YOU DIDN'T KNOW

The "Night of the Long Knives" was a grisly act of revenge ordered by Hitler, Himmler, and Göring on June 30, 1934, partly against Ernst Röhm and the leadership of the SA but also against just about everyone who had tried to stop Hitler's rise to power in 1932 and 1933. The highest ranking of the victims was General Kurt von Schleicher, who had served briefly as chancellor. At the time of the purge, however, von Schleicher was out of power. The greatest danger to the Nazi regime at the time was the SA. It consisted of some two million troops and Röhm had been ambitious to turn it into Germany's principle army, over which he, and not Hitler, would exert control. The "Night of the Long Knives" (a term adopted by the Nazis themselves), thus, was the result of a deadly struggle for supreme power in Germany.

Heinrich Himmler.
(U.S. Holocaust Memorial Museum)

The German Army After the Purge

Thanks to the purge, Hitler, Himmler, and Göring had rid themselves of their major enemies. While it had not participated in the bloodbath, the military had looked the other way, allowing the unholy triumvirate to eliminate a direct threat to the primacy of the army on the German scene. Ever since Bismarck, the German army had been practically a state within the state, a law unto itself, facing few if any challenges to its budgetary demands. With the Night of the Long Knives, the army was back in its old position of power—or so it seemed.

And, indeed, the generals had good reason to be smug. In a speech delivered on July 13, 1934, Hitler stated that the army was to remain "the sole bearer of arms." But they hadn't looked closely enough at what Hitler and other top Nazis were busy doing. They were developing and expanding two new instruments of power, the SS and the Gestapo.

The New Instruments of Power

Understandably, most people assume the Nazis invented the concentration camp. In fact, the dubious credit goes to the British army. During the Second ("Great") Boer War, fought on the veld (plains) of South Africa between 1899 and 1902, General Herbert Horatio Kitchener devised the idea of rounding up the wives and children of his enemies, the Boer guerrillas, and incarcerating them in huge barbed-wire compounds guarded by tall watchtowers. Given the poor food and lack of sanitation, thousands of people died in these camps, an eventuality that earned Kitchener the nickname "Butcher of the Veld." The camps were condemned throughout the European continent. Ironically, the loudest protests came from Germany.

The Nazis were quick to adopt the idea. Within days of the takeover of power, Hermann Göring, whom Hitler had appointed Minister of the Interior for Prussia, authorized the first Nazi concentration camps at the end of February 1933.

Experimental Camp Dachau

The original purpose of the camps was to aid the regime in suppressing civil liberties by taking dissidents out of circulation. Heinrich Himmler, however, soon expanded the mission. As president of the Munich Police, he announced on March 21, 1933, the opening of an "experimental" concentration camp at Dachau. It would hold 5,000 prisoners.

Reichsführer-SS Himmler as always thought in the most chilling of terms. People were arrested and put into the camps for "protective custody." But it was not the prisoners' protection that interested Himmler. His objective was to protect the Nazi regime against "racial traitors and Bolshevik agitators," people who (in Himmler's judgment) might interrupt the efficient workings of the state. Under Göring, people were thrown into the camps because they had protested or otherwise acted against the Nazi Party or the government. Under Himmler, people were imprisoned because of what they *might* do—or simply because of who they were.

TERMS AND TRANSLATIONS

"Based on Article I of the 'Decree of the *Reich* President for the Protection of People and State' of February 28, 1933, you are taken into protective custody in the interest of public security and order. Reason: suspicion of activities inimical to the state." Note the word *suspicion*. In the western democracies, a person arrested may not be detained indefinitely on the basis of suspicion. Sooner or later, the authorities must plea bargain or put the suspect on trial. This obviously was not the case under Himmler: Suspicion was enough to arrest and hold as long as deemed necessary.

Hitler's Henchmen and the Gestapo

For Himmler, it was not enough to merely confine suspects. In an SS order issued in April 1933, he wrote: "A great deal of potentially useful information can be extracted from suspects. Even if suspicion of treasonable activities proves to be unfounded they can often be persuaded to give information that will lead to other suspects. Such information is usually readily given under duress, threat, or promise of release."

Himmler's Dachau underlings, men such as Adolf Eichmann, a future architect of the Holocaust, were given carte blanche to interpret Himmler's instructions however they wished. They often obtained information by flogging, beating, or otherwise torturing their victims. Those who resisted long enough were often shot or hanged to discourage resistance in others.

People don't just put themselves in concentration camps. A secret police force, the Gestapo, was assigned to round up dissidents, race traitors, and other undesirables.

TERMS AND TRANSLATIONS

Gestapo was short for *GEheime STAatsPOlizei*—Secret State Police.

Unlike the SA and the SS, which were active during the rise of Hitler, the Gestapo did not come into existence until after the Nazis had been installed in the government. Operating originally in Prussia, the organization got its name after Göring had purged the state police and put Nazi supporters in all posts. These persons were the core of the new Gestapo. Its headquarters was established at 8 Prinz-Albrecht Strasse in Berlin, a building that soon became notorious as the Gestapo's chief interrogation center.

After Göring became increasingly involved in plans to build up a German *Luftwaffe* (air force), control of the Gestapo passed into the hands of Himmler, who transformed it into a national institution. Under Himmler, the Gestapo became involved in every aspect of terror practiced by the Nazis. In time, this meant the abuse of prisoners of war, the operation of slave labor programs, murderous excesses in the administration of occupied territories, brutalities and killings in the concentration camps, and the persecution and mass murder of the Jews.

Hitler's War on the Jews

Some of the Nazis' crimes were not committed until the outbreak of World War II. The regime's war against the Jews, however, began from the start, and, from the start, it was led by the Gestapo.

Nazi Germany has been the object of intense historical study since the end of World War II. Scholarly debates have raged over Hitler's motives in his quest for power. Some argue that he was a sincere ideologue, a true believer in the mythologies of German destiny he and his chief propagandist, Josef Goebbels, sowed among the masses. Others believe that the power was everything, and ideology was therefore nothing more than a tool to Hitler, to taken up or discarded as the political situation required. Those who stress the importance of ideology believe that Hitler was a rabid anti-Semite, while those who hold that his only objective was acquisition of power believe that the Jews were neither more nor less than a means of generating the level of racial and cultural hatred indispensable in stirring the masses to tribal militancy.

Anti-Semitism

Hatred of the Jews was hardly original with Hitler. Anti-Semitism had been endemic throughout Europe for centuries. Some countries, such as Holland, had always been highly tolerant, even welcoming Jews. Others, especially France, had long traditions of anti-Semitism. The world witnessed this in 1894, when a Jewish French army officer named Alfred Dreyfus was tried and, on blatantly fabricated evidence, convicted of committing treason by passing military secrets to the Germans. He was shipped off to the infamous Devil's Island penal colony. Thanks to popular protests, he was given another trial in 1899. Once again, he was found guilty—but pardoned. At last, in 1906, under intense political pressure from the left, the French army totally exonerated him, and he was reinstated into the service with a promotion from captain to major. (He went on to fight with distinction and valor in World War I.)

The "Dreyfus Affair" tore French society apart, in large measure over the issue of anti-Semitism. In Russia, however, no one—at least no one who was not Jewish—had qualms of conscience about anti-Semitism. Jews had long been confined to special territories ("the pale of settlement"), which were periodically subjected to violent raids called pogroms. The world outside of Russia often condemned this situation, but most Russians accepted it.

The Holocaust, however, started neither in France nor Russia, but in Germany. Why Germany?

The roots of the Holocaust go back at least to the rise of German nationalism during and after the Napoleonic wars. When the armies of Napoleon crossed the territories of the many Germanies, they brought with them the ideals of the French Revolution, especially liberty and equality. In practice, this meant the liberation of Jews, particularly in cities like Frankfurt, which had previously restricted Jews to ghettoes. As many Germans saw it, Jews were the beneficiaries of the French conquest and occupation. Whatever folk prejudices Germans may have long harbored against them, the Jews were now sharply defined as the enemies of the spirit of German nationalism.

In the course of the nineteenth century, German public opinion generally became more liberal and tolerant. But as economic unification reached its peak under Bismarck, many Germans—farmers, artisans, small businessman, and the like—began to blame their reduced status on the Jewish financiers. The view was without factual merit. Banking and finance were hardly the sole province of Jews. But it is human nature to look for scapegoats and then to find scapegoats among those identified as "foreign devils" or simply "the other." To many in overwhelmingly Christian Germany, Jews loomed as devils.

In the late nineteenth century, the era of Bismarck, no Holocaust erupted, but there was plenty of anti-foreign feeling in Germany, and it was aimed most particularly against the Slavs and the Jews. On any given day, German bookstores had reams of anti-Semitic tracts for sale.

It was World War I that created the conditions in which the Nazis' prolonged mass attack against the Jews would unfold before and during World War II. By the middle of 1916, World War I was going badly. Tens of thousands of young men were being killed or wounded at the front, hardships were mounting at home, and the government produced no decisive victories that could make up for the sacrifices. Something was going wrong, but nobody blamed Kaiser Wilhelm II or his top generals. To do so was not the German way. Nor could anyone accuse the soldiers, who were, after all, fighting so valiantly. The target of opportunity, as usual, was the Jews.

Once the war was over and Germany had to face the facts of defeat, the building anti-Semitism exploded. Newspapers and books demanded the exclusion of Jews from public life. State and national legislators regularly introduced anti-Semitic bills. And a booklet called the *Protocols of the Elders of Zion,* a forgery purporting to be a Jewish plot to take over Germany, received wide attention.

Anti-Jewish Legislation

Germany by the late 1920s and early 1930s was filled with hate, paranoia, and a feeling that Jews had caused every one of the nation's misfortunes. The idea took hold that all would be cured and Germany redeemed if only the nation could rid itself of the Jews. Street-corner orators invoked the mantra: "*Deutschland erwache, Juda verrecke.*" "Germany awakes, Judea kicks the bucket."

From the start of his quest for power, Hitler intended to make the Jews "kick the bucket." On April 7, 1933, the Third Reich promulgated its first anti-Jewish law. Titled "Law for the Restoration of the Professional Civil Service," the measure forced the retirement from governmental posts of all "non-Aryan"—by which was meant ethnically non-German—officials. The war against the Jews had begun. Much more was to come.

The Least You Need to Know

- In the first year of Nazi rule (1933–1934), previously influential institutions such as the labor unions, the free press, and the like collapsed under the pressure of their Nazi opponents.
- In the Night of the Long Knives, Hitler, Göring, and Himmler eliminated their SA enemies. Goebbels took little part in this brutal fight. How did he escape being purged? His skills as a propagandist were enormously valuable to Hitler.
- With the SA out of the way, the Nazi regime turned to using concentration camps and the Gestapo to suppress all leftist opposition.
- The Third Reich commenced an all-out war against the Jews, beginning with those who lived within the Reich itself.

Life in Nazi Germany: 1934–1936

Hitler and the Nazis were now in power; no substantial group could or would challenge that power. Certainly not big business: Hitler was going to support their interests. The military? The Prussian officers may have looked down their aquiline noses at Hitler but he held out the promise of restoration of their former military preeminence in German life.

Then what about ordinary Germans? With the bloody efficiency of the Night of the Long Knives now a fact of history, there wasn't much appetite for dissent. Besides, Hitler positively appealed to German patriots. He promised to free Germany from the shackles of the Treaty of Versailles and to give Germany the global power the treasonous surrender to the Allies had denied it. Hitler appealed to a national, racial, and quasi-tribal sense of collective birthright and destiny.

A combination of intimidation and appeal to German pride created momentum for the Nazis, but what were the deepest roots of Hitler's growing power?

Big business and the army, of course, and such organs of terror as the Gestapo. But could these institutions by themselves have enabled Hitler and the Nazis to enforce their tyranny? The legion of historians who have addressed this question conclude that Hitler triumphed because the German people overwhelmingly supported his triumph. Most Germans either acquiesced in or actively favored the tyrannical regime of Adolf Hitler.

The question has often been asked: Were ordinary Germans fully aware of the nature and content of that tyranny? The evidence that they were is overwhelming. We now know that a vast array of information about Nazi assaults on the churches, the press, the courts, the Jews, and others deemed to be social outsiders was widely published and read by the German population. Indeed, the people themselves helped single out suspected enemies and did so in a spirit of cooperation and patriotism.

In short, Hitler didn't do it alone. He mobilized the masses to enact his will. He and his cohorts did so with undeniable brilliance.

German Culture During Nazi Rule

Once in power, the Nazis lost no time in wooing the public with glittering showmanship. Central to their political theater was a dazzling mythology that even included a calendar of feast days. These swastika-emblazoned occasions coincided—by no accident—with traditional Christian German holidays as well as more ancient Germanic pagan feasts and observances. The Nazi propaganda machine exuberantly wove together Christian and pagan rituals to create a secular religion in which the one true god was Adolf Hitler.

The god's birthday, May 20, was celebrated nationwide with shop window displays of his photograph wreathed as if it were a holy icon. By night, there were torchlight ceremonies, fire being a powerful and ancient pre-Christian symbol. Even when viewed today on grainy newsreel footage, the nighttime spectacles are stirring—or chilling. May Day was reclaimed from the Communists and restored to its pagan roots as a celebration of rebirth. It was an occasion for more torchlight parades and swastika displays. The summer solstice, June 22, another ancient Teutonic holiday, saw more of the same. All the displays of fire evoked the principle of life—*German* life—and by implication, death to others.

Other celebrations reinforced the propagandistic union of the ancient and the modern. At Stralau, a town near the Baltic, with swastikas draping the front of the municipal hall, a man dressed in Nordic-looking animal skins and carrying a trident marched down the steps in a yearly Nazi-era ritual. Following him were young women dressed like sea nymphs, and behind them came other young women in peasant dirndls, full-skirted dresses with tightly laced bodices. The ceremony revived an ancient folk festival that honored a year's success in the harvest of fish. Germany—under Adolf Hitler—was a place of boundless bounty and endless fertility.

Every year on the anniversary of the failed 1923 Beer Hall *Putsch*, Hitler flew to Munich to deliver a celebratory speech in the beer hall that started it all.

But the greatest ceremony of all took place annually at Nuremberg (Nürnberg) on the northern edge of the Bavarian Alps. This Nazi Party festival was celebrated in late September, at the time of the autumn equinox, with its promise of snowfalls to come in those beautiful mountains. The orgy of celebration lasted a week. After Hitler opened the ceremonies with one of his grandiose speeches, a series of extravaganzas followed: Worker's Day, in which Nazis paraded not with rifles, but with shovels polished to gleaming brilliance; Hitler Youth Day, featuring marches by uniformed teenagers; Party Leaders' Day, with parades of 150,000 marchers; Army Day, with mock battles fought using weapons that were becoming increasingly abundant in open defiance of the Treaty of Versailles; and, above all, Closing Day, with flags, banners, brass bands, torches, and hundreds of thousands of uniformed Nazis marching in lockstep unison past Hitler's reviewing stand.

These rituals were profoundly seductive. The Nazi regime was consolidating its conquest with irresistible cultural glamour.

Burning of Literature

The celebrations that glorified the rise of Nazi power unfolded against a deliberately negative counterpoint. While the festivals were intended to create fanatical loyalty, a program of suppression was aimed at eliminating all sources of dissent.

Some four and a half months after Hitler became chancellor, his propaganda chief, Goebbels, used a torchlit parade for a most special purpose. At midnight on May 10, 1933, thousands of students trooped to a square at the end of Berlin's grand boulevard, *Unter den Linden,* facing the University of Berlin. They carried textbooks with them. Instead of reading these, they filed by and threw them in a pile, which they set on fire. With Goebbels looking on approvingly, the students made the fire blaze higher and higher by hurling in more classics of modern German literature, including the novels of Thomas Mann, Stefan Zweig (the Viennese writer who had observed the first reaction of his government to the assassinations in Sarajevo), and Erich Maria Remarque (author of the worldwide best-selling antiwar novel *All Quiet on the Western Front [Am Westen Nichts Neues]*).

Goebbels had majored in literature, and he knew what he was doing. He directed the students to pitch in classics from beyond Germany's frontiers: works by Proust, Zola, Freud, H. G. Wells, Helen Keller, Upton Sinclair, Jack London, and many others. Under Goebbels's guidance, the students were expressing contempt not so much for modern literature as for modern liberal thought, thought that questioned authority, that preached humanity, that called for tolerance, that criticized war—thought that might in any way undermine the Nazi order.

MODERN DAY PARALLELS

Lots of American college students from time to time would love to burn their books. The frustrations of student life can be great. But imagine a campus on which students raid the library and throw hundreds or thousands of the works kept there onto a bonfire. They would be destroying much of their own culture. It has not happened here, but it did over and over in Nazi Germany.

Nazification of German Culture

The Nazi regime banned all forms of modernity and liberalism in art and drama. Before production, every book or play had to go to a censor for approval. In music, Bach, Beethoven, and Brahms were fine. The works of Felix Mendelssohn, however, who had been born into a Jewish family but converted to Christianity, were banned. All "Jewish" composers were outlawed, even if they had converted to Christianity. As the Nazis saw it, the Jews were members of a race, not adherents of a religion. You could change your religious affiliation, but you could not change your blood.

One composer received the unquestioning endorsement of the Nazi Party. It was Richard Wagner (1813-1883), whose epic nineteenth-century works, still cherished as masterpieces, evoked the mythological Teutonic past. They were not only perfect as idealizations of Nazi values and rule, they were the favorite music of Hitler himself. "At the age of twelve, I saw ... the first opera of my life, [Wagner's] *Lohengrin*," he wrote in *Mein Kampf*. "In one instant I was addicted. My youthful enthusiasm for the Bayreuth Master knew no bounds." And for Hitler and the Nazis, there was a bonus: Wagner had been a rabid anti-Semite.

Through Goebbels, Hitler was leading the Nazification of German culture. Countless people have asked how so refined a people as the Germans could have accepted Nazi rule. In large part, it was because the Nazis so skillfully co-opted German culture, elevating and twisting the elements that served their propagandistic purposes while suppressing, burning, banning, or killing whatever worked against their program.

The Nazis and the Churches

Christianity, of course, was part of German culture and tradition. But churches from time to time have defied temporal authority. The Nazis were not about to countenance any such defiance.

The Nazi war against Christianity started slowly. Hitler himself had been born a Catholic, and although in *Mein Kampf* he had made disparaging remarks about Rome, in a speech given on March 23, 1933, he praised Christianity as essential "for safeguarding the soul of the German people." Four months later, Berlin even entered into a concordat with the Vatican, promising that in Germany the Catholic Church could "regulate her own affairs."

It did not take long for the Nazis to break this promise, whereupon church-state relations eroded badly. In an effort to ensure the racial "purity" of the German people, the regime passed a "Sterilization Law," and forced sterilizations began in January 1934. Under the law, some 300,000 to 400,000 people were sterilized, most following a diagnosis of "feeblemindedness." Such disorders as schizophrenia and epilepsy were also grounds for sterilization. Men were typically subjected to vasectomy, women to ligation of their ovarian tubes. The use of x-rays or exposure to radium was tried on an experimental basis to destroy the male testes. It is not known how many people died as a result of surgical and radiation-related procedures, but the number may be assumed to be in the thousands, with the greater risk of mortality being among women. Contrary to popular belief, the "Sterilization Law" did not target Jews. Gypsies, another "racial" group the Nazis persecuted, were sometimes sterilized, not because of their "race," but because of their position as outcasts who undermined the social order. The same held true for homosexuals, whose sexual orientation was considered at least partially hereditary.

It should be noted that court-ordered sterilization was common in early twentieth-century Europe and even the United States. But no country carried it out as extensively as Nazi Germany, and German Catholics objected vehemently. They considered sterilization, like abortion and even birth control, a sin. Catholic protests triggered Nazi reprisals. One of those murdered during the Night of the Long Knives was Erich Klausener, leader of the Catholic Action League. The regime also arrested priests and nuns, typically charging them (falsely) with "immorality" or "smuggling foreign currency." Catholic magazines and newsletters were censored, and Nazi undercover agents even violated the sanctity of the confessional.

BET YOU DIDN'T KNOW

Early in 1960, a movie called *Counterfeit Traitor* reached the cinemas. Starring William Holden and Lillie Palmer, it was based on a true story. Holden played an American businessman based in neutral Sweden during the World War II. While pretending to be neutral himself, he did business in Nazi Germany. In the course of his many trips to the Reich, he gathered valuable military intelligence, which he passed along to the United States embassy in Stockholm. Palmer played his lover and contact in Germany. When she realized that the information she was giving him enabled Allied bombers to kill scores of German children, this woman, a staunch Catholic, went to a church to confess. She told all to the priest—who proved to be a Gestapo agent. It was the sort of trick the Nazis really used.

Catholicism

By 1937, the Catholic clergy in Germany had had enough. After they reported the Nazi misdeeds to the Vatican, Pope Pius XI issued a papal encyclical titled *Mit Brennender Sorge ("With burning sorrow")*. The Vatican accused the Nazis of violating the concordat and formally accused Hitler and his gang of "suspicion, discord, calumny, of secret and open fundamental hostility to Christ and His Church."

Although he had issued *Mit Brennender Sorge,* Pius XI, like his successor, Pius XII, would be criticized after the war for having failed to do much to protest the persecution of German Jews, to protest the Holocaust, or to aid Jews to escape the clutches of the Third Reich. There is no doubt, however, that *Mit Brennender Sorge* was practically a declaration of spiritual war against Nazi Germany.

TERMS AND TRANSLATIONS

Let's break down *Mit Brennender Sorge. Mit* is easy; it means "with." For the verb **brennen,** take the English verb *burn* and reverse the *u* and the *r.* You get "brun." This is close to *brennen.* At some point, when the German-speaking Saxons shipped over to the British Isles, there supposedly occurred something called the "great vowel shift." *Brennen* means "to burn." For the word **sorge** the connection to English is the word *sorrow.* In German and English the first three letters are the same. How the *ge* in the German became the "row" in English, who knows. Regardless, *Mit Brennender Sorge* translates as "With Burning Sorrow," a pretty tough statement about the Nazi regime.

Protestantism

While Austria and southern Germany were predominantly Catholic, most of the rest of Germany during the Nazi era was Protestant, with the principal denomination being Lutheran. The instigator of the Protestant Reformation was German, of course. Martin Luther broke with a notoriously corrupt Catholic Church in 1517, but he left his own dubious legacy to Germany. A violent anti-Semite, he urged that the Jews' "synagogues and schools be set on fire, that their houses be broken up and destroyed, and they be put under a roof or stable like the gypsies, in misery and captivity as they incessantly lament and complain to God about us." Luther also preached a doctrine of absolute obedience to the state.

In contrast to Germany's Catholics, the nation's Lutherans generally welcomed the rise of Hitler. In particular, Pastor Martin Niemöller, the nation's leading Lutheran cleric, saw the Nazis as bringing about a "national revival" after "years of darkness" under the Weimar Republic. (A patriot, Niemöller was a U-boat commander in World War I.)

In 1933, Hitler named Ludwig Müller, a noted theologian, as *Reichsbischof* (Reich Bishop), the official head of religion in the Nazi government. Müller oversaw the folding of the Protestant churches into the regime itself, as congregations were required to pledge "One People, One Reich, One Faith."

After a year of this, even Niemöller had had enough. Breaking away from what was now the state-controlled Lutheran Church, he founded in May 1934 an alternative denomination he called the "Confessional Church." Niemöller and his like-minded colleagues began to use their pulpits to denounce the regime.

The result was inevitable. Before the end of 1935, Nazi agents had arrested several hundred pastors of the Confessional Church. A leader of the anti-Hitler opposition, Niemöller preached on June 27, 1937, what would be his last sermon in the Third Reich:

> We have no more thought of using our own powers to escape the arm of the authorities than had the Apostles of old. No more are we ready to keep silent at man's behest when God commands us to speak. For it is, and must remain, the case that we must obey God rather than man.

Pastor Niemöller was arrested early in July, was imprisoned in Berlin, and sent to Dachau, one of the regime's most infamous death camps. Somehow, he survived both the camp and the war and lived to 1984, when he died at the age of ninety-two. Of his experience with the Nazis, he famously said, "First they came for the Socialists, and I did not speak out—because I was not a Socialist. ... Then they came for me—and there was no one left to speak for me."

We should not let the outcry of the Vatican or the heroic protest of Pastor Niemöller deceive us. For the vast majority of Germany, Catholic or Protestant, the loss of freedom of religion did not matter much. If they wanted to, they could still go to services, listen to the familiar dogmas, and sing the old hymns. Like most other Germans, it was the promised glories of Nazism, as reported to them in the state-controlled press, that most stirred their spirit.

The Media

Under Nazi rule, the state seized control of the media. Newspaper publishing and movie production remained nominally in private hands, but Goebbels's Ministry of Propaganda and the Chamber of Films, a government entity, oversaw every aspect of what reached the public. Freedom of the press in Nazi Germany ceased to exist. Editors occupied their posts by virtue of their racial purity and willingness to slavishly print each day's news stories as dictated from Berlin.

The movie industry was much the same, except that films could produce results more spectacular than anything in the papers. Hitler's favorite motion picture director was a beautiful former actress turned prodigiously gifted director named Leni Riefenstahl. Her specialty was the documentary film. Her feature-length portrayal of the 1934 Nazi Party congress at Nuremberg, *Triumph des Willens* (*Triumph of the Will*), is still regarded as a masterpiece of film making. Using cameras placed on airplanes, flagpoles, and cranes, she captured Hitler's dramatic entrance into the Luitpolt Arena as the soundtrack carries the strains of Richard Wagner.

Tightly regulated, the media in Nazi Germany served one purpose only: to glorify Adolf Hitler and the Third Reich. Such also became the purpose of education.

Education

Hitler was a secondary-school dropout and an art-school reject. He had little affection for the public schools or the universities. Indeed, his contempt for professors and the academic life runs like a bright red thread through the pages of *Mein Kampf*.

In the end, he had little use for any form of conventional education, whose purpose is the discovery of truth. Instead, Hitler and his coterie saw education as a means of molding the loyalty of the young to the service of the Nazi regime. In a speech given in November 1933, Hitler stated: "When an opponent declares, 'I will not come over to your side,' I calmly say, 'Your child belongs to us already. ... What are you? You will pass on. Your descendants, however, now stand in the new camp. In a short time they will know nothing else but this new community." And on May 1, 1937, he boasted: "This new *Reich* will give its youth to no one, but itself will take youth and give to youth its own education and its own upbringing!"

The regime lost no time Nazifying the schools and the universities. Old textbooks were discarded (or burned), and *Mein Kampf* became the heart of the curriculum. Teachers and professors had to join the National Socialist Teachers' League, which, by order of a new statute, was made "responsible for the execution of the political coordination of all teachers in accordance with the National Socialist doctrine." Service in the SA, the SS, or the Hitler Youth became a prerequisite for employment as a schoolteacher, and all applicants were vetted for their ideological "reliability." Secret police agents penetrated the schools to ferret out any signs of disloyalty. The National Socialist Association of University Lecturers, an organization run not by academics but by party hacks, made sure that professors did not depart from the party line.

The effect of party control over the schools and universities was disastrous. Jews, of course, were purged from all teaching positions. History and literature became exaltations of a mythical Teutonic past. Something called "racial science" entered the standard curriculum. Science itself became *German* science, so that students studied *German* physics and *German* mathematics. German science was science without Jews or "Jewish ideas." For instance, the theories of Albert Einstein, a Jew who was among the greatest physicists of the twentieth century, were ignored as if they had never existed. Einstein himself became a nonperson and was fortunate enough to escape the Reich. He became a resident scholar at the Princeton Institute for Advanced Study in 1933, thus narrowly escaping almost certain death in a concentration camp. He was naturalized as a U.S. citizen in 1940.

For the Nazis, the *real* education of the young was to take place outside school and university walls. Boys were required to enter the *Hitlerjugend,* or Hitler Youth. After swearing an oath of allegiance to Hitler, members of the group would devote much of their time—time when normally they would have been in school—to camping, hiking, marching, and, in fact, to military drilling.

BET YOU DIDN'T KNOW

The *Hitlerjugend* oath stated: "In the presence of this blood banner, which represents our Führer, I swear to devote all my energies and my strength to the savior of our country, Adolf Hitler. I am willing and ready to give up my life for him, so help me God."

The regime did not forget the girls. Young women were enrolled in the *Bund Deutscher Mädel* (League of German Maidens) and, like the boys, were sent out to drill and march. Their only real duty was to be healthy; for healthy mothers breed healthy children, and the Reich wanted healthy children, racially pure children, and plenty of them.

The Courts

As Nazi education existed to serve the state, not to pursue truth, so the justice courts were to serve the Reich, not to pursue justice. In the United States and other Western democracies, the courts serve justice and guard against abuses of power by those in positions of authority. This means that courts must be independent of the legislative and executive branches of government. In Germany, there was no daylight between the courts and the regime. The law? *Hitler* was the law.

In 1936, Dr. Hans Frank, the Nazi commissioner for justice, made this point perfectly clear: "The National Socialist ideology is the foundation of all basic laws," he told an audience of judges, "especially as explained in the party program and in the speeches of the Führer."

Frank elaborated. Even now, his words are chilling:

> There is no independence of law against National Socialism. Say to yourselves at every decision which you make: "How would the Führer decide in my place?" In every decision ask yourselves: "Is this decision compatible with the National Socialist conscience of the German people?" Then you will have a firm iron foundation which, allied with the unity of the National Socialist People's State and with your recognition of the eternal nature of the will of Adolf Hitler, will endow your own sphere of decision with the authority of the Third Reich and this for all time.

The message for all judges was plain enough: Hand down your verdicts according to the guidelines promulgated by Hitler. This essentially meant that anyone who crossed Hitler should be found guilty of treason. Sometimes, judges did get confused. In 1934, for example, a court in Berlin tried a businessman charged with bribing a government official. The evidence of guilt was clear and straightforward. The judge, therefore, should have sentenced the defendant to prison. But the official he was accused of bribing was Hermann Göring. Orders were issued from on high, and the open-and-shut case dismissed.

This sort of thing destroyed the prestige of Germany's court system. As the courts inevitably retreated, the SS began to take their place—and, by the late 1920s, the primary judicial task of the SS was the pursuit and destruction of the Jews.

The Nazi Vision of Struggle

Hitler titled his political autobiography *Mein Kampf,* "My Struggle." The Nazi ideology imposed the concept of struggle on everyone, however, so that life in Germany became, for all intents and purposes, "Our Struggle."

As the historian Peter Fritzsche explains in his *Life and Death in the Third Reich,* the Nazis saw political life in "crude Social Darwinist terms," as a constant struggle between peoples. "Even as they built up a militarized racial state, which appeared almost unassailable to its opponents," Fritzsche writes, the Nazis "repeatedly imagined the demise of Germany at the hands of Poles, Bolsheviks, Jews, and other enemies." They imagined that these people would do to Germans what the Nazis were already doing to those they did not consider properly and purely German. The enemies of the Nazis would, if they could, confine or sterilize or kill the German people. The Nazi vision of life and history was, in a word, "embattled," and this, according to Frtizsche, "helps explain the fantasies of extreme violence the Nazis harbored. ... Life and death were ... deeply entangled in the Third Reich."

Toward War and the Holocaust

Nowhere were life and death more deeply entangled than in the Nazis' persecution of the Jews. For a time, between 1933 and 1935, the regime concentrated on enacting anti-Jewish legislation. New laws deprived Jews of their jobs, their businesses, and even their homes. The implication of the Nazi vision of struggle—the glorification of Aryan culture, the official contempt for religion, the use of the media and the schools to inculcate an Aryan ideal, and the deliberate weakening of courts that might have provided justice for minorities—pointed in a single direction. It was toward the "final solution" to what Hitler and fellow Nazi leaders called the "Jewish question."

By the approach of 1936, the same SS that was already supplanting the civil justice system was on the verge of becoming the principal instrument of the final solution. A standard passage in the indoctrination of SS troops read: "The Jew is a parasite. Wherever he flourishes, the people die. Elimination of the Jew from our community is to be regarded as an emergency defense measure."

When Hitler came into power, the civil government was in charge of "answering" the Jewish question. Initially, the SS did little more than maintain the Himmler–Heydrich filing system in Munich. After the SA was crushed, however, the dividing line between the state and the party became invisible. Himmler and Heydrich rushed in to take over the government's anti-Jewish functions.

For a time, that function may have seemed relatively benign. In 1934 and 1935, SS officials largely confined themselves to discussing how to encourage Jewish emigration. But by 1936, SS documents revealed a new and terrible direction. On August 28, an SS officer who at the time was Adolf Eichmann's superior at Dachau, put that new tone in writing:

> The Jew is a 100 percent enemy of National Socialism, as proven by the difference in his race and nationality. Wherever he tries to transmit his work, his influence, and his world outlook to the non-Jewish world, he discharges it in hostile ideologies, as we find it in Liberalism, especially in Freemasonry, in Marxism, and not the least in Christianity.

The document continued:

> We shall unremittingly fulfill our task, to be the guarantors of the internal security of Germany, just as the *Wehrmacht* [the army] guarantees the honor, the greatness, and the peace of the Reich from the outside. We shall take care that never more in Germany, the heart of Europe, can the Jewish–Bolshevik revolution of subhumans be kindled internally or by emissaries from abroad. Pitilessly we shall be a merciless executioner's sword. ...

The next chapter turns to Hitler's preparations for a war abroad. All the while, however, the SS, at Hitler's behest, was making preparations for a war at home—a war against the Jews.

Some apologists for Nazi Germany have claimed that the Holocaust came about only after Germany was at war. The extermination of the Jews, they have argued, was a means of national defense. As the documents just quoted show, the Nazis were planning the Holocaust well before Germany embarked on World War II. What is more, whether within Germany or wherever German forces invaded, the war against the Jews was never defensive. It was a major dimension of an aggressive, all-out struggle to subjugate the peoples of Europe and, ultimately, the world.

The Least You Need to Know

- ☸ The Nazis used every available instrument—newspapers, the radio, movies, as well as parades and other such extravaganzas—to laud the ideal of Aryan racial purity.

- ☸ The Nazi Party deliberately tried and largely succeeded in eliminating or reducing any and all institutions, such as the churches, the schools, and the courts, that might have threatened the Nazi rulers with alternative centers of power and influence.

- ☸ The Nazi vision of history was struggle—struggle for survival and struggle for supremacy. The rise of Hitler and Nazism was a preparation for global warfare, among the primary targets of which were the Jews—in Germany, in Europe, and, ultimately, in all the world.

CHAPTER 13

The First Steps Toward Conquest: 1934–1936

IN THIS CHAPTER

⭐ How the Third Reich broke the Versailles Treaty

⭐ Germany's attempt to occupy the Rhineland

⭐ The 1936 Olympic Games, Germany's propaganda tool to exhibit the superiority of the pure Aryan athlete

Up until now, the Nazi Party's control was concentrated in Germany, but just as the Bolshevik Revolution could not be confined to Russia, so the rise of the Nazis looked beyond the Fatherland. A program of conquest begins with looking beyond the borders of one's own country. Hitler started his with neighboring Austria, the land of his birth and earliest disappointments.

The Anschluss and the Dollfuss Murder

In the earliest pages of *Mein Kampf,* Hitler made clear that he would seek a Greater Germany, with Austria joined to the Third Reich. To realize this goal, Hitler sent agents into Austria almost as soon as he came into power. Their task was to undermine and facilitate the overthrow of the government in Vienna. This accomplished, they were to bring about the absorption into the Reich. The agents had plenty of help. Hundreds of thousands of Austrians were ardent Nazis and, citing the obvious ethnic bonds between Germany and Austria, they clamored for what they called *Anschluss,* annexation by the Third Reich.

TERMS AND TRANSLATIONS

The verb **schliessen** means "to lock or to close." The prefix *an* carries the sense of motion toward something. So, the noun *anschluss* means "union"; it can also mean "a highway" or "rail junction."

But the passion for *Anschluss* was hardly universal. The Austrian chancellor, Engelbert Dollfuss, wanted no part of a union with the Third Reich. Dollfuss was a tiny man—the Viennese nicknamed him "Millimetternich," after Prince Klement von Metternich, the leading statesman at the Congress of Vienna—but his determination was great. Outlawing both the Socialist and Nazi parties, he had set up a dictatorship modeled on that of Mussolini, Hitler's own early object of emulation.

Forced underground, Austria's Nazis turned to terror. In July 1934, at just about the time of the Night of the Long Knives, they blew up a power station in Vienna. Dollfuss responded with a threat to execute any Nazi caught with explosives.

A week or so later, Dollfuss was meeting with his cabinet. Suddenly 10 Nazis, garbed in uniforms stolen from the Austrian army and police, burst into the chamber. One of them shot the chancellor in the neck and chest and two others dropped him, bleeding but still alive, on a sofa.

While the ministers were held as prisoners, the Nazis occupied the chancellery for some six hours. As they did so, Dollfuss bled to death. The time for Austria's joining the Third Reich seemed at hand.

But those who wanted such a union would have to wait. During the Nazi break-in at the Austrian chancellery, one cabinet member was absent. This was Minister of Education Kurt von Schuschnigg. When he learned what was going on, he ordered Austrian soldiers to surround the building. Inside, the gun-toting Nazis got nervous. One of them telephoned the German embassy in Vienna. A German official arrived on the scene, arranging with von Schuschnigg what he thought was a truce. The gunmen, he was assured, would let the other cabinet ministers go if they could have safe conduct to the German border.

It was a trap. The moment the Nazis left the chancellery, von Schuschnigg had them arrested. In short order, the leaders were hanged, and von Schuschnigg became the new chancellor.

The Dollfuss murder nonetheless shocked the outside world. Headlines in New York proclaimed a "war scare." In London, the *Times* regarded the assassination as making the very word "Nazi stink in the nostrils of the world." And in Rome, no less a figure than Benito Mussolini took the murder very personally. At the time of the killing, Dollfuss's wife and two children had been vacationing with the Mussolini family at an Adriatic resort. After putting the widow on a plane back to Vienna, an angry Mussolini sent 50,000 Italian troops to the Brenner pass, on Italy's frontier with Austria.

Alarmed, the German government denied that it had had anything to do with the Dollfuss murder. Hitler himself claimed that he wanted only to set German–Austrian relations on the path of peace.

In the face of Mussolini's military action, Hitler did nothing: There was no confrontation with Italy. The reason was simple: Germany was too weak for a military response. But Hitler did learn a valuable lesson from the Dollfuss affair. Germany, he believed, had to rearm (in violation of the Versailles Treaty), and do so as soon as possible.

The Rearmament of the Third Reich

The rearmament proceeded in strict secrecy. Goebbels instructed his newspapers not to use the phrase "General Staff." The treaty had forbidden such a group even to exist. The government stopped publication of the list of its officers, and in June 1934, Admiral Erich Räder, in charge of the navy, wrote that the "Führer demands complete secrecy …"

Secrecy about what? Hitler had ordered construction of a new submarine fleet, a major breach of the Versailles document. But it was not the only one. In 1933 and 1934, the German navy began the construction of two battle cruisers. At 26,000 tons apiece, once finished they would exceed the Versailles limit by 16,000 tons. (These warships eventually would be dubbed the *Scharnhorst* and the *Gneisenau*, named for Prussian generals who took part in the defeat of Napoleon at Waterloo.) Hitler furthermore mandated the expansion of the army by October 1, 1934, from 100,000 men to 300,000 men. Versailles limited the German army to 100,000 officers and men.

Göring, too, was busy. He had taken on the job of minister of aviation. On paper, this meant building civilian airplanes. In reality, Göring was letting contracts for war planes. Under the banner of a group calling itself the League for Air Sports, pilots were learning how to handle military aircraft.

The Treaty of Versailles had been signed only a decade and a half before. Gross violation of the treaty demanded that the Allies respond. Invasion was the obvious response. And that was something the French had already done at the end of World War I, when they occupied the Ruhr Valley. When the Great Depression began draining financial reserves, Paris considered the Ruhr occupation too costly to maintain and left. But French spies remained in the region, and their secret reports to Paris must have raised alarms. For the great factories of the Ruhr Valley were as busy as they had been before the World War I. After 1919, the Western Allies had ordered Krupp, the mighty munitions maker, to get out of the gun-making business. Krupp had been making munitions since the Thirty Years' War of 1618-1648 and it was not about to stop now. In secret, its factories defied the Allies' order. Later, after World War II had gotten under way, Gustav Krupp, nominal head of the firm during the war, bragged that "the basic principle of armament and turret design for tanks had already been worked out in 1926. ... Of the guns being used in 1939 to 1941, the most important ones were already fully complete in 1933."

Much the same was true of I. G. Farben, the German chemical giant. During the World War I, Farben scientists had figured out how to make synthetic nitrates, vital ingredients of fertilizers—and high explosives. After the British blockade had shut off shipments of naturally mined nitrates from Chile, the Germans turned successfully to Farben's synthetics. After the war, the Allies prohibited the company from reentering the synthetics business. In defiance of the ban, Farben continued to research not just synthetic nitrates, but synthetic oil and rubber. As early as the mid-1920s, Farben had figured out how to make gasoline from coal. Later, it discovered that coal and other raw materials that abounded in Germany could yield artificial rubber as well.

During World War I, the British embargo badly crippled the German war machine. In the run-up to World War II, however, Germany was self-sufficient in the production of both oil and rubber.

That left one raw material still wanting: iron and steel. Germany had no significant iron deposits and had to import the ore from Swedish mines via Narvik, a port in northern Norway. Hitler planned a solution to maintaining the flow of iron imports. When the time was right, he would invade Norway.

BET YOU DIDN'T KNOW

The British economist John Maynard Keynes diagnosed the Great Depression as a case of shrunken consumption. His remedy was massive spending by the biggest consumer of all, government. Recent economic scholars have asked if Keynes's theory influenced Nazi economic policy. In fact, in a 1971 lecture, economist Joan Robinson, who had been a colleague of Keynes, said, "Hitler had already found how to cure unemployment before Keynes had finished explaining why it occurred." It was deficit spending for the purpose of rearming the Reich. Hitler reasoned that this would produce thousands of jobs. He was right, and by the mid-1930s joblessness in Germany was gone. In the foreword to the German edition (1936) of his monumental *General Theory of Employment, Interest and Money*, Keynes wrote, that his theory "is much more easily adapted to the conditions of a totalitarian state, than ... under conditions of free competition."

Allied Responses to Germany's Rearmament

Early in 1934, the Reich Defense Council had sent out contracts to thousands of munitions plants. The hope was that they could operate in secret, but the volume of production was so great that, by the end of the year, the Allies were fully aware of what Germany was doing.

How did London and Paris respond?

They argued—with one another. London decided to accept Germany's rearmament as a *fait accompli*—an accomplished fact that no one could do anything about. In the spring of 1934, the

British foreign secretary, Sir John Simon, even proposed to Germany an arms parity treaty. Aghast, the French protested, arguing for intervention.

As it turned out, the arms parity treaty never came into existence—although Germany and Great Britain would sign a naval limitation treaty. Hitler saw in the soft British attitude an opportunity to score a diplomatic victory. The Treaty of Versailles had given France control of the Saar, that little coal-rich corner of the Ruhr Valley where the Rhine turns northward, for a period of 15 years, after which the people of the region could vote on whether to become French or rejoin Germany. In January 1935, they voted by a margin of 10 to 1 to return to the Reich. Hitler used the occasion to promise publicly that he would make no claims to Alsace and Lorraine. Bismarck had taken those territories, but Versailles had given them back to France. Hitler was relinquishing nothing to which Germany had any right. Nevertheless, his pledge created a feeling of relief in London. The British government had made a fateful choice. It chose to trust Adolf Hitler.

Hitler's "Peace"

Hitler's moment had come. On March 16, 1935, he formally announced the creation of an army of half a million men. This was his most brazen violation of the Treaty of Versailles. Once again, however, he sought to mollify the Allies. Germany was not looking for war, Hitler said, and in a May 21 speech to the *Reichstag* (meeting in its restored building), he underlined his peaceful intentions:

> The blood shed on the European continent in the course of the last 300 years bears no proportion to the national result of the events. In the end France has remained France, Germany Germany, Poland Poland, and Italy Italy. What dynastic egotism, political passion, and patriotic blindness have attained in the way of apparently far-reaching political changes by shedding rivers of blood has, as regards national feeling, done no more than touched the skin of the nations. It has not substantially altered their fundamental characters. If these states had applied merely a fraction of their sacrifices to wiser purposes the success would certainly have been greater and more permanent. … National Socialist Germany wants peace because of its fundamental convictions. And it wants peace also owing to the realization of the simple primitive fact that no war would be likely essentially to alter the distress in Europe. … The principal effect of every war is to destroy the flower of the nation. … Germany needs peace and desires peace. …

It sounded sincere. Yet the cold, hard fact was that if Hitler *said* he wanted to avoid a war, what he next *did* could not have been better calculated to produce a war. His first act came the following winter.

The Treaty of Versailles not only mandated Germany's disarmament but also separated East Prussia from Germany proper, forbidding a union of Germany and Austria. In addition, it ordered the permanent demilitarization of the Rhineland.

In the thinking of most Germans, and not just Hitler, the Rhineland had a special significance: It was the region that historically France had used to weaken Germany. Adolf Hitler wanted the Rhineland under his complete authority. He decided to march a German army into it.

The Occupation of the Rhineland

In April 1935, Jean Dobler, the French consul in Cologne (Köln) reported that everywhere he went, through the narrow medieval streets of the city, high along the banks of the Rhine, or out into the fertile German countryside, he saw swarms of men erecting barracks, building depots, and laying out airfields. All this was just what the Rhineland would need to shelter a German force of occupation.

Back in the consulate, Dobler fired off two cables to Paris, warning his government of the developments. He received no acknowledgement.

On November 21, 1935, officials in the French embassy in Berlin were frowning with puzzlement. The French ambassador, André François-Poncet, had just rushed in from a session with Hitler. Entering his private office, the ambassador left the strictest orders that he was not to be disturbed.

The other embassy officials could not help but notice the ambassador's alarm. Was it something Hitler had said?

It was indeed.

Hitler had launched into a tirade against the recently signed Franco–Soviet Pact, in which the two nations agreed, in principle at least, to resurrect the pre–World War I alliance against Germany. As Hitler saw it, this was the old encirclement that Kaiser Wilhelm II found so threatening. Hitler intimated to the Frenchman that he would emulate the kaiser and take preemptive action.

François-Poncet cabled Paris with a warning. Like Consul Dobler, however, he received no indication that Paris would act.

Weeks passed. On the last day of 1935, in a black and bitter mood, the ambassador repeated his message. Once again, silence.

François-Poncet's Plea for Peace

On March 2, 1936, François-Poncet called again at Hitler's chancellery. He wanted to plead for peace. SS guards outside Hitler's office requested that he wait in the antechamber. The Führer, they explained, was in an urgent meeting.

Suddenly the door flew open. Through it stepped a figure familiar to the French ambassador: General Werner von Blomberg, the German chief of staff. He was obviously upset.

Von Blomberg having left, the French ambassador was admitted into Hitler's inner sanctum. France had no intention of attacking Germany, François-Poncet began to say—but Hitler cut him short. The Franco–Soviet Pact, he screamed, was criminal, a grave menace to Germany.

Thinking it useless to continue against the Führer's tirade, François-Poncet rose from his chair. He reiterated: France wants peace, not war. Then he put on his coat—pausing when Hitler spoke his name.

Suddenly grinning, Hitler asked François-Poncet one small favor. Would the French ambassador keep his visit a secret for just a few days?

François-Poncet agreed, but soon learned why Hitler had made the request. General von Blomberg had gone straight to his senior generals with orders to mobilize the troops.

The French Sit Idly By ...

March 7, 1936 (five days after the meeting between the French ambassador and Hitler) was the date set for the German army to march into the Rhineland. Hitler's pretext was the imminence of French attack. The German generals protested. Surely, they argued, the *Wehrmacht* (army) was still too small and weak to risk a war.

Yes, von Blomberg conceded to the objectors, it was a considerable gamble. But he would send only a token force into the Rhineland, and if the French counterattacked, he would retreat immediately.

So it was that, on the chilly, misty morning of March 7, 1936, helmeted and gray-coated German troops marched across the Hohenzollern Bridge across the Rhine. Even the name of the bridge, that of the family of the exiled Kaiser Wilhelm II, was in keeping with Hitler's use of symbols. But the march was more than symbolic. In defiance of Versailles, Hitler was putting guns and soldiers on the border of France.

Surely, there would be hell to pay.

On the morning of the occupation, the French ambassador to Great Britain scurried to No. 10 Downing Street, only to find that Prime Minister Stanley Baldwin and the rest of the British cabinet had decamped for a weekend in the countryside. At a dinner party the next week, Baldwin told Pierre Flandin, the French foreign minister, that "if there is even one chance in a hundred that war would follow [a counterattack by France in the Rhineland] I have not the right to commit England. England is simply not in a state to go to war." He was leaving the job to France, and, absent British backing, France chose to do nothing.

The French talked. They conferred with each other, they negotiated with their allies, and they orated in the chambers of the League of Nations. But when the three battalions of Germans marched into the Rhineland, the French failed to act. Had they done so, Hitler later admitted, "we would have had to withdraw with our tails between our legs."

War did not break out, not in 1936, anyway. The Third Reich nonetheless celebrated the occupation of the Rhineland as if it had been a great victory. Next, eager to demonstrate that Germany was once again a great power, Berlin acted as host of the 1936 Olympic Games. Not only would this garner international prestige, it would provide a competitive occasion to exhibit the racial superiority of Germany's Aryan athletes.

The Nazi Olympics: Symbol of Virility

As athletes from around the world gathered in Berlin in the summer of 1936 for the Eleventh Olympiad of the modern era, the rulers of the Third Reich were nervous. Much of their propaganda had stressed the superiority of "pure" Germans in all aspects of life, including sports. Since the first modern games, held in 1896, however, the dominant national group had been the Americans.

The leadership in Berlin could have explained that fact away by pointing to the vast population of the United States and to the large part of that population descended from Germany. By 1936, however, many on the United States team were African Americans. To Nazi ideologues, black people were subhuman. What, then, if black athletes walked away with a lot of medals? Hitler made it clear that this could not be allowed to happen.

The Olympic Setting

The Nazis were determined to use the Olympics as the ultimate form of propaganda to legitimatize the Nazi regime in the eyes of the world. Back in February 1935, the government had opened the Olympic Exhibition in a Berlin museum. The exhibition included a display of photographs of Germany's most famous athletes as well as models of the yet-to-be-erected Olympic Stadium, the Olympic Village, and other facilities. On view also were photographs of the ruins of the Olympic Stadium in ancient Greece and plaster sculptures of classical Greek athletes.

Germans for generations had venerated the Greeks as the master race of classical antiquity. The regime, therefore, was drawing a direct visual link between the ancient Hellenes and the modern Germans—both superior people.

True to their origins, the Nazis also made special efforts to spread the excitement into the rural regions. Throughout the winter and spring of 1936, a caravan called the *Olympia-Zug* descended upon small-town Germany. This was an extraordinary event. The procession consisted of four huge Mercedes-Benz trucks, each flying swastikas and hauling two trailers. Arriving in a town early in the morning, the trucks would stop in the plaza, parking on the cobbled streets and under medieval gables. Workers then stretched the trailers—built like accordions—so that townspeople could enter a series of exhibition rooms. Inside, visitors could watch movies about the Olympics and gawk at the copies of classical artifacts.

At every stop, the message of the Olympia-Zug was the same. The Olympiad of 1936 was going to put on display for all the world to see the virility of the German people. Every German was invited to witness the games.

TERMS AND TRANSLATIONS

Olympia-Zug. As in the English word *tug*, **zug** has to do with pulling or hauling. So it can refer to a train or a truck; the **Olympia-Zug** was a caravan of trucks.

The Olympic Complex

In Berlin, construction of the Olympic complex was proceeding rapidly. Located on the western edge of the German capital, the stadium was the largest ever built—anywhere. Even so, it occupied no more than one twentieth of the area of the total Olympic complex. Surrounding the stadium was a huge array of practice fields, racetracks, parking lots, dormitories for the athletes, and even a new subway station.

Connecting the compound to Berlin itself was also a special boulevard, called the *Via Triumphalis* (Triumphal Way). With this, the Nazis trumpeted their claim that Germany was derived from the Roman Empire.

The avenue ran almost ten miles from the kaiser's palace and the *Lustgarten* (Pleasure Park), along *Unter den Linden* (Under the Linden Trees) and through the *Brandenburger Tor* (Brandenburg Gate), out to the western suburbs. Swastikas lined every yard of the boulevard.

The Olympic procession marched along the *Via Triumphalis*. And when the athletes reached the front gate of the stadium, over which hung the five interlocking circles of the Olympic banner, a German brass band sounded the official welcome.

The German Caesar

The Olympiad was scheduled to open on July 31, 1936. At first, however, the rituals had nothing to do with sports. Josef Goebbels had seen the Olympics as a chance to stage the greatest Nazi show yet seen, and the star of the show was not the athletes, but Adolf Hitler.

Garbed in the brown uniform of a Storm Trooper and wearing high leather boots, Hitler left the chancellery that day in an open touring car. Behind him followed a long row of open-top Mercedes bearing an array of dignitaries, politicians, and Olympic officials. The column moved slowly along the *Via Triumphalis*. Some 40,000 Nazi guardsmen held back the crowd that lined the boulevard 20 to 30 people deep.

When the procession reached the stadium, Hitler stepped down from his automobile, greeted the rows of assembled athletes, who were standing at attention, and then walked alone through the Marathon

Gate. He emerged into the stadium, facing the huge crowd of spectators, a fanfare of 30 trumpets announcing his arrival. As the Führer took his seat of honor, Richard Strauss, the aged composer of *Thus Spake Zarathustra* and other masterpieces, conducted an immense orchestra and chorus of 3,000 voices in a performance of the German national anthem *"Deutschland über alles"* and the Nazi Party anthem, the *"Horst Wessel Lied"* (the "Horst Wessel Song"). This was followed by a version of the "Olympic Hymn" composed by none other than Strauss himself.

Once the music ended, Hitler was approached by a small girl, corn-silk blond and wearing a blue dress. She handed the Führer a bouquet of flowers. One hundred thousand spectators sighed tenderly. Hitler, after all, was known for his love of children.

A great bell announced the start of the parade of the athletes. As always it was a colorful event. Some details, however, were out of the ordinary. Passing below Hitler's booth, the Austrian team gave the Nazi salute. The crowd cheered loudly. To the surprise of almost everyone, the Bulgarians goose-stepped by. The French gave a salute that looked like the Nazi one—although they later claimed that it was the traditional Olympic salute. The British, however, did not even lift their eyes to the "Tribune of Honor." For this affront, they were booed.

Last in the alphabetical list of the foreign teams was the *Vereinigten Staaten*, the United States. On passing below the booth, all the previous groups had lowered their national flags. The Americans refused to do so.

Hitler didn't have time to put on one of his rages. Just as the undipped American flag passed beneath his reviewing stand, the German team, striding eight abreast, emerged from the Marathon Gate. They were uniformed in white and all wore yachting caps—perhaps in tribute to the yacht-loving Kaiser Wilhelm II.

Standing in his booth, Hitler walked to a microphone. For once, he had no speech to make. He declared simply: "I announce as opened the Games of Berlin, celebrating the 11th Olympiad in the modern era."

Let the Games Begin

After the opening ceremonies, Germans were confident that their athletes were going to overwhelm all others, even the mighty Americans. Some of the German athletes, to be sure, did superbly well, helped by Germany's rigging of some of the scoring. But even the American point tabulation put Germany in first place overall.

For Hitler, this was not enough. He wanted the athletes of the Reich to demonstrate specifically their superiority over those of "lesser" races. It was much to Hitler's consternation, therefore, that the star of the 1936 Olympics was an African American student from Ohio State University named Jesse Owens. During the track and field competitions, held between August 2 and August 9, 1936, Owens swept to Gold Medal victory in every event he entered.

As the host of the Berlin games, the Führer personally awarded all the medals and shook all the hands of the winners. When it came to Jesse Owens, Adolf Hitler could not bring himself to take the black man's hand. The snub spoke volumes. Hitler, however, was untroubled. Shrugging off the evidence against Aryan superiority, he set out next to annex Austria.

The Least You Need to Know

- Hitler's first step in regaining Germany's former rank as a great power was that of rearmament. The Treaty of Versailles sharply restricted Germany's military strength. Betting correctly that the British and the French would not enforce the treaty, Hitler proceeded to rebuild the armed forces.

- The occupation of the Rhineland, carried out in 1936, was also a violation of the treaty. Again, as Hitler calculated, the Allies did not respond.

- The Nazis intended the Berlin Olympic Games of 1936 to demonstrate the physical superiority of the pure Aryan race. The Germans did field the best team overall, but through his own victories, Jesse Owens, an African American, belied the Nazi race theories.

In Spain and Austria: 1936–1938

The year 1936 was pivotal. With Germany's rearmament, the occupation of the Rhineland, and the public orgy of Aryan virility at the Berlin Olympics, the post-World War I period was not merely over but, for Nazi Germany, exorcised. With this, the pre-World War II period had begun.

The Rhineland invasion was martial but peaceful. It was a triumph, but what Hitler wanted was a shooting war. Conveniently for him, one was already under way, in Spain. Better yet, it was a contest between the forces of leftist liberalism and hard-right fascism. Hitler chose to intervene in the Spanish Civil War (1936-1939) on the side of Francisco Franco, who, like Italy's Mussolini, was a fascist. Not only would the intervention give Hitler a possible ally in Franco, it would demonstrate the superiority of fascism (an ideology closely identified with Nazism), and, most of all, showcase the appallingly efficient violence of which a reborn post-World War I Germany was capable.

Dress Rehearsal in Spain

Indeed, the German intervention in the Spanish Civil War was a full-dress rehearsal for the much greater war of European conquest to come. Most specifically, it afforded an unparalleled opportunity for Germany's brand-new Luftwaffe (air force) to hone the tactical skills needed for *blitzkrieg*, the new type of "lightning war" Hitler's generals were preparing to unleash on Europe—perhaps on the world.

Strategically, German action in Spain would lead to an understanding between Nazi Germany and Fascist Italy. This *entente*, in turn, would lead directly to Hitler's annexation of Austria.

Run-Up to Civil War

Back in 1931, a quick revolution in Spain pushed Alfonso XIII off the Spanish throne and ushered in a democratic Spanish Republic. It was a noble experiment, but the republic rapidly proved itself even weaker than its counterpart in Weimar. Below what was a seemingly peaceful surface, great tensions erupted.

Catalonia, a Catalan-speaking region around Barcelona, which had long harbored a strong passion for nationhood separate from Spain, now demanded independence. The Madrid government responded by conceding a degree of autonomy, but it was not enough.

While Catalonia seethed, Spanish peasant farmers throughout Spain clamored for ownership of their own land and an end to the quasi-feudal tenant-farming system under which they labored. Again, Madrid sought to mollify dissent by breaking up some of the larger estates. But, as with the Catalonian demands, the response was insufficient to satisfy the peasants.

Worse, the steps the republic took toward liberalization outraged the great landowners, who swore revenge against the republican leaders of the country. Much as the monied interests in Germany sided with the Nazis in a corporatist state, so the landed gentry of Spain looked to emerging fascism. Not only did the republican government undermine their economic supremacy, it opposed their religious identity. Many of the liberal Spaniards loyal to the republic were virulently anti-Catholic. The land-owning class, in contrast, were faithful adherents of the Church.

In 1933, the government fell into the hands of the landowners, the Catholic clergy, and their conservative allies. The new regime overturned the republican land reforms, crushed strikes among leftist coal miners, and brutally repressed the Catalan independence movement.

February 1936 saw a general election in Spain. The people went to the polls divided among a bewildering array of parties and factions; however, the fragmented groups generally—but far from harmoniously—identified with either the left or the right. On the left were republicans, socialists, anarchists, and Communists. Many uneasily united in what was called a Popular Front. On the right were monarchists, clerics, army officers, and landowners, who banded together more homogeneously than the left. They were known collectively as the Falangists, or Spanish Fascists.

Still, the Popular Front won the election. It was a victory wholly unacceptable to the Falangists. Shortly after the votes were counted, certain officers associated with the right plotted a takeover of the government. Their leader was a controversial and charismatic general, Francisco Franco.

Spaniards Say *"No Pasaran"* to Francisco Franco

A De Havilland DH.89 Dragon–Rapide, a British-made short-haul, twin-engine, biplane airliner made largely of plywood, had been parked for days at an airstrip in the Canary Islands, just off the southwestern tip of Morocco. Its papers indicated that it had been chartered by a group of British tourists. Early in the afternoon of July 18, 1936, however, and much to the surprise of its English pilot, three Spanish men, dressed in civilian business suits, climbed aboard and ordered him to fly to Spanish Morocco, immediately south of Morocco. Their destination was Tetuán, the Spanish colonial capital.

The pilot, a man named Cecil Bebb, was in for another surprise. Once over land and nearing Tetuán, he was told to fly low enough to let his passengers get a close look at the group of men gathered on the runway. Assuring himself that those below were friendly, one of Bebb's passengers, obviously the leader of the other two, told him to set the plane down.

While the airplane was taxiing to a stop, that leader slipped off his suit and pulled on the khaki uniform of a Spanish general. The aircraft stopped, and Francisco Franco stepped out of the cabin to a round of salutes from those gathered by the runway.

Faced with the rebellion, the republican government in Madrid tried to purchase weapons abroad. Neither Paris nor London, however, was willing to authorize such sales. The French and British governments feared that the civil war in Spain would spread into a wider war in Europe. In fact, at the request of the British and the French, 27 other governments, including that of the United States, laid embargoes on weapons sales to Spain and refused to take sides in the conflict.

The policy of nonintervention, however, was a farce. Three countries—the Soviet Union, Fascist Italy, and Nazi Germany—all sent military equipment to Spain. The Soviets sided with the Loyalists, as the supporters of the republican government were called. Germany and Italy aligned themselves with the Franco-led fascist rebels.

For about a year, even with German help, Franco's forces failed to make much headway. They did eventually surround Madrid, laying siege while German bombers dropped their loads on the city. The air raids, however, failed to destroy the morale of the capital. On the contrary, the determination of the Madrid residents to hold out only stiffened. *"No Pasaran!"* (They shall not pass!) they proclaimed, a phrase that echoed French General Robert Nivelle's defiant declaration during the Battle of Verdun in World War I: *Ils ne passeront pas!*

The city dwellers heard those words chanted regularly over the radio by Dolores Ibarruri, called *La Pasionaria,* "the impassioned one." Once a staunch Catholic, she had become a Communist. Spanish workers viewed her as a revolutionary saint. She was the real inspiration of Madrid's resistance.

The Raid on Guernica

By the end of March 1937, Franco realized that to conquer Spain he would need to do something new. He turned to his German advisers for their thoughts. Starve Madrid into submission, they counseled. Undoubtedly, the German officers in Spain remembered well the effect the British naval blockade had on their own civilian population during World War I. Take the farmlands! Take the coal and iron mines in the north, up in Basque territory! If you can't overrun Madrid yet, go after Bilbao, on the Bay of Biscay! (Bilbao was a major industrial center.) Take Durango! (Durango was a northern industrial city.) Let us Germans use those cities to test a new technique of aerial warfare we have developed. (It was the combined use of high-explosive and incendiary bombs. The explosives reduced buildings to rubble, which made effective kindling for the incendiary munitions.)

Franco went north. As he did so, a German air unit called the Condor Legion followed along. It hit Bilbao and Durango. Then, for no reason of military necessity, the Condor Legion unloaded on Guernica.

About 18 miles east of Bilbao, Guernica was a town of some 7,000 inhabitants. Isolated for centuries by the mountains of northern Spain, it was the cultural and religious center of the Basque region. Full of churches and convents, the town centered on a large plaza, a gathering place formed by a railroad station, a hotel, a public school, and the municipal hall. Right in the middle of the plaza stood the sacred oak of Guernica, a symbol of Basque independence. Early in 1937, the tree bloomed. Some of the town's people thought it a bad omen.

They were right.

At 4 P.M. on April 26, 1937, two nuns went up into a church in the center of the town and began to pull the bell. They called down, *"Aviones! Aviones!"* (Airplanes! Airplanes!) Sure enough, in just a moment, bombers from the Condor Legion were overhead. Bombs rained on the plaza in front of the railway station. Wrote one survivor, "A group of women and children were lifted high into the air, maybe 20 feet or so, and they started to break up. Legs, arms, heads, and bits and pieces flying everywhere."

Before nightfall, eight more waves of planes from the Condor Legion appeared over Guernica. By the time they left, roughly 2,000 persons were dead, and all the buildings around the plaza smashed to bits.

Hitler may have been proud of the performance of his Luftwaffe, but he also knew that he now had a public-relations disaster on his hands. Berlin sent the Condor Legion strict orders to say nothing about the attack. But the news got out anyway. Although Franco's propagandists claimed that the town had been destroyed by retreating Loyalist troops, foreign sympathizers of the Spanish republic charged Franco with war crimes.

BET YOU DIDN'T KNOW

In Paris, the Spanish artist Pablo Picasso, who had already built a reputation as one of the world's preeminent painters, was inspired to create a large canvas (137.4 inches by 305,5 inches) called simply *Guernica*. Using a stark palette of gray, black, and white, it employed his trademark explosive "cubist" style to evoke the horror of the air raid. It created a sensation, which brought worldwide attention to the Spanish Civil War, along with condemnation of the barbarism of the role Germany had chosen to play in it.

Despite almost universal condemnation of the raid on Guernica, Hitler reaped one great benefit from it. Up to this time, Benito Mussolini had regarded Hitler with a mixture of pity and contempt. He knew the Führer admired him and sought to emulate his success. Yet he saw Hitler as a clownish upstart, not to be taken altogether seriously. Now, at last, Mussolini (*Il Duce*, "The Leader," as he referred to himself) was impressed—impressed and a little afraid. Hitler, it seemed, would stop at nothing.

As we have seen in Chapter 13, Mussolini had reacted with rage to the Dollfuss murder. He felt close to the Dollfuss family and, just as important, he regarded Austria as lying within Italy's sphere of influence. After all, during its wars of unification in the 1860s, Italy had expelled the Austrians from Lombardy and Venetia; then, with the Paris peace talks of 1919, Italy had acquired Trieste, which had been the major Austro–Hungarian port on the Adriatic. Like a lot of other Italians, Mussolini had begun to regard Austria as almost an Italian colony.

But Guernica changed Mussolini's thinking. Despite his imperial pretenses, Il Duce knew that, in battle, Italy would be no match for Germany. If Hitler wanted Austria, Mussolini would let it be known, he could have it—and, what's more, he would welcome an alliance with the Führer.

The Hossbach Memorandum

Well before the outbreak of World War II, we come now to Nazi Germany's first advance beyond the nation's traditional borders. It is time to ask: What was Hitler really after?

On the afternoon of November 5, 1937, six officials were summoned for a secret meeting in Hitler's office at the Chancellery. In attendance were Field Marshal Werner von Blomberg, commander in chief of the German army; General Werner von Fritsch; Chief Admiral Erich Räder; Hermann Göring, head of the *Luftwaffe*; and Baron Konstantin von Neurath, the foreign minister. The sixth man was a mere colonel, Friedrich Hossbach. A staff officer assigned to Hitler, his function at this meeting was to take notes.

The men were seated at a big round table, with Hitler, as usual, doing most of the talking. He began by harping, as always, on Germany's need for *Lebensraum*, "living space," but the question was: Expansion where? For a while, Hitler talked about overseas colonies, only to speculate that these might simply be too expensive to acquire and maintain. Expansion, therefore, would have to take place in Europe.

That raised the next question. Where in Europe?

It did not take Hitler long to offer an answer. The quest for *Lebensraum* would begin next door, with Austria and that hated product of the Treaty of Versailles, Czechoslovakia. Their proximity made them obvious targets as well as convenient sources of food and raw materials for Nazi Germany. They would also offer ready space for emigration—once, that is, Austria and Czechoslovakia had been cleared of racial "undesirables."

But there was a problem. "Germany," according to Hossbach's memorandum of the meeting, "had to reckon with two hate-inspired antagonists, Britain and France. … Germany's problem could only be solved by means of force and this was never without risk." Hitler added: to both London and Paris, "a strong German colossus in the center of Europe would be intolerable."

A few of the men around the table were shocked. They believed that if Hitler was talking about going to war, as he seemed to be, he was putting Germany on the road to disaster. Fritsch pointed out that the Czechoslovakian defenses were potent indeed. Blomberg contended that France was militarily superior to Germany, even if Paris had to take on Italy at the same time as it engaged against Germany. And Neurath did not even see much likelihood of a war between France and Italy.

Hitler was unfazed by these doubts, which he largely dismissed. The meeting lasted until after dark, when Hitler ended it with the comment that he might move "as early as 1938"—just a few months off.

As for those who had raised the doubts, Hitler did not forget them. Within three months of the meeting, Blomberg, Fritsch, and Neurath were all out of office. Neurath's replacement as foreign minister was Joachim von Ribbentrop, whose qualifications for the diplomatic job were that he had been a champagne salesman, could speak several languages, and, far more important than the first or second, was Hitler's unquestioning poodle. As for the ennobling "von" in his name, it was acquired because an aunt had adopted him. He was a workingman, not a member of the nobility.

If Hitler could have removed Blomberg, Fritsch, and Neurath immediately, he would have, but engineering the end of their careers took some time. Blomberg, for example, was popular in the army, and Hitler could not get rid of him until his Gestapo spies discovered that the general, a widower, in early 1938 married a young woman who had been a prostitute. The Gestapo also went to work framing Fritsch on a charge of homosexuality. He demanded a trial, and, for once, a Nazi court handed down a verdict of not guilty. By then, however, Hitler had forced his resignation.

With the three dissenters out of the way, Hitler on February 4, 1938, had a decree broadcasted by radio throughout the Third Reich: "From now on I personally take over the command of all the armed forces."

Consider Hitler's position at that moment. He must have thought he was on the top of the world. He had long since crushed the German left. He had made a mockery of those institutions—the press, the schools, and the courts—that in the Western democracies often stood independent of state power. Many Germans still attended their churches, but hundreds of Protestant clergy, who had refused to toe the Nazi line, were without jobs or in jail. In the Catholic south, anti-Nazi priests had been jailed on charges of pederasty. (Sadly, as we know today, sometimes such charges are valid. In Nazi Germany, however, they were attached only to those who opposed the regime.)

Strikes and labor walkouts were strictly forbidden. But, thanks to rearmament and public-works projects, jobs were plentiful, pay was good, and workers were generally content. In short, Hitler was in total command of the home front. Abroad, as we know from the Hossbach memorandum, he worried about France and Great Britain. But he was confident that neither of those powers regarded Austria as an area of serious interest.

Hitler's Threats Against Austria

All through 1937, Austria's Nazis, with money and encouragement from Berlin, renewed their terrorizing tactics. Bombs went off all over the country, and violent demonstrations gave rise to the rumor that the Nazis were planning to kill the new chancellor, Kurt von Schuschnigg, as they had murdered Dollfuss, his predecessor.

Against this background of intimidation, Hitler ordered the head of the government of Austria to meet with him in his Alpine retreat at Berchtesgaden. The session took place on February 12, 1938.

When they met in the frosty mountain air, Schuschnigg, the possessor of upper-class Austrian politeness, commented eloquently on the beauty of the view. But Hitler was not of an upper-class Austrian background. Pointedly, he interrupted, saying that he wasn't there to discuss scenery. Then came the customary tirade:

> You have done everything to avoid a friendly policy. … The whole history of Austria is just one long act of high treason. That was so in the past and is no better today. This historical paradox must now reach its overdue end. And I can tell you right now, Herr Schuschnigg, that I am absolutely determined to make an end of all this. The German Reich is one of the great powers, and nobody will raise his voice if it settles its border problems.

Hitler was talking about annexing Austria. Schuschnigg was taken aback, asking just when Austria had been so treasonous.

Hitler ignored the question. Resuming his rant, he proclaimed:

> I have a historic mission, and this mission I will fulfill because Providence has destined me to do so. … Who is not with me will be crushed … I have chosen the most difficult road that any German ever took; I have made the greatest achievements in the history of Germany, greater than any other German. And not by force, mind you. I am carried along by the love of my people …

Saying that he was willing to accept all that, Schuschnigg offered to reach an understanding. But an understanding was not what Hitler had in mind:

Listen, you don't really think you can move a single stone in Austria without my hearing about it the next day, do you? … I have only to give an order, and in one single night all your ridiculous defense mechanisms will be blown to bits. You don't seriously believe that you can stop me for half an hour, do you? … I would very much like to save Austria from such a fate, because such an action would mean blood. After the army, my SS, and the Austrian Legion [Austrian Nazis] would move in, nobody could stop their just revenge—not even I.

Hitler then laid out specific demands. In fulfilling them, Austria would essentially be giving up its sovereignty. The Austrian Nazi Party, which was outlawed (at least on paper), must be made legal. Arthur Seyss-Inquart, an Austrian attorney who was already state councilor in the Austrian cabinet (the position was roughly equivalent to attorney general), was to be named minister of the interior, in charge of all law enforcement. Nazis were to head up the ministries of defense and finance.

Hitler wanted it all. In Austria, Nazis would control the courts, the police, the army, the navy, and the money. What else was left? That was Schuschnigg's question, only he didn't dare ask it. Instead, defeated, he signed a piece of paper agreeing to everything.

Austria's "Resistance"

Once back in Vienna, however, Chancellor Schuschnigg decided to stand up to Hitler. On February 24, 1938, in a speech to the Austrian parliament (it was called the *Bundestag* and—we must make no mistake about this—its members were loyal supporters of a one-party, dictatorial regime), he declared: "Thus far and no farther!" Austria, he proclaimed, would never give up its independence. He ended with a stirring chant: "Red-White-Red [the Austrian national colors] until we're dead!"

The response to the speech?

That very day, in Graz, a town in southern Austria almost at the border of Yugoslavia, a huge crowd of Nazis marched into the square, pulled down the red-white-red Austrian flag, and ran up the German swastika in its place.

TERMS AND TRANSLATIONS

Red, in German, is *rot*; dead is *tot*. So Schuschnigg's "red-dead" rhyme worked in German as well as it does in English.

Normal governance in Austria began to collapse. As minister of the interior, Seyss-Inquart, the first of the major Hitler collaborators, did nothing to quell further Nazi demonstrations. Alarmed, lots of Austrians pulled their money out of the banks and made plans to flee the country. Tourists suddenly stopped coming. From New York, Arturo Toscanini, the internationally famed symphonic and operatic conductor, cabled that "because of political developments in Austria," he would not appear at the Salzburg Festival. Each summer, that festival, dedicated to the music of Mozart, drew tens of thousands of visitors. Foreign firms withdrew their investments. Suddenly, lots of people in Austria were out of work. The country stood on the brink of economic disaster. And all the while the Nazis were marching in the streets.

Now the streets of Vienna and other Austrian cities were full of leftists, eager and willing to do battle with the Nazis. What they wanted in turn from the chancellor was a chance to reactivate their own Social Democratic political party and run candidates for seats in the Bundestag. Believing that he had no choice, Schuschnigg scheduled a nationwide election to be held on March 13.

SUPPORTING ACTORS

Desperate, Schuschnigg did something that played right into Hitler's hands. As chancellor, he had sworn to defend Austria's sovereignty. But that did not mean he was a left-winger—quite the contrary. Assuming power after the murder of Dollfuss, Schuschnigg had clapped lots of left-wingers, workers, trade union leaders, strikers, and Social Democrats, in jail. Like Hitler, he believed in authoritarian, one-party, right-wing rule. On March 4, however, he let the leftists out of their cells.

Hitler Moves

News of Schuschnigg's election plan sent Hitler into a rage. Just what a Hitler rage could produce was detailed in an entry from the diary of General Alfred von Jodl, chief of operations in the German army: "Führer is determined not to tolerate [the Austrian election]. The same night, March 9 to 10, he calls for Göring. General v. Reichenau is called back from Cairo Olympic Committee, General v. Schobert [commander of the military district on the Austrian border] is ordered to come …" Hitler was gathering his top generals in preparation for action.

The next morning, March 10, Hitler told them of his decision. He was going to launch a military occupation of Austria.

Certain that France and Great Britain would do nothing to stop him, Hitler saw only one question: How would Mussolini react? A telephone call solicited from Philip of Hesse, a German prince who had married a daughter of the late king of Italy, provided the answer. Mussolini did not object at all.

Over the wire Hitler almost gushed: "Please tell Mussolini I will never forget him for this … Never, never, never … I shall stick with him whatever may happen, even if the whole world gangs up on him."

The Nazi Invasion of Austria

At 5:30 A.M. on March 11, 1938, Schuschnigg's bedside telephone rang. On the line was his chief of police. The officer reported that the Austrian–German border at Salzburg had just been closed. Dressing quickly, the chancellor rushed to his office. There he learned from intelligence reports that German units in the Bavarian military district had mobilized. Their destination, presumably, was Austria.

At about 10 A.M., Schussnigg had a visitor, his own minister of the interior, Seyss-Inquart. The latter produced an ultimatum from Berlin. Schuschnigg must resign and cancel the election. He had until noon to telephone Göring, saying that he had taken these steps. Otherwise Germany would invade.

Time was short. The chancellor made some quick inquiries. Could he throw a police cordon around Vienna? The answer came back: So many of the policemen were Nazis that members of a cordon would welcome the invaders. Could he make an appeal to world opinion? From the foreign ministry, also under Nazi control, came the sneering news that Mussolini would not lift a finger—and neither would the British and the French. As for Stalin, he would do nothing to help his own leftist allies in Vienna.

So that was that. At about 4 P.M., Schuschnigg canceled the voting and resigned. But he had missed the ultimatum's deadline. So, Germany invaded anyway.

Not that it was much of an invasion. When the German troops crossed the frontier at Salzburg on Saturday, March 12, the townspeople welcomed them with flowers and Nazi flags. A group of locals tore down the border station that had separated the two countries. Later in the day, when Hitler's Mercedes limousine entered Austria, heading along the country road toward Vienna, peasants by the roadsides scooped up pieces of earth the tires had touched.

When Hitler reached Vienna in the late afternoon, he made the inevitable speech.

> I believe that it was God's will to send a boy from here into the Reich, to let him grow up, to raise him to be the leader of the nation so as to enable him to lead back his homeland into the Reich.

Almost immediately, Hitler banned the use of the word *Österreich,* Austria. Austria was now officially part of the Third Reich.

Austria Under the Nazis

Wholly absorbed into Germany—a plebiscite taken shortly after the German-Austrian Anschluss (Union) had 99 percent of the Austrians voting for such unity—Austria ceased to exist as a nation. For a short time, the Germans called it *Ostmark* (East boundary or frontier, as when you mark something off), but even that sounded too dignified for a noncountry. So, they simply referred to Austria by its various *Gaue* (districts), such as Salzburg or the Tyrol. Vienna became just a regional administrative center, indeed an increasingly shabby, down-at-the-heels city.

BET YOU DIDN'T KNOW

Hitler was allowing Vienna to rot away. It was his revenge for the way he had been treated, or thought he had been treated, during his earlier years as a bum in the city.

Socialists and Communists were publicly whipped. Jews were made to scrub the streets and clean latrines. Kurt von Schuschnigg ended up in the concentration camp at Dachau, not to be freed until the arrival of American troops in 1945.

Overseeing the former chancellor's arrest and shipment to Dachau was Reinhard Heydrich, the number two man in Himmler's SS. Over the course of the next two years, Vienna would see a good deal of Heydrich. For the Holocaust, in which Heydrich would play a major part, was now truly underway.

The Least You Need to Know

- The horrors of the Spanish Civil War may seem a bit removed from the subject of Nazi Germany. But they weren't really: At Guernica, Nazi bombers inflicted hideous, and wholly uncalled for, suffering.

- As the Hossbach memorandum, eventually captured by the Allies, revealed, Hitler after the Rhineland occupation was definitely planning conquests in Central and Eastern Europe.

- The first step in that drive was to be the annexation of Austria. Upon that bloodless conquest, Austria as such ceased to exist.

"Peace for Our Time" 1938–1939

On November 7, 1938, Herschel Grynszpan, an unemployed, 17-year-old Polish Jew living in Paris, entered the German embassy in that city and shot to death Ernst vom Rath, one of the officials working there. The youth's motivation, he said, was revenge for the way Nazi Germany was treating his fellow Jews. When word of the assassination reached Berlin, the infuriated Hitler orchestrated the worst *pogram* in Germany to that date.

Kristallnacht

Vom Rath had been scheduled to deliver a speech commemorating the Beer Hall *Putsch*. Propaganda minister Josef Goebbels gave the speech in the slain official's place, adding "the Führer has decided that ... demonstrations should not be prepared or organized by the party, but insofar as they erupt spontaneously, they are not to be hampered."

What followed was a nationwide orgy of anti-Jewish riots—truly, a *pogrom*—aided and abetted by the regime. Within just three days of Grynszpan's confession, vandals systematically hit synagogues and Jewish stores and homes. Because of the shards from broken windows that littered the streets, the orgy came to be known as *Kristallnacht,* or Crystal Night. Ninety-one Jews were killed, 20,000 were arrested, and a fine levied against all German Jews came to one million marks.

TERMS AND TRANSLATIONS

Pogrom is a Russian word meaning "like thunder." It is an organized and often officially sanctioned massacre or persecution of a minority group, especially against the Jews.

When Jewish merchants tried to collect insurance for all the damage done to their businesses, the Nazis confiscated the payments. After all, went the official excuse, if the Jews hadn't been there, nothing would have happened.

An obscenity in itself, Kristallnacht was the Nazi regime's signal that violence against Jews was not just the policy of the Third Reich, it was, in effect, the duty of German citizens. Historians deem the event to be the beginning of the Holocaust.

Target: Czechoslovakia

The next step in Hitler's plan was Czechoslovakia. Like Austria, Czechoslovakia had a German-speaking population. Unlike Austria, however, that population was a minority. Thus, with the impending annexation of all Czechoslovakia, Hitler could no longer claim that he was simply trying to unify German-speaking peoples.

Created as a nation by the Treaty of Versailles, Czechoslovakia was shaped rather like a fish. The narrow tail, the region called Slovakia, was on the east, bordered by Poland, Hungary, and a swatch of Romania. Where we might locate the gills is what is today the Czech Republic, and its capital, Prague; Hungary and Austria lay to the south. The head of the fish was the Sudetenland, nuzzled into the side of Germany, with Dresden above and Munich below.

Because of its proximity to Germany, German speakers largely inhabited this last part of Czechoslovakia, forested and mountainous. When Versailles created this multi-ethnic country, it expressly barred the unification of the Sudetenland with Germany. But when Austria was joined to the

Reich in the Anschluss, a clamor arose among the Sudeten Germans: Why can't we do the same? Hitler thought it was a very good question.

Map of Czechoslovakia.
(Eric Stevens)

Why not do to Czechoslovakia what he had done with Austria?

Hitler realized that attempting to annex Czechoslovakia would be a high-risk move. Austria was just a dysfunctional little country, attractive to tourists but no one else. Besides, much of Europe and the world already thought of Austria as German. Czechoslovakia was another matter altogether. The Allies had deliberately designed it as a barrier against both Russian *and* German expansion. As we heard Hitler say in the previous chapter, the last thing the British and French wanted was a German super-power in the center of Europe.

But extending Germany into the heart of Europe was precisely what Hitler *wanted* to do. Besides, the Sudetenland was the industrial center of Czechoslovakia and would be a valuable and productive addition to the Reich. The clamor of the Sudeten Germans was to Hitler a siren song. He became determined to act. All he needed was a plausible pretext to offer the world.

Sometimes a good pretext is not very hard to find. Early in the morning of September 13, 1938, a pair of Czech policemen on bicycles rode through Eger, a town in the Sudetenland, and stopped outside the Victoria Hotel. While one rang the doorbell, the other pulled a piece of paper from his pocket. The document was a search warrant. A Czech judge had learned that the hotel was the headquarters of the Sudeten Nazi Party and that it contained a cache of illegal weapons. The two policemen were supposed to investigate.

They did not get very far. While they were waiting for someone to open the door, a bullet fired from a window above hit one of the officers, killing him almost instantly. The other officer tried to escape on his bicycle, but was too panic-stricken to mount it and instead ran around a corner. In short order, he reported the incident to his police headquarters.

In response to the report, two Czech police motorcycles, followed by a squadron of armored cars, descended on the Victoria Hotel. The armored cars pulled up to the front of the hotel and opened fire, sending artillery shells through its second-story windows. A Czech officer demanded through a megaphone that those inside surrender immediately. By way of an answer, those inside returned fire and tossed down a hand grenade. One of the Czech police officers was killed.

Czech army units were summoned. Mortar troops took up positions, fired their high-trajectory rounds, and demolished the roof of the hotel. Still, those holed up inside maintained their return fire. At last, about noon, a white flag appeared in one of the windows. The Czech troops entered the building.

They found in the upstairs rooms eight men dead, all of them Sudeten Nazis. There were two survivors. One was the rifleman, who early in the morning had killed the Czech bicycle cop. The other was Karl Hermann Frank, number-two man in the Sudeten Nazi Party. When the shooting began, he had slipped out a back door of the hotel and, obtaining a car, had driven to the nearby town of Asch. There he had told his chief what was going on. Returning to Eger, Frank surrendered, confident that he would not spend much time in jail.

The leader of the Sudeten Nazis to whom Frank had reported was Konrad Henlein. When Hitler became chancellor of Germany in 1933, Henlein was a gymnastics teacher. His profession put him very much in tune with the Nazi emphasis on the physical fitness of youth. He also eagerly embraced the rest of the Nazi ideology, so much so that by 1935 he had organized the Sudeten branch of the party and was receiving a substantial subsidy from the German foreign office. Under Henlein's leadership, the Sudeten Nazi Party caught on with Czechoslovakia's Germans. Soon, they were agitating for the unification of the Sudetenland with the Third Reich.

The Sudeten Germans claimed that the Czechs, who made up the majority in Czechoslovakia, discriminated against them. Although the evidence for this is sketchy, it may well have been true. Indeed, the Slovaks made much the same claim against the Czechs. Forced ethnic combinations did not often work well in Europe. The fact that Czechoslovakia had been hurriedly cobbled together by the Versailles commissioners did not promote a feeling of true nationhood among these ethnic Germans, Slovaks, and Czechs. The artificial "instant" country was ripe for action by Henlein and his Nazi *fifth column* that Berlin financed.

TERMS AND TRANSLATIONS

The term **fifth column** is derived from the Spanish Civil War. In a radio broadcast, Queipo de Llano, a general fighting on the side of Franco, tried to frighten the defenders of Madrid by stating that they were under attack by four of Franco's columns and by a fifth column of secret Franco supporters inside the city. The phrase came to mean disinformation and subversion by foreign agents. It was widely applied to the work of Nazi agents in various parts of Europe.

On hearing the news of Eger from Karl Hermann Frank, Henlein, a pudgy-faced man who wore eyeglasses and had a deceptively mild manner, was overjoyed.

"Our comrades have fallen in the battle for freedom, killed by the Czechs, but they will not be forgotten," he exclaimed to Frank. "I must inform the Führer at once. Adolf Hitler can now demonstrate to the world that Sudetens and Czechs can never live together, that it is useless to go on negotiating, that the only place for the Sudeten Germans is back home in the Reich!"

For Hitler, the Eger incident was lucky indeed. Two days later, Neville Chamberlain, the British prime minister, was scheduled to fly out of London to meet with the Führer. On both sides of the German–Czechoslovakian border, agitation for unification had been intense. To Chamberlain, as well as to the French premier, Éduard Daladier, the situation was critical. They were not concerned about the woes of one ethnic group or another. What is more, the indifference of France and Britain to Franco's fascist takeover of power in Spain suggests that they probably didn't even care much about whether Czechoslovakia remained a democracy. Chamberlain and Daladier were also aware that, as a means of containing Germany, the Sudetenland was ultimately ineffective. Ethnically German and geographically adjoining the Reich, it was, for all practical purposes, already part of Germany.

But there was more to Czechoslovakia than the Sudetenland. The leaders of Britain and France regarded non-Sudeten Czechoslovakia as still key in keeping Hitler and Germany out of Eastern Europe. It went back to the old balance-of-power principle. As Chamberlain saw it, preventing the rise of any superpower in Europe was the essential ingredient of national security. That was the lesson of Napoleon's rise, and Hitler had all the potential of being a new Napoleon.

Yet Chamberlain understood that Great Britain was in no position to fight a land war on the European continent. Like France, Britain had rushed to demobilize and disarm at the end of World War I. British and French families had lost so many of their sons in war. They had sacrificed so much of their treasure. France—though a victor—suffered terrible devastation, since most of the fighting on the Western Front had taken within its borders. The European democracies threw down their weapons. Wanting no more wars, they rendered themselves incapable of fighting.

True, the Royal Navy was still potent, far stronger than the German fleet. But the army was once again very small. How was a British military force even to march to the defense of Czechoslovakia, much less carry out that defense?

Chamberlain believed Britain had no course other than to avoid war. He needed to work out a compromise with Hitler. In the middle of September 1938, he flew to Munich to meet with the man he called "Herr Hitler." He believed—he hoped—he could negotiate a settlement.

The Munich Conference and the Myth of Appeasement

History has not been kind to Neville Chamberlain. The story of his meeting with Hitler—actually, there were two, one in mid-September 1938 and the other at the end of the month—has been told over and over. It has been told as the tale of a British politician, a nice enough chap armed only with an umbrella, humiliated by a thug into giving away the Sudentenland in return for a piece of paper promising peace. The event was labeled with the word Chamberlain himself used to describe his policy toward Nazi Germany: *appeasement*.

To be more accurate, Chamberlain called it "*active* appeasement," and he intended it as a strategy to put off war long enough for Britain to move a reluctant rearmament program along. Chamberlain actually believed war was likely. He wanted to buy time to give his country a fighting chance.

But all of this strategic thought is lost in the usual telling of the Tale of Appeasement. The account by Harold Nicolson, English author, historian, and member of Parliament is typical. Chamberlain and an aide, Sir Horace Wilson, a member of the British cabinet, flew to Germany with "the bright faithfulness of two curates entering a pub for the first time; they did not observe the difference between a social gathering and a roughhouse; nor did they realize that the tough guys assembled did not either speak or understand their language," Nicolson writes. "They imagined that they were as decent and as honorable as themselves."

"We should have traveled with about 50 secretaries and an imposing array of bodyguards," Sir Horace Wilson later admitted; they had only taken one secretary, a detective from Scotland Yard, and a foreign office expert on Central European affairs with them. "Instead we had this tiny delegation, and for a great power we looked puny. We didn't know any better."

The small British party landed at the Munich airport. The British ambassador and Joachim von Ribbentrop, the German foreign minister, were waiting for them by the runway. A special train took them to a hotel at Berchtesgaden, Hitler's hideaway. After changing clothes, they started in two cars up the mountain slope. Both sides of the winding road were lined with black-uniformed, jackbooted SS troops. Wilson later recalled "thinking to myself as we climbed the mountain past all those guards, 'I wonder if we'll come out of this alive. I wonder if we will ever get down again.'"

When the cars came to a stop at the top of the mountain, Hitler was standing by the steps to the villa. Wilson recounted:

> I remember I wasn't at all impressed with his uniform. He looked just like a draper's assistant [essentially, a store clerk]. He greeted Neville Chamberlain and we all went inside for tea.

The weather had changed by this time and it had begun to rain. We were taken into this large room with a great picture window which was supposed to look down on Salzburg, but all it looked down on at that moment was rain and mist. We all seated ourselves around a large table. Hitler sat next to [Chamberlain], with Schmidt [the German] translator, on [Chamberlain's] right, and then Göring, [Field Marshal Wilhelm] Keitel, then me and [William] Strang [the foreign office European expert] and Neville Henderson [the British ambassador to Germany]. I was sitting right opposite Hitler, and I was glad of that. It gave me the opportunity of having a good look at him. When I was a negotiator on the Ministry of Labour, I always liked to be sitting in a position where I could take a good look at my adversary so that I could size him up and see what sort of chap he was. I looked at Hitler. I didn't like his eyes, I didn't like his mouth; in fact, there wasn't very much I did like about him.

Chamberlain and Hitler Dialogue

What Chamberlain thought of Hitler is hard to say. As they opened their discussions, however, he stayed calm and to the point:

> **Chamberlain:** This business of the Sudeten Germans isn't really our affair, you know. We are only interested in it because of Great Britain's interest in the maintenance of peace.

> **Hitler:** How can you talk about peace when peace in Czechoslovakia has already ceased to exist? Let me make it clear once more that I am determined to solve this problem one way or the other. It can no longer be tolerated that a minor country like Czechoslovakia should treat the great 2,000-year-old Reich like an inferior.

> **Chamberlain:** But look here. I am a practical man. How can it be arranged in a practical manner that the Sudeten Germans can be brought back into the Reich? … Why worry about a new frontier? Why not a resettlement?

This was indeed a practical suggestion: If the Sudeten Germans thought themselves persecuted, why not welcome them into Germany itself? Hitler exploded.

> **Hitler:** Don't you realize that whole districts in the Sudetenland have already been evacuated by the people? Ten thousand refugees are already on German soil! … This persecution of German nationals must stop, and I am determined to put an end to it!

The argument continued for quite a while, and then Chamberlain made a considerable concession to Hitler: He was prepared, he said, to discuss with cabinet colleagues back in London whether Great Britain should accept "the separation of the Sudetenland from Czechoslovakia on the basis of self-determination."

When the British party returned home, the cabinet acquiesced in Chamberlain's proposal. At the end of September, Chamberlain and Hitler met again outside Munich. Daladier and Mussolini were also at the conference.

Hitler's Supposed Peace

This time Hitler made a formal pledge that if he could have the Sudetenland, he would then pursue a policy of peace.

Landing again at the Heston Airport outside London, Chamberlain climbed down from the airplane and held aloft a piece of paper. It was a promise of peace, and it bore Hitler's signature. Later, at 10 Downing Street, the residence of the British prime minister, Chamberlain leaned out a window and said to a crowd below, "Peace is at hand!"

While Chamberlain was celebrating in London, Hitler returned to Berlin in triumph. Standing in an open Mercedes limousine, the Führer extended the Nazi salute to the huge crowds that lined every street and intersection to the chancellery. Just a few days later, on October 3, 1938, the German army moved into the Sudeten region of Czechoslovakia. Shortly afterward, Hitler made another triumphal entry, this time into Karlsbad, just across the border in the western tip of Czechoslovakia.

BET YOU DIDN'T KNOW

Did Hitler realize the precarious nature of his situation? Probably not. When he rode in triumph into Karlsbad, he noticed a Czech fort standing on a hilltop. Offended by its presence, he ordered German artillery to blast it into ruins. Guns fired away and shells hit the fortress, but nothing happened: The fort was too solidly constructed to be knocked down by Hitler's artillery. "Well," Hitler said, "it doesn't matter if the will of the people collapses."

Now, like Austria, the Sudetenland was part of what the Nazis called Greater Germany. Hitler had won a substantial victory. Or had he?

Britain's New Policy

What was widely seen as Britain's betrayal of Czechoslovakia was the culmination of a series of events in what amounted to a war the Allies lost without firing a shot. The British acquiesced in the German reoccupation of the Rhineland in March 1936; the *Anschluss* (unification) with Austria in March 1938; and now the annexation of the Sudetenland in October of that year. Eleven months would pass before Nazi Germany (along with the Soviet Union) invaded Poland, and Great Britain (and France) responded by declaring war on the Third Reich. What at last pushed Chamberlain and the British government over the edge?

The usual explanation is that the members of the British government, perhaps feeling guilty over the settlement imposed on Germany by the Versailles Treaty, perhaps naïve and gullible, and perhaps even favorably inclined toward the Nazi dictatorship, appeased Hitler. The usual explanation, however, is inadequate and distorted. Chamberlain has been called a coward and a fool. He is rarely given credit for at the very least also being a realist. Whatever else Chamberlain may have been feeling, he went to Munich keenly aware that his country was militarily unprepared for war—a war that would involve not only Germany but, quite likely, Mussolini's Italy as well.

Research by the historian Simon Newman *(March 1939: The British Guarantee to Poland* [Oxford University Press, 1977]) reveals that, almost from the moment of Hitler's takeover of power, the British government was determined to block German expansion into Eastern Europe, even though it had allowed its military power to decline following World War I and, with the Great Depression, had little money with which to rearm. London instead sought to checkmate Hitler by signing a series of economic and trade agreements with the countries of Eastern Europe. These would give those nations privileged entry into the British home market. In return for this access, the Eastern European nations agreed to raise barriers against German trade and investment. London's idea was to contain Nazi Germany by non-military means.

The trade agreements did not succeed in halting the spread of German influence across all of Eastern and Southeastern Europe, but they may have slowed it. As for appeasement, it did manage to buy eleven months before Hitler broke his word by ordering, in the middle of March 1939, an invasion of Bohemia and Moravia (now the Czech Republic). During the 11 months between Munich and the invasion of Czechoslovakia, Britain had engaged in an ambitious rearmament program. It was now at least more prepared for war than it had been when Chamberlain signed the Munich Agreement.

The invasion of Czechoslovakia awakened the most ardent appeasers to the true extent of the danger posed by Hitler's aggression. At this point, it was clear that he would stop at nothing. So, the British government resolved to finally take action against Nazi expansionism.

The reality behind the uniforms and the bluster was that Germany, like Great Britain, was not fully prepared for war in 1938 or, for that matter, 1939. Despite its own rearmament program, its forces remained relatively weak and untested. When the armies of the Third Reich had entered the Sudetenland, one of the German generals remarked that a single determined Czech peasant with a blunderbuss probably could have stopped them.

Not without apparently good reason, Hitler grossly underestimated the will of the British people in March 1939.

The Nazi Conquest of Czechoslovakia

On October 21, 1938, less than a month after his talks with Prime Minister Chamberlain, Hitler sent a top-secret directive to his top military officers. He told his leaders that the armed forces must be prepared for the following:

- Securing the frontiers of Germany
- Occupying the Memel district
- Liquidating the remainder of Czechoslovakia

Memel was a German-speaking port on the Baltic that the Versailles Treaty had taken from Germany and given to Lithuania. Its recapture (along with the corridor in Poland that separated Germany from East Prussia) would complete the reunification of the German Empire of old.

BET YOU DIDN'T KNOW

Slovakia had plenty of grievances against the Czechs, or so they claimed. Hitler's hope was to set Slovakia up as an "independent" country. Hungary, soon to become a German ally, was to grab off the eastern tail of the fish of Czechoslovakia.

But Hitler was looking beyond the Bismarckian borders. Perhaps he thought that Eastern Europe, once its Jews had been expelled or killed, would provide the *Lebensraum* his growing empire required. Perhaps he believed that the oil deposits of Romania and the grain fields of Ukraine would make Germany at last self-sufficient, immune from another British naval embargo. Perhaps he was becoming a megalomaniac, envisioning himself as the new—Teutonic—Napoleon. Perhaps all three of these motives stirred within him. For whatever reasons, Adolf Hitler wanted to be ready at any time to crush Czechoslovakia.

His directive continued:

> The preparations to be made by the armed forces for this contingency [an attack of Bohemia and Moravia] will be considerably smaller in extent than those for *Fall Grün* ["Case Green," the code name given to a contingency plan for a two-front war]; they must, however, guarantee a considerably higher state of preparedness since planned mobilization measures have been dispensed with. The organization, order of battle, and state of readiness of the units earmarked for that purpose are in peacetime to be so arranged for a surprise assault that Czechoslovakia herself will be deprived of all possibility of organized resistance. The object is the swift occupation of Bohemia and Moravia, and the cutting off of Slovakia.

The fall of Czechoslovakia came about with startling ease. Throughout the winter of 1939, Czech president Emil Hácha tried to stop the political disintegration of his nation by purging the leaders in Slovakia and Ruthenia, the latter being the easternmost province. In both districts, officials of government had been agitating for alliance with the Nazis. Hácha, however, lacked the authority to dismiss them. When he pushed too hard, Slovakia responded by proclaiming its independence, and Hungary demanded that Prague's troops leave Ruthenia.

Desperate, Hácha and his foreign minister went to see Hitler in Berlin, pleading for mercy. The Führer showed none at all. Instead, he demanded that Hácha sign away the little that was left of his country's sovereignty.

By daybreak, March 15, 1939, German troops entered Bohemia and Moravia. Although a blizzard hit Prague that morning, people were out on the streets, going to work as usual or making last-minute preparations for the German occupation of their ancient city. The Germans were quick to arrive.

That night, Hitler arrived in Prague. He announced to the world, "Czechoslovakia has ceased to exist." To underscore the magnitude of his triumph, he spent the night in Hradčany Castle, the traditional home of the kings of Bohemia.

BET YOU DIDN'T KNOW

An American diplomat, George F. Kennan, happened to be outside in Prague. At about 10 A.M., he encountered a German armored car stopped in the middle of a narrow street. Trying to find his way to the German legation, the driver had become lost. A crowd of embittered Czechs down on the street refused to tell him the way. The soldier in the turret sat huddled up against the driving snow, nervously fingering the trigger of his machine gun as he faced the group of people. The armored car moved on without incident.

The Fate of the Jews in the Former Czechoslovakia

Hitler proclaimed Bohemia a German "protectorate." Among the Nazis first acts was to "protect" the nation's Jews. Heinrich Himmler of the SS and Karl Hermann Frank, number-two Sudeten Nazi, took charge. Himmler's published rationale for what was to follow:

> For a thousand years the provinces of Bohemia and Moravia formed part of the *Lebensraum* of the German people. … Czechoslovakia showed its inherent inability to survive and has therefore now fallen a victim to actual dissolution. The German Reich cannot tolerate continuous disturbances in these areas. … Therefore the German Reich, in keeping with the law of self-preservation, is now resolved to intervene decisively to rebuild the foundations of a reasonable order in Central Europe.

For Hitler and Himmler, rebuilding a "reasonable order" in the former Czechoslovakia meant getting rid of the Jews. About 120,000 Jews lived in Bohemia and Moravia. Under the Czechoslovak Republic, they had enjoyed full civic and religious freedom. On June 21, 1939, Himmler issued a decree that placed them all under direct "German jurisdiction." What this meant was that the Reich first isolated the Jews and then expropriated their property without compensation. These were the first steps toward expulsion of the Jews from Bohemia, Moravia, the Sudetenland, Austria, and Germany itself.

But where were they to go?

Some in the German government thought that Palestine was a good idea. For a long time, Zionists had been pressing for a Jewish homeland there. But Palestine was a British "mandate," and, yielding to Arab opinion, resisted further Jewish immigration into the region. Besides, resettling the Jews in Palestine could be construed as further appeasement of Nazi Germany. And the days of appeasement were at an end.

For the Jews of a conquered Czechoslovakia—for the Jews of all Europe—the options were rapidly being closed.

BET YOU DIDN'T KNOW

Soon after Pearl Harbor, following instructions from the federal government, authorities in California, Oregon, Washington, and British Columbia *expropriated* properties owned by Americans of Japanese birth or descent. "Expropriation" is a legal term for theft, and the expropriation of property was the initial move in sending the victims to "internment" camps in the inland western states. The great injustice done by the U.S. government to Japanese immigrants and Japanese citizens during World War II fell far short of the mass murder inflicted by the Nazis on Europe's Jews.

The British Pledge to Defend Poland

The Nazi invasion and seizure of Czechoslovakia made clear Hitler's next move. In anticipation of this, at 2:52 P.M., March 31, 1939, Prime Minister Chamberlain appeared before the House of Commons, its galleries packed. His statement was terse, very much to the point: "I now have to inform the House that … in the event of any action which clearly threatened Polish independence …. His Majesty's Government would feel themselves bound at once to lend the Polish Government all support in their power. They have given the Polish Government an assurance to that effect."

The line was at long last drawn. If Hitler invaded Poland, Great Britain would declare war on Germany.

The Least You Need to Know

- Seeing the success of Austria's Nazis in joining up with the Third Reich, the Sudeten Germans clamored for the same. Money and agents from Germany helped stimulate the agitation.

- The old story that the British appeased Hitler at Munich, accepting the unification of the Sudetenland with Germany in exchange for Hitler's promise of peace, is a vast oversimplification, even a myth. When Hitler first rose to power, the British government was determined to prevent the emergence of a super-Germany in Central and Eastern Europe.

- As long as the states of Eastern Europe could stand up as bastions against German expansion, Great Britain did not need to go to war. The dismemberment of Czechoslovakia proved that those barriers would not stand.

- London pledged formally to declare war on Germany if Hitler invaded Poland. That, of course, was precisely what Hitler was planning.

The Dark Summer: 1939

Slovakia was now an "independent" country, although so heavily influenced by decisions in Berlin that it was a client, if not a puppet, of Germany. Moravia, Bohemia, and the Sudetenland were now all provinces of the Third Reich. Helping itself to Ruthenia, the easternmost part of the former Czechoslovakia, Hungary became an ally of Nazi Germany. In April 1939, Hitler's other ally, Benito Mussolini, took over control of Albania across the Adriatic to the east. Hitler also seized Memel from Lithuania and made demands for Danzig and the Polish Corridor. That he would drive into southeastern Europe and the Soviet Union seemed only a matter of time. All this set off alarm bells in London and Paris. Great Britain followed its guarantee to Poland with similar ones to Romania and Greece. In the spring and summer of 1939, the British and the French tried to forge an anti-German pact with the Soviet Union. (France already had an understanding with the USSR, but it was by no means a solid treaty, and its alliance with Czechoslovakia, which had proved worthless to the Czechs, had been negated.)

Like his counterparts in the West, Stalin appreciated the German danger. But Poland and the three Baltic republics, Latvia, Estonia, and Lithuania, refused to accept the presence of Russian troops on their soil, even as a defense against Germany. Understanding their fears of Russia, the British and the French refused to put pressure on those small countries. Stalin, in turn, thought the British and French hypocritical. After World War I, Poland had taken more territory from Russia than the peace settlement allowed, pushing its eastern border well into Byelorussia, almost to Minsk. The Allies had done nothing to stop the Poles then. So, Stalin and his comrades wondered, whose side were the British and the French really on? Could it be that they actually hoped the Soviet Union would take the brunt of a war with Nazi Germany? A distrustful Stalin rebuffed an alliance with Britain and France.

In the meantime, Hitler was making louder and louder noises about Danzig and the Polish Corridor. With each shrill demand, the Führer took Europe closer and closer to war.

Danzig and the Polish Corridor

Danzig (today the Polish port city of Gdansk) was a town of about 400,000 persons in 1939, almost all of them German. That was not surprising. Danzig was, as it had been for centuries, an important German trading center, once a key member of the venerable Hanseatic League, which had been formed in the fourteenth century as a protective association of northern German and other Baltic and North Sea ports. During its heyday, which lasted to the end of the fifteenth century, the league dominated the commercial history of Northern Europe. Even in the sixteenth and seventeenth centuries, when Poland was its nominal ruler, Danzig existed virtually as an independent city, a rich emporium for many products, but especially grain and timber. Because the merchants of the Hanseatic League built their homes over their warehouses, the ports of the association all displayed high-gabled houses that rose above cobblestone streets. So it was with Danzig, which bore a striking physical resemblance to Amsterdam, Brussels, Lübeck, and Memel.

Danzig.
(Culver Pictures)

Such had been Danzig for centuries. With the German defeat at the end of World War I, however, the question arose: What should be done with Danzig? At the Paris peace talks, Poland argued convincingly that it needed a corridor to the Baltic. If Poland was to serve as part of the anti-aggression buffer in Eastern Europe, the peace negotiators had to provide it with a way to survive. Since survival depended on commerce, Polish representatives argued, the need for a corridor of land through Germany to the sea was obvious.

The Allies bought the idea. But they had no intention of turning Danzig itself over to Poland. The Allies had fought against Germany, but they retained a high regard for German culture, and Danzig was an important German cultural center. This meant, among other things, that the houses in Danzig were swept and painted, the city government was clean, and the dockworkers were skilled. And although they accepted the idea of Polish independence, the Allied leaders regarded the Poles as dirty, uncouth, and backward. To preserve the culture of Danzig, the peace negotiators at Paris worked out a compromise. The city and its suburbs would be called the Free City of Danzig, administered by a high commissioner appointed by the League of Nations.

As for the Polish Corridor, it was established as a strip of land that varied between 50 and 100 miles wide. At the west end of the strip was Germany proper; to the east was East Prussia; at the top was Danzig. Yet while the corridor was called "Polish," the people who lived in it were overwhelmingly German. Despite the arrangements made in Paris, they persisted in thinking of themselves as German, and they sneered at the Poles under whose rule they now lived. To the Germans living in the corridor, the Poles were inferior intellectually, socially, and morally. The corridor-dwelling Germans could not forget that for centuries it had been the duty of the Teutonic Reich to hold back the Slavic tide from the east. Not for a moment from 1919 to 1939 had these Germans accepted the circumstance into which the peacemakers of Paris had cast them.

At least two British statesmen also found the notion of a Polish Corridor troublesome. Not long after signing the Treaty of Versailles, David Lloyd George, one of its framers, allowed that he could not imagine any arrangement better calculated to produce another war than the corridor through Germany. Austen Chamberlain, the older brother of Neville and a leading Conservative politician in Britain, added the observation that the Polish Corridor was not worth the bones of a single British soldier.

BET YOU DIDN'T KNOW

If Germans wanted to travel by land between Germany proper and East Prussia, by Polish law they could do so only in trains that were sealed with all curtains closed. Hitler himself asked a group of visiting Americans how they would like to take such a train between Texas and New Mexico with a Mexican corridor lying between. Practically all Germans, even many Jews, believed that the Reich had the right to redress the grievance that was the Polish Corridor.

Hitler Unnerves Colonel Josef Beck

In 1938, Hitler asked Colonel Josef Beck, the Polish foreign minister, if Warsaw would allow the Reich to lay down a six-lane *Autobahn* through the corridor. Beck's response was a blunt, no.

TERMS AND TRANSLATIONS

Bahn in German means "path," "track," or "course." So an *autobahn* is a highway. A *bahnhof* is a train station.

By January 1939, however, Hitler was no longer asking. And that made Beck nervous. When he stopped *asking*, Beck knew, Hitler generally started taking. But then came the dismemberment of Czechoslovakia, which prompted the British guarantee of Polish sovereignty. The theft of Czechoslovakia gave Beck reason to fear, but the guarantee gave him reason for hope. He accepted that guarantee (as he said), between "two flicks of my cigarette ash."

Warsaw now had an assurance of safety.

But did it really? During the May 1939 celebration in Berlin of Hitler's fiftieth birthday—Hitler's birthday had already become an occasion for compulsory public celebration—one of the dignitaries present was Grigore Gafencu, the foreign minister of Romania. Joachim von Ribbentrop, his German counterpart, informed him that the Danzig situation was "impossible," and, in a private interview with Hitler, the Führer screamed on and on about the British guarantee to Poland. Why, Hitler demanded to know, did Britain care about Danzig? Danzig and the corridor were properly German! They had been German for centuries! Great Britain, Hitler opined, was trying to encircle the Reich, to use Danzig as a pretext for going to war!

At this point, Hitler's natural paranoia, his perpetual feeling of victimization, was tuned to its highest pitch. One more twist of the tuning peg, and the string would snap.

That twist came not from any British diplomat, but from German newspapers, which suddenly carried reports of acts of Polish violence toward Germans. Populations in Eastern Europe were far from homogeneous. Poland was peopled by ethnic Poles and ethnic Germans—a great many of them. According to the papers, ethnic Poles were on a rampage, setting fire to German real estate firms, attacking members of choral societies with bludgeons, and smashing the windows of German-owned stores.

Hitler ordered retaliation by men who loved to retaliate: the Storm Troopers. In mid-May, a group of SA men attacked a Polish customs post on the East Prussian border, beat up the officials, and abducted them. With the Polish guards on ice, trucks carrying German-made weapons roared past the customs post and into Danzig. The contents of the trucks were quickly distributed to the German-speaking majority within the city. Street orators began to demand the return of Danzig to the Reich. Swastikas and banners with Nazi slogans adorned every major corner. The speechmakers were preaching to the converted.

With the crisis heating up, the Polish government fanned the flames still higher. Beck already had the guarantee from London; now, in the early summer of 1939, he also extracted a promise from Paris. If war broke out between Germany and Poland, the French pledged, they would attack the Reich from the west. We can presume that the French thought their promise would ease things a bit. Quite the contrary, without consulting London and Paris, Colonel Beck informed the Germans in Danzig that he would meet any attempt to join Germany with force.

"You want to negotiate at the point of a bayonet," the German ambassador complained to Beck. Beck replied: "That is your method!"

Danzig Descends into Chaos

Danzig itself was descending into chaos. The few Polish students in the city and their German counterparts engaged in fistfights. University classes closed down. More weapons were smuggled into German hands in Danzig.

Then, in early June, Dr. Goebbels showed up. As a speaker, he was almost as spellbinding as Hitler himself. "We are not gathered here today, citizens of Danzig, to decide whether this great city should return to the Reich, but *when!*" Goebbels told a huge crowd gathered in the main square. "Soon, comrades, soon! There is not much time to waste. Just like the Jewish whores who try to sneak into our beds and rob us of our manhood, so do the Poles and the British scheme to steal our land and our people. All we ask is what rightfully belongs to us. Danzig is German. It must return to Germany. … Already the Polish in Warsaw talk about claiming East Prussia and German Silesia. And don't fool yourselves, if we let them they will go farther than that. They will claim that their frontier should be on the Rhine. … But will we let them? We will not let them! We will drive them out of Danzig!"

In Warsaw, Beck proved himself nearly as skilled a demagogue as Goebbels. "We in Poland do not recognize the concept of peace at any price," he told the Polish parliament. "There is only one thing in the life of men, nations, and states which is beyond peace, and that is honor."

It was almost as if Danzig the place no longer mattered. The quarrel between Nazi Germany and Poland (which was every bit as nationalistic, undemocratic, and anti-Semitic as Germany) had raised Danzig to the level of principle.

And that principle was the mastery of Eastern Europe. Long before the Nazis, Germany had asserted the right to that mastery. "Let us put Germany in the saddle," Otto von Bismarck exhorted the Reichstag on March 11, 1867, "it already knows how to ride." Rearmed by 1939, Germany under Hitler seemed to positioned to assert mastery anew. Poland stubbornly opposed any such extension of German power. But what could Poland do about it? With an army on horseback, armed with lances, the country's military was mired in the Middle Ages—no match at all for German airplanes and tanks. So, Poland had to rely on France and Great Britain for its defense.

The British King Eats a Hotdog and Finds an Ally

Could London and Paris effectively come to Poland's aid? As events would soon reveal, no. In its initial onslaught, Germany would prove unstoppable. Yet, in June 1939, far from Central Europe, an event occurred that spelled, in the fullness of time, Nazi Germany's doom.

We must travel, at this dark juncture, to Washington, D.C.

Late in September 1938, Britain's King George VI received a letter from President Franklin D. Roosevelt. The British monarch was planning to visit Canada in June 1939. Would he care to add the United States to his itinerary? Roosevelt asked. The king jumped at the invitation.

At exactly 11 A.M., Friday, June 8, 1939, the royal train with a blue and silver central car pulled into Washington's Union Station. In an unusual gesture, FDR himself had been driven to the station. Standing beside Mrs. Roosevelt on the platform, the president—who, stricken by polio or (according to some recent medical experts) Guillain-Barre Syndrome, had been unable to walk since August 1921—balanced himself on the arm of a White House aide. When the train stopped, U.S. Secretary of State Cordell Hull, followed by King George and Queen Elizabeth (she became the Queen Mother, who died in 2002 at the age of 101) stepped down from the car. Secretary Hull, who had met the royal couple at the Canadian border, introduced them to President Roosevelt. As they shook hands all around, the Marine Band played "The Star-Spangled Banner" and "God Save the King." Then the party left the station in a motorcade that rode to a point of First Street, just below the Capitol Dome. Two huge American flags flew in front of the Capitol. The king, dressed in the full uniform of a British admiral, snapped a salute, and the huge crowd of American onlookers went wild. The motorcade then headed for the White House.

BET YOU DIDN'T KNOW

In the course of the weekend visit, the first time a British monarch had set foot in the United States, the royal couple visited Mount Vernon (where George VI laid a wreath on the tomb of George Washington), the New York World's Fair, and the Roosevelt mansion in Hyde Park, New York, overlooking the valley of the Hudson River. At Hyde Park, the royals attended an Episcopal service at St. James's, FDR's parish church, and, under the gawking gaze of onlookers held back by police barriers, His Majesty wolfed down a hot dog, drank a beer—and asked for seconds. It was an affirmation of democracy beyond any that could have been made in a mere speech. From Hyde Park, the young couple returned by train to Canada, a personal bond between the heads of state having been forged.

During an evening conversation in the library of FDR's ancestral house, in Hyde Park on the Hudson, the president and the king chatted about the "firm and trusted friendship" between Canada and the United States. We know this from the king's diary. Roosevelt indicated that he wanted access to the British naval base at Trinidad. From there, if the navy of a resolutely neutral United States spotted a German submarine, it would fire away and worry about the consequences later. Roosevelt stopped short of promising an Anglo-American alliance. But, the president assured the king, "If London was bombed, the USA would come in."

The consequences of this promise were immense. King George VI left Hyde Park with an assurance that, if it went to war with Germany over Poland, and Britain was indeed menaced, the United States would come in, much as it had in 1917-1918. The conversation in the president's library stiffened the British resolve to face Hitler down in Eastern Europe.

The First Lady, King George VI, the president's mother, Queen Elizabeth, and Franklin D. Roosevelt seated on the veranda of the Roosevelt home in Hyde Park, New York.
(Franklin D. Roosevelt Presidential Library)

The Nazi-Soviet Pact

That was early summer 1939. Two months later, in August, the world received the shocking news that Nazi Germany and the Soviet Union—avatars of diametrically opposed political systems, rightwing Nazism and leftwing Communism—had signed a pact of "non-aggression." With this, any hope that the British government may have had of allies encircling Germany with a 1914-style Triple Entente was shattered. The so-called Ribbentrop-Molotov Pact, named for the German and Soviet foreign ministers who negotiated it, gave Berlin a free hand in Poland.

It was a geopolitical earthquake. To understand how it happened, we must look at the world from the points of view of Josef Stalin in Moscow and Adolf Hitler in Berlin.

To Stalin, Nazi Germany was unquestionably the enemy. The Nazis had murdered or exiled thousands of his fellow Communists. As Soviet propagandists painted them, the Nazis, not the Western democrats, were the ultimate champions of capitalism. Stalin did not doubt that, given the opportunity, the Nazis would be the deadliest of military foes.

Yet, Stalin reasoned, it had been the Allies, not Germany, who had in 1919 invaded revolutionary Russia, It was the United States, Britain, France, Poland, and Japan that marched in, determined to strangle the new Soviet government in the cradle, before it could even take control of Russia. At the postwar peace settlement, the Allies blithely sheared the Baltic states away from the old Russian Empire and gave Poland their blessing to expand at Russia's expense. And, come the 1920s and 1930s, those same Allies treated the Soviet Union as an international pariah. Only now, at the eleventh hour, in 1939, were the British and French making overtures of alliance to Moscow.

Why, Stalin asked, should he accept their hand in friendship now?

It was universally understood that Stalin trusted no one, maybe not even himself. There can be no doubt at all that he did not trust Britain or France. He believed, with good reason, that their true motive was to induce Russia and Germany to fight each other—cancelling each other out, so that Britain and France could move in to scoop up the spoils.

No, Stalin didn't trust *any* of the European powers. He did distrust Germany a little less than he distrusted France and Great Britain. This assessment was a result of recent history, and it was also based on a certain fellow feeling Stalin had for Hitler. They were, after all, both totalitarians. They both knew what they wanted. They were absolutists, rulers without the ambiguities and ambivalences that plagued the leaders of democracies. Hitler was indeed a devil. But, to Stalin, he was a devil he believed he knew, as he knew himself.

But what about Adolf Hitler? As a Nazi, he was the de facto enemy of Soviet Communism. Ideologically, there could be no two ways about that. Yet as the head of a nation he intended to lead to a position of imperial dominance far greater than anything the kaisers had dreamed of, he had more urgent concerns than ideology. He feared that London and Paris intended to recruit Poland and Russia as allies in the encirclement—and strangulation—of Germany. Paranoid delusion? Kaiser Wilhelm II believed he confronted a similar situation, and World War I had proven him right.

Then there was America. Immediately after the armistice was signed in November 1918, an American journalist asked Paul von Hindenburg a blunt question: Who won the war against Germany? The chief of the German General Staff, co-architect with Erich Ludendorff of Germany's Eastern Front victories and its nearly war-winning Western Front offensives, did not hesitate in his answer. "The American infantry," he said. Hitler knew what every German knew: It was the intervention of the United States that defeated Germany in 1918. Nor could Hitler take comfort in the neutrality of the United States in 1939. The nation had refrained from entering World War I from its outbreak in 1914 to April 1917, but when it entered, it entered in war-winning numbers and intensity. Hitler had good reason to believe that if the United States joined the British, French, and Russians, Germany would again be doomed.

By splitting off the Soviet Union from the Anglo–Franco–Polish—and possibly American connection, Hitler sought to nip the encirclement in the bud. If he succeeded in this, he might well be able to defeat France quickly, just as Germany would have done in World War I had its commanders not foolishly deviated from the Schlieffen Plan. The key was to embrace the Soviet Union—now.

The Molotov-Ribbentrop Pact proves the historical folly of dismissing Adolf Hitler as a madman or even an ideological extremist. Evil he was. Mad he was not. In fulfilment of an immoral and obscene vision for the world, Adolf Hitler was capable of rational pragmatism. To be sure, he despised the Soviet regime, with its Communist system, Jews in places of political prominence, and a Slavic population Hitler believed were racially inferior to the Aryan Germans. But he needed a Soviet alliance, and so he held his nose and made one.

Hitler's Telegram

On August 19, 1939, a coded telegram went out from Hitler at Berchtesgaden to the German embassy in Moscow. There, Friedrich Werner von der Schulenburg, the German ambassador, was to deliver the message (decoded and translated into Russian) to Stalin. It read:

> M. STALIN, MOSCOW:
>
> THE TENSION BETWEEN GERMANY AND POLAND HAS BECOME INTOLERABLE. IN MY OPINION IT IS DESIRABLE NOT TO LOSE ANY TIME. I THEREFORE PROPOSE THAT YOU RECEIVE MY FOREIGN MINISTER ON TUESDAY, AUGUST 22, BUT AT THE LATEST ON WEDNESDAY, AUGUST 23. I SHOULD BE GLAD TO RECEIVE YOUR EARLY ANSWER.

Then, at 10:50 P.M., August 21, the teletype machine in the villa made a noise. Hitler raced to read the message:

> TO THE CHANCELLOR OF THE GERMAN REICH, MR. A. HITLER:
>
> I THANK YOU FOR THE LETTER. I HOPE THAT A GERMAN-SOVIET NON-AGGRESSION PACT WILL BRING ABOUT A DECIDED TURN FOR THE BETTER IN THE POLITICAL RELATIONS BETWEEN OUR TWO COUNTRIES. THE SOVIET GOVERNMENT HAS INSTRUCTED ME TO INFORM YOU THAT THEY AGREE TO MR. VON RIBBENTROP'S ARRIVING IN MOSCOW ON AUGUST 23.
>
> J. STALIN

The following morning, Ribbentrop, the foreign minister, flew from Berchtesgaden to Berlin, where he collected thirty-some officials, photographers, and reporters. Thereafter, with a stopover in Königsberg in East Prussia, Ribbentrop, his party flew on to Moscow.

BET YOU DIDN'T KNOW

Hitler was extraordinarily nervous the night he sent the telegram to the German Embassy. Unable to sleep, he paced up and down in front of the big plate glass window looking onto the mountain tops. In the middle of the night, he telephoned Göring, who was in Berlin: The government had had no response from Moscow. Dawn came, and Hitler could see the sun rise over the mountains to the east; still nothing from Moscow. The day dragged on—later Hitler said that it was the longest day of his life—and he watched the sun set over the mountains to the west. Still nothing. Outside the window all went black.

Von Ribbentrop's Meeting with Stalin and Molotov

When the Germans disembarked from their aircraft at the Moscow airport, they stood at stiff attention as a Red Army band struck up the "Internationale," the Communist hymn to revolution, followed by the "Horst Wessel Lied," the Nazi ode to the destruction of the Communists. The visitors then passed through two rows of Soviet troops who held aloft flags bearing the hammer and sickle, and flags emblazoned with swastikas. A motorcade took Ribbentrop and his delegation to the Kremlin.

After lunch within the Kremlin walls, Ribbentrop sat down with Marshal Stalin and Vyacheslav Molotov, the new Soviet foreign minister. Molotov was "new" because, as a gesture of goodwill toward Berlin, Stalin had unceremoniously dumped his predecessor, Maxim Litvinov, a Jew.

Through translators, the Nazi emissary and the two Soviets quickly agreed upon the desirability of a nonaggression pact. Now bargain making began in earnest. If Germany got Danzig, the corridor, and most of central Poland, what would Russia get? The answer soon emerged. The Soviets could help themselves to the remainder of Poland plus the Baltic states. These latter included Finland and Bessarabia. Neither of these were Germany's property to give. Finland was a proudly independent nation, and Bessarabia a province of Romania. Taking Finland would require a war—quite a costly war, as it turned out—and acquiring Bessarabia would require the compliance of Romania. But Germany would not interfere in Russia's efforts to acquire these territories.

With the bargain concluded, the conferees agreed to make their pact public—except, of course, for the part about carving up portions of eastern Europe between themselves. Though set down in writing, that was to be kept secret.

Yet it was an open secret. A stunned world not only realized that the Soviets had effectively given Germany permission to go to war, but it was clear to everyone that the two powers intended to divide Eastern Europe between themselves.

The Invasion of Poland

On the morning of September 1, 1939, Hitler walked to a microphone in front of the Reichstag. On a raised dais, directly behind and above him, sat Göring. On the wall behind Göring, a huge swastika hung suspended from the talons of a sculptured eagle with its wings spread wide. And before this tableau the entire body of the Reichstag was standing at attention, right arms thrust stiffly forward in the Führer salute.

When all took their seats, Hitler began to speak. He was wearing a uniform of *Feldgrau*, field gray, instead of his usual light brown Nazi Party uniform. He drew attention to this, pointing out that he was wearing the "sacred coat" of the German troops in World War I. He wore it because, six hours earlier, in the predawn darkness, the air, land, and sea forces of the Third Reich began the attack on Poland.

The first shots were fired at Danzig. Two days earlier, the *Schleswig-Holstein,* a German navy training ship, had steamed into the harbor of the old port city. The captain announced that he was paying a courtesy visit.

Even as the captain and his crew looked out at the picturesque gabled houses built by medieval merchant-princes, they knew that this would be no courtesy visit. The training vessel *Schleswig-Holstein* had been built as a battleship and was equipped with 11-inch guns that were very much in working order. As soon as the sun rose on September 1, 1939, these guns spoke, blasting away at the island fortress that guarded the sea approach into Poland. Overwhelmed and outgunned, the Polish garrison surrendered quickly.

The "courtesy visit" of a German ship was not the only deception on that day. DURING THE NIGHT OF AUGUST 31, 1939, A PRISONER from one of Adolf Hitler's concentration camps—his identity is unknown to history—was dressed in the uniform of a Polish soldier, taken to the German town of Gleiwitz on the Polish frontier, and there shot by the Gestapo. On September 1, Adolf Hitler informed the Reischstag, the people of Germany, and the world that this "Polish soldier" had been shot during an attack by the Polish army on a German radio transmitter at Gleiwitz. It was, Hitler pointed out, yet one more example of Polish aggression, and it was the final straw. There was now more than enough reason to go to war—a war, he told the German legislators, that had in fact begun at 4:30 that very morning.

In addition to the firing on Danzig, the attack across the Polish border included a massive air component, as Luftwaffe dive bombers hit Polish airfields, and a surge of ground forces. The invaders included about 2.5 million troops, elements of the German army as well as Soviet units. They were opposed by some 280,000 men of the Polish army, 30 infantry divisions, 11 cavalry brigades (armed with lances!), two mechanized brigades, and supporting units.

The Poles fought valiantly, but the numbers were against them. They were not only outmanned, but were vastly outgunned, facing modern aircraft and tanks with obsolescent warplanes and ground forces anchored by nineteenth-century cavalry. They also faced a new tactic, the *Blitzkrieg,* or "Lightning War," which hit with great speed, great violence, and close coordination among infantry, armor, ground-support aircraft, and bombers. Most of the Polish air force was destroyed on the ground. As for the dive bombers, Junkers Ju 87s, called "Stukas," they were armed not only with bombs, but specially equipped with sirens intended to magnify the psychological effects of their downward sweeps upon the front lines. The German infantry was heavily mechanized, with motorcycles, troops transported by truck, and the Panzers, newly designed and fast-moving German tanks.

The genius of Blitzkrieg was its use of aircraft to disrupt the enemy's rear lines as ground forces hit the front lines. Avenues of communication and retreat were thus disrupted, and the chaos created was intense. This was compounded by hordes of fleeing civilians, their earthly belongings piled onto wagons or wheelbarrows, their horses terrified, their few trucks and automobiles breaking down. The refugee columns were endless. Moving east, they collided with Polish reinforcements being sent west to meet the German onslaught.

Within two days, led by General Wilhelm von Keitel and his principal aide, General Alfred Jodl, the German invaders had brought Poland to the edge of defeat. All that remained were the mopping-up operations.

It was at the end of those two days, on September 3, when Poland was essentially lost, that France and Great Britain declared war on Germany. The prelude to war was over. Europe's second great war of the twentieth century had begun.

The Organization of the Holocaust

With the beginning of World War II in Poland, so began, in full earnest, the Holocaust. To this point, Nazi treatment of the Jews had been brutal and sometimes deadly, as during the *Kristallnacht*. The regime had forced many Jews to abandon their businesses. Jewish doctors, dentists, and lawyers were not allowed to offer their services to Aryans. Jews were obliged to carry identity cards and, from October 1938 onward, all Jewish passports were stamped with the letter J. Early on, Nazi authorities explored ways of encouraging Jewish emigration, but most of the world did not welcome refugees of any kind, and they were particularly indifferent to Jews.

All of this was horrific enough. But now a program of systematized murder—mass "extermination"—was about to begin. It would not be a "counterpoint" to Hitler's war. It would not be a "side effect" of his military campaigns. The Holocaust was a central aim of Nazi strategy.

The invasion of Poland was the end of so-called civilized warfare. Through a chain of command consisting of Heinrich Himmler and then Reinhard Heydrich of the SS, and passing down to Hans Frank, Reich governor of the province of Poland, Hitler issued one of his most monstrous orders. Five *Einsatzgruppen* were to enter into Poland on the heels of the primary invasion force. These Einsatzgruppen were organizations of professional killers whose mission was not to defeat the enemy army but to commit mass murder among tens of thousands of officials, priests, and intellectuals. The objective was to deprive the Poles of their natural leaders.

In September 1939, the Einsatzgruppen did not yet specifically target Jews. (They would first begin doing this when Hitler turned against Stalin and invaded Russia.) But they were members of the SS, the organization charged with answering the "Jewish question." The SS high command soon realized that Poland, remote from the German population but adjacent to Germany, would be an ideal place to build new concentration camps—camps intended to imprison Jews, camps that would soon be used to murder them.

TERMS AND TRANSLATIONS

The term **Einsatzgruppen** is a little complicated. The *gruppen* is easy: It's the plural of "group." Now as for *einsatz*—*ein* is "in." *Satz* comes from *setzen*, "to set." So *einsatz* means something "set in," inserted.

The Least You Need to Know

- ○ Provoked by Hitler and local Nazis, the Danzig crisis came to a head in the summer of 1939. Against Polish protest, Hitler demanded the return of Danzig and the "Polish corridor" to the German Reich.

- ○ Spoiling for war, Hitler's one major concern was that the Soviet Union would intervene on behalf of Poland. The Führer neutralized this danger in August 1939 with the Soviet-Nazi Non-Aggression Pact (Molotov-Ribbentrop Pact).

- ○ The German invasion of Poland on September 1, 1939, was the opening battle of World War II. It also opened the first phase of the Holocaust.

PART 4

The Rising Tide

Here you'll find a Nazi Germany seemingly unstoppable, on the road to what many feared was world conquest. Faced with the German juggernaut, countries large and small—Poland, Denmark, Norway, Holland, Luxembourg, Belgium, France, Yugoslavia, and Greece—fell like bowling pins. In the North African desert, General Erwin Rommel, the famed German tank commander, appeared to be on the brink of taking control of the Suez Canal. Then he began to run out of gas.

Germany's resources, it turned out, were limited, and Hitler's reach soon exceeded his grasp. By the end of 1942, Rommel had lost the fight and was squeezed out of North Africa by the advancing British and Americans. Despite this loss and all it portended, Hitler unilaterally dissolved his non-aggression pact with Joseph Stalin and invaded the Soviet Union.

Life in the Third Reich: 1939–1940

The Treaty of Versailles forced Germany to accept all the blame for World War I. This was both historically inaccurate and morally unjust. World War II, however, was another matter. Without question, it was Germany's aggressive rearmament and mobilization, followed by its invasion of Poland, that started the war. It is even fair to say that Adolf Hitler himself started World War II, but he did not do it alone. The people of Germany and Austria also made the war a fact.

Another thing is quite certain: When the war broke out in Poland, ordinary Germans and Austrians had no idea what was in store for them. At first, things were eerily quiet—abnormally normal—in both Germany and Austria. On September 10, 1939, William L. Shirer, an American foreign correspondent posted to Berlin, wrote in his diary (later published as the classic *Berlin Diary*):

> Life here is still quite normal. The operas, the theaters, the movies, all open and jammed. *Tannhäuser* and *Madame Butterfly* playing at the Opera. The Metropol, Hitler's favorite show house, announced a new revue Wednesday. One week after the Anglo–French declaration of war the average German is beginning to wonder if it's a world war after all. He sees it this way. England and France, it is true, are formally fulfilling their obligations over Poland. For a week they have been formally at war with Germany. But has it been war, they ask? … The industrial heart of Germany lies along the Rhine close to France. From there come most of the bombs that are blowing up Poland with such deadly effect. Yet not a bomb has fallen on a Rhineland factory. "Is that war?" they ask.

The Arms of Krupp

Although it manufactures only a few weapons now, the Ruhr Valley today is still hard at work. If you fly over the area you see forests of smokestacks poking up through the smog as if they were cathedral spires. But this is nothing new. Even back when Nazi Germany first went to war, the Ruhr Valley was the heart of the industrial economy.

In that economy, no company, or rather combination of companies, was more significant than Krupp, an arms manufacturer since the sixteenth century. The German government for a long time had allowed the formation of cartels, huge trusts designed to crush competition and fix prices. Krupp was the biggest trust of all, and for Krupp and the entire Ruhr Valley, business was booming. Government contracts were plentiful. For this, Alfred Krupp, scion of the family dynasty and head of the enterprise in 1939, was most grateful. Personally, he had no use for Adolf Hitler, but as long as he was paying for weapons, the Krupp firm would support him, including political financing and lots of it.

Partly thanks to a German television documentary titled *Hitler's Money,* originally aired in 2002, we have comprehensive knowledge of how much financing Hitler received from Krupp and other big businessmen. In today's money, the sum was well over $3 billion. In return, Alfred Krupp and his colleagues made billions more from their war work. They were, by any measure, war profiteers.

By the standards of a democracy, even a highly capitalistic one like the United States, Nazi economic policy was thoroughly corrupt. It ran on a system of pay to play, one hand washing the other, or whatever else you choose to call a quid pro quo. The large industrial concerns greedily milked the government as a cash cow, in return kicking back large sums to support the Nazi Party.

Corrupt as it was, the system stimulated the economy, created employment, and engendered a level of prosperity higher than elsewhere in Depression-era Europe. Many Germans owned cars, and the big cities supported an array of fashionable boutiques. Well-dressed city-dwellers frequented lively cafés. Disappearing rapidly was the shabby, bedraggled look of the Depression years. The German public felt hopeful. Hitler, as they saw it, had snatched them from the brink of starvation as well as humiliation. Rearmament revived the economy and defied the Treaty of Versailles. Other nations did not love Nazi Germany, but they respected it. Adolf Hitler was widely regarded as the savior of the German nation. And now he was also the valiant victor in the war against Poland, a country he had portrayed as a threat to the good life that had come at last to Germany.

Hitler's Appeal to the Germans

Before the attack on Poland, many of Hitler's top generals were anxious about the prospects for an army untried on the field of battle. With an Anglo–French threat of war looming over their heads, they feared that they might be marching toward disaster. Hitler proved them wrong—at least in the short run, against the valiant but outnumbered and outclassed forces of Poland.

- ✪ It's hard to overstate the degree of Hitler's popularity after his victory in Poland. With that, he had delivered everything he had promised. Given the enormity of Hitler's crimes against humanity, it seems immoral to think of him as a politician. Yet he was. Politicians who fail to deliver on their promises quickly fall from popular favor. But Hitler had delivered, and the German people rewarded him with their loyalty. After all, he Rose to power and, as he promised, demolished the Communist left.

- ✪ Hitler rearmed Germany and, in so doing, brought about an economic recovery as well as a recovery of national prestige.

- ✪ Under the Nazis, Germany reoccupied the Rhineland—traditionally the source of the nation's industrial might.

- ✪ Hitler unified Germany and Austria, fulfilling a nationalistic dream that had evaded even Bismarck himself.

- ✪ Hitler brought the Sudetenland into the Reich; as he said he would, he dismembered a Czechoslovakia that, his propagandists had told the German people, posed a serious military threat.

- ✪ Hitler retook Danzig and destroyed the Polish Corridor, eliminating the barrier between Germany proper and East Prussia.

- ✪ Hitler brought those backward Poles under the German heel—providing space for German emigration and a place for disposing of the Jews.

In the process of all this, the Führer became a wealthy man, partly through immense royalties from *Mein Kampf,* partly from the bribes he received or extorted from businessmen, and partly from simply looting the nation's treasury. Nazi Germany was a kleptocracy (a nation ruled by thieves). The hierarchy of the Nazi governing class resembled nothing more closely than it did an organized crime establishment such as the Mafia.

Hitler lived well, having come a very long way from homelessness in Vienna. He built a house in Munich for Eva Braun, his paramour; he started the reconstruction in Poznan, Poland, of a palace originally built for Kaiser Wilhelm II; and he continued to maintain his mountaintop villa at Berchtesgaden in the Bavarian Alps. If anything, the display of his success increased the admiration of the German people.

Hitler, Frau Morell, and Eva Braun.
(Culver Pictures)

BET YOU DIDN'T KNOW

Although he projected an image of austere celibacy, a leader "married" to the Reich, Hitler had a mistress. The daughter of lower-middle-class Bavarians who disapproved of her relationship with him, Eva Braun was a shapely, blond, pretty young woman who doted on him. Hitler usually kept her hidden away at Berchtesgaden and refused to marry her—until the day before the couple committed suicide together.

We also know from the 2002 German television documentary that Hitler personally spent millions on lavish gifts and payments to buy the loyalty of politicians and businessmen—and to keep them dependent upon him. Hitler was the central wheel in a vast political machine. But money pressed into the hands of his cronies and cronies-in-the-making did not account for Hitler's popularity with the German masses. Nor alone would his string of political and military victories account for the reverence the people offered him. As for his private personality, he was nasty, mediocre, and bizarre;

that is, he was not charismatic in any conventional sense. A one-time tramp, he never quite shed the aura of poverty and squalor that had been his early lot. Yet about him rose an extraordinary cult of personality, the "Hitler cult."

TERMS AND TRANSLATIONS

The dictionary defines a **cult** as a system or community of religious worship and ritual, especially one focusing on a single deity, spirit, or person. More specifically, a **cult of personality** is created by the use of propaganda, mass media, and grandiose public displays to build an idealized image of heroism and infallibility that commands unquestioning adulation.

The Hitler Cult

The Hitler cult was widespread and pervasive. It made use of dramatic symbols, mass media, and grand public displays to systematically endow the Führer with a public personality. The cult elevated him to the status of a demigod.

Europe between the two world wars was fertile soil for the sprouting of such cults of personality. Mussolini in Italy and Stalin in the Soviet Union come most immediately to mind. Franco in Spain was a lesser version of these three figures. As different as they were from one another, the cults of Hitler, Mussolini, Stalin, and Franco share certain elements. They all led mass movements; they all fabricated an image of heroic leadership; and they all used propaganda, symbolism, and mass media to endow themselves with quasi-divine qualities.

The cultists present their object of worship as a figure engaged in a battle against some existential evil. For Mussolini, it was Communism and whatever nation or people dared oppose Italy in its quest to regain its rightful Roman imperial heritage. For Stalin, it was the evils of capitalism, including fascism (despite his shocking pact with Hitler). For Franco, it was Communism, anarchy, and the forces opposed to the Catholic Church. For Hitler, the enemy, increasingly, was the Jews—the Jews and their supporters in all the nations that threatened to encircle, isolate, and smother "Germania" (the classical Roman term, often adopted by Nazi propagandists, for the geographical region of Germany).

The Hitler cult began in the mid-1920s, after Hitler's release from Landsberg prison. It soon became embellished with gestures and symbols rooted in German history, heritage, and mythology. The obligatory cry of "Heil Hitler" (Hail Hitler!) and the stiff-armed salute (in emulation of the fascist "Roman salute" used in Mussolini's Italy) were tokens of absolute devotion to the leader. As for the Nazi Party's principal symbol, the swastika, it was a pseudo-religious image derived from ancient Buddhist iconography.

In the early 1920s, of course, the Nazi Party represented no truly mass movement. For those who voted for him in the early 1920s, Hitler had come to represent *Kampf*—struggle—just as the title of *Mein Kampf* had boasted: the struggle of the "little man" against society's "big battalions." It was the struggle against what so many saw as the moral decadence of the Weimar Republic. It was the struggle of a humiliated Germany against a hostile world that had wronged it in the 1914-1918 war and its aftermath.

So pervasive did the Hitler cult become that it is sometimes hard to remember that, during his rise, he often failed to win popular elections. How, then, did the Hitler cult spread as rapidly as it did throughout much of the German population?

At least three things came into play. First, given the decrepitude and factionalism of the Weimar system, Hitler offered a new face and a fresh hope. A great many Germans were prepared to give him a chance. Second, in his lightning thrust toward power, he demonstrated supreme confidence. Even if he did not win outright, he always played the game like a winner. Third, he appealed for striving, commitment, and sacrifice. In a German nationalist context, he appealed to idealism and patriotism. He offered the German people purpose and a renewal of pride.

All this came to culmination in Hitler's victory over Poland. As most Germans saw it—especially when they read the accounts in government-controlled newspapers—that victory was not only triumphant, it was also virtually cost-free. The economy was strong and most people were more prosperous than ever before.

Most of all, Hitler had been *right*. Like King Midas, everything he touched had turned to gold—so that the future itself suddenly seemed golden. A defeated population was lifted up. Suddenly, it was good to be German. And no cohort believed this more sincerely than Hitler's most ardent supporters, the youth of the nation.

SUPPORTING ACTORS

Working behind the scenes, Propaganda Minister Josef Goebbels used the state-controlled media to present Hitler as the one and only German leader, the "Symbol of the Nation." Hitler's cluster of "virtues"—his strength, determination, and vision (broadcast endlessly through all the media)—were precisely what the Germans craved. When Hitler harped on the need to rid Germany of its enemies at home and abroad, the people heard him—and heeded him.

The Hitler Youth

The *Hitlerjugend*—Hitler Youth—dated to the very origin of the Nazi Party in 1922. By 1933, it was the only official youth organization of the Nazi Party, and it served not only to indoctrinate German youngsters, boys (*Hitlerjugend*) and girls (*Bund Deutsche Mädel*, League of German Girls), into the Hitler cult, but was also a paramilitary organization that prepared German youth for service in the armed forces. After World War II, one former Hitler Youth explained how the indoctrination worked:

> No one in our class ever read *Mein Kampf*. I myself only took quotations from the book. On the whole we didn't know much about Nazi ideology. Even anti-Semitism was brought in

rather marginally at school—for example via Richard Wagner's essay, "The Jews in Music" … Nevertheless, we were politically programmed: to obey orders, to cultivate the soldierly "virtue" of standing to attention and saying, "Yes, Sir," and to stop thinking when the magic word "Fatherland" was uttered and Germany's honor and greatness were mentioned.

Preparation for "membership" in the Hitler cult thus began in childhood, at the age of 10, as training in reflexive obedience. There was no argument, discussion, or debate. In such an educational and cultural climate, war came to seem normal and violence legitimate. Hitler's victories abroad between 1936 and 1939 led Germans to take pride in a Führer who combined violent threats, claims of legal right, and risk-taking to produce success. At bottom, however, the Hitler cult was a cult of authority and kneejerk obedience to it.

The conversion of children into essentially obedient soldiers—long before they were conscripted into actual military service—was a key step in the "purification" of the "Aryan race." The motto every child learned was *Ein Volk, Ein Reich, Ein Führer*—One People, One Empire, One Leader. That "One People" was the German people, who were idealized as decedents of the Aryan race. As the Nazis saw it, the Aryans were the original speakers of the Indo-European languages and were the "purist" sub-race of the Caucasian race. Purification of the German Reich meant purging the Jews, of course, but it also went beyond this group to include anyone considered unworthy of membership in what the Nazis believed was the "master race."

Social Outcasts

In part, the master race already existed, and in part it had to be cultivated over time by culling out from the German "stock" not only Jews but others who were unable to play positive, productive roles in society. Communists and other political undesirables were to be purged, as were Gypsies and, in many cases, people of Slavic origin. In addition, those deemed *Lebensunwertes Leben* (literally, "life unworthy of life") were to be eliminated. These included certain criminals, "degenerates," chronic dissidents, and, most of all, people with congenital cognitive and physical disabilities (so-called feebleminded individuals, epileptics, schizophrenics, those with cerebral palsy, muscular dystrophy, the deaf, and the blind.) "Elimination" of "life unworthy of life" was accomplished for the most part through involuntary sterilization. Early in 1939, however, Hitler authorized the murder, either by lethal injection or deliberate starvation, of severely handicapped infants. At about the same time that the Molotov-Ribbentrop Pact was concluded, the policy of "euthanasia" was extended to some adults. These included not only those who were physically deformed but also those suffering from developmental disabilities and some illnesses. In 1939, about 200,000 adult Germans were categorized as "life unworthy of life." In six mental hospitals throughout Germany, the regime constructed gas chambers that could induce death through the introduction of carbon monoxide. These facilities received some 72,000 persons from all over the Reich, all of whom were asphyxiated in the hospital facilities. In 1941, a rare display of public pressure induced Hitler to call a halt to the program. He did not, of course, stop the Holocaust.

TERMS AND TRANSLATIONS

Eugenics is the study of hereditary improvement, especially of human improvement, by genetic control. The horticultural and agricultural sciences have long known how to make new and improved varieties of plants; horse owners breed stallions and mares to produce Kentucky Derby winners. The Nazis proposed doing the same with human beings. Although eugenics was taken to horrific extremes in the Third Reich, it was not unique to Hitler's Germany, but was popular even in nineteenth- and early-twentieth-century America.

The Emerging Holocaust

In January 1939, only eight months before the start of the war in Poland, Hitler went before the Reichstag to make a statement that received wild approval: If "international Jewish finance inside and outside of Europe succeeds in involving the nations in another war," he proclaimed, "the result will not be the bolshevization of the earth and the victory of Judaism but the annihilation of the Jewish race in Europe." That same month, he also informed the Czech foreign minister that "we are going to destroy the Jews. They are not going to get away with what they did on November 11, 1918."

The two statements—to the Reichstag and to the Czech foreign minister—contain a massive self-contradiction. Hitler asserts that the Jews both started the World War I and ended it. No matter. For Hitler, the Jews existed to be blamed, period. By pinning "another war" on "international Jewish finance," Hitler was getting ready to blame the Jews for the war *he* was about to start. Moreover, it was a war he himself was concocting to both justify and carry out the Holocaust.

A Speculation

If Hitler was so determined to see the return of Danzig and the Polish Corridor to Germany, why did he not simply take them and stop? Why the broader war against Poland? The popular assumption is that he had a kind of ungovernable lust for conquest. Perhaps. More likely, however, he saw Poland as a convenient space in which to expand and the home of Europe's largest population of Jews. By invading Poland, Hitler could create a war fever in which the German people would regard the mass murder of Jews as a military necessity. This became a key message in German propaganda. The attack on Poland, which embroiled Nazi Germany in a war with France and Great Britain, may have had as its ultimate objective the murder of European Jews.

The Nazi Solution

The documented fact is that, even while the war was unfolding in Poland, Nazi leaders were developing a new "solution" to the "Jewish question." Hitler intended (as he told associates) to turn Poland into a slave state, the inhabitants of which would be compelled to serve the master race of German settlers. The first step of this enslavement would be forcing some three million Polish Jews into ghettos. Later, they would be transferred to a reservation near Lublin, southeast of Warsaw.

Only a month after the German invasion of Poland, Heinrich Himmler, in his role as Reich commissioner, took over the "Germanization" of Poland. This meant that Poland's Jews, or at least those west of the Soviet zone, were wholly at the mercy of the SS. Between December 1939 and February 1940, accordingly, 600,000 Jews in Danzig and the former Polish Corridor were forced from their homes, prodded into cattle trucks, and shipped into the Polish territories annexed by the Third Reich.

But the plan went awry. In German-occupied Warsaw, Hans Frank, the Nazi official in charge, protested that he already had about 1,400,000 Jews under his jurisdiction. The addition of hundreds of thousands more was causing a strain on food supplies. He began, therefore, to withhold food from Jews.

Semi-starvation was cruel and often lethal, but it did not yet amount to the Final Solution. The problem of food shortages, however, did finally raise that fatal issue. At the highest levels of the German government, the question was being asked: Instead of feeding Jewish slaves in the factories of Poland, why not simply kill them?

BET YOU DIDN'T KNOW

Wherever they lived, Polish Jews were forbidden to move—the regime wanted to keep tabs on them—and they were required to obey a curfew; wear the yellow star to identify them on sight, and perform slave labor, chiefly in newly constructed German factories.

The Austrian People and Hitler's War

The Austrian popular response to the start of the war was similar to that in Germany itself. When news of the German invasion of Poland reached Vienna, people were stunned. "I heard Hitler's speech [declaring war on Poland] at the Carlton," an Austrian diplomat wrote; "the club was packed with listening guests. Everybody with grave expressions. No applause. A small crowd of people on St. Stephen's Square. Those near the loudspeakers raised their arms during the national anthem. Those standing farther away not at all. Everywhere depressed spirits. Vague hopes of a short local war. Not one trace of enthusiasm."

As it did in Germany, the mood in Austria soon changed. The remarkable success of the *Blitzkrieg,* Lightning War, in Poland rid Austria of its fear of military disaster and unleashed both admiration and rejoicing. Within days, Austrian troops who had fought alongside German counterparts were showered with flowers, food, and cigarettes. And they were favored with more than that. "In the euphoria of reunion," an Austrian official reported, "no one was offended that formerly prevailing bourgeois morals are no longer being observed."

Few cared about the breakdown of "traditional" sexual morality because Austria, like Germany, had a new morality, the Hitler cult, which superseded all else. Hitler, after all, was the local boy who made good. Hitler worship even began replacing Austria's traditional Catholicism.

The one Austrian tradition that remained—and was stronger than ever—was anti-Semitism. Led by Arthur Seyss-Inquart, the Austrian Nazi whom Hitler had put in charge of Vienna, party members throughout the country stepped up the abuse of Jews. In one town, Türkenschanze, Nazi militants demanded that Jewish homes post identity plates; in another, Kettenbrücke, Jews had to wear the Star of David.

The Winter of Discontent

As in Germany, Austrian Nazis were willing to blame the Jews for all woes. Despite the joys of autumn 1939, the advent of winter brought plenty of despair. In both Germany and Austria, the winter of 1939-1940 was harsh and created severe shortages of just about everything needful: milk, flour, coffee, meat, and vegetables. All available foodstuffs were being routed to the military, not civilians. The regime in Berlin responded to the shortages not by diverting some food from the armies, but by imposing stricter rationing on the civilians. This succeeded only in slowing production and delivery and making the food shortages more acute. Because of the demands of the armed forces, shoes and clothing also became scarce.

Next, in the midst of this unseasonably cold winter, came the coal crisis. Rural peasants could cut down trees for fuel, but the city-dwellers had no alternative to scarce coal. Adding to the pain was a tax increase. War, after all, cost money. To offset the burden on the public, the Reich printed more money. This brought on the demon that had so afflicted Weimar Germany: inflation.

Still, during this early period of the war, the news from the front was generally very good—even spectacular. Yet the cold, the hunger, the currency of dwindling worth—all this foreshadowed far greater hardships to come.

Life, nevertheless, went on. It was pinched and harder than usual, but even if people sometimes went hungry, the food allotments were adequate to prevent out-and-out starvation. Most of all, the war itself seemed remote—because it was just that: far away.

The Phony War

The Germans called the first eight months and one week of World War II, from September 3, 1939, to May 10, 1940, the *Sitzkrieg*, or Sitting War. The French name for it was the *drôle de guerre*, or "funny war." British prime minister Neville Chamberlain used the term "twilight war." But American journalists in Europe coined the phrase that really caught on. They called it the "Phony War."

All the terms express the popular perception of the early months of World War II, but they miss the bigger picture. For one thing, there was nothing at all phony about the war at sea. On September 3, 1939, shortly after Germany and Russia began carving up Poland, a German U-boat torpedoed and sank the British liner *Athenia*. Another U-boat slipped into the harbor at Scapa Flow, the British naval base at the northern tip of Scotland, and sank the battleship *Royal Oak* (October 14, 1939). The British in their turn trapped the German cruiser *Graf Spee* in the waters of the Rio Plate, which flowed into the Atlantic at Montevideo, Uruguay. The attack damaged *Graf Spee* so severely that the crew scuttled the vessel to prevent its capture (December 17, 1939).

While the seas were roiled with warfare, all sides were preparing for major combat on land. Although the Royal Navy was much more potent than the German High Seas Fleet, as was true during World War I, and although they had made strides in building up its Royal Air Force (RAF), the British were struggling to enlarge their army. Eventually, by December 1939, London could deploy the four divisions of the British Expeditionary Force (BEF) to northeastern France. Although the British officers looked upon the French troops with contempt—General Alan Brooke wrote of "men unshaven, horses ungroomed, clothes and saddlery that did not fit, vehicles dirty, and complete lack of pride in themselves and their units"—this British contingent was a mere drop in the bucket of France's 100 divisions. Besides, France was defended by the Maginot Line. A chain of interconnected fortresses and strong points on the country's eastern border, the Maginot Line was never intended to stop a German invasion, but it was designed to exact a heavy toll on the invaders and also to slow them down, to buy time during which large numbers of French troops could be deployed wherever needed to confront the enemy.

MEMORABLE PLACES

Named for a French minister of defense, André Maginot, the Maginot Line was constructed between 1930 and 1935 as a system of concrete and steel fortifications that ran all the way from Switzerland to Luxembourg along the French–German frontier. With heavy artillery encased in bombproof casements, the line was never intended to be impregnable, but it was meant to delay an invader long enough for the French army to mount an effective defense.

The Maginot Line was a modern wonder of military architecture, a true state-of-the-art fortification. However, it did not cover the border between France and Luxembourg. Part of the reason was budgetary, and part of the reason was the presence of the thick woods of the Ardennes Forest. French military strategists believed the density of this tract prevented any massive attack, especially by mechanized vehicles. (This assumption proved fatally wrong.) The Maginot Line also did not parallel France's frontier with Belgium. French planners reasoned that they could safely deploy many of the army's 100 divisions at the Belgian border, from which they could mount a defense or even a counterattack.

The Germans had their own variant (although not so formidable) of the French fortification system, the so-called West Wall. The British nicknamed it the Siegfried Line, a title made popular by a passage in a British music hall song: "We're going to hang out the washing on the Siegfried Line." This system of fortifications ran just inside the German frontier, facing the Maginot Line. Like its French counterpart, the Siegfried Line was defensive. It is difficult to believe, given the terrifying success of the German invasion of France, but Hitler had only 23 divisions to hurl against France's 100. Moreover, most of Germany's land forces were extensively mechanized, and repairing and refitting the tanks, armored cars, and airplanes used in the Polish campaign would take time.

So, until spring 1940, the land war on the Western Front hardly seemed a war at all. Hitler, however, understood that the *Sitzkrieg* could not last forever. It was he who ended it by landing in neutral Denmark and Norway on April 9, 1940, thus bringing the real war to the West.

The Least You Need to Know

- Undergirding Nazi Germany's successes in war was its industrial prowess. The heart of the German economic machine was the Ruhr Valley, home of the great arms maker, Krupp.

- Key to understanding Hitler's early political and military victories is his hold on the German and Austrian people. He was the object of a cult of personality and had especially great appeal for the German youth, who were systematically molded into zealous Nazis.

- Bent on creating a pure Ayran master race, Hitler and his associates unleashed a horrific program of euthanasia, mostly targeting the physically and mentally handicapped, who were deemed "life unworthy of life."

- The persecution of the Jews, now not only in Germany but also in Czechoslovakia, Austria, and Poland, moved forward. Under the direction of the SS, the first phase of the Holocaust concentrated the Jews in closed ghettos in Polish cities and towns.

- After the fall of Poland, the principal combatants, Nazi Germany on one side and France and Great Britain on the other, engaged in an eight-month period of preparation known as the Phony War, September 3, 1939-May 10, 1940.

From Norway to *Blitzkrieg:* 1940

Adolf Hitler believed in miracles. He called them *Wunderwaffen*—Wonder Weapons—and he placed great faith in them. Some historians have accordingly judged him to be deluded, perhaps mad. The thing is, some *Wunderwaffen* actually worked, and even more came close to working.

We think of the atomic bomb as the weapon that ended World War II, when the United States dropped "Little Boy" and "Fat Man" on Hiroshima and Nagasaki in August 1945. The Nuremberg war crimes trials, held by the Allies from 1945 to 1946, revealed that the Nazis were trying to develop atomic weapons from the very start of the war. One of the Nazi defendants in that trial, Albert Speer, an architect by profession and designer of Germany's military production during the war, made a startling statement. At war's end, he said, Germany was only two years from having an atomic bomb. German scientists had been working on the weapon for years.

The Self-Inflicted Wound

Hitler, Speer pointed out at Nuremberg, had failed to create the atomic *Wunderwaffe* because his Nazi policies had driven out of Germany most of the country's best scientists, especially the physicists (many Jewish), who could have delivered the weapon earlier.

Not all the eminent personages who fled Germany were Jewish, but those who left certainly made up an intellectual elite perhaps unmatched in any other country. Among them were—

- ✪ The Nobel Prize–winning novelist Thomas Mann and his wife, Katya
- ✪ Dr. Sigmund Freud and his daughter, Anna, who made their way to London
- ✪ Erich Maria Remarque, the author whose famed novel *All Quiet on the Western Front* (*Am Westen Nichts Neues*) had exposed the horrors of front-line warfare
- ✪ Erich Leinsdorf, the young conductor of the Salzburg Festival Orchestra, who landed a job conducting Wagner for the Metropolitan Opera Company
- ✪ Furniture designer Marcel Breuer and architect Walter Gropius, who in Germany had founded a school of modernist design called the *Bauhaus* (Build House)—condemned by the Nazis as decadent—and who ended up teaching at the Harvard School of Design
- ✪ Another *Bauhaus* architect named Ludwig Mies van der Rohe
- ✪ The scholar Hannah Arendt who, starting in 1940, taught at the New School for Social Research in New York City

But by far the most famous outcast of the Nazi era was a Jewish physicist, Albert Einstein, who left Germany and found refuge at the Institute of Advanced Study at Princeton. Doubtless, Albert Speer had Einstein in mind when he testified at Nuremberg.

The Nazi Atomic Bomb Program

"Dear Mr. President," began an August 1939 letter from Einstein to President Franklin D. Roosevelt, alerting FDR to the alarming growth of German nuclear weapons research. Einstein wrote in deliberately nontechnical terms and avoided hysteria, but he was nevertheless blunt: "it is conceivable … that [in Germany] extremely powerful bombs of a new type may be constructed." He went on to explain that "a single bomb of this type, carried by boat and exploded in port, might very well destroy the whole port together with some of the surrounding territory."

This might have sounded like science fiction, except for one detail Einstein was careful to include: "I understand that Germany has actually stopped the sale of uranium from the Czechoslovakian mines which she had taken over …"

This last statement was enough to prompt the president to authorize what came to be called the Manhattan Project, America's own top secret atomic bomb program. Einstein made clear his opinion that, if Germany was prohibiting the export of uranium from Czech mines, and thus the sale of the ore to Great Britain, which was also working on an atomic bomb, then Germany could be assumed to have a development program up and running.

The Super-Bomb Memorandum

Einstein's letter to FDR was triggered by a conversation with the brilliant physicist Leo Szillard, a Hungarian-born Jewish citizen of Germany who fled to London and then to New York and a professorship at Columbia University. With fellow physicist Enrico Fermi—who fled Mussolini's fascist Italy because his wife was Jewish—Szillard developed the idea of a nuclear chain reaction, the very key to creating an atomic weapon. Szillard was alarmed by the news that German physicists had discovered nuclear fission ("atom splitting," the essential first step toward achieving a chain reaction), and he talked Einstein (far more famous than he) into writing the letter to the president.

The fears of both Szilard and Einstein were very well grounded. A document titled "Memorandum on the Properties of a Radioactive Super-bomb," classified top secret, made the rounds of the top scientists in the United States early in 1940. In part, it read:

1. The United States believed that the super-bomb would be practically irresistible.

2. The bomb could probably not be used without killing large numbers of civilians.

3. "… It is quite conceivable that Germany is, in fact, developing this weapon …"

4. It must be realized that no shelters are available that would be effective and could be used on a large scale. The most effective reply would be a counter-threat with a similar weapon."

Led by one of the greatest of modern physicists, a theoretician named Werner Heisenberg, Germany was indeed coming into "possession of this weapon."

The Search for Heavy Water

Working in a Berlin laboratory, Heisenberg in early 1941 had reached the point of designing a so-called heavy-water reactor, a device in which a controlled chain reaction could be produced—again, a step essential to creating a weapon.

But where would the German scientists obtain heavy water? Germany had no facilities for producing it. It turns out that Norway did. Near the town of Vemork, the Norwegians had built an establishment called the High Concentration Plant, which specialized in the production of heavy water.

BET YOU DIDN'T KNOW

Containing more hydrogen than ordinary water—it is ^2H_2O rather than H_2O—deuterium oxide, or "heavy water," is used as a neutron moderator in certain kinds of nuclear reactors.

The American memorandum ended with the words, "The most effective reply [to a German atomic bomb] would be a counter-threat with a similar weapon." Who else might develop a "similar weapon"? Believe it or not, Japan, which was leaning toward an alliance with Germany and therefore posed no threat to the Nazi regime.

Yet another nation working on the bomb was Great Britain. At the Cavendish Laboratory of Cambridge University, British scientists were engaged in atomic research, and they also needed heavy water.

Both Germany and Great Britain thus had a good reason, then, to cast longing eyes toward Norway, which not only was a source of heavy water, but had a strategically critical ice-free port, Narvik. The major raw material lacking in Germany's Ruhr Valley was iron ore. This had to be imported, and the closest mines to Germany were in northern Sweden. Ever since the start of Germany's industrialization, iron ore had been hauled from those Swedish mines by land to Narvik, and then by sea along the Norwegian coast to Germany.

Map of Denmark and Norway

Even in peacetime, the Norwegian coastal route was vital to the German industrial economy. Britain and France also were short of iron ore. Without steel, they could never hope to carry out their war with Hitler. During the Phony War, therefore, both sides, Germany versus France and Great Britain, prepared to seize Narvik as well as the heavy-water facilities of Norway. Never mind that Norway was a neutral country.

The Race to Norway Is On

On April 9, 1940, at a Berlin press conference, Ribbentrop, the Nazi foreign minister, gloated: "Gentlemen," he said to the reporters, "yesterday's Allied invasion of Norwegian territorial waters represents the most flagrant violation of the rights of a neutral country. … However, it did not take Germany by surprise … It was the British intention to create a base in Scandinavia from which Germany's flank could be attacked. The plan included the occupation of all Scandinavia—Denmark, Norway, and Sweden. The German government has the proofs that French and British general staff officers were already on Scandinavian soil, preparing the way for an Allied landing."

Much of Ribbentrop's claim was sheer nonsense. Nevertheless, it was true that the Allies and the Germans had been racing to claim Norway, and the Germans had won.

Allied plans for the disruption of the flow of iron ore to Germany had been in the works ever since the German conquest of Poland. Appointed First Lord of the Admiralty in September 1939, Winston S. Churchill began searching for a satisfactory plan of action. But he was not yet in the commanding position of prime minister, and, like any other bureaucrat, he found that his ideas had to be vetted by committees—British committees, French ones, military and economic staffs, and so on. The deliberations took time. In fairness, there were grave considerations to be debated. In its war with Germany, Great Britain counted on the neutrality of the Scandinavian countries. How would neutral Norway respond to a *British* attack on its territory? Churchill had no good answer.

Then an event in a country adjacent to Scandinavia intervened. On November 30, 1939, Stalin's Red Army invaded Finland, the Molotov-Ribbentrop Non-Aggression Pact having given the Soviets a free hand along the Baltic. The heroic resistance of the Finns in what was called the Winter War won the hearts of much of the world. This gave Churchill an idea. If Great Britain and France chose to come to Finland's defense, they would *have* to cross the territory of Sweden and Norway. In so doing, Churchill suggested, they could overrun the Swedish iron ore mines and be positioned to invade Norway.

In a bilateral conference held on February 5, 1940, the British and French high commands both approved Churchill's plan. Unfortunately for the Allied planners, however, Finland surrendered on March 13, 1940. This nullified the Finnish pretext for invading Sweden and Norway.

In Paris, the government of Éduard Daladier fell from power on March 21, 1940. The French electorate was outraged by the lack of assistance given to Finland and the failure to carry out the wider war against Hitler. Daladier was replaced by Paul Reynaud, who was immediately under enormous political pressure to take action—somewhere, anywhere. Churchill likewise thirsted for action. Britain and France, therefore, organized a joint flotilla to take Narvik and other northern Norwegian ports, no matter the diplomatic consequences.

This was on April 5, 1940, and as the naval staffs in Paris and London knew full well, up along the high Norwegian coast the ice was about to melt. Iron ore shipping would soon resume. The Allies had to move fast.

At that point Churchill threw a new spice in the pot. As long as we are headed to Narvik, he asked, why not lay mines in the Rhine River? Debate over this step consumed another valuable day, and the slow-moving convoy of Allied ships did not rendezvous in the English Channel and start northward until April 7.

Denmark and Norway

German spies, in the meantime, were active. They alerted the top brass in Berlin to the Allies' movement. Hitler responded by unleashing a new *blitzkrieg*—the lightning war—which had proved so devastating in the invasion of Poland. The Nazi strike up through Denmark and Norway was so fast that when Allied troops landed near Narvik and the other ports, they found that the Germans were already there. The British and the French beat a hasty withdrawal from the Norwegian coast, and as fast as they could go. The Danish–Norwegian campaign practically ended with a snap of the fingers.

Hitler did face one setback. After his own surprisingly costly (perhaps as many as 363,000 Red Army casualties) victory over Finland, Stalin ordered the deportation from all the lands he had seized around the Baltic of the 100,000 or so resident Germans. He was afraid that, as in Austria, the Sudetenland,

and Danzig, Hitler would use these German-speakers as a pretext for an eventual invasion of the Soviet Union.

Hitler was outraged over this forced exodus of ethnic Germans. For the moment, however, he did nothing about it. He was now casting his eyes toward the west.

The Schlieffen Plan Revised

From a point along the Maginot Line just outside Strasbourg, France, a pair of young French sentries gazed through the narrow slit in their concrete pillbox. It was shortly before dawn on May 10, 1940. The sun was about to peek over the hills of Germany to the east, and the bridge that led across the Rhine to the Nazi fortifications at Kehl still glittered with innumerable lights. But soon the river would ripple and flash in the sunshine, the air would become dry and clear, and the sky would grow blue and cloudless and warm. One of the sentries leaned against the barrel of his 75mm cannon, knowing that he would soon be off duty far below in the subterranean bowels of the fortification, sound asleep on his bunk. In the underground barracks, his comrades were already stretching and yawning as they climbed out of bunks, waking to take their watch on another boring day in the Phony War. Like the sentries far above them, they were weary, restless—and, they felt, perfectly safe.

Their safety was about to be revealed as a cruel illusion. After the success of his Scandinavian venture, Hitler believed that the time had come to eliminate the danger from France and Britain on the western frontier. It is doubtful that Hitler planned to invade the British Isles. Although his Luftwaffe could certainly bomb London and other English cities, his navy was not strong enough to cross the English Channel for an amphibious landing and invasion. Besides, he may well have deemed a full-scale war between Germany and Great Britain, almost cousin nations, irrational. Indeed, fascism had been gaining popularity in Britain, at least before the British government cracked down on British blackshirts after the declaration of war.

All the same, if Germany could knock the French out of the war and deprive the British of a base on the continent, the kind of base they had in World War I, the Reich would be secure on its Western Front. It would be free to break the non-aggression pact with the Soviets and turn against Russia.

Hitler and his top generals spread out their maps and dusted off the old Schlieffen Plan. The basic idea still seemed valid: The German armies would wheel through neutral Belgium—and this time through neutral Holland as well—driving along the English Channel coast and striking down toward Paris in a flanking attack on the mass of the Anglo-French armies.

Two points particularly encouraged the revival of the Schlieffen Plan. First, with the addition of airplanes and tanks—fast tanks at that—the German forces could move much faster than it had in 1914. Second, because Germany was not yet going to war with the Soviet Union, there would be no need to divert troops to the Eastern Front, as the German high command had done—fatally—in the autumn of 1914.

Still, there was a problem, and it seemed to be a big one. Although the Maginot Line possessed no offensive capability, it did present a formidable defense, which freed up the French to position huge numbers of troops along the otherwise undefended Belgian frontier. This presented the German army with a much more formidable defense than Poland could possibly have mustered.

Once again, Hitler's generals were jittery. They were not at all certain of success. But Hitler had an idea. The objective of the original Schlieffen Plan had been to encircle the French from the north. But what if this time the Schlieffen Plan was simply turned upside down, encircling all those French defenders (who were deployed along the Belgian border) by attacking from the south?

From the south? the generals asked, aghast. *But how?*

By advancing through the Ardennes Forest, just above the Maginot Line, Hitler offered.

"Impossible!" the generals sniffed. *"It's impassible."*

Back in the time of the Roman Empire, most of central Europe had been covered with forests so thick that they were practically jungles. In his classic account, *The Gallic Wars,* Julius Caesar gnashed his teeth over the difficulty of fighting the German tribes in those forests. Throughout the two hundred or so centuries since Caesar, most of the woodlands had given way to pastures and croplands, but the dense Ardennes Forest remained. And it surely *did* present obstacles. Hitler, however, was unimpressed by them. He was convinced that his armored units could traverse the woods successfully. The Führer thus having ended all debate, the generals positioned their forces to advance through the Ardennes, just above the Maginot Line and well below the French troops deployed along the Belgian frontier.

Before dawn on May 10, 1940, just as those two French sentries were about to go down for breakfast and turn in for the day, the 19th German Armored Corps under the command of General Heinz Guderian was rumbling along through the Ardennes Forest, their lights extinguished. In the lead were the *Panzers* (Panthers), the superbly engineered German tanks, the armored cars, and the up-armored motorcycles. Next followed the troop trucks, the heavy field artillery, and the supply echelons. Finally, stretching for 50 miles to the rear, came the columns of German athletes, the elite corps of the Nazi infantry, the blond supermen of the Third Reich.

It was pitch-dark in the mountains, and, with headlights doused, the drivers had to exert the utmost care to avoid ending up in the roadside ditches. The sound of the motors was getting on everyone's nerves. More and more troops who had been quartered in the forest were getting under way; more and more armored vehicles were emerging from the approach roads to join the main columns of tanks. The men were anxious. What awaited them once they crossed into France?

As it turned out, they need not have worried. *Luftwaffe* (air force) crews were also up and about in their *Stukas* and *Heinkels,* droning off toward Holland and Belgium, diverting French attention northward. The bombers were perpetrating an enormous feint in a highly successful effort to persuade the French that Hitler was launching the old, northern-oriented version of the Schlieffen Plan.

Before noon, May 10, 1940, the German armored units had not only driven through the Ardennes Forest—proving Hitler right and convincing him that he was a greater strategist than any of his generals—they had also crossed the rivers into France, and they began their race to the English Channel.

They would not be seduced into attacking Paris, not right away. Their objective, assigned by Hitler, was to attack the French armies from the rear. Within days, they did just that. The result was a rout—a French defeat at once costly, humiliating, and utterly demoralizing.

Escape from Dunkirk

The retreating French as well as members of the British Expeditionary Force withdrew in large numbers to Dunkirk, just west of the Belgian border on the English Channel. Their only hope for salvation from total annihilation was amphibious evacuation. That seemed a very slim possibility, however. So, essentially, the French and British were fighting the German onslaught with their backs to the "wall" that was the water's edge.

The story of Dunkirk, from which most of the British Expeditionary Force and many French troops escaped between May 26 and June 4, 1940, has usually been portrayed as a saga of utmost heroism. There was indeed plenty of that. While a BEF and French rearguard held off the final German onslaught, a motley fleet of 693 ships, among them 39 destroyers and 36 minesweepers plus 77 civilian fishing trawlers, 26 yachts, and an assortment of other small craft—all crewed by British civilians who volunteered to save "our boys"—snatched from the port of Dunkirk 338,226 soldiers, including 140,000 French troops, who would otherwise have been killed or captured. The evacuation was carried out under continuous *Luftwaffe* attack.

But there was more to the story. Large numbers of British officers deserted their men to climb aboard the first boats to arrive. Once on English soil, many of those rescued were so demoralized that they threw their weapons out of train windows. Some, upon meeting their wives, changed into civilian clothes and simply walked home. Publicly, in a moving speech to the House of Commons on June 4, Winston Churchill, who on May 10 had succeeded Chamberlain as prime minister, celebrated the deliverance of so much of the BEF. Privately, however, he told some of his ministers that Dunkirk had been "the greatest British military defeat for many centuries."

Despite all the attention it has received, the escape from Dunkirk was only one episode in the larger story: Hitler's utter humiliation of the Allies in the Battle of France.

The Fall of France

Twelve days after the evacuation from Dunkirk, France surrendered. Hitler's upside-down version of the Schlieffen Plan had worked brilliantly, catching the huge French armies from the rear and causing general panic. With the French in rapid retreat everywhere, the Germans marched into Paris almost unopposed.

Thereafter, along with the ministers of the government, what remained of the French army fled, first to Tours in the Loire Valley and then to Bordeaux on the southwestern coast. But it was all over. On June 16, 1940, Premier Paul Reynaud formally surrendered.

The Germans immediately allowed the formation of a new French government. Headed by Marshal Philippe Pétain, the aged hero of World War I, it established its capital in Vichy, a southern resort town. The Vichy government was allowed to administer the southeastern two fifths of France. The rest of the country fell under direct Nazi rule.

In the north of France, Hitler savored a moment of victory. At the end of World War I, on November 11, 1918, Marshal Ferdinand Foch, then the French commander in chief, officially accepted the German surrender aboard a railroad carriage on a siding at Compiègne on the edge of the fields of Flanders. The French later erected a monument on the spot. Now, on June 22, 1940, Hitler entered France and stopped his procession at that monument.

Having in advance of his arrival ordered Marshal Foch's railroad car to be extracted from its place of honor in the Musée de l'Armée (Army Museum) in Paris and returned to Compiègne, Hitler stepped aboard and read the terms of surrender to a French delegation. They spelled out the geographical limits of Vichy authority, but they made no demands on France's overseas empire. Under German and Italian supervision (at the last moment, Mussolini had entered the war on the side of Germany), the French were to disarm their warships in their home ports.

BET YOU DIDN'T KNOW

William L. Shirer, an American correspondent, was watching Hitler on June 22, 1940. Hitler's face, he wrote, was "alive with scorn, anger, hate, revenge, triumph. He steps off the monument and contrives to make even this gesture a masterpiece of contempt. … He glances slowly around the clearing. … Suddenly, as though his face were not giving quite complete expression to his feelings, he throws his whole body into harmony with his mood. He swiftly snaps his hands on his hips, arches his shoulders, plants his feet wide apart. It is a magnificent gesture of defiance, of burning contempt for this place and all that it has stood for in the 22 years since it witnessed the humbling of the German Empire."

All this the French delegates found more or less acceptable. Then Hitler made one more demand. France was to turn over all the anti-Nazi German refugees who had found shelter on French soil. By this, Hitler meant primarily that he wanted the escaped Jews of Germany handed over. One of the French officers, General Charles Huntziger, protested, but Wilhelm Keitel, soon to be appointed chief of the High Command of the Armed Forces, cut him short. "Warmongers and traitors," the German informed the Frenchman bluntly, were to be extradited "at all costs." In that moment began the French participation in the Holocaust.

The Least You Need to Know

- Well before the United States began its Manhattan Project, Nazi Germany had embarked on research intended to develop the atomic bomb.

- Early in April 1940, the Germans on the one side and the British and French on the other engaged in a race to conquer Norway. Ships along the Norwegian coast were like a huge conveyor belt, transporting iron ore from northern Sweden to the factories of the Ruhr Valley in Germany.

- Hitler wanted to avenge Germany's defeat in 1918. So, he adopted a variant of the Schlieffen Plan, encircling the French armies through the Ardennes Forest and thus from the south, enabling German armored units to approach the French forces from the rear.

- With the French surrender, Nazi Germany was engorged, controlling Norway, Denmark, Holland, Belgium, and Luxembourg. As thoroughly and ruthlessly as he could, Hitler proceeded to impose on those captured countries the same racist policies that had enveloped the Third Reich.

The Occupied Countries: 1940–1941

On many occasions, after the German troops had marched into Paris, they acted like farm boys seeing the big city for the first time in their lives. They gawked at the Eiffel Tower, took snapshots of the Arc de Triomphe, and ogled the girls in the dance halls. They seemed nothing like conquering heroes. Some, to be sure, had affairs with the French. But, on the whole, the Parisians treated them with disdain. So did most of the people in the other conquered countries, even when the Germans brutalized local populations. Wherever they went, the Germans made themselves thoroughly loathed, more disrespected than feared.

As for the terms of French surrender to the Nazis, the Armistice of June 22, 1940, established German occupation of three-fifths of France north and west of a line through Geneva and Tours, extending to the Spanish border. This gave the Kriegsmarine (German navy) access to all French Channel and Atlantic ports—an extremely valuable strategic advantage. Internally, all persons who had been granted political asylum (including tens of thousands of Jews) were to be surrendered to occupation authorities. As an added humiliation, France was obliged to pay Germany the costs of occupation: 400 million French francs a day.

There were some concessions to France. The nation was permitted a minimal army, and, while the navy was disarmed, Hitler did not demand the surrender of its vessels. To do so, he believed, would provoke the French to continue to fight from their colonial possessions—which Hitler also allowed the French government to retain, recognizing that he could not afford to spare troops to occupy the French colonial empire. Finally, France was allowed to administer an unoccupied two-fifths of its territory in the south. It was administered as a German client state from Vichy by a government Marshal Pétain headed.

Brigadier General Charles de Gaulle's Escape from France

The surrender of the French army had been thorough—except for the fraction of forces that were evacuated from Dunkirk and one more very important, very tall French officer, a brigadier general named Charles de Gaulle.

On the morning of June 16, 1940, the very day of the French surrender, a British general named Edward Spears was in Bordeaux. Fluent in French, he had been serving as a special aide to Churchill, who gave him a unique assignment: bring safely out of France the sole French general officer willing to continue the fight against Germany.

On June 17, de Gaulle announced that he was driving Spears to the Bordeaux airfield to see him off on his return flight to Britain. In addition to the British and French general, the car carried de Gaulle's aide de camp, Lieutenant Geoffroy de Courcel, and a trunk with documents snatched from the French war ministry.

En route to the airfield, the car inched past abandoned and wrecked vehicles as well as slow-moving streams of refugees. Policemen loyal to Marshal Pétain stood guard at crossroads and intersections. Anyone of them could have arrested de Gaulle and Spears. But they were not stopped—until they reached the airport gate. There a guard peered into the car. He demanded to know why an Englishman was seated with two French officers in an automobile headed for the runway. Within a matter of days and throughout World War II, no figure would be more universally recognizable—save, perhaps, for Adolf Hitler—than the six-foot-five de Gaulle. At this point in the war, however, he was just a brigadier general in a defeated army. No one recognized him. When de Gaulle explained that he was seeing Spears off, the guard waved the men through.

Spears drove on, spotted the twin-engine De Havilland Dragon Rapide—a small civilian airliner—and acknowledged the energetic waving of the pilot, who was standing beside the tail of the plane. The pilot walked over to the car to work out plans for departure. He immediately saw a problem. The heavy trunk could easily shift in flight, causing the light biplane to crash. His solution was to lash it inside the fuselage. But he didn't have a rope—and he certainly did not advise spending time searching for one, not when de Gaulle was liable to be arrested at any moment.

Couldn't they just leave the trunk behind? the pilot asked.

No, General de Gaulle snapped.

The trunk contained, among other sources of valuable strategic information, lists of names of persons remaining in France who could be trusted to join him in organizing the resistance. Someone, he said, would have to find a rope. Brusquely he gave de Courcel the order, and the lieutenant set off on the double to find one.

Spears later wrote that he rated this "high among the unpleasant periods of waiting I have experienced. The possibility of de Gaulle's departure from Bordeaux being detected was increasing. Somebody was sure to think of him in the course of the morning; then steps would be taken to locate him."

Sitting beside Spears in the car, de Gaulle chain-smoked gold-tipped cigarettes, seemingly oblivious of the danger.

Not so Spears. De Courcel had not yet returned, and "if it occurred to anyone that [de Gaulle] had gone, the aerodrome would be the natural place to look for him." And in the bright summer sunshine, someone would sooner or later be able to spot him. Yet there was still no de Courcel.

Spears was frightened. He looked first out through the windshield of the car, and then he climbed out and up onto a wing of the aircraft to search for any sign of the missing aide. "Some would remember having seen me in the car with [de Gaulle]," Spears wrote. "That would be the clue. Then there would be a telephone call."

Spears gazed over the tops of all the parked airplanes. Nothing.

He was in despair. He gazed this way and that across the airport, and then started to clamber down again from the wing. Then something caught his eye.

From under the wing of the next plane came someone running. It was Lieutenant de Courcel. As fast as his "stilt-like legs" were going, Spears thought the man was "moving in slow motion." But he was dashing, tightly clutching a ball of twine. The trunk was secured, and Charles de Gaulle was on his way to London. Until August 25, 1944, and the liberation of Paris by the Allies, he would be the heart, soul, and strategic mind of "Free France."

De Gaulle's Attempt to Rally a French Resistance

Two days after his escape, General de Gaulle made a broadcast to France from a BBC radio studio. "*Á tous les français*" ("To all Frenchmen"), he began. His brief talk was printed up in the form of posters, and some of the French who joined de Gaulle in London—mostly survivors of Dunkirk—smuggled those posters into France:

> France has lost a battle! But France has not lost the war! The government of the moment has capitulated, giving way to panic and delivering the country into servitude. However, not all is lost. Out in the free world, immense forces have not yet entered the fray. One day, these forces will crush the enemy. It is necessary that on that day France is present at the victory. Then she will recover her liberty and her grandeur. Such is my goal, my only goal!

That is why I invite all French people, wherever they find themselves, to join with me in action, in sacrifice, and in hope.

Our nation is in danger of dying. Let us struggle to save her!

Vive la France!

From London, on June 18, 1940, de Gaulle proclaimed the beginning of resistance to the Nazi occupation. Only a few joined him, but he had taken his stance.

Acts of French Heroism

Back on the continent, citizens of France and other occupied countries engaged in individual acts of heroism. Some of their deeds are recorded in photographs. Despite a German ban on tributes to Belgium's *World War I Unknown Soldier,* a retired veteran sneaked flowers past Brussels policemen and placed them on the monument. A young Norwegian couple sitting on the grass of a public park arranged stones to form the monogram of King Haakon VII, who had fled the Nazi invasion. On the back of his silk jacket, a jockey at the Longchamps Racecourse, in the lovely Bois de Boulogne on the west side of Paris, wore the Cross of Lorraine, once the emblem of Joan of Arc and now the symbol of Charles de Gaulle and his Free French movement. In Amsterdam, Dutch patriots spread their national flag beside an Amsterdam canal where the Germans had shot 29 of their compatriots—executed in reprisal for a Dutch attempt to assassinate the local SS chief.

Negligible Resistance

Such heroic actions were undeniably brave. But they were isolated and individual acts, part of no organized, general movement of resistance. After the World War II, occupying Allied forces discovered that almost nobody would confess to having been a Nazi or a collaborator with Nazis. In fact, at the war's end, just about everyone in the occupied countries claimed to have been a member of the resistance. But it wasn't so. The pattern varied from country to country, but the overall theme was similar to that of France: surrender, resignation, and even collaboration.

This is not to condemn these subjugated populations. Heroism is celebrated precisely because it is exceptional behavior. But the truth is the truth, and the fact is that, after the German victory over France and during the Battle of Britain, when it appeared that Hitler might even invade the British Isles, the continental resistance was small, even negligible. With a few exceptions, all the territory from northern Norway to the Swiss border and from eastern Poland to Brittany, the French peninsula that jutted out into the Atlantic, was a geographical extension of militarized Nazi Germany.

BET YOU DIDN'T KNOW

The massive air campaign in the skies over England during the summer of 1940 was fought to determine air supremacy over the British Isles. If Germany was to have any chance of eliminating its English foe, it had to destroy the Royal Air Force (RAF). The greatest German aerial offensives took place in the middle of August. They succeeded in knocking out most of Britain's airfields. Before the destruction was complete, however, Hitler and Göring, head of the *Luftwaffe,* decided to divert their effort to bombing London. This act of terrorism caused extensive damage and human devastation, especially in the East End of the capital. But it also meant that British pilots were able to concentrate their efforts on destroying incoming bombers whose course was known. By the middle of September, Germany had lost the Battle of Britain. "Never in the field of human conflict," Churchill declared in a speech to the House of Commons, "was so much owed by so many to so few"—by which he meant the pilots of the RAF. It was indeed what Churchill called it: Britain's finest hour.

Poland

A stocky, dark-haired, balding man, Hans Frank was the *Gauleiter* of Poland. A lawyer and an early Hitler supporter, his loyalty had led to his installation in Wawel Castle, the ancient site of Polish kings. He told his wife, Brigitte, that she was going to be the queen of Poland. Once the Germans had subdued that nation, he certainly conducted himself as if he were the monarch. Resplendent in flaring breeches and shiny black boots, he held his official receptions in the throne room. Beneath ancient tapestries, he entertained guests with long tables burdened with Polish hams, cheeses, and bottles of vodka.

TERMS AND TRANSLATIONS

Gau means "district," and *Leiter* translates as "leader."

The guests, needless to say, were not Jews. They were the Nazi elite: men like Josef Goebbels, propaganda minister, and Alfred Rosenberg, the Nazi Party's chief theorist. They also included a stream of "Aryan" movie stars, musicians, and opera singers, a parade of celebrities arriving in Frank's royal railway carriage to take part in his royal parties.

Despite his regalt pretensions, however, Hans Frank knew full well that he served only at Hitler's whim. And he would survive in Wawel Castle just as long as he did his master's bidding. His central mission was to dispose of the Jews. Thus, under Hans Frank in 1940 and 1941, Poland turned into a diabolical machine of death. Jews were arrested, consigned to ghettos, and packed off in freight trains to concentration camps. Auschwitz in southern Poland quickly became the most infamous. Those who weren't killed immediately were forced to work as slave laborers. Those who could work survived as long as they could labor. Many were worked to death, succumbed to diseases spawned in overcrowded and filthy conditions, or were shot at the whim of their guards.

Frank focused on the Jews, but he did not stop with them. Gypsies and disobedient Poles also became his victims. Rumor had it that he himself was "tainted" with Jewish blood, but this did not curb his rapacity.

Frank also enriched himself through black-market corruption. His wife, Brigitte, loved to shop for bargains in the Warsaw ghetto. In their desperation, Jews sold whatever valuable personal belongings—furs, gold, carpets—had not been stolen from them. Prices were, of course, rock-bottom. A sensitive being in her way, Frau Frank was acutely aware that the Jews hated her. Eventually, she took her loot and retreated to a mansion in Bavaria for a life separate from her husband. As for the Jews of Poland, the worst was yet to come.

Denmark

As brutish as they were, the Nazis did know where their bread was buttered—in Denmark. Being a heavily agricultural country, Denmark was a major supplier of meat and butter to the Third Reich. The food supply of Nazi Germany thus was highly dependent on Denmark. Lots of Germans could eat only as long as Danish farmers were willing to produce and sell.

Even though their nation was occupied by Nazi thugs, the Danes were able to drive a hard bargain. They insisted on—and they got—the right to self-rule under their constitutional monarch. Even more astounding is the degree to which they coerced the Nazi occupiers to leave "their" Jews alone. About 8,000 Jews lived in the country, most of them in the charming capital city of Copenhagen. They would have been easy targets for the Nazis, but, needing the cooperation of the Danes, the occupiers moderated their persecution.

King Christian X on one of his daily horseback rides through the streets of Copenhagen.
(U.S. Holocaust Memorial Museum)

Norway

The handful of Jews—about 1,800—living in Norway were not so lucky. In April 1940, Nazis desecrated the synagogue in the port town of Trondheim. Soon afterward, Nazi authorities decreed that no Jews could leave Norway. Jewish businesses were confiscated, and hundreds of Jews were arrested.

Unlike Denmark, Norway—at least official Norway—sanctioned Nazi rule as well as Nazi anti-Semitism. The reason was that the nation had been sold out to Hitler's Germany by a man named Vidkun Quisling.

Formerly a military officer serving on the Norwegian general staff, Quisling became the leader of a small group of Norwegians who believed in Nordic racial superiority and were therefore enthusiastic supporters of the Nazis. Early in the 1930s, Quisling was appointed defense minister by a right-wing conservative government. He used his powerful post to lash out at the leftist political parties. From this position, he organized the Norwegian equivalent of the Nazi Party.

When, on April 9, 1940, the Norwegian government fled from Oslo, the invading Germans set him up as head of a pro-German, anti-British government. In his capacity as prime minister, Quisling insisted that Norwegian schools revise their textbooks, bringing them into line with the Aryan, anti-Semitic slant of those in Nazi Germany. When the history teachers refused to go along with this, Quisling had them arrested. Of the 1,000 or so teachers incarcerated, about 500 were sent to work as dock hands at an Arctic port near the Finnish border. He also revived a defunct passage in the nineteenth-century constitution that had declared Jews and Jesuits to be illegal immigrants. Quisling was laying the groundwork for the deportation of Norway's Jewish community.

For selling out his nation and ruling it as the puppet of a Nazi regime, Vidkun Quisling lost his life (he was executed by firing squad on October 24, 1945) and gave the English language a new word, *quisling*, to describe any treasonous puppet.

TERMS AND TRANSLATIONS

A **quisling** is a traitor who serves as the puppet ruler of the enemy occupying his country.

The Low Countries

Under Quisling's rule, some 700 Norwegian Jews were arrested and sent to the concentration camps. The rest managed to slip across the frontier into neutral Sweden. The Jews in the Low Countries, however, fared worse. There was nowhere for them to go, except into hiding within the small nation, and Holland was a tough place in which to hide. Densely populated, it had no hills or forests to speak of. Most important, after the German invasion of France, every country on Holland's borders was Nazi-occupied. The sea afforded no viable avenue of escape. Danish fishermen regularly smuggled

Jews out of Copenhagen and across a narrow sound into Sweden, but fishing boats out of Holland were immediately on the high seas and easily tracked by German coast guard cutters. Dutch Jews were trapped.

When the Germans marched through the country in May 1940, about 1,140,000 Jews lived in Holland, most descended from families that had been fully integrated into Dutch life for centuries. On the whole, Jews were accepted as being fully Dutch. Some of Rembrandt's favorite subjects for his paintings were Jews.

None of this mattered to the Nazis. In the autumn of 1940, the German occupiers instituted thorough-going anti-Semitic measures. As always, Jews were defined in racial terms, and all Jewish business owners had to register with the authorities as Jews. In November, Jewish professors at the universities at Leiden and Delft lost their jobs. When outraged Dutch students protested, the Nazis closed the classrooms altogether. Next, Jews were barred from using buses and taxies; they couldn't buy tickets to the theaters; and they couldn't check books out of the public libraries. Early in 1941, Nazi hoodlums—some of whom were Dutch—began to beat up Jews at random.

By early 1941, persecution of the Dutch Jews was thoroughly systematic. All Jews had to register as such and were then summarily forced into ghettos separate from the rest of Dutch society. In July, SS chief Heinrich Himmler ordered the shipment of Jews out of Holland and into the concentration camps, mainly in Poland.

Most Gentile Dutch were sympathetic to the Jews, and quite a few tried hard to help. Here and there, farmers took in Jewish children. Some city dwellers gave Jews refuge in their attics or basements.

BET YOU DIDN'T KNOW

The most famous of Dutch refugees was the Frank family of Amsterdam, whose 13-year-old daughter, Anne, began to keep a diary. Published after the war, it would become world-famous under the title *The Diary of a Young Girl*. Secretly harbored above an Amsterdam business beginning on July 6, 1942, the family was arrested on August 4, 1944. They were sent to camps, and, in March 1945, Anne died of typhus in Bergen-Belsen—just days before advancing British and Canadian troops liberated it.

The fate of Anne Frank was typical of the Dutch Jews. Aside from individual Dutch families willing to risk their lives, there was simply no one able to help them.

Belgium afforded somewhat more protection than Holland. There, Queen Elizabeth, who had refused to flee, made personal pleas to Nazi authorities, which saved thousands of Jews from deportation to the camps. Joseph-Ernest Cardinal van Roey, the highest-ranking Roman Catholic in the country, ordered all his institutions to give help to the Jews—at least as far as they could. Priests and nuns, schools and hospitals, joined in a massive effort to conceal Jewish families. So did a well-organized Jewish underground.

At the start of the Nazi occupation, some 65,000 citizens of Belgium were Jewish. 25,000 of them survived. Ghastly as the toll was, it was higher than in most of the occupied countries.

France

The French, by and large, took a different attitude toward the Jews in their country. Unlike Scandinavia and the Low Countries, France had a long history of anti-Semitism. When the Germans invaded France, Reichsführer Hermann Göring made a speech to the gauleiters who were going to rule the country:

> What happens to the French is of complete indifference to me. Maxim's [the famous restaurant] must have the best food for us but not for the French. … I intend to plunder in France, and profitably. There will be such inflation in Paris that everything will go for smash. The franc will not be worth more than a well-known type of paper used for a certain purpose.

Göring was true to his word. Clothed in the sky-blue uniform of the chief of the *Luftwaffe*—a costume he designed personally—he accompanied Hitler to Compiègne to celebrate the victory over France. But he didn't stay long. Instead, he slipped away to Paris, where he studied art—not for the sake of aesthetic edification but rather for theft. His aides then spread out all over Occupied France, cataloguing and then seizing paintings, sculptures, carvings, and furniture of any value whatsoever. (In France, they confined their looting to works in private hands, for fear that theft from the great museums—such as the Louvre—would trigger a popular revolt.) If the owners were Gentiles, they had to sell at ridiculously low prices; if they were Jewish, the property was declared "ownerless" and simply hauled away.

In September 1940, German authorities promulgated the first of their anti-Semitic measures in occupied France, defining as Jewish anyone who had at least two Jewish grandparents and ordering a census of the Jewish communities. Once identified as Jewish, business owners were required to post bilingual signs: *Jüdisches Geschäft* and *Entreprise Juive*: "Jewish business." The lettering was in black on a yellow background.

Most of the French treated their German occupiers with icy disdain. Signs appeared on lampposts and cemetery gates reading: "For Germans only." Referring to the weather in Russia—after the war there began going very badly for the German invaders—a few placards made a sardonic joke: "Frost—the best method against pests."

In the spring of 1941, few if any were joking. In May, the Paris police willingly cooperated with Nazi authorities in rounding up nearly 4,000 foreign-born Jews (most of whom were refugees from Germany and other occupied countries to the east) and herding them into a sports stadium. They were shipped on cattle trains to an internment camp in northeastern France. By the end of 1941, 30,000 more Jews had been "removed," all with the willing assistance of French authorities.

Under Philippe Pétain, the record of unoccupied Vichy France was equally shameful. In October 1940, the Vichy regime interned more than 7,000 Jews who had fled from Germany and Austria. They were hauled by train to camps in the Pyrenees where, during the winter of 1940-1941, about an eighth of them died of disease, starvation, or exposure.

It was just the beginning. In the spring of 1942, widespread deportation directly to the death camps in the east began. An order from Himmler of the SS stipulated that within three months France was to send 100,000 Jews to Auschwitz. French authorities in rural France did their best to comply. Most of the Jewish refugees, however, were in Paris, where, on the night of July 16, 1942, several thousand gendarmes fanned out through the darkened streets, tracking down Jews whose names and addresses had been established in the census. Police agents called the operation the *grande rafle,* the "clean sweep," but it is even better known as the *Rafle du Vel' d'Hiv*—the "Vel' d'Hiv Roundup," named after the *Vélodrome d'hiver,* the "Winter Velodrome," an indoor bicycle-race stadium where those arrested were initially confined.

From various sources, anonymous telephone calls, notes in mailboxes, and whispered warnings, many of the refugee Jews knew that the roundup was coming and were able slip out of the city. Others, seeing no alternative, committed suicide. Nevertheless, on the night of the *Rafle du Vel' d'Hiv* , the police arrested 12,884 Jews.

Fewer than 400 of those rounded up returned alive from the concentration camps. Of those arrested, 4,051 were children.

The Vichy regime did not last much longer. In November 1942, British, Canadian, and American forces under the leadership of General Dwight D. Eisenhower successfully invaded Morocco and Algeria. Although both had remained French colonies, Vichy had failed to defend them against the Allied attackers. To seal off the southern French coast from another such invasion, the Germans took over power in what had been Unoccupied France. Vichy now was a government in name only.

Thus Hitler completed his conquest of France. Not satisfied, he looked to the whole basin of the Mediterranean for further gains.

The Least You Need to Know

- For the conquering Nazis, Poland became a vast source of loot. They also turned Poland into a killing field.
- Denmark was spared the worst of what happened in Poland, partly because the Danes were seen as quasi-Aryan (unlike the Slavic Poles) and, even more, because the Nazis knew they needed the produce of Danish farms. The Danes, who had no anti-Semitic tradition, were able to mitigate the persecution of their Jewish citizens.
- Although various Dutch and Belgian Gentiles offered hiding places to the Jews, their efforts were not well organized. By 1942, the anti-Semitic terror in Holland and Belgium was widespread.
- The French collaboration with the Nazis was outright, voluntary, and on a large scale, both in Occupied and Unoccupied (Vichy) France. The tradition of French anti-Semitism was nearly as ingrained as it was in Germany.

Taking the War to Germany: 1941–1942

Despite the resounding victories in Scandinavia and Western Europe, Berlin greeted the New Year 1941 without much joy. On New Year's Eve, the German capital was nearly deserted. Instead of fireworks, searchlights scuttled across the black of the sky, scanning the heavens for signs of British bombers. Only a few buses were out in the snow-covered streets; their interior lights were turned off, and the top halves of their headlights were hooded with black. No street lights were turned on, and whatever parties took place did so behind shuttered windows. Berliners were experiencing what had become a nightly event: the blackout.

Retaliation Begins

The physical darkness paralleled the spiritual bleakness that had settled over the city. People felt depressed and anxious, not the least of them the foreign correspondents. "I vegetated on through the long black night of the second war winter," wrote Howard K. Smith, a young reporter with United Press (today United Press International, UPI) and later an esteemed television commentator. "I was losing my eagerness to see and learn in a tidal wave of despair. My lethargy was not unique. Already old names, long connected with news from Berlin, were disappearing for the simple reason that their owners were sick at heart. … The pressure that forced them, one by one, to desert Berlin, was finally christened with a name. Those of us who remained called it the 'Berlin Blues.' The name stuck, to describe those awful pits of gloom each of us fell into with periodic regularity, and which grew more severe as the war wore on."

One of those who left was William L. Shirer, the American reporter who had chronicled first-hand the rise of the Nazi regime. (See Chapter 17 for more information.) He had left just before the New Year. Once he was well away from the Reich, Shirer lashed out against "the Nazi blight and the hatred and the fraud and the political gangsterism and the murder and the massacre and the incredible intolerance and all the suffering and the starving and the cold and the thud of a bomb blowing the people in a house to pieces, the thud of all the bombs blasting man's hope and decency."

But now the bombs were starting to rain down on Germany itself, and the German people were in disbelief. After all, they had defeated France and occupied most of Western Europe. Hitler and his legion of propagandists had told the German people that all was well, that not only did the Reich rule much of the Continent, the nation was quite invulnerable to retaliation.

Yet the retaliation was a reality. At first, the people hardly dared to ask the question: Had Hitler lied?

The Bombing of Germany Commences

The Germans could not deny that they had set themselves up for revenge. After the failure of Germany's fighter planes to defeat the RAF in the Battle of Britain, Hermann Göring authorized a new phase of the air war, the massive and relentless bombing of Britain.

But that was far from his original intention. The first German air raid over England set out on the morning of August 24, 1940. It was a Saturday and for once the skies over southeastern England were clear and bright—"*Luftwaffe* weather," some Britons worried.

They were right to worry. By 9 A.M., more than 100 German bombers, protected by long-range *Messerschmidt* Bf 109 fighters, were up from their new air bases in France and over the English Channel, hitting a British RAF airfield near Dover first. Soon, the mass of bombers darkened the sky as the aircraft rumbled on toward London. Outside the British capital, they demolished two more RAF landing strips.

They had not yet hit London itself. Göring had strictly forbidden that step. Why? Nobody knows. Perhaps he fancied himself marching in triumph from an undamaged Buckingham Palace to the undamaged Houses of Parliament. Or, given the consequences of unrestricted submarine warfare in World War I—the entry of the United States into the fray—he feared that terror-bombing the British nation's capital would push the world too far. Possibly, Göring even foresaw that, far from demoralizing the British public, bombing of London would only serve to galvanize the people behind the war effort. When some of Göring's air commanders expressed pleasure over being given a crack at the British capital, Göring was aghast. "Would the people of Berlin capitulate under terror bombing?" he demanded. "I do not believe it. I cannot see the people of London pleading for mercy either." Hitler backed him up—at least at first.

But, on the night of August 24, two German bombers flew off course and, desperate to get back safely to their home bases, dropped their bombs to save fuel. They didn't realize that they were over London. London, after all, was living under a blackout. The bombing was an accident, as the German high command realized.

Did the British realize it, too? They did not act as if they did. For, the next night, August 25, RAF bombers unloaded over a Berlin suburb. With this, all restraint was gone.

"When the British declare that they will increase their attacks on our cities," Hitler told an audience, "then we will raze their cities to the ground. We will stop the handiwork of these night air pirates, so help us God! When the British air force drops 3,000 or 4,000 kilograms of bombs, then we will, in one raid, drop 300,000 or 400,000 kilograms. … In England they are filled with curiosity and keep asking: 'Why doesn't he come?' Be calm. Be calm. He is coming! He is coming! … The hour will come when one of us will break, and it will not be National Socialist Germany!"

The Nazis Bomb the Coventry Cathedral

Now it was London, not the RAF fields, that became the primary target for Nazi air raids. From September 7, 1940, to May 10, 1941, the Luftwaffe conducted what the British called "the Blitz," eight months and four days of air raids night and day, whenever the weather permitted. It was a horrific ordeal for the people of London, but ending the bombing campaign against RAF bases was a fatal German strategic error. As long as the RAF could fly, the German bombers would be shot out of the sky, and the British bombers would keep flying over Germany.

The damage to London, especially on its working-class East End, was appalling. The Germans focused on the London docks. They also targeted other English cities, mainly industrial towns. The single most shocking air raid was against Coventry, a manufacturing center about 100 miles northwest of London. During a 10-hour-long attack on the night of November 14, 1940, German bombers dropped hundreds of tons of bombs, killed more than 500 persons, and wounded another 800. The attack leveled some 100 acres of factories and homes—and it gutted the ancient cathedral at Coventry.

Coventry emerged as a symbol of British resilience and the desire for vengeance.

The resilience was apparent overnight. The vengeance took some time. For German bombers based in Belgium and northern France, skipping across the English Channel and dropping their bombs was relatively easy. British penetration into German air space was altogether another matter. London and Berlin are about 700 miles apart. Bombers guzzled gas, and fuel tanks were comparatively small. Navigational devices were rudimentary, and the German ground-based antiaircraft artillery was not only potent, but concentrated in France as well as Germany. Moreover, swift and maneuverable German fighter aircraft were based throughout occupied France, ready to shoot down the lumbering British bombers.

Despite the long odds, British engineers made remarkable technological strides. The development of radar, combined with the breaking of the German "Enigma" codes, enabled RAF fighters to shoot down many incoming Nazi bombers, while airborne radar and radio homing devices improved long-distance navigation for British bombers. Vastly improved bombsights enabled bombardiers to more accurately pick out strategic targets—such as factories and refineries—in Germany.

The British needed all the technology they could muster. They confined themselves to nighttime raids, since the exposure of daylight was just too hazardous. They also began to mount bigger and bigger raids. Although they still attempted to identify key industrial targets, the enlarged raids engaged in so-called carpet bombing, sowing huge amounts of ordnance on German cities, doing to Germany's civilian urban population what the perpetrators of the Blitz were doing to London and other English towns.

Throughout 1941, the British air attacks on Germany became more and more accurate; British bombers at one point, without destroying the factories, spread terror throughout the Ruhr Valley. Still, much of the British strategic bombing effort was hit or miss. Compelled to invest in pilots and aircraft to defend against *Luftwaffe* raids, the RAF lacked the resources to transform the RAF into a long-range bombing fleet.

Germany Declares War on the United States

The nation's circumstances began to change, however, just four days after aircraft of the Japanese Imperial Navy bombed Pearl Harbor, Hawaii Territory, on December 7, 1941. This was followed by a declaration of war on the United States by Japan's ally, Adolf Hitler.

Maybe this made sense. In the summer of 1941, the United States, still officially neutral in World War II, joined the British in the Battle of the Atlantic, helping to track down German submarines and even assisting the British in sinking the mighty German battle cruiser *Bismarck* on May 26-27, 1941. Washington also extended enormous financial and military assistance to Great Britain. The latter, a program called Lend Lease, swapped U.S. World War I-era destroyers to the Royal Navy in exchange for leases on British bases in the Caribbean, close to the United States. In a sense, then, Hitler's declaration of war may well have been neither more nor less than an acknowledgment of what was actually going on: a de facto alliance between Great Britain and the United States.

In the short run, the Japanese attack on Pearl Harbor was a devastating blow to the U.S. Pacific fleet, and the German declaration of war was terrifying. In longer, strategic terms, both moves spelled doom for Imperial Japan and Nazi German, and promised the salvation of Great Britain.

By the summer of 1942, U.S. pilots and air crews, as well as U.S. heavy bombers (mostly B-17 Flying Fortresses and B-24 Liberators) were swarming into RAF air bases in East Anglia. The American fliers and their aircraft brought a new strategy and a new confidence into the air war against Germany.

The strategy had to do with the American rejection of nighttime bombing in favor of daylight attacks. The British-based Eighth U.S. Air Force took the day shift, employing visual precision bombing to hit German strategic targets, while the RAF was left to continue the nighttime carpet bombing raids. Germany was being pounded day and night.

The American B-17s and B-24s were superior to anything the British could put in the air. Moreover, thanks to the manufacturing capacity of the United States, Boeing and Consolidated turned out B-17s and B-24s, respectively, in outrageous numbers: 12,731 B-17s and 19,256 B-24s by war's end. When he declared war on the United States, Adolf Hitler did not have a clue as to the kind of aircraft that Boeing, Consolidated, and other manufacturers were capable of making, let alone the speed and quantity with which they could make them.

Both major types of U.S. heavy bombers could fly higher than any British bomber and were far better armed. The typical U.S. "heavy" bristled with 10 .50-caliber machine guns, which made them formidable foes to incoming *Luftwaffe* fighters. The American bombers also carried the fabled and super-secret Norden bombsight, so accurate that, it was said, a bombardier could "drop a bomb in a pickle barrel" from 20,000 feet.

Such precision bombing, carried out in daytime, appealed to the American frontier pride in marksmanship. At first, the British resisted the hazardous daylight strategy, but soon saw its advantage. By mid-1942, American bombing raids over Germany were wreaking havoc with the industrial production of the Third Reich—albeit at heavy cost to Eighth Air Force crews, who alone suffered half of U.S. Army Air Force casualties in World War II: 47,000, including 26,000 killed.

BET YOU DIDN'T KNOW

The American air crews' swagger was expressed in "nose art," painted decorations on bomber fuselages, usually just below or slightly forward of the cockpit. The imagery was often in the style of the American "pin-up" magazines, including scantily clad women with such suggestive names as "Ima Vailable" and "Dinah Might." A lot of the British started complaining that the trouble with their Yank allies was that they were "overfed, oversexed, and over here."

Hitler and his followers in Nazi Germany had good reason to fear the effect of the Americans on the course of the war. Did Hitler begin to think that perhaps he had gone too far? Had he been less aggressive against Great Britain, would the United States have stayed out of the war? Was going so far as to declare war on the U.S. such a good idea after all?

Indeed, Hitler did vividly comprehend the consequences of yet another American intervention in a European world war. He had been afraid of it all along. Yet as if obsessed—and perhaps he was—he embarked next on a course of action that could not have been better calculated to ensure his own doom. He extended the war even farther.

Hitler Lays Out the Balkan Campaign

Hitler's attack on the Balkan peninsula stemmed from a lot of things. In 1940, his ally Mussolini had invaded Greece and Albania. *Il Duce*'s entry into the Hellenic peninsula, however, had led him to a swift defeat, and the Albanians were slowly but surely driving the Italians out. With the Italians in retreat, Great Britain was placing troops in Greece. (Throughout the nineteenth century, Greece had been a British protectorate, and the Greek and British royal families were united by blood.) With the British nearby, the Yugoslavs in turn were resisting German demands for cooperation that included trade concessions and cooperating with the Reich's anti-Semitic policies. Moreover, Yugoslavia had just undergone a palace coup. The pro-German regent, Prince Paul, had been replaced by the pro-British King Peter II.

Did Hitler believe that the British, under Churchill, were planning an attack on the German homeland from southeastern Europe? Churchill called the region Germany's "soft underbelly," and, back in World War I, when he was First Lord of the Admiralty, Churchill had launched the Gallipoli campaign in precisely this "underbelly" region. For the British, that effort had led to disaster; but the objective of getting at Germany from the south was not unreasonable. Hitler may have feared the same objective again.

There is an additional rationale for Hitler's Balkan attack. As early as the beginning of 1941, the Führer was laying plans for the invasion of the Soviet Union. This meant that a British-supported Greek-Yugoslav anti-German bloc was unacceptable, because it threatened the flank of his prospective drive toward the east. To Hitler, therefore, the Balkan threat had to be removed.

The German invasion of the Balkans began on April 6, 1941. Joining Germany in the assault were Hungary, Romania, and Bulgaria, all of which saw an opportunity to exploit German military power to increase their own holdings in the region. Besides, Hungary, Romania, and Bulgaria all had governments enthusiastic about Hitler's anti-Semitism. Murderous hate was hardly the exclusive province of Nazi Germany.

German-Occupied Europe

The invasion had a political as well as a military purpose. The largest state in the Balkans, Yugoslavia, was the last intact remnant of the Versailles Treaty. It had been part of the Allied-conceived *cordon sanitaire* (sanitary corridor) designed as a buffer against aggression in Eastern Europe. Like Czechoslovakia, it contained a host of ethnic groups, some of which were at odds with each other. In particular, the Serbs, living largely but not exclusively in the portion of Yugoslavia that had been

Serbia, tended to be Eastern Orthodox in religion. The Slovenes, living in the north along the border of Hungary, and the Croats, who were concentrated along the Adriatic coast, were Roman Catholic. Wanting to break away from the Yugoslav union and form an independent country, the Croats were strongly pro-Nazi.

The Germans gave the Croats what they wanted, the separate country of Croatia (which exists again now). With German support, the *Ustaše*, a Nazilike paramilitary Croat unit, carried out pogroms against local Jews and Serbs. In this way were sown the seeds of hatred that led to the Balkan wars of the 1990s.

Serbian Sentiments

The Germans had little difficulty overrunning the rest of Yugoslavia, and they did so with a vengeance. After the palace coup in Belgrade, which had taken place in the middle of March, the Serbian people had made clear where their sympathies lay. The new king was distinctly anti-German, and when he assumed the throne, crowds in the street shouted anti-Nazi slogans and even spat on the automobile of the German ambassador.

None of this meant that the Serbs were pro-Western. (Although those who staged the coup had had encouragement from an American named William "Wild Bill" Donovan, who became the director of the OSS [Office of Strategic Services] and the very first director of the CIA [Central Intelligence Agency].) In a way, what was going on was a replay of what had led to World War I. Serbia saw Hitler as the latest Austrian threat. Serbian sympathies, as in 1914, lay with Russia. The Serbs considered Hitler to be like the "mad counts of Vienna" in 1914: bent on crushing Serbia.

So, while the Croats attacked Serbs in their own territory, the Nazis went after Serbs and Jews in Serbia and Bosnia. Peter II, the new king of Yugoslavia, and the leading members of his cabinet fled the country, setting up a government-in-exile in London. Lesser members of the defunct government landed in Nazi prisons.

Then came the Jews. Of the 12,000 Jews who had lived in old Serbia, about two thirds were residents of Belgrade. Within a week of the German invasion, the Nazis began to register the Belgrade Jews, forcing them to wear the identifying Star of David. Next, following the usual pattern, the Nazis stripped them of their homes and businesses and proceeded to "Aryanize" Serbia. Jews were interned—Yugoslavia did not have concentration camps—or executed in mass shootings. By mid-November 1941, in Serbia, the Nazis had murdered 5,000 male Jews. In December, they rounded up most of the women and children and shot them to death, too.

A few Jews escaped the roundup. But, as in France, there were Serb collaborators, who willingly hunted down the Jewish survivors, turning them over to the Nazis. By the beginning of 1942, Yugoslavia no longer had a "Jewish problem."

Isolating Thrace

The German assault in the meantime had continued southward into Greece. The attack began on April 12, 1941; this time Italian and Bulgarian units joined the German attackers. Facing them were combined Greek and British forces.

Isolating Thrace—the part of Greece that extends over to Turkey and lies just below Bulgaria—the Germans and the Bulgarians started down the Aegean coastline. On the western side of the Balkan peninsula, the Italians and the Germans grabbed the Dalmatian coast, soon trapping much of the Greek army in Albania. In the center of Greece, the Germans took on the British (mostly units of Australians and New Zealanders), quickly forcing them into retreat toward Athens.

German bombers reached Athens early in the morning of April 26. At about 4 A.M., an American scholar working in an archeological institute in the Greek capital heard "a blast of ungodly sound and weird blue light. ... The whole southern sky flamed over Piraeus [the port by Athens], an unearthly brilliance that silhouetted the calm Parthenon to stark ghostly beauty. ... From neighboring houses came sounds of maids screaming, and the wild cries of a macaw. Nothing in all the sound effects of catastrophe in Hollywood films could match the crashing thunder, the crackling individual blasts under the greater roar, the howl of the dogs, and human shrieks."

Down in the harbor, all was madness. A British tanker, hit by German bombs, blazed away. The flames leaped to a British supply ship loaded with dynamite. A destroyer valiantly attempted to tow it away, but before it reached the breakwater, the supply ship exploded, obliterating the destroyer and shattering windows ashore a dozen miles away, in Athens. Refugees started to flee the city. The British government admitted that it could give Greece no more help. Soon, Greece surrendered, King George II fleeing for safety to Alexandria.

The Assault on Crete

Next came Crete, a mountainous, 160-mile-long island below Greece and Turkey at the southern extremity of the Aegean Sea. Crete served as a British naval and air base; it lay within striking distance of Romanian oil fields that Germany needed badly. For Göring, Crete offered a chance to regain a reputation largely lost in the failure of the Battle of Britain. The skies of the Mediterranean would give him another go at the British. And this time, he believed that he was assured of victory.

Thanks to ULTRA—the British decrypts of top-secret German military communications—British high command knew exactly what the Germans were planning and when. All the same, the British forces on Crete were too weak to defend the island, and the German assault came on the morning of May 20, 1941. Shortly after 6 A.M., a flight of *Stukas* appeared in the blue sky over the island. They dived, screamed, strafed, and bombed, just as they had over the mountains of Greece.

It got worse. From the ground, the British on Crete next saw contingents of large aircraft in mass formations. Many towed huge gliders, which looked like "young vultures following the parent bird from the roost." Suddenly, the sky was full of specks, most of them white, but some also red or green or black or yellow, floating to earth and looming ever larger. The Germans were landing both glider and parachute troops.

They hit the ground running, and by May 27, Crete was in German hands. Hitler's forces were now in a position to command the eastern end of the Mediterranean.

Like many Austrians and Germans, Hitler had a special reverence for classical antiquity. Accordingly, he ordered his forces in Greece and Crete to treat the Greeks with all due consideration.

Not so the Jews.

The ghastly Nazi pattern repeated itself. Throughout Greece, Jews were evicted from their homes, humiliated, and arrested. By July 1942, about 10,000 Greek Jews, rounded up for forced-labor battalions, died in malaria-infested swamps. At the same time, Jewish businesses were smashed or taken over.

Outwardly, as always, Nazi Germany was all-powerful. Beneath the efficient military surface, however, was the stench of anti-Semitism.

BET YOU DIDN'T KNOW

ULTRA was the special security classification the British gave to information gained from breaking the code of the standard German radio enciphering machine, called the ENIGMA. Just before the outbreak of the war in September 1939, Polish agents had given the British and the French reconstructed copies of the German machine. Just how the Poles got hold of an original machine is a mystery, even today. Nonetheless, believing their codes safe, the Germans persisted in using ENIGMA until the end of the war. This was a major blunder.

The Italians Surrender in the War in the Desert

In North Africa, the Germans were proving just as potent militarily as they had been in the Balkans. Ironically, however, North Africa would bring Hitler his second intimation of vulnerability.

Back on June 10, 1940, Italy had declared war on France and Great Britain. Mussolini had then given a speech from the marble balcony of his office in the *Palazzo Venezia* in Rome. After announcing the declaration of war, he exhorted the crowd gathered below: "Italian people! Rush to arms and show your tenacity, your courage, your valor!"

He wasn't sending troops to fight against the British on their home island. He wasn't that foolish. What he had in mind was the expansion of his own empire from Libya, already an Italian colony, eastward into Egypt, Somaliland, and Ethiopia, areas largely under British control. Because Great Britain was fighting for its life above the English Channel, Mussolini figured that the time was ripe for picking off British interests along the Suez Canal. For the Italians, descendants of the Roman Empire, this shouldn't be a problem.

On June 28, 1940, Mussolini issued orders for the invasion of Egypt. He called it the "great reward for which Italy is waiting." Preparations took most of the summer, but Mussolini kept telling his people, "We are a revived nation! We can fight!" Finally, on September 13, the Italians pushed out of Libya and into Egypt. They moved with five infantry divisions, seven tank battalions, and 80,000 troops—against 36,000 British troops in Egypt. Great odds. What they didn't realize was that they had embarked on the road to disaster.

At first the advance went well. In only four days, as they followed the Mediterranean coastline, the Italian legions reached Sidi Barrani, an oasis 60 miles into Egypt.

Here the British contested the advance, and things started going wrong for the Italians. Their troop-bearing trucks ran up against desert boulders and fell apart. The landscape was barren, the sun was broiling hot, and the food for the enlisted men went bad. The officers had a good enough time of it, since their own food was refrigerated, they had liters of wine, and they slept on clean sheets.

On December 9, 1940, both officers and men were hit by a manmade storm. Having built up their forces, the British counterattacked, converting the Italian advance into a retreat and the retreat into a rout. Chasing the Italians back across the desert, the British—mostly Australians, in fact—reached the Libyan port town of Tobruk on January 22, 1941. The Aussies overran the place, using captured Italian tanks painted with white kangaroos so that their comrades would not mistake them for the enemy.

At Tobruk, the Italians gave it up for good. Surrendering en masse, they boarded troop ships as prisoners of war. Disgusted by his ally's failure, Hitler decided to make his own run for the Suez Canal. He sent a full contingent of German tanks under the command of a distinguished officer who had emerged as one of the heroes of the attack on France, Lieutenant General Erwin Rommel.

Rommel Is Triumphant

A courtly officer of keen intelligence and tremendous energy, Rommel handled his desert tank corps with great tactical brilliance. His orders from Berlin had been to engage in defensive action only. By the time he reached Africa, however, he sensed that he could easily wage an offensive. So it was. On March 31, 1941, Rommel opened his first desert campaign, sweeping the British almost entirely out of Libya and back into Egypt. On June 21, 1942, he took back the Australian-held fortress at Tobruk. Next, he penetrated into Egypt much farther than the Italians had gone, to a way-station 50 miles west of Alexandria. It was called El Alamein.

Speaking to the House of Commons, Churchill paid Rommel a rare tribute: "We have a very daring and skillful opponent against us, and, may I say across the havoc of war, a great general."

Augmenting Rommel's reputation as a great general was the fact that, for once, the murderous SS didn't follow in the path of regular German army victories. Libya, of course, was a lightly populated country with very few Jews. Rommel's military successes were not marred by the usual Nazi atrocities.

Rommel, however, was far from perfect. Like many brilliant generals, he was arrogant. He also spent so much time on the front lines that he neglected the nitty gritty of any military campaign: the rear-echelon matter of logistics and supply.

Overextended across the hostile desert, Rommel's supply lines were getting choked. For Hitler and the general staff in Berlin, the building of air defenses around the German cities, the war in the Balkans, and the invasion of the Soviet Union (Chapter 21) took priority over North Africa. If the situation were ideal, Hitler would have given Rommel everything he needed to liberate Egypt from the British. But the situation was far from ideal—and getting farther every day. Germany's war resources were finite and dwindling. The Russian campaign had gone from triumphant to ruinous and was consuming more and more of Germany's capacity to wage war.

With American aid, the British in Egypt were building up their own supplies, preparing to meet Rommel at El Alamein. The new British commander in the theater was General Bernard Law Montgomery, soon to be known as Montgomery of Alamein.

Rommel Withdraws from El Alamein

Shortly after dusk on October 23, 1942, Monty—as his adoring men called him—launched an attack on the German forces at El Alamein. Although Rommel's troops were well dug in, the British hit with an overwhelming superiority of personnel and equipment.

The German commander knew he could not hold out. On November 2, 1942, he radioed Hitler, asking permission to withdraw. Hitler's response: "… there can be no other thought but to stand fast, yield not a yard of ground, and throw every gun and every man into the battle. … As to your troops, you can show them no other road than that to victory or death."

Although he was not a Nazi himself, Rommel had admired Hitler. The unthinking message quickly ended that admiration. What Rommel saw as the insanity of Hitler's order was the beginning of his greater disillusionment with the Führer. A lapse in the fanatical loyalty Hitler demanded of his generals, it would ultimately lead to Rommel's death.

In defiance of Hitler's command, Rommel withdrew from El Alamein. The British victory there marked the beginning of the end of the North African war. The outright downfall of Nazi Germany began with Hitler's invasion of the Soviet Union in the summer of 1941.

SUPPORTING ACTORS

After defeat in North Africa, Rommel was later stationed in France to fend off the expected American-British invasion. Again, however, he was not given the resources to do the job properly. By this point, he had come frankly to doubt Hitler's leadership.

The Least You Need to Know

- ⊘ From the start of the Balkan campaign to Rommel's push into the Egyptian desert, Nazi Germany enjoyed a considerable string of victories.

- ⊘ Even in Yugoslavia and Greece, the Nazis instituted their systematic efforts to destroy the local Jewish populations. In Yugoslavia, they had substantial help from the Catholic Croatians, who went after not only Jews but Serbs as well.

- ⊘ By this point in the war, Hitler had received two warnings—intimations of Germany's vulnerability. One was the start of the strategic air war against the German homeland. The other was the defeat of Germany's most respected general, Erwin Rommel, in North Africa. Had Hitler heeded the warnings, Nazi Germany might have survived—at least longer than it did. Instead, Hitler pushed on heedlessly.

Barbarossa: 1941–1943

By the middle of 1941, the European theater of war had settled into something of stalemate. The Germans were bombing Britain and the British were starting to bomb Germany. The Atlantic Ocean was the scene of significant naval fighting. German submarines were sinking thousands of tons of foodstuffs and other commodities bound for Great Britain, but the Royal Navy, with American assistance, was becoming increasingly successful in defeating the submarine menace—even though the United States had not yet entered the war officially.

The Consequences of Hitler's Invasion of the Soviet Union

It's easy to look back in hindsight and say that American entry into the war was inevitable. In mid-1941, however, America's entry into the conflict was far from certain. "America First" isolationists in Congress, the press, and elsewhere—the most famous of whom was Charles Lindbergh, the aviator—seemed to hold sway.

But then, in the summer of 1941, Hitler invaded the Soviet Union. As he did, an apparently unlikely thing happened. For almost a quarter of a century, the overwhelming majority of Americans—and the American government—had seen the Soviet Union as global public enemy number one. This remained true even with the rise of fascist Italy under Mussolini and Nazi Germany under Adolf Hitler. Stalin had the reputation of being the breaker of nations. With good reason, too. Even American Communists saw Stalin's entering into the 1939 pact with Hitler as an act of betrayal, and the Soviet invasions of Poland, the Baltic states, and Finland left just about any remaining U.S. sympathizers horrified.

Then Hitler invaded the Soviet Union and, almost overnight in the eyes of the American public, Stalin the butcher became kindly and heroic old "Uncle Joe," a beleaguered leader sticking up for his people. As American sympathy for the plight of the Russian people rose, so declined the influence of the isolationists.

Didn't Hitler realize the effect his attack on Russia would have on American public opinion? If he did, did he care? Was he so obsessed with the idea of *Lebensraum* that he could not grasp the consequences of his war with Russia? Or was there something else, too? Had Hitler trapped himself in his own mythic image as the Führer Invincible? Had he so accustomed the German people to victory that he could not resist going after yet another victory—his biggest so far?

These are old questions, and the answers are still probably anybody's guess. But one thing is certain: By the summer of 1941, Hitler's public image of omnipotence and omniscience had never been so visible to the people of Germany. Hitler's image, as expressed in paintings and sculpture, and mounted almost everywhere for the public to see, had never been more pompous.

Image-Making at Its Most Grandiose

Hitler as an art critic? Very much so. He knew what he liked and he foisted it—relentlessly—on the German public. He couldn't stand what we call modern art. The paintings of Van Gogh, Gauguin, Picasso, Chagall, and Modigliani (the last two of whom were Jewish) he condemned as decadent. With that judgment, down they came from museum walls. Hitler wanted the public to see nothing but heroically idealized paintings and monumental sculpture. Soon, all manner of representations of powerful Aryan men and nubile Aryan women went on display. Without artistic merit, these were, as Hitler saw things, propaganda gold.

Indeed, such art was so important to Hitler that he created a formal arts bureaucracy. Its function was to censor what the public saw. Those artists who met the Aryan criteria were showered with patronage, favorable criticism (Goebbels banned all negative criticism of Nazi art), and (best of all, perhaps) exemption from military service. As the party leadership saw it, the Nazi artists were performing a valuable national service already. The new art was intended to awaken Teutonic pride, turn that pride toward war, and, when the battle came, sustain the spirit of German nationalism.

Josef Goebbels at a microphone.
(Eric Stevens)

The art that Hitler loved the most was devoted to the subject of himself. In a studio filled with heroic statuary and busts of Nazi notables, a sculptor named Josef Thorak created a Hitler head, many times life size, looking determined, even-featured, and indeed quite handsome.

Hitler found all this intoxicating. His artistic ambitions frustrated in youth, Hitler was now the very *subject* of art. The allure of the sculptures and such led him to believe in his own heroic myth.

It was a trap. For, to sustain the myth he needed to sustain the forward momentum of idealized Nazi heroism. If he stopped conquering, Nazi Germany would stagnate, inertia would set in, and, soon, his personal popularity and the support of the German masses for the Nazi regime would fade.

In a very real sense, Hitler had ceased to be a person and had become the Führer, exalted above mere humankind. To remain the Führer, he had to lead. Otherwise he might find himself reliving his humiliating days in Vienna—or worse.

In that spirit, in July 1941, Hitler launched his biggest campaign ever: an invasion of the Soviet Union. He called it "Operation Barbarossa."

TERMS AND TRANSLATIONS

In Italian, **Barbarossa** means "Red Beard." It was the name given to a Greek-born Turkish pirate of the mid-sixteenth century who raided Spanish ports and shipping, captured Algiers, Tunis, and Nice, and for three or four years ruled the Mediterranean. As a code name, Operation Barbarossa was obviously intended to deceive the Soviets about the imminence of the attack. Like America's own military code names, such as Operation Just Cause and Desert Storm, it was also supposed to inspire the troops to victory. The choice of this particular designation, however, contained a startling irony: the original Barbarossa's rule in the Mediterranean was short-lived indeed.

The Nazi Attack on the Soviet Union

Winter hung on late in Russia in 1941, at least in Moscow and Leningrad. Snow was on the ground on May Day, and the chilly fogs were still rolling in from the shores of the Baltic well into June. Even the summer carried the promise of winter again, for late June was unseasonably cool. Despite these omens, Hitler plunged ahead.

Operation Barbarossa, Hitler's scheme for the betrayal and rapid defeat of Russia, started off in grand style. From a series of points along the borders of Poland and East Prussia, a massive force of three million soldiers, riding everything they could climb on, from *Panzers* and armored cars to motorcycles, bicycles, and horses, swarmed into the Soviet Union in what proved to be history's largest military assault. The attack went swimmingly, in some cases almost literally. At some points, German soldiers waded across streams in Lithuania, Byelorussia, and the Ukraine.

German engineers threw up pontoon bridges as fast as they could, enabling the infantry to cover as many as 30 miles a day. The *Panzers* moved even faster. By sundown on the first day, June 22, 1941, German armored units had penetrated more than 50 miles into the vastness of the Soviet Union.

The advance was so swift and so sudden—Stalin and the top officials of the Soviet Union had ignored intelligence warnings of the impending assault—that at one point a German motorcycle unit startled a group of Soviet recruits who were just learning to march. The pace was exhausting. But as in the great triumph the year before in the Low Countries and France, General Heinz Guderian stood high in the turret of his tank and urged his forces ever onward.

By July 10, thousands of Russian troops were dead or prisoners of war. German armored units were approaching Smolensk, more than 300 miles into the Soviet Union.

Even General Franz Halder, the German chief of staff and a man by nature cautious, was ready to celebrate. He had doubted the wisdom of taking on the Soviet Union, with its vast terrain and brutal winters. "It is probably no overstatement," he now however wrote in his diary, "to say that the Russian campaign has been won in the space of two weeks."

Map showing the German advances into the Soviet Union.

The Early Successes

Unfortunately, as seen from Halder's point of view, Russia was an underdeveloped country. The farther the German columns penetrated eastward into the countryside, the worse the roads became—if roads even existed. Maps soon proved almost useless. Moreover, Russia spread eastward like an enormous funnel. The Germans had begun their advance in three coordinated columns. The farther they ranged ahead, however, the farther apart they had to spread. And the farther apart they spread, the more the Russians were able to mount effective resistance, often in the form of guerrilla bands operating from hiding in the fields, marshes, and forests that lay between sparsely populated villages and a few great cities.

And those guerrillas were fighting unfairly, or so went the German lament. The Russians were breaking the rules of war, using what German commanders denounced as "Asiatic tricks." They would lie on the ground pretending to be dead, then leap up and shoot at the soldiers passing over them. Or they would wave white flags of surrender, then fire at those coming to capture them.

The German troops heard such tales up and down the Russian front. In response, many of them murdered Russians who were genuinely trying to surrender or who were already prisoners. Atrocities raged back and forth. "Our ranks got thinner every day," recalled a German colonel who led a regiment into Ukraine. "Numberless cemeteries full of our dead appeared along our route."

Impoverished and disorganized, though, the Russian guerrillas could not stop the German juggernaut. The regular Russian army—the Red Army—was nearly as impotent. The German strategy was to direct the northernmost of its three columns up through the Baltic states toward Leningrad (today St. Petersburg); the column in the middle was to head past Bialystok, Minsk, and Smolensk toward Moscow; and the third was to penetrate the Ukraine, moving toward Kiev.

Germany Takes Ukraine

In passing through Ukraine (where at first the Ukrainian population welcomed the Germans as liberators from Stalin and other Soviet oppressors), this third column on June 30 cut off three Russian armies. Some of Hitler's commanders in the field wanted to take Kiev, the Ukrainian capital, but he decided otherwise. Bypassing the city, therefore, the German forces pushed on to the Dnieper River that flowed into the Black Sea. Ukraine was now under Hitler's control.

Or at least that is what Hitler's general told him. In fact, no sooner had the Nazis arrived than the Ukrainians set up their own government, separate from that of the Soviet Union. Five days later, the SS knocked it over and jailed its members. In Berlin, Hitler carved Ukraine into four pieces.

The southern hunk he gave to Romania, one of his Eastern European allies; another piece he turned over to Nazi authorities in Occupied Poland. The other two parts fell under the direct control of the *Wehrmacht,* the German army.

Sent to administer these latter two parts of Ukraine, Erich Koch, a Nazi bureaucrat, boasted to his assistants: "I am known as a brutal dog. For this reason I was appointed *Reichskommissar* [regime leader] of the Ukraine. I am expecting from you the utmost severity toward the native population."

Koch's aides took him at his word. To encourage the spread of disease, they tore up sewers and other sanitary facilities. They stopped the shipment of food to hungry areas. And they sent away inhabitants for slave labor in Germany. From Kiev alone, 38,000 Ukrainians were sent off in cattle cars.

"There is no Ukraine," Koch declared. "We are the master race!"

Collaborationist Ukrainians accepted his doctrine, joining the Germans in the murder of Jews. One of the worst massacres of World War II took place at Babi Yar, a large gully near Kiev. In two days in September 1941, more than 35,000 Soviet prisoners, Ukrainian partisans, and Jews were executed—their bodies dumped into a mass grave.

BET YOU DIDN'T KNOW

Although their languages are similar and they share a common history, Russians and Ukrainians are not the same people. There is a Ukrainian museum in Toronto that shows graphically Ukrainian suffering at the hands of the Russians. So, when the Germans showed up, the Ukrainians at first thought they had the promise of liberation.

Russia Retreats

Operation Barbarossa was an astounding success so far. In only two months of fighting, the Germans had cost the Russians nearly two million men, dead or wounded. Germany controlled a swath of Soviet territory that was almost 500 miles wide. Up along the Baltic, the Germans had pushed to within 100 miles of Leningrad. In Ukraine, they had overrun half the region, were on the Dnieper, and were ready to advance to the industrialized areas beyond the far bank of the river. And in the central zone, the German forces were only 200 miles from Moscow.

At this point, all the Russians could do was retreat, trading territory for time, or so they hoped. Stalin was prepared to evacuate Moscow.

This was at the end of August 1941. In Russia, winter comes early and stays long. But not usually this early. In this last full month of summer, the nights were turning quite chilly. The German commanders in the field knew that they had to move fast, before the season set in and the winter left them immobilized for months. So, General Guderian, in command of the middle column, believed that he had to strike immediately toward Moscow. Once Moscow fell, he believed, Russia would surrender, and Nazi Germany would have won its greatest victory ever.

Then Hitler intervened.

MEMORABLE PLACES

In Wolf's Lair, a forest shelter complex that served Hitler as a forward headquarters, General Halder kept talking about Moscow. But Hitler would not be dissuaded. "The Führer right now is not interested in Moscow," Halder told aides. "All he cares about is Leningrad."

Conflict over Goals

To the German commanders on the ground, it seemed so easy: Push on just a few days more, take Moscow, and the war on the eastern front would be over. Ordinary soldiers agreed. As they moved east of Smolensk, German troops pounded hand-painted markers along the roadsides. They read "To Moscow."

But Hitler refused to go that way. Perhaps he realized that exactly 129 years before he launched his attack on the Soviet Union, Napoleon had also marched to Moscow—and captured it. But it proved a hollow victory. Napoleon found a mostly deserted city, and he gained no real leverage over the czar. There was no Russian surrender. Instead, Napoleon suffered a fatal overextension of his supply lines and, with this, ultimate defeat in a brutal Russian winter. Perhaps Hitler feared the same fate.

Whatever his reasons, however, Hitler was adamant about his change of plans. Back in July, he had given orders for the infantry to march to Moscow. Now, as August gave way to September, he split the central column in two. Half of the units, commanded by Guderian, headed for Ukraine. "This means that my *Panzer* Group would be advancing in a southwesterly direction," Guderian complained to his diary, "that is to say toward Germany."

The other half of the central column, led by General Hermann Hoth, was to head for the Baltic. There it was to help the northernmost column in the capture of Leningrad.

The Siege of Leningrad

Built in the early eighteenth century by Peter the Great as a Baltic port and as what he called his "window to the West," Saint Petersburg—under Soviet rule called Leningrad—was known as the Venice of the North. Bridges arched its many canals, waterways separating the numerous islands on which the town was constructed. Facing one another over the Neva River were the cathedral-fortress of Saints Peter and Paul and the graceful spire of the Admiralty Building.

In World War II, Leningrad was a city of great beauty and great vulnerability. The Soviet armies had retreated eastward in a gigantic contracting semicircle, leaving Leningrad exposed to attacks from three sides. The Finns (who, eager to avenge the Winter War, had aligned themselves with Hitler) were poised to attack overland from the northwest. The German *Kriegsmarine* (navy) was poised to sail across the Baltic and attack from the sea. And the invading German columns were marching overland from the west and the south. Only Lake Ladoga, on the outskirts of the city's east side, offered Leningraders any hope of escape by evacuation.

On September 4, 1941, Joseph Stalin cabled Winston Churchill that the Germans were close to Leningrad. He withheld the more alarming information that the enemy now controlled the rail lines and had cut off communication between Moscow and Leningrad. He also failed to mention that he was on the verge of surrendering Moscow.

What saved Leningrad—if a salvation it was—was the determination of the local Red Army commanders and the citizens of the city to simply hang on. In the end, Hitler never captured Leningrad, but for some 900 days his army laid intensive siege to the city while subjecting it to continual bombing and artillery barrage. Food supplies were all but completely cut off. Once emergency reserves were exhausted, Leningrad sustained itself—barely—by shipping supplies over Lake Ladoga. When winter set in and the lake froze, sleds and trucks were driven across the ice. It did not take the Germans long to identify the supply route, which they bombed continually.

The flow of supplies dwindled to a trickle. Soviet authorities enforced strict food rationing. Those violators who were not summarily shot were sent to the front to work in Red Army labor units.

The rationing did little good. Starvation and the Russian winter set in at about the same time. Throughout the long, dark, cold months, Leningraders died by the thousands, often collapsing where they stood. The streets and public squares were heaped with corpses. A total of 632,000 Leningraders died during the siege, 4,000 on Christmas Day 1941 alone.

The wonder is that Hitler's troops did not simply take the dying city, which surely presented an even less resistant objective than Warsaw had been. Historians have been torn between assigning two different motives. Either the Wehrmacht was overstretched here, or perhaps the commanders were engaged in a war of terror. Even more than possession of the city, they may have wanted to inflict horrendous suffering on the Russian people.

Sadism on a mass scale was part of the Nazi military's stock in trade. Following close behind the invading Wehrmacht forces throughout the Soviet front was the notorious SS *Einsatzgruppen* ("inserted groups"). Their explicit task was the extermination of hundreds of thousands of Jews and other so-called enemies of the Nazi state.

The Masters of Death

The *Einsatz* operation defies even the most brutal of imaginations. Yet it really happened. The first phase of the plan, opened at the same time as the German invasion of the Soviet Union, called upon the *Einsatzgruppen* to slaughter the Jews of the Soviet Union. Between 1941 and 1943, these executioners murdered *en masse* some 1.5 million Jews. Their usual method was to round up a group of victims, force them to dig a long trench, line them up with their backs toward the trench, and then shoot them down. Their bodies fell into the trench, which made a convenient mass grave.

The Russian *Einsatz* operation was a prelude to the second phase of the Nazi plan of "racial" extermination. Unleashed in December 1941, this operation targeted Jews in the occupied countries of Western Europe.

An operation of this size needed support. We now know that, in addition to the "ordinary soldiers" and SS men who carried out the mass murders, the Berlin government recruited economists, architects, and lawyers—pillars of the German community—to lend their expertise to various aspects of what quickly evolved into the Holocaust.

To the Gates of Stalingrad

As expected, the howling winds and deep snowfalls of the Russian winter of 1941–1942 stopped the German advance and exacted a terrible toll of suffering, privation, and death on German invaders. The coming of spring provided warmth, but it was, if anything, even more lethal to a massive army on the move. What had been ice and snow melted, churning the vast Russian landscape into a glutinous mud that made movement impossible. Add to this the spring freshets that caused the many rivers of Russia to overtop their banks in floods of Old Testament proportions.

Summertime allowed the Germans to move forward again. The invading force was much reduced, but still very large. Intending to finish the Russians off, the Nazis drove hard toward the southeast, moving beyond the Black Sea and advancing to the Volga River. There, a good 1,000 miles from the borders of the Third Reich, they reached a city called Tsaritsyn before the Soviet era and then named after Stalin—Stalingrad. (In 1961, it changed names again, becoming Volgograd.)

Stalingrad—that name made it an all the more appealing target for Hitler. By the same token, Stalin was moved to order his namesake defended to the death. The German plan was a classic pincers attack, with columns converging from two directions. The offensive was scheduled to start on August 23, 1942, and it began well. Then the German Sixth Army encountered remarkably heavy resistance. They were held on the outskirts of the city in a pitched battle and resorted to bombarding the Red Army until Stalingrad was almost completely leveled. Once finally inside Stalingrad, the Germans soon discovered they had laid claim to a ruin and were about to be caught in a trap.

During November 19-23, 1942, the Soviets conducted Operation Uranus, which led to the encirclement of the entire German Sixth Army inside the city it had captured. The enemy that laid siege to Leningrad was now about to suffer its own siege. This would be bad for the Sixth Army, and it would be bad for the Third Reich. The Battle of Stalingrad was the first a major turning point of World War II in Europe and the beginning of the end for Nazi Germany.

The Least You Need to Know

- ✪ Increasingly megalomaniacal, Adolf Hitler believed that his judgment could never fail—hence the invasion of the Soviet Union.
- ✪ At the outset, the invasion went so well that most foreign reporters predicted the quick collapse and surrender of the Soviet Union.
- ✪ The Germans inflicted unimaginable suffering on the Soviet people, suffering that was neither explicable nor justifiable by any military motive. As for the Jews of the Soviet Union, the Nazi program of anti-Semitic persecution was now a campaign of outright genocide.
- ✪ German forces occupied Stalingrad, only to be encircled in the Battle and Siege of Stalingrad in 1942-1943, one of World War II's epic battles and the turning point of the war in the east.

PART 5

The Decline and Fall of Nazi Germany

For Hitler and Nazi Germany, the invasion of the Soviet Union was the beginning of the end. To put it in terms of Greek tragedy, it laid bare the regime's fatal flaw: hubris. The product of a vast overextension of resources, the invasion of Russia weakened Germany enough in the occupied countries to allow the rise of serious resistance. It revealed that Germany simply lacked the material and manpower to fend off a U.S.-led Allied landing in France and drive to the Rhine. Moreover, Hitler and his henchmen continuously diverted badly needed military personnel from the combat fronts to bring the Holocaust to its hideous climax.

In the end, the once apparently invincible Nazi military machine was unable to prevent the destruction of Germany. Germany's surrender, when it came, was the bitter fruit of total defeat, as you'll see in the following chapters.

From Conquest to Decline: 1943

It may be hard to do, but for the moment put aside the criminality of Adolf Hitler and his regime and look instead at what has happened so far from an international perspective. Among the things that fueled Nazi Germany's drive for dominance of the European continent was a national sentiment of resentment. Almost to a person, whether Nazi or not, Germans had felt maligned by the Treaty of Versailles and vehemently denied the treaty's allegation that Germany had been the sole cause of World War I. By the end of 1942, they had punished their accusers—the British, the French, and the Russians. To many, Germany appeared to be the master of Europe.

The Fragility of Nazi Triumph, 1942-1943

Almost throughout Hitler's rise to power, Great Britain had contested the Nazi bid for mastery. As we have seen, the notion that Britain under Prime Minister Chamberlain ignominiously appeased Hitler is mostly a distortion and a myth. Appeasement was a bid to gain time for British rearmament. When Britain and France drew the line at the German invasion of Poland in September 1939 and declared war, both nations were better prepared militarily than they had been even a year or two earlier. Nevertheless, the British were deceiving themselves if they believed they could stop Hitler on the European continent.

Soon, Britain was the sole European democracy standing, and while the English Channel was a barrier against a Nazi invasion, it would not stop *Luftwaffe* air raids, and it would not help Britain put together an effective counteroffensive on the Continent. Prime Minister Winston Churchill understood that securing victory against Germany would require doing everything possible to bring the United States into the war—even if this meant relinquishing the UK's once unquestioned lead voice in international affairs.

In any case, Hitler's Germany was on the make. By the end of 1942, Germany seemed to have replaced Great Britain as the world's leading power. Appearances can be deceiving, however, and the Nazi invasion of the Soviet Union was turning out to be an action that was ensuring an equal and opposite reaction.

Slowly, in response to the Nazi onslaught, the Red Army retreated, and then regrouped, and then avenged the Mother Land. Stalingrad marked the ultimate extension of Nazi power into the Soviet Union. When the Germans were defeated there, the Russians came howling after them like wolves out of the Siberian forest.

In the end, Great Britain and Nazi Germany had something in common. They were both like aging racehorses who suddenly could not keep up the pace. The Anglo–German contest for the mastery of Europe gave way to the division of that continent between the new steeds, the United States and the Soviet Union.

Stalingrad and the German Retreat

"My Führer," asked General Heinz Guderian, the tank commander, "why do you want us to attack on the East at all this year?"

"You are quite right," Hitler answered. "Whenever I think of this attack, my stomach turns over!"

The brutal Russian winter of 1942-1943 at last yielded to spring, and all along an Eastern Front that stretched the nearly 2,000 miles, from Leningrad to the eastern part of the Black Sea, the Germans were experiencing a terrible foreboding. By the start of February 1943, the Germans had lost the crucial battle of Stalingrad. Combat had fallen into two phases: the German attack and occupation of the city, which had lasted from August to November 1942, followed by the Soviet counteroffensive, which began in mid-November and ended with the surrender of the German Sixth Army on February 2, 1943.

Most of Stalingrad lay on the west bank of the Volga River. Friedrich Paulus, the German general in charge of the offensive, believed that once he could cross the river, the Soviets would be finished. His strategy had called for his infantry and light armored units to approach the city from the northwest with a *Panzer*—heavy armor—army moving in from the southwest. The city was supposed to fall quickly. To Paulus's chagrin, the Red Army held the Nazi pincers apart. The Germans did not reach even the city outskirts until September 1942. Throughout that month and all October, a German bombardment completely destroyed Stalingrad. In November, the Germans had entered an almost wholly deserted city. As the ancient Caledonian chieftain Calgacus reportedly said of the Roman victory at the Battle of Mons Graupius in northern Scotland in A.D. 83 or 84, "They make a desert and call it peace." The fruit of Nazi triumph was very often desolation.

For the Nazis, it would prove even worse than desolation. Red Army commander Marshal Georgi Zhukov sent two Soviet columns across the ice of the Volga River, closing in on the Sixth Army occupiers of the ruins of Stalingrad from the north and the south. The besiegers were besieged. Trapped inside the devastated city, General Paulus appealed to Hitler for permission to surrender. Hitler refused, and Paulus obeyed. Fighting through the snow, the Soviets forced their own way back into the city, destroying the Sixth Army and taking 400,000 German soldiers prisoner. Only 5,000 of them would survive captivity.

BET YOU DIDN'T KNOW

Conditions in the Soviet prisoner of war camps had been brutal. In 1955, when the Soviets finally released those still imprisoned, the German survivors numbered no more than 5,000.

Hitler's Strength Wanes

Stalingrad sapped the *Wehrmacht* in the east both figuratively and literally. Morale collapsed—and was sometimes enforced in the armies of the Western Front by threats that any lack of enthusiasm would be rewarded by a transfer to the Eastern Front, which had become synonymous with doom. There was every reason for the prevailing crisis of confidence. The eastern armies were significantly diminished—the entire Sixth Army had ceased to exist—and yet the Red Army was continually growing in manpower and combat effectiveness. Little wonder that Hitler, in conversation with General Guderian in the spring of 1943, confessed to nausea.

His problems, of course, were much more serious than a bellyache. His prestige both at home and among his European allies demanded a show of strength and a demonstration of triumph. Yet the strength and will of his military machine were oozing away. This fact was becoming obvious through-out the network of Nazi allies. Mussolini had begun looking for a way out of the war. Romania's

Marshal Ian Antonescu and Hungary's Admiral Miklos Horthy, the fascist dictators of their respective small countries, were hoping to make contact with America and Great Britain. They wanted to negotiate a separate peace, along with protection from both Hitler (their ally) and Stalin (their enemy).

At home, Hitler's support was also starting to erode. The availability of the most basic consumer goods and services was rapidly drying up. Boys as young as 16 and men as old as 65 were being called up for military duty. Women between the ages of 17 and 50 had to work in the munitions plants. Under the leadership of Albert Speer, war production increased. He doubled the output of airplanes and tanks and tripled that of artillery. But he did so at the cost of multiplying slave labor and of looting and stripping the civilian economy. Discontent was growing.

Realizing that he could no longer attain victory over the Soviet Union, and yet needing that victory for political and personal reasons, Hitler proposed a compromise. Throughout his career, he had been an unyielding extremist. Now he sought a middle way. On March 13, 1943, the Führer told his top generals, "It is important for us to take the initiative at certain sectors of the front if possible before the Russians do, so as to be able to dictate their actions in at least one sector."

Gathered around Hitler in the Wolf's Lair encampment in East Prussia, Hitler's generals pored over their maps. Where, they asked each other, could they find a spot to fight a battle and be reasonably sure of victory? After much deliberation, they came up with the Soviet city of Kursk.

Outsmarted at Kursk

Kursk was not far from the Don River border between Ukraine and Russia. It was far from Moscow, which lay to the north, and far from Stalingrad, to the southeast. In fact, it had no inherent value either to Germany or Russia. But it happened to be situated in the middle of a salient—a bulge—Red Army had punched into the German lines. A salient is dangerous for two reasons. First, it is a well-supplied position from which the enemy may attack in at least three directions, and thereby outflank one's position. Second, as an encroachment into your territory, a salient represents a terrible psychological threat. Hitler and his generals reasoned that, if they could take Kursk, they could at least drive the Soviets back and straighten out the front. At the very least, this might transform a losing campaign into a stalemate.

Some historians dispute the numbers, but it is generally believed that the Battle of Kursk was the largest armored fight in history. It was fought in two phases, the German offensive spanning July 5-16, 1943, and the Soviet offensive extending from July 12 to August 23 of that year. The Germans went into the battle with nearly a million troops, 2,700 tanks and assault guns, 10,000 heavy artillery weapons, and 2,000 aircraft. Absolutely confident of victory, Hitler ordered the offensive, code-named *Zitadelle* (Citadel), to start on July 5.

It began with every promise of victory. As in the early days of the war, the German armies gobbled up the land—but there was an incredible expanse of land to gobble. The vast Russian steppe that formed the battlefield was far greater than anything encountered in Holland or Belgium.

The Soviets' Marshal Zhukov took advantage of the vast space for maneuvering. He let the Germans advance while he carefully prepared a counterattack. Unaccountably, German military intelligence, among the best in the world, broke down. Hitler's generals assumed they had the superior numbers. They did not suspect the truth: that the Red Army here had somewhat more than a million men, and, even more important, substantially outgunned the Germans. Against 2,700 tanks, Zhukov mounted more than 3,300 tanks and armored vehicles. Against 10,000 heavy artillery pieces, Zhukov had 20,000. Where the Germans could launch 2,000 aircraft, the Russians had nearly 3,000.

And numbers weren't the whole story. Zhukov ringed Kursk with six concentric defensive belts encompassing some 6,000 miles of trenches. Moreover, between the circles of trench was a total of some 22,400 antitank mines.

It was a build-up of hardware that the Germans could not have imagined. They had failed to account for the huge volume of U.S.-supplied equipment that poured into Russia via the southern ports. German intelligence also failed to notice that Stalin had ordered most of the great Soviet war plants to be evacuated from the west and moved east of the Ural Mountains, in Siberia, far out of Hitler's reach. Remote though this made them from the front, the factories were very close to sources of the iron ore and steel-making facilities necessary to turning out weapons in massive quantities. What is more, while the Nazis exploited slave labor, the Soviets appealed to patriotism, which drove the free Russians to work much harder in the desperate defense of their homeland than slaves ever would. In addition to spirit, the Russian commanders possessed largeness of vision. They extended rail lines into the salient and brought in some half-million carloads of supplies. They transformed Kursk into a vast citadel.

In the opening of the attack, the Germans advanced some 30 miles into the salient; however, it was so large that they had another 100 miles to go before they could choke the Russian position off. In a series of tank duels—supported by fighter and fighter-bomber attacks from the air—Zhukov effectively tied off the eastern end of the salient, holding the Germans within the 30 miles into which they had advanced. It was a case of quite literally bagging the enemy. At the end of the first phase, the Germans had lost 70,000 men killed, along with virtually all of their *Panzer* tanks, more than 800 heavy guns, nearly 1,400 aircraft were shot down, and 5,000 motor vehicles were destroyed or captured. The next step for the Russians was the phase two offensive, which defeated the Germans who were struggling to hold onto the towns of Orel and Belgorod. Red Army casualties were heavy, with at least 160,000 killed or wounded. But Hitler had lost his war with Russia—and, ultimately, that meant he was doomed to lose the war in the West as well.

Rommel's Expulsion from North Africa

The fate of the Germans in North Africa was also turning dark by late 1942. After the Second Battle of El Alamein (October 23-November 11, 1942), General Erwin Rommel's *Afrika Korps* began a dismal retreat toward Tunis. Rommel knew full well that he could not hold on any longer. As in Russia, Hitler refused to allow retreat, yet he made no provision for resupplying his forces in the desert with fuel, transport, and reinforcements. Short of everything needful, Rommel confronted the British out of Egypt (freshly supplied by the United States) and the U.S. forces crossing Morocco and Algeria. These two allies squeezed Rommel in an ever-tightening grip. By the time the German Sixth Army was under siege at Stalingrad, Rommel's North Africa campaign was over. The general and many of his top aides managed to escape Allied capture, but by early 1943, nearly 300,000 Germans and Italians in North Africa had surrendered to British and American forces.

What had gone wrong for the Germans in North Africa? And why had Hitler sent them there in the first place? After all, Nazi Germany had no vital interest in the region. Hitler's plans for the acquisition of *Lebensraum* was centered in Europe. But perhaps he saw in North Africa a road to Egypt and the British colonies east of Suez. Yet, surely, Greece and Crete would have afforded far better and easier jumping-off points to fight the British for their Egyptian possessions.

Ultimately, the only plausible explanation for Hitler spreading his forces thin by venturing into North Africa was his desire to support his ally Mussolini. It is understandable to want an ally, but Mussolini's military was so singularly inept that one is tempted to ask: With allies like these, who needs enemies? Indeed, the Italian dictator had refrained from joining Hitler's war until he saw that the Germans were certain to defeat France. He joined arms with Hitler to pick up his scraps. If Hitler was now placing his faith in Mussolini as a military asset, he was revealing himself as tragically naïve.

The North Africa campaign, like Operation Barbarossa in Russia, succeeded in bringing nothing but loss and suffering to all combatants and, in the process, stretching Germany's resources beyond their limits. Perhaps believing his own mythology, perhaps convinced that he was indeed a man of destiny, Adolf Hitler had made the mistake fatal to so many of history's tyrants. He pursued infinite goals with finite resources. In so doing, he left Germany vulnerable to attack from the south, from Sicily up through Italy, a country that by 1942 was virtually a German colony.

The Allied Invasion of Sicily and Italy

When the Americans and British landed on the southern coast of Sicily in mid-July 1943, a combined German–Italian force at first put up a vigorous resistance. It soon crumbled. Even so, roughly 230,000 defenders, mostly Italian, were still on the island, and General Dwight D. Eisenhower, Supreme Allied Commander in Europe, was determined that these troops not be allowed to escape to the mainland, where they would be available for future battle. Ike, as Eisenhower was familiarly called, sent forces under British General Bernard Law Montgomery—Montgomery of El Alamein—along with U.S. Major General George S. Patton Jr., on a mission to take Messina, only three miles from the toe of Italy. The objective was to capture and hold Messina to cut off the Italian-German escape route to the mainland. The race was on—and while it was ostensibly a race to take Messina before the enemy, Monty and Patton, intense rivals, were also racing one another.

In the end, the Allies rounded up most of the Italians, but the German commanders succeeded in moving almost all of their personnel and equipment across the strait to Italy. At the beginning of

September, the Allies invaded Sardinia and Corsica before landing on the Italian peninsula itself—on the toe of the famous boot from Sicily; on the shinbone at Salerno from Sicily and North Africa; the heel at Taranto from Bizerte, Tunisia. On October 1, 1943, the Americans entered the port of Naples and the British, having crossed the peninsula on the east, overwhelmed the German airfields at Foggia. On November 8, Eisenhower ordered the assault on Rome.

At the same time, the Soviets had pushed beyond Kiev along the Dnieper River. The city of Smolensk, near the border of Latvia and Lithuania, was about to fall to the Red Army.

In both Russia and Italy, the Germans continued to put up fierce and shockingly effective resistance—in Italy, taking a great toll on both the British and Americans. The mountainous terrain of Italy was better suited to the German fighting style than the vast Russian steppes. In Italy, there was plenty of opportunity for digging in and creating formidable defensive positions. From November 1943 until very nearly the end of the war, the Allies fought their way up the Italian peninsula. The taking of Rome on June 4, 1944—an event overshadowed by the Allied D-Day Landings on Normandy two days later—was a bright spot in the grim campaign, but the fighting continued to exact a heavy cost on both sides until the end of the war. Still, Germany's alliance with Italy disintegrated throughout the long campaign. From almost the moment of the Allied landing in Sicily, leaders of Italy's Fascist Party realized that their country's defeat was imminent, and they put Mussolini under arrest. Hitler dispatched a daring raid led by an SS commando officer named Otto Skorzeny to rescue his ally. On September 12, 1943, the raiders succeeded in liberating *Il Duce* from his captors.

Hitler ordered Mussolini reinstalled as head of a puppet government at Lake Garda, well to the north of Rome in the Italian Alps. But Mussolini's power was a sham, and few Italians were deceived. Fascist leaders set about looking for an honorable way to surrender to the Allies.

They realized that not even the Germans could hold on forever. Indeed, the Nazi defense of Italy was running up against the same problem Rommel had faced in North Africa: a lack of resources.

It is often said that under Hitler, Nazi Germany had to fight a two-front war, West and East. This is mistaken. Hitler fought on numerous fronts. In addition to the Western Front, there was the Russian front, which devoured just about all the men and materiel Berlin could throw at it; there was the North African front; and there was the Italian front.

And there was yet another front. Call it the resistance.

The Resistance

Well before dawn on July 4, 1943, a half-dozen Frenchmen, all dressed in black, slipped away from a locomotive roundhouse at Troyes, an industrial town about 100 miles southeast of Paris. They disappeared into the night. For half an hour or so, nothing happened. Then an explosion shook the station. German sentries started to investigate, but before they could learn much, there was another explosion.

Then another, and another. By the time the sun rose, 13 bombs had gone off, destroying 6 locomotives and severely damaging 6 more.

Three months later, a pair of Frenchmen disguised as shipyard workers talked their way aboard a German minesweeper anchored at Rouen, downstream from Paris on the Seine River. In the middle of the night, an explosion ripped the ship apart and, within minutes, only the top of its funnel was visible above the surface of the water.

On January 7, 1944, two British paratroopers landed near the southern French town of Figeac. Even before they could bury their parachutes, the French foreman of a local airplane factory greeted them. The factory where he worked turned out propellers for the *Luftwaffe*. The three men went into a cheese shop, which belonged to another covert operator, and fashioned bombs, which they covered in cheese. The owner of the shop, still wearing a chef's hat, carried the large cheese balls across town, and the foreman, who had a key, let the men into the plant. In the middle of the night, the aircraft factory went up in flames—and produced no more propellers for the *Luftwaffe*.

These and similar covert operations were coordinated from London. General Charles de Gaulle's Free French organization played a part in the missions, but his funding and personnel were limited. Taking an even greater role in developing anti-German sabotage missions was a British army unit called the British Special Operations Executive (SOE).

BET YOU DIDN'T KNOW

The SOE was comparable to America's Special Forces.

Placing trained agents not only in France but also in Belgium, Holland, and Scandinavia, the SOE would radio coded messages, transmitting orders to saboteurs. SOE aircraft flying out of Britain air-dropped guns, ammunition, and *plastique*, a puttylike explosive concoction that resistance fighters could shape to fit almost any space. It was a very useful, very portable, and very destructive substance.

The Germans were nearly defenseless against such sabotage. Dutch resisters blew up Nazi trucks. Danish resisters demolished a Copenhagen sports arena the Germans used as a military barracks. Most important, with the help of British SOE agents dropped in by parachute, Norwegian agents went after the plant manufacturing heavy water for the Nazi atomic bomb project. Although the plant was heavily guarded and was situated in the deep gorge of a river, the British and Norwegian saboteurs made their way, undetected, down an icy slope and into the plant. On the night of February 27, 1944, they wrapped their *plastique* around tanks of heavy water and detonated the explosive. In the morning, they also blew up a ferry transporting heavy water to Germany. The saboteurs then escaped by skiing to Sweden. The Nazi atomic bomb program never recovered from these two attacks. Resistance radio operators on the ground also directed RAF bombers to pinpoint targeting of German manufacturing and munitions facilities.

The resistance did not have a decisive strategic impact, but their attacks accomplished three things. They forced the Germans to divert manpower from the Soviet and Italian fronts. They demoralized the occupying forces. And, even more important, they gave hope to the civilian populations held captive throughout occupied Europe.

There was great risk and high cost, not only to the members of the resistance, but to the civilian populations among which they operated. The Germans instituted draconian and terroristic policies of reprisal for resistance attacks. Perhaps they would shoot 10 locals, usually chosen at random, for every German soldier the resistance killed. In response to the assassination of Reinhard Heydrich, the "Protector" of Bohemia and Moravia (and a leading planner of the Holocaust), by Czech Resistance fighters, the SS carried out the total destruction of the Czech village of Lidice in June 1942, murdering some 340 men, women, and children.

The reprisals never succeeded in ending resistance activities. The more the Germans tried to stave off attacks by various resistance groups, the bolder the attacks grew. Never decisive, the resistance nonetheless created a slow but relentless drain on German warfighting capacity. This was added to the drain on resources the Nazis' overextension inflicted on themselves. Carrying out the Holocaust required a massive commitment of manpower and logistics. No matter the cost, however, Hitler's Germany pursued its campaign of genocide with increasing, not diminished, fervor.

The Holocaust at its Most Terrible

The *Einsatzgruppen* were vicious but they weren't efficient. Those tasked with implementing the Final Solution simply could not kill fast enough. Shooting Jews consumed precious ammunition and time. It also had a negative effect on the morale of ordinary soldiers, who may have had no particular love for Jews, but who did not relish gunning down men, women, and children, a mission even they found disturbing.

On January 20, 1942, Reinhard Heydrich—the "Butcher of Prague," who was destined to fall victim to assassins of the Czech resistance—convened the so-called Wannsee Conference, named after the stately mansion, expropriated from a deported Jewish family, in the Berlin suburb of Wannsee. Heydrich summoned Nazi leaders to discuss a comprehensive solution to the "Jewish question"—not just in Germany, but in all Europe. At Wannsee, Heydrich defined the meaning of "Final Solution" as a policy of genocidal annihilation of Europe's Jews through a combination of slave labor and mass murder. It was at Wannsee that the use of lethal gas in specially built extermination camps was set forth.

The deportation of Jews to the first death camp gas chambers began in late 1942 and built up momentum early in 1943. On February 16, SS chief Heinrich Himmler ordered the "liquidation" of the Warsaw ghetto. Jews resisted with whatever weapons they could find, but after six weeks, the ghetto uprising was crushed. From then on, special freight trains deported Jews from Minsk, Vilna, and other Soviet cities; from the Baltic states; and from France, Italy, Hungary, Greece, and Slovakia.

Nothing was allowed to slow the pace of the Holocaust. During the desperate Battle of Stalingrad, the *Wehrmacht* High Command ordered a halt to all civilian train traffic, so that trains could be reserved for exclusive army use. Himmler intervened with Hitler, who gave him all the trains he wanted. For Hitler and the Nazi regime, it seemed, killing Jews was more important than saving Germany from the vengeance of Stalin and the Soviet Union.

Himmler and the other Final Solution conspirators took great pains to avoid revealing to the outside world what was happening in the death camps. The world beyond the Nazi sphere did not understand what he understood: that the destruction of European Jewry was a glorious cause, one that must be pursued even at the risk of the defeat and ruin of the Third Reich itself.

Just when the German forces were starting to retreat from the Eastern Front and when the entire country was facing the inevitability of a massive Allied attack on the Western Front, the campaign of genocide was accelerated, expanded, and intensified.

Was this mass murder a symptom of mass insanity?

A growing number of high-ranking German military officers believed it was. Just one month after the Americans, Canadians, and British landed at Normandy on June 6, 1944, a group of these elite German warriors tried to kill the Führer to whom they had taken a blood loyalty oath.

SUPPORTING ACTORS

Were "Hitler's Henchmen" crazy? Judge for yourself. On October 4, 1943, Himmler addressed an SS gathering with the following words:

I am referring to the evacuation of the Jews, the annihilation of the Jewish people. This is one of those things that are easily said. "The Jewish people is going to be annihilated," says every party member. "Sure, it's in our program, elimination of the Jews, annihilation—we'll take care of it." And then they all come trudging, 80 million worthy Germans, and each one has his one decent Jew. Sure, the others are swine, but this one is an A-1 Jew. Of those who talk this way, not one has seen it happen, not one has been through it. Most of you know what it means to see a hundred corpses lie side by side, or five hundred, or a thousand. To have stuck this out and—excepting cases of human weakness—to have kept our integrity, this is what has made us hard. In our history, this is an unwritten and never-to-be-written page of glory …

The Least You Need to Know

- ✪ The Battle of Stalingrad marked the farthest geographical extension of Nazi power.
- ✪ The start of the retreat from Stalingrad coincided with two other critical developments: Rommel's expulsion from North Africa and the ensuing Allied invasion of Sicily and Italy. The German defense of the northern half of Italy was bitter but costly. It put a tremendous strain on Germany's increasingly scarce resources.

- At the same time, the resistance movements in the occupied countries of Scandinavia and Western Europe were becoming ever more potent. In themselves they could not stop the German war machine. But they certainly could give it a lot of flat tires.

- The Holocaust was reaching its terrifying conclusion. It was an act of mass killing but it was also one of mass madness. At a time when the Nazi regime needed all available resources to stem the rising Red tide to the east, the Holocaust represented a massive diversion of those resources into genocide.

- Recognizing the disastrousness of the Holocaust diversion and the ineptitude of Hitler's military leadership, a group of top-ranking German army officers concluded that the only way to save the Reich was to get rid of Hitler. They entered into a conspiracy to murder him.

The Reich under Duress: 1943–1944

Nazi Germany had been based on delusion all along. True, the desire to overturn the unjust Treaty of Versailles was both real and justifiable. (Even many British and French leaders believed the treaty was fundamentally unfair.) And the war and the suffering and the killing, they were certainly no delusion. The Holocaust, although it defied comprehension, was all too real. But the ideas on which Nazi ideology were based—a master race, the evil of the Jews— were the products of delusion. Even more, the notion that Nazi Germany could implement these ideas by conquering Scandinavia, the Low Countries, France, the nations of the Mediterranean and North Africa, and the Soviet Union, *and* fend off the power of the United States in the bargain—these made up a delusional belief in a military, economic, and political impossibility.

Maintaining the delusion of Nazi life had been easy early in the war. While Hitler enjoyed military successes, most Germans continued to deny the limits of their nation's power. But by 1943, the successes were fewer and fewer, and the delusion began to crumble. Increasing numbers of Germans became, if not chastened and contrite, at least more realistic. At the height of this new realism, in 1944, a cadre of military officers even plotted to kill Adolf Hitler in the hope of negotiating peace with the Allies.

The Normandy Landing

Between 1942 and 1944, Adolf Hitler ordered the construction of perhaps the most spectacular system of fortifications ever conceived. It was called *Atlantikwall*—the Atlantic Wall—a coastal defense system built of steel and reinforced concrete by slave labor, interconnecting 18 major fortresses, bristling with heavy coastal and medium field artillery, and extending along the entire coast of occupied Norway in the north and, below that, from Denmark down to the French border with Spain.

The Atlantic Wall was most heavily defended along the French coast, and it was here, at Normandy, on June 6, 1944, that the British, Canadians, and Americans executed the greatest amphibious assault in the history of the world. Hitler and his high command were stunned—all, that is, except for Erwin Rommel, who had been put in charge of fending off just such an attack. He understood that any fixed fortification could be overcome. He knew the assault would come.

In all honesty, many Allied military leaders thought an assault on the Atlantic Wall at Normandy was doomed to fail. All along the English Channel coast, slave laborers had constructed remarkably well-designed reinforced concrete pillboxes which held machine guns, antitank weapons, and artillery. Below the pillboxes, the landing beaches were sown with mines. Rommel had placed elaborate obstacles just offshore, including explosive Teller mines mounted on tree trunks designed to blow up incoming landing craft, and sharp steel girders arranged to rip out the bottoms of these boats.

The impregnability of the Atlantic Wall was a real possibility, not another mere delusion, but the Allies understood that the landings *had* to be made, and that they *had* to succeed. If the assault on Europe failed, the consequences would have been grave. America might well have turned from Europe, concentrating its efforts on the defeat of Japan. In that case, Great Britain would have stood alone again, and Hitler would have been able to transfer troops from the west to the Eastern Front, perhaps turning the tide against the Soviet advance. By the time the American forces returned to Europe—if they ever returned—the Nazis might have made themselves the undisputed master of the entire continent.

The make-or-break stakes were the very highest. Even the bold Winston Churchill advocated continuing the strategy of nibbling away at the edges of the Third Reich, continuing the sabotage, counterattacking perhaps in Greece, launching an invasion of France on its southern coastline, eating away at the "soft underbelly" of Europe in what would be a war of attrition. It might have worked, but it almost certainly would have extended the war many years.

In the end, Dwight D. Eisenhower, the American general who had been appointed Supreme Allied Commander in Europe, backed by U.S. Army Chief of Staff General George C. Marshall and President Franklin D. Roosevelt, persuaded Churchill. "Ike" and his party were all for betting everything on one massive assault, very carefully planned and prepared for. The prelude to it was an elaborate campaign of deception. Artisans from the film studios of Hollywood and London collaborated with military planners to create convincing military props—dummy tents and buildings along with dummy landing craft near the mouth of the Thames, for example—to give the appearance of a vast Allied army forming up at Dover for an invasion of northern France at the Pas de Calais, near Dunkirk. Here, the

English Channel was at its narrowest, making it the most likely place for an invasion. The props and the obvious strategic logic were augmented by fake radio broadcasts to reinforce the deception. Phony intelligence was disseminated identifying George S. Patton, Jr., already famed as the best general in the U.S. Army, as the commander who would lead the invasion. In the run-up to June 6, the Eighth U.S. Air Force launched hazardous bombing raids near the Pas de Calais. As the Germans saw it, this confirmed the place of the landing. No enemy would risk so many bombers and crews on a mission of deception.

But that is just what the Americans did. And the ruse worked. General Rommel moved his armored units toward the Franco–Belgian border. One entire German army—the Fifteenth—was moved to the area of the Pas de Calais, leaving Normandy less well defended than it would otherwise have been. When the Normandy landings began on June 6, German intelligence at first insisted that *these* were the ruse, intended to draw away strength from the Pas de Calais, site of the *real* invasion yet to come. By the time Rommel—who, on D-Day, was back in Germany, on leave to celebrate his wife's birthday— returned to his post, the Allies were already on the shore in force.

Eisenhower's own intelligence units had understood that the Germans were deceived. Thanks to the breaking of the German Enigma codes early in the war, the Allies received a steady stream of "ULTRA" decrypts, which told them of defenders' move to the east. Indeed, this knowledge persuaded Eisenhower and his aides to pull the trigger on the great invasion. Had they possessed one more piece of information, they would have been even more encouraged: The German treasury was nearly bankrupt.

TERMS AND TRANSLATIONS

ENIGMA was the ciphering machine used by the Germans; the British had come into possession of one of these machines. ULTRA was the special security classification given by the British to information gained from breaking the codes sent out by the ENIGMA machine.

Bombs Away

If Hitler had not followed his delusion by invading the Soviet Union, he would have had a much better chance of successfully defending the Atlantic Wall and the entire Western Front against the Allied invasion. Perhaps he could have defeated it altogether.

The same applies to the ever-mounting Allied air campaign against Nazi Germany. The effort against Russia drew resources away from German air defenses. More Allied bombers survived to drop their ordnance on German cities and factories.

The British air raids of 1942 stunned and staggered Germany. The RAF's Wellington and Halifax bombers had the range to reach any city in Germany, drop a huge tonnage of explosives, and return to bases in Britain. Sir Arthur "Bomber" Harris, marshal of the Royal Air Force, not only advocated strategic carpet bombing of German cities—which meant targeting civilian populations—he approved the combination of high-explosive and incendiary ordnance. The high explosives reduced buildings to rubble—kindling to be ignited by the next phase of bombing with incendiary loads. The idea of an incendiary attack was less to knock out vital industry than to spread fires throughout civilian urban areas. It was terrorism, intended to strike at the morale of the population.

BET YOU DIDN'T KNOW

Life in Nazi Germany had been growing progressively tougher. Because of the demands of the eastern front and damage inflicted by British bombing, ordinary Germans in 1941 were plagued by food shortages. So-called sugar had been made of wood pulp, sausages from beechwood nuts, and beer from whey. Malnutrition had been increasing and so, according to the testimony of many doctors, had the incidence of cancer. Public health was in rapid decline.

By 1943, the high-explosive/incendiary formula had been perfected, and, on the night of March 9 and 10, the RAF celebrated the tenth anniversary of the Nazis' seizure of power by unloading terrific devastation on Munich, the Bavarian city that had given birth to the Nazi movement. By the time the Wellingtons and Halifaxes turned back toward home, more than 200 citizens of Munich were dead, more than 400 wounded, and almost 9,000 made homeless.

BET YOU DIDN'T KNOW

All over Germany in 1943, underground shelters such as subways were overwhelmed with people seeking safety from the night bombings. Mob scenes ensued at the entrances and, in the hysteria, people in many cities were crushed to death. In London, the Blitz tended to build camaraderie. In Germany, the relentless raids turned citizens against one another.

The United States Army Air Forces began participating with the RAF in bombing missions as early as 1942, but it was not until January 2, 1944, that the Eighth U.S. Air Force was born and assumed bombing operations independent of the RAF. As mentioned earlier, unlike the RAF, which confined itself to nighttime carpet bombing missions, the Americans were brazen enough to do precision bombing by daylight. This enabled aircrews to more precisely target strategic objectives such as factories and military installations. But the Eighth Air Force also hit civilian neighborhoods, and thus the hell faced by ordinary Germans became a 24-hour ordeal. The first independent U.S. raid, on March 18, 1944, killed 172 residents of Munich and wounded nearly 300 more. Four thousand were made homeless. The losses in other German cities were similar.

Although the Allied air raids took a heavy toll on air crews, they exposed Hitler's inability to retaliate effectively and revealed the essential weakness of Germany's air defenses. The major attacks were so devastating to industry that the regime turned increasingly to slave labor for factory work. The effect on urban dwellers was horrific. Propagandists tried to explain the destruction away by blaming the attacks on "Jewish brains" in Washington and "nigger" pilots who hated the white race. Such familiar appeals to racism, however, were wearing thin on the German population. More and more Germans were becoming hostile to the Nazi regime. Some even began to participate in acts of resistance within the borders of Germany itself.

Schindler's List

The regime had always had its opponents. Back in 1939, Johann Georg Elser, an unemployed carpenter from Württemberg, a town near Munich, had gone into a backroom of a Munich beer hall where Hitler was scheduled to speak, carved a hole in a pillar, and inserted a time bomb. The device functioned very well, but, as luck had it, Hitler's speech ended ahead of schedule, and he and his entourage left before the bomb detonated. Indeed, more than twenty-six assassination attempts are recorded against Hitler between 1934 and Operation Valkyrie, the major attempt of July 20, 1944, which we will discuss shortly.

Assassination was not the only vehicle of opposition. In 1941 and 1942, conspirators in Munich printed and distributed anti-Nazi tracts signed, "White Rose," the work of University of Munich students. The core group began its work on June 27, 1942, and was arrested by the Gestapo on February 18, 1943. Among those White Rose members subsequently convicted of high treason and executed (she was guillotined on February 22, 1943) was 21-year-old Sophie Scholl, daughter of liberal politician and anti-Nazi Robert Scholl, who, remarkably, survived the Nazi era. Sophie's final words are still haunting:

> How can we expect righteousness to prevail when there is hardly anyone willing to give himself up individually to a righteous cause? Such a fine, sunny day, and I have to go, but what does my death matter, if through us, thousands of people are awakened and stirred to action?

In those same years, an American woman, Mildred Fish-Harnack and her husband, Aviv, as members of a resistance group called the Red Orchestra, helped political dissidents escape and provided economic and military intelligence to Washington and Moscow. In 1943, they were discovered, arrested, and executed.

Because of the popularity of Steven Spielberg's 1993 *Schindler's List*, an Academy Award–winning movie based on the 1982 historical novel by Thomas Keneally, much of the world knows something of the role played by a few German Gentiles in helping Jews escape certain death in the Holocaust. Born in 1908 into a German-speaking family in Moravia, a region that would become part of Czechoslovakia, Oskar Schindler grew up to become a traveling salesman. Like many Central Europeans, he was fluent in several languages, and he was a gifted salesman, with an easy charm that allowed him to ingratiate himself into many influential circles. After the Nazis came into power in Germany, he became a spy for the Reich. In 1939, he set up an enamelware factory in the Polish city of Krakow where, manufacturing utilitarian dishes and cooking vessels for the German military, he used slave labor, including many Jews.

Outwardly, Schindler, a member of the Nazi Party, was just another German war profiteer. In 1940, a year after Schindler set up his business, the Nazis built the Auschwitz concentration camp, not far from Krakow. The next year, they established the ghetto at Krakow, forcing the Jews there to live behind brick walls and barbed-wire fences, awaiting eventual deportation to Auschwitz or some other death camp. Some, however, were sent to Schindler's factory, where they were astonished to find themselves in the hands of an employer who treated them humanely.

With the New Year of 1942, mass killings began at Auschwitz. Aware of the murders, Schindler, at great risk to himself, began passing whatever information he could obtain to Jewish underground organizations. It did not much help, and in 1943, the Nazis built Plaszów, a slave labor camp near Krakow. They moved the city's Jews either into it or directly to the extermination camps. Using his contacts, his charm, and bribes that gradually bankrupted him, Schindler obtained permission from the authorities to open a "sub-camp" in his factory. There his Jewish laborers were safe from Auschwitz, at least for the moment.

In the autumn of 1944, as the Allied armies were crossing the northern European plain toward Nazi Germany, Schindler pulled off a massive deception. The authorities closed the Plaszów slave camp, preparing to send its inmates to the gas chamber. Wanting to save as many of them as he could, Schindler went back to his hometown in Moravia. There he located an abandoned textile plant and saw that it could be used to manufacture artillery shells. Bribing various officials, he obtained permission to set up a new operation there. With the help of a Jewish personnel clerk, he compiled a list of roughly 1,100 Jews slated to be moved from Plaszów to Auschwitz. These particular Jews, he persuaded his bribed officials, were necessary to run his Moravian shell plant. In this way, he got permission to move them there.

Schindler, however, had no intention of making shells to aid the Reich. He was determined instead to use his plant as a safe haven for the relative handful of Jews on his list. Some made it safely to his plant, others did not. Schindler's list was full of deletions and typed-in additions. He had to pretend that his factory was for real. All his skills as a sleazy salesman came into play. He made some shells, mostly designed to fail. He also purchased shells from other factories and passed them off as his own.

In the meantime, the Jews in Schindler's plant lived in a state of high anxiety. What if the lies and bribes should fail? What if Schindler lost his remarkable courage? What if the Nazis, in their lust to achieve their greatest aim, the eradication of European Jewry, cared less about getting shells than they did about murdering Jews?

BET YOU DIDN'T KNOW

Schindler continued to bribe officials and even launched an affair with a female SS guard. His saintliness was built on a foundation of "sin."

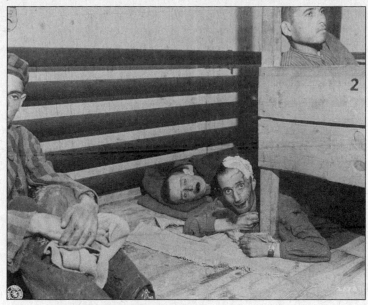

Slave laborers in their bunks at a concentration camp.
(Holocaust Museum)

Oskar Schindler and his wife, Emilie, were always in danger themselves. In the eyes of the Nazi authorities, helping Jews was even worse than bribing officials. Many of those who took the bribes still saw Schindler as a criminal. For the Schindlers and their Jewish workers, it was only a matter of time. If the Americans, the British, or the Russians did not arrive soon, the Schindlers would surely perish together with the Jews.

BET YOU DIDN'T KNOW

Near the end of the war, Schindler and his family, fearing capture by the Russians, made their way across Czechoslovakia to neutral Switzerland. The trip was harrowing, but Schindler's silver tongue, along with the diamonds he had hidden in his suitcase, eased their way to safety.

The Road to the Wolf's Lair

Men like Schindler were rare. Their existence revealed not only human decency in unexpected places, but the inexorable deterioration of the Reich. The decay of loyalty to the Nazis in general and to Hitler in particular was even more widespread in the upper echelons of the *Wehrmacht*. Veteran military commanders increasingly recognized that the total defeat of Germany was only a matter of time. Beyond question, the Allies were closing in. The only remaining question was *How could the devastation of surrender be limited?*

Unlike a relatively few righteous German Christians like Oskar Schindler, the *Wehrmacht* officers cared little or not at all about the fate of the Jews. Some of the anti-Hitler military conspirators have been portrayed as heroes seeking national liberation and moral salvation. In fact, most were simply trying to save their own necks. As harsh as the Treaty of Versailles had been on Germany, the terms of surrender for this new war promised to be much worse—especially for anyone in power. Early in the conflict, President Franklin D. Roosevelt made it publicly clear that he intended to treat those who had launched Germany's aggressions as war criminals.

All German soldiers and officers were required to take an oath of personal loyalty to Adolf Hitler. The officers who participated in the plot to kill the Führer on July 20, 1944, claimed that they had switched their allegiance from him to the German state. Maybe so. But, clearly, they also wanted to be able to present themselves to the soon-to-be-victorious Allies as the "good Germans."

Claus von Stauffenberg

The central figure in the plot to kill Hitler was Claus Philipp Maria Schenk Graf von Stauffenberg, a handsome young Wehrmacht lieutenant colonel, an officer descended from the Prussian aristocracy (*graf* means "count"). Stauffenberg compiled an outstanding record at the infantry school at Dresden and the cavalry academy at Hanover and was commissioned a second lieutenant in 1930. Rising rapidly through the officer ranks, he served as a captain in the Battle of France (May 10-June 25, 1940) and was then transferred to North Africa. During this service, his staff car was strafed in an Allied air attack, and he was grievously wounded. Flown to an army hospital in Munich, he was promoted to lieutenant colonel and remained hospitalized through the summer of 1943. By the time of his release from the hospital, he had lost his right hand and forearm, his left eye, and the last two fingers of his left hand. During his extensive medical treatment, he impressed his doctors and fellow patients by refusing any of the painkillers offered him. This demonstration of valor brought him to the attention of military higher-ups, and his uncle, a Prussian general, arranged his appointment to the army general staff. After all, he was a brilliant officer who could no longer fight in the field.

There was only one catch. Stauffenberg was to serve under General Friedrich von Olbricht. Olbricht was a bespectacled, slender, balding, mild-looking officer who, when Stauffenberg reported for duty in August 1943, asked a decidedly pointed question. Was he prepared to commit himself to an attack on Hitler's life?

Stauffenberg, who had already lost so much in Hitler's war, answered yes.

Three Vital Questions

Under the cover of doing his staff work in the War Ministry on Berlin's Bendlerstrasse (now renamed the Stauffenbergstrasse), Stauffenberg labored at his real job, organizing the assassination of the head of the Third Reich. Consulting with other like-minded officers, he realized that he would have to find answers to three vital questions:

- ✪ First, how and when should Hitler be killed? This seemed the easiest of the questions to answer: Hitler was spending most of his time at *Wolfsschanze* (Wolf's Lair), his Eastern Front headquarters in the Masurian woods outside of Rastenburg, East Prussia (today Kętrzyn, Poland).

- ✪ Second, how, after an assassination, should a new government be set up to negotiate surrender to the Allies on the best terms? Stauffenberg and his co-conspirators did not want to repeat the disaster of Versailles.

- ✪ Third, what steps could be taken to ensure that, in the wake of the assassination, extremist units, such as the SS, did not seize power?

Operation Valkyrie

The answer to all these questions evolved into a secret plan called Operation Valkyrie, named after the warrior maidens in *Die Walküre,* the second opera in Richard Wagner's epic "Ring Cycle" (*Der Ring des Nibelungen*). In the opera, the Valkyries hover over the battlefield and conduct the souls of slain heroes to Valhalla.

Operation Valkyrie involved a bold deceit. Olbricht went to Hitler to tell him that, because of the Allied bombing of Germany, the hardships, and the fear of imminent defeat, there was arising the strong possibility of a popular revolution. This part of the scheme was hardly far-fetched. To forestall a threat to the security of the Reich from the inside, he recommended creation of a special Home Army. Germany, he advised, needed to be divided into domestic military districts, each under the command of an officer who could move fast to quell anti-Reich actions.

Hitler saw the logic of Olbricht's argument and authorized the creation of such a force and such an organization of districts. What Hitler did not suspect was that Olbricht's intention was to issue secret orders to the Home Guard commanders to suppress SS response to the assassination.

The Olbricht scheme addressed both the second and third questions. But that left the first: how to kill Hitler.

Officers higher than Stauffenberg began putting together the elements of a plot. Someone had to be able to get physically close to Hitler at Wolf's Lair. That individual would have to earn Hitler's trust, as well as the trust of the SS guards, who never left the Führer's presence. The ideal candidate, it occurred to them, would be a bona-fide war hero, preferably someone who had been visibly wounded. Hitler would trust a hero, and the SS guards would be unlikely to thoroughly search a valiant warrior who had given so much to his country.

The brass approached Stauffenberg with this proposal. He volunteered instantly, and the plan was fleshed out. Stauffenberg would go to Wolf's Lair on the pretext of delivering reports from the War

Ministry. Given his reputation, such a trip would be easy enough to arrange. The papers would be in his briefcase—along with a bomb. If an SS officer opened the briefcase, it would be game over for the conspirators. But if the briefcase, hand carried by a high-ranking hero, went uninspected, the plot might just succeed.

The bomb would be equipped with a pencil detonator inserted into a kilogram of *plastique* (plastic explosive). A simple time-delay fuse, the pencil detonator was a thin brass tube with a copper section on one end containing a glass vial of copper (cupric) chloride ($CuCl_2$) solution. When the copper part of the tube was crushed, the chemical would leak out, eroding a wire that held back a spring-loaded striker. Once the wire was completely eaten away, the striker would hit a percussion cap, which would detonate the plastic explosive.

At the appropriate time, Stauffenberg was to open the briefcase, use a small pliers to crush the tube, close the briefcase, and place it where the explosion would be certain to kill Hitler.

The question was, could Stauffenberg, with his right hand gone and only the thumb and next two fingers remaining on his left hand, do the job? He assured the others that he could. In the meantime, to avoid arousing suspicions, he continued to perform all his normal duties at the War Ministry. At night and in the secrecy of his Berlin apartment, he practiced the maneuvers of opening the briefcase and manipulating the pliers.

The Assassination Attempt

On the morning of July 20, 1944, Lieutenant Colonel Claus von Stauffenberg woke up early. As previously arranged, a staff car from the War Ministry picked him up at 6:15; in the car was Lieutenant Werner von Häften, Schauffenberg's *aide-de-camp* and almost literally his right-hand man. Häften was in on the plot. Together, they rode through the Berlin suburbs to an airstrip at Rangsdorf, which lay beside a small lake about 40 minutes from the city. At 7 o'clock they were airborne, Stauffenberg with the bomb in his briefcase. Two hours later, they landed at Wolf's Lair.

TERMS AND TRANSLATIONS

Wolfsschanze. Wolf is clear. *Schhanze* has two meanings: The first is the same as the English word *chance;* the other is *trench,* hence also, *entrenchment.* So, while we usually translate *Wolfsschanze* as Wolf's Lair, which sounds Teutonic, the term really referred to Hitler's heavily fortified "entrenchment," or forward command post.

At the airport by Rastenburg, the nearest town to the command post, another automobile was on hand to take the visitors to the Führer. The drive wound its way through open countryside, then into a dark and gloomy forest, where wolves might once have been abundant indeed. But pity any wolves still lurking about. The forest floor was heavily mined. Uniformed SS guards lined the roadway, and the car had to pass through checkpoints at two concentric and encircling fences.

Before getting out of the vehicle, Stauffenberg initiated the fuse. Time was of the essence. If Hitler, notorious for his late arrivals, did not show up at the meeting inside the conference room as scheduled, Stauffenberg, and not Hitler, would be dead.

For once, however, Hitler was on time. Besides Hitler, 20 other officers were gathered around a large conference table on which maps were spread. Stauffenberg positioned himself near Hitler, set down the brief case, and then pushed it with his foot as close he could to his target. A few minutes later, Stauffenberg received a planned telephone call, excused himself, and left the room to take it. Instead, he left Wolf's Lair and, once through the door, he bolted back to the car. Häften was already there. Ducking inside the vehicle, he ordered the driver to return to the airport immediately. The driver did not understand what was going on, but he did as he was told.

Just as the automobile cleared the second checkpoint, at 12:42 in the afternoon, the men inside the car heard an explosion. Then the alarms went off. Stauffenberg was certain Adolf Hitler was dead.

Hitler's Revenge

Of the 24 people in the conference room with Hitler, 20 were injured in the blast. A stenographer was killed instantly, and three officers later succumbed to their wounds. Hitler survived, suffering some burns, a perforated eardrum, and apparently some damage to his right hand, which was probably temporary.

It is believed that Colonel Heinz Brandt, standing closest to Hitler, had either deliberately or accidentally moved the briefcase behind one of the heavy wooden pillar legs of the table. This shielded Hitler and several others from the direct force of the blast. (Brandt did not survive.)

Ignorant of this outcome, Stauffenberg and Häften flew back to Berlin. By nightfall, however, the SS had determined that Stauffenberg was the would-be assassin. In short order, he was apprehended and executed.

The SS dragnet expanded. In the end, some 7,000 suspected conspirators were arrested, of whom 4,980 were either executed or committed suicide. Many of those judged to be the leaders of the conspiracy were hanged from piano wire, left to die as slowly and painfully as possible. Among those arrested was none other than General Erwin Rommel. This presented Hitler with a problem. For Rommel was widely regarded as a great hero. The SS gave him the choice of standing trial or taking poison. If he chose suicide, he was assured, his family's safety would be assured. On October 14, 1944, Rommel took the poison. He was given a state funeral, befitting a hero of the Reich, Nazi propaganda reporting that he had succumbed to wounds sustained earlier.

The Least You Need to Know

- The success of the Allied landing in Normandy, combined with the Soviet advance from the east, was the beginning of the end for Nazi Germany.

- As Nazi Germany crumbled, resistance movements gained in momentum. The kind of resistance associated with Oskar Schindler—action to thwart the Final Solution—was rare, but was nevertheless a symptom of the disillusionment growing toward the Hitler regime.

- The most dramatic manifestation of domestic German resistance was Operation Valkyrie, the July 20, 1944 attempt to kill Adolf Hitler.

- The Valkyrie conspirators hoped to take over the German government and conclude an immediate peace with the Allies on terms as favorable as they could secure. Instead, the assassination plot failed, mass arrests followed, and Hitler continued in power.

CHAPTER 24

The "Thousand-Year Reich" at Years Eleven and Twelve: 1944–1945

Instances of readiness to risk their lives in opposition to the Hitler regime occurred not only among Stauffenberg and the other martyrs of the German military aristocracy but also among the humbler members of German society. Here and there simple people of the working class decided to voice their opposition to Hitler. Some of them secretly wrote and disseminated postcards criticizing the Führer for his waste of German youth in an unnecessary war. Such humble acts may be less dramatic than the assassination attempt at Wolf's Lair, but these gestures and deeds were powerful indeed, coming from people accustomed to obeying those who ruled them. When "agitators" were caught, their fate was inevitable, but by late 1944, it was becoming increasingly clear that the fate of their persecutors was also inevitable. For Hitler, the ugly death of Benito Mussolini was an omen.

Mussolini's Execution

After his fall from power in mid-1943, Mussolini was placed under arrest, only to be liberated in a daring raid led by SS commando Otto Skorzeny on July 20, 1944. Il Duce was flown to Germany and put on a train to Wolf's Lair, where Hitler—less than two hours after his brush with death—met his fellow dictator at the railway station and promptly took him on a tour of the scene of the bomb blast.

It was as if Hitler intended to convince Mussolini that he, like the Führer himself, was invincible. For Hitler had plans for the man whose rise he had emulated in the 1920s and 1930s. He sent him back to Italy—the far northern portion of the country that the Allies did not yet control—and installed him as the head of state of something the pair called the Fascist Republic of North Italy.

Mussolini's new headquarters was on Lake Garda, near the Brenner Pass, which led through the Alps, a location that might have afforded him a quick escape if things went bad. Things soon went bad. In the early spring of 1945, when it was obvious that Germany was in retreat everywhere, Mussolini decided to flee Italy. His thought was that he would make his way to neutral Switzerland. En route along the shore of Lake Como, he and his mistress, Claretta Petacci, were intercepted by partisans—Italian guerrillas who sided with the Allies. He was hiding in a German truck, dressed in the heavy coat of a German enlisted soldier and wearing a German helmet.

The partisans gave Petacci a chance to leave Mussolini. She declined to do so. The next morning, the couple was shot in front of the ornate gate of a ponderous villa. Petacci, it is said, tried to shield Mussolini's body with her own. It was a gesture in vain. Both bodies were taken to Milan, where they were hung upside down, by the heels, from a high fence in front of a filling station. The mob spat on them, beat them, and mutilated them.

BET YOU DIDN'T KNOW

Il Duce (Mussolini) had once said to a biographer: "Everybody dies the death that corresponds to his character." Mussolini had fooled his people, and they, in turn and at the end, fooled him into believing that they were his eternal supporters. Now he was dead.

Stalin's Next Target: Berlin

Throughout the autumn of 1943 and the winter of 1943-1944, the Soviet army ground steadily ahead, gradually forcing the Germans back to a line about 300 miles west of Moscow. In May 1944, however, as the spring rains became torrential and the rivers rose, the Soviet advance stalled.

At this point, Hitler thought he might be able to recoup his losses. Studying the military maps of the Eastern Front in the spring and summer of 1944, he saw that the German line was actually a bulge, with the Red Army almost at Estonia in the north, the bulk of the German forces still ballooning toward Byelorussia, and another extension of the Soviets into Poland in the south. What, Hitler and his intelligence officers asked, was going to happen next? Allied bombing and partisan warfare were already pushing the Germans up and out of Crete, Greece, and Yugoslavia. So, much of southeastern Europe was now up for grabs. The Russians had long wanted to get their hands on Bulgaria, Romania, and Hungary, and the Germans could no longer stop them. Furthermore, once the Soviets had Hungary (the strategists in Wolf's Lair calculated), they could go on into Austria and then Bavaria, in southern Germany itself.

Believing that Stalin would be unable to resist the temptation of such a southern strategy, Hitler in May 1944 stripped much of his strength from the Baltic states and the bulge into Byelorussia, and sent those forces south. Hitler was very proud of this move: At last he had outsmarted Stalin! The truth was, however, that he had played directly into the Soviet dictator's hands.

Stalin could afford to wait. Most of southeastern Europe was his for the taking—whenever he wanted it. He had instead set his sights on the much bigger and more meaningful prize: Berlin itself. So, while the flood waters of May 1944 rose, crested, and receded, Stalin and his commanders used the pause in the fighting to plan an assault upon the bulge in the German line.

Operation Bagration

There was nothing subtle about the Soviet scheme. It was named Operation Bagration, after Pyotr Bagration, the Russian warrior-prince who had won fame by defeating another invader from the west, Emperor Napoleon I. The starting date for the new Soviet offensive was June 22, 1944, exactly three years after the opening of Hitler's invasion of the Soviet Union.

The Soviets prepared well for the attack. A fleet of some 12,000 trucks (many supplied by the United States under the Lend-Lease program) transported a force of two and a half million to the front. Supporting them were more than 5,000 tanks—the Soviet T-34 tank was legendary, rivaling even the vaunted German *Panzer*—some 7,000 fighter aircraft, and at least 31,000 field guns and mortars. During a month and a half of preparations, the Soviets moved 100 trainloads of ammunition, food, and fuel to the front.

No one could hide a buildup of this magnitude, and Hitler's intelligence officers warned him of what it portended. Hitler was now in full denial mode, however, and he refused to heed the warnings. The massing of Soviet forces on the eastern bank of the Dnieper River, he told his aides, was only a ruse. Stalin was going to go south! No doubt!

Soviet Assault

The Soviet assault that opened on June 22, 1944 was a juggernaut: unstoppable. Aircraft equipped with precision bombsights took out German artillery all around the bulge at the battlefront. At 4 A.M. on June 24, Red Army artillery opened fire in a barrage whose magnitude left the Germans in disbelief.

On June 28, six days after it had begun, the Soviet attack was a complete success. Dazed by the catastrophe, thousands of German soldiers threw down their weapons and surrendered. Those who did not surrender rushed westward in a panicked retreat that can fairly be described as a rout. Nothing now stood in the way of a Soviet march into Poland—and it was through Poland that the route to Berlin lay.

MEMORABLE PLACES

Observing the bombardment from a village on the Dnieper, Vasily Grossman, a Soviet reporter, wrote:

> The pounding blows of the headquarters artillery, the thunder of the divisional cannon, the heavy strokes of the howitzers, the sharp, rapid reports of the regimental guns merged in an uproar that shook the very foundations of the earth. Through the rumble of the artillery came a piercing whistle, like an enormous locomotive letting off steam.

> Hundreds of fiery sickles rose into the air and fell into the German trenches. The trench mortars of the Guards had opened fire. A cat ran down the deserted village street, dragging its tail in the dust. It must have been mewing desperately, but its cry could not be heard. The leaves were trembling on the Byelorussian maples, oaks, and poplars. In the deserted houses windowpanes were shattered, brick stoves fell crumbling to the floor, and doors and shutters swung wildly.

Then the Soviet tanks and troops moved forward, supported by aircraft. Grossman continued:

> The sky was in tumult with the rhythmic roaring of the dive bombers, the hard metallic voices of the attack planes, the piercing whine of the fighters. Fields and meadows were splashed with the darting outlines of hundreds of planes.

The Western Front

In the meantime, after landing successfully on the beaches of Normandy, the Allies—the British, Canadians, Americans, and a small contingent of Free French under the leadership of General de Gaulle—expected to make rapid progress across northern France. Once Normandy and Brittany to the west were under control, Allied planners thought, they could dash on to Paris, and then launch a massive drive across northern France and Belgium into Germany. Estimates were that all this would take about three months. There was talk of an end to World War II in Europe by Christmas 1944.

By the middle of June 1944, however, the invaders were way behind schedule. The Germans still held Caen, the major city in Normandy, and Cherbourg, a key port on the Channel coast. The Allied advance was nowhere near Paris. Not only were the Germans fighting back fiercely, the Allies had made a critical tactical error. Much of Normandy east of the landing beaches was so-called hedgerow country—the French called it *bocage*—dense thickets of hawthorn, brambles, vines, and trees centuries old that often stood as much as 15 feet high. This thick growth demarcated the property lines of the Norman farmers. Moreover, the shrubbery often concealed ancient stone walls. In effect, individual fields looked as if they were surrounded by the walls of forts. They might as well have been. Worse, these natural forts were surrounded by narrow lanes and drainage ditches. Together, the features of the terrain brought the Allied advance to a crawl. Despite all the planning that had gone into the Normandy landings and the breakout toward the east, somehow no one had taken into account the salient feature of the landscape—the hedgerows.

Tanks were bogged down in the lanes and ditches, and when they tried to crash through the brush they often upended or exposed their thinly armored undersides to German bazooka fire. Infantrymen also had to proceed with the utmost caution. The hedgerows were so thick that Allied soldiers sometimes would step around a bend only to find themselves eyeball-to-eyeball with a German counterpart. Finally, the hedgerows gave all the advantage to the defender, providing nearly perfect cover and concealment for machine-gun nests. As for the lanes, clear passage through the hedgerow country, these were thickly sown with mines.

Nevertheless, the Allies substantially outnumbered the Germans and—Germany's scarcity of resources was showing up again—the defending tanks and airplanes were running out of fuel. As usual, Hitler dismissed this problem as a fantasy. By the end of June and the beginning of July, he was ranting and raving, demanding that his forces in France create a new Dunkirk.

But no Dunkirk was in the offing. Everywhere along the slowly eastward-moving Normandy front, Allied artillery repulsed counterattacks. By July 10, 1944, most of Normandy was in Allied hands.

Operation Cobra

Also on July 10, Omar Bradley, the American general Eisenhower considered his right-hand man in the field, devised a plan for a breakout from hedgerow country. Operation Cobra, as he called it, stepped off a week later. By this time, some American tanks had been fitted with improvised battering rams to break through the hedgerows. Called "salad forks," these were an inspiration of a Sergeant Curtis G. Culin Jr., who had the idea of welding steel prongs—some of them fashioned from the girder-like anti-landing craft obstacles—onto the front of some M-4 tanks to transform them into dozers. On August 19, Cobra resulted in a decisive German defeat on the banks of the Seine River. There the Allies caught the enemy in a hurricane of tank and artillery fire. Flames from German ammunition dumps jumped skyward as ammunition exploded. So many fleeing Germans crowded onto a bridge at the same time that it collapsed, sending hundreds into the river in a tangled mass.

As a Canadian soldier later remembered:

> Germans charred coal-black, looking like blackened tree trunks, lay beside smoking vehicles. One didn't realize that the obscene mess was human until it was poked at. I remember wishing that the Germans didn't have to use so many horses. Seeing all those dead animals on their backs, their legs pointing at God's sky like accusing fingers, their bellies bloated, some ripped open … That really bothered me.

The defeat was the worst the Germans had suffered since Stalingrad and Tunisia. That night, in a pouring rain, American soldiers walked single-file over a narrow dam on the Seine, each man touching the one ahead to keep from falling into the water. In the morning, engineers laid the first of many temporary bridges across the flow. The Allies now had a clear shot at Paris.

The Liberation of Paris

Generals Eisenhower and Marshall were in favor of temporarily bypassing Paris to keep driving the Germans back onto Germany and, ultimately, to Berlin. But President Roosevelt, Prime Minister Churchill, and General de Gaulle overruled them. Paris meant too much to France and the world not to be liberated as soon as possible.

Starting at 8 A.M., August 25, the first of the Free French armored units entered the outskirts of the City of Light. Followed by an American infantry division, de Gaulle's tanks had come to liberate Paris. Their arrival touched off one of the most tumultuous celebrations in history.

Despite gunfire from remaining German occupiers and their collaborators, Parisians poured out onto the streets to welcome their liberators. They showered their Free French soldiers with champagne and flowers and smothered them with hugs and kisses. And they gave the Americans exactly the same. Along the route to the center of Paris, open windows displayed the long-forbidden French tricolor flags. People cried out, *"Vive de Gaulle!"*

Riding into the city at 4 P.M., de Gaulle first established his headquarters at the Ministry of War, the same building from which four years earlier he had departed with his trunk-load of documents pertaining to the building of a resistance. Then he proceeded to the Arc de Triomphe where he headed a victory parade down the *Champs Élysées*, the same grand boulevard along which the Nazis had paraded when Paris fell to them.

While de Gaulle's triumph was taking place, thousands of German occupiers suddenly became German prisoners of war. The people of Paris exacted their revenge. They cut up or shot portraits of Nazi leaders and ripped down swastikas, setting them afire. When General Dietrich von Choltitz, the former military commander of Paris, was hauled off to jail, people spat on him and clawed at his uniform. They did not know that hours earlier, by disobeying orders from Hitler to burn Paris to the ground—SS men had planted explosive charges on all the great bridges across the Seine—Choltitz had saved the city.

BET YOU DIDN'T KNOW

Parisians also assaulted French women who had been mistresses of the Nazis. Their heads were summarily shaved and their breasts, bared, were painted with swastikas. Forced to parade this way through the streets, some were made to display signs that proclaimed, "I whored with the *boches*"—the French derogatory word for Germans.

In the meantime, the great triumphal parade was nearing its climax, heading out of the Champs Élysées and around the Place de la Concorde on the way to the Cathedral of Notre Dame. Just at that point, the marchers heard a gun going off. Thousands of people fell to the pavement or took cover behind vehicles parked along the street.

General de Gaulle, however, sought no refuge. Walking straight and tall, he approached a waiting car that took him to the *Hôtel de Ville*—city hall—where he stopped briefly. As he reemerged from the building, rifles and machine guns went off from nearby windows and rooftops. Apparently, the Germans were making their last stand in Paris. Soldiers in the parade began firing back.

Indifferent to the danger, de Gaulle rode on to the cathedral. There was more shooting there; yet, calmly and without hurry, General de Gaulle entered through the massive front doorway. In the gloom inside, still more shooting broke out from the balconies high above the nave. De Gaulle, unfazed, strode 200 feet down the aisle to his place of honor in a pew facing the altar. "He walked straight ahead in what appeared to me to be a hail of fire," a BBC correspondent reported, "without hesitation, his shoulders flung back. It was the most extraordinary example of courage that I've ever seen."

De Gaulle stayed at his place in front of the nave throughout the singing of the *Magnificat*. When he left the cathedral, an American journalist wrote, he "had France in the palm of his hand." His performance went a long way toward purging the humiliation of 1940 and reclaiming the honor of France.

Battle of the Bulge

But Hitler was not yet finished. There was a natural temptation among the Allies to regard the liberation of Paris as a token of the liberation of Europe itself. Eisenhower and the other top Allied commanders knew this was not the case.

Even as the German armies were streaming back across France and Belgium in the late summer of 1944, the Führer was mulling over the idea of a counteroffensive against the Allies. If he could deal them a major setback and aggravate jealousies between the British and American high commands, then maybe he could win a separate peace and finally hurl everything against the ever-advancing Soviet army.

His thoughts returned to where, turning the Schlieffen Plan upside down, he had scored his major strategic triumph in 1940: the Ardennes Forest. Hitler believed—correctly—that Eisenhower and the other Allied commanders were making the same mistake the French had made in 1940. They regarded the Ardennes Forest as impenetrable by modern vehicles of war. Since the Ardennes was a natural barrier, they threw the weight of their forces to the north of it. Hitler figured that if he could feint with armored units toward Antwerp, almost at the Belgian North Sea coast, he could lure Eisenhower away from the Ardennes region altogether. With the position thinly defended, he could launch a major advance through it. Might this win the war? Hitler may have thought so. But while that eventuality was unlikely, a major breakthrough to the west would certainly have resulted in heavy Allied casualties.

Hitler called the plan *Wacht am Rhein* (Watch on the Rhine). Its target date was December 6, 1944. He ordered absolute secrecy. Sensing perhaps that the Allies might have broken German codes—which, through ULTRA, they had indeed done—years earlier—he forbade any radio or telephone traffic concerning the operation. All preparations took place at night. Not until the first day of December were the corps and division commanders given their orders, and not until the night of December 5 and 6 were the troops given their operational orders.

The German secrecy was remarkably effective. At dawn on attack day, some 200,000 German troops made their way through the snow of the Ardennes Forest and, coming up from the rear, took the American army in Belgium by total surprise.

Most of the American units in this sector were battle weary. It was assumed that the sector would be quiet and that they would be given a much-needed opportunity to rest. Instead, the fighting turned out to be the biggest pitched battle in which American soldiers had ever engaged—not just in World War II, but ever. Every indication was that the armies of the Third Reich were beaten, exhausted, hardly capable of defending themselves. And now, suddenly, they were mounting a massive offensive.

Because the Germans pushed heavily into the middle of the Allied lines, driving that portion into a westward retreat, the fight has been called the Battle of the Bulge. Officially, it was the Battle of the Ardennes.

As the scope and depth of the German attack became apparent, General Eisenhower realized that the enemy had succeeded in splitting his forces in two, making communications between his troops down near Luxembourg and up near the Belgian coast impossible. By December 20, the 101st Airborne Division and the 10th Armored Division, holding the southern Belgian town of Bastogne, were surrounded, outnumbered, and under heavy siege.

On December 22, the commanding officer of the *Panzer* corps laying siege to Bastogne sent officers into the town with a message, demanding surrender. Brigadier General Anthony McAuliffe, acting commanding officer of the 101st Airborne, received the message from one of his aides. He was confused, thinking that the Germans were offering to surrender *to him*. When the aide explained that, no, they were *demanding* surrender, McAuliffe replied: "Us? Surrender? Nuts!" And so, "Nuts!" became the typically brash, utterly dismissive, and exuberantly irreverent American response to the German demand.

The Germans celebrated Christmas by mounting a huge bombardment of Bastogne. But for the trapped Americans, help was on the way. Under the command of General George S. Patton, elements of the Third U.S. Army broke through the siege lines on December 26 and liberated the town and its beleaguered defenders.

Heavy fighting followed, during which Patton drove the German offensive into headlong retreat by January 22, 1945. The "bulge" that gave the battle its popular name was eliminated, and the back of the *Wehrmacht* was effectively broken. The German army would never mount another offensive.

The Battle of the Bulge slowed the Allied advance and delayed the end of the war. Both sides had suffered terrible casualties: the Germans 100,000 and the Americans about 81,000. They both had lost heavily in weapons and equipment—800 tanks each, and the Germans 1,000 airplanes. The difference between these casualties was that the Americans could replace men and equipment quickly. For the Germans, the losses were absolute and final.

The Holocaust Continues

Militarily, World War II in Europe was at an end. And yet Hitler's soldiers kept fighting, killing, and dying, and his SS, even in retreat, continued to carry out the Final Solution. All over the parts of Europe the Nazis still occupied, SS men, sometimes joined by local Nazi supporters, Latvians, Poles, Hungarians, and others, continued the destruction of the ghettos into which the Jews had been forced. Labor camps were closed down, and the Jews who had worked for survival were shipped to the gas chambers of the death camps.

In the chaos of the war's waning days, some Jews managed to escape the camps and the Nazi dragnet. Perhaps 10,000 took refuge in the forests, struggling for survival amid a hostile nature. Others, having somehow equipped themselves with forged papers, tried to survive in the cities by passing themselves off as Aryans. In the forests, anti-Semitic peasants sometimes led the Gestapo to Jewish caves and other hiding places. In the cities, local police, spies, blackmailers, and the like exposed Jews who had tried to pass as Christians.

As the winter of 1945 gave way to spring, most of those who had sought to hide had been exposed. Each day, the number of surviving Jews dwindled.

Throughout Central and Eastern Europe, entire Jewish communities were gone. There were no synagogues, no Jewish schools, no Jewish life. In Poland, blood-soaked books in Yiddish and Hebrew strewn along the banks of the Vistula were all that remained of the thousand-year-old civilization of the European Jews. By the end of the war, the staggering magnitude of the genocide would be known. Six million European Jews had been murdered.

The Destruction of Dresden

Winston Churchill was sometimes at odds with his own air marshal, General "Bomber" Harris, who unapologetically advocated unlimited strategic bombing of German cities and their civilian inhabitants. Churchill thought the policy was uncivilized. As the full extent of the Holocaust became increasingly apparent with each concentration camp the advancing Allies liberated, such moral compunctions diminished. Many in the Allied nations—leaders as well as ordinary citizens—had come to believe that the German people deserved to suffer.

Situated some 100 miles south of Berlin, Dresden was one of Germany's most ancient and beautiful cities. Established in the thirteenth century, it boasted much of Europe's finest baroque and rococo architecture. Its galleries and museums housed masterpieces by the likes of Holbein, Vermeer, Rembrandt, Rubens, Botticelli, and Canaletto. Dresden contained an engravings collection that, by 1945, numbered at least a half million pieces. The city was long famous worldwide for its delicate, exquisitely lacelike porcelain figures and figurines. For centuries, Dresden had been a center for music and musicians—Bach, Handel, Telemann, Wagner, Richard Strauss, all had spent creative time here. The sculptures and bas-reliefs on the public buildings were from the classical age of Greece. The sky-line of bridges and spires was unsurpassed anywhere in Europe.

Fortunately for Dresden, it was a city of no military value and had therefore been spared strategic bombing by the Allies. Then, during February 13-15, 1945, RAF and U.S. Army Air Forces bombers destroyed Dresden. All of it.

They made use of the high explosive-incendiary combination that had been so destructive in the past. Indeed, the fire-bombing was so extensive that it created a phenomenon called a firestorm, a conflagration that effectively creates its own swirling wind system, which sustains and intensifies the fires initially set off by the bombing. Some 25,000 Dresden residents perished, mostly in the fires. If the Allies had lost the war, the bombing of Dresden would surely have brought trials for war crimes. If there was any justification for the bombing—beyond simple vengeance—it was the hope that the horror would hasten a German surrender.

The Least You Need to Know

- Mussolini's death foretold the fate of his ally to the north, Hitler.
- The Soviet westward advance in 1944-1945 became an unstoppable force. Hitler's delaying tactics proved irrelevant. For despite the long-standing economic and technological backwardness of the Soviet Union, Hitler had committed the fundamental error of overextending all his resources.
- No matter how determined the German resistance to the Normandy landings and inland advance was, they were overwhelmed by the superiority of Allied (especially American) numbers, firepower, and sheer economic prowess.
- With the intensification of the Holocaust and the utter yet gratuitous destruction of Dresden, Nazi Germany was plunging toward a Wagnerian immolation.

Immolation Scene: 1945

At the end of *Die Götterdämmerung (The Twilight of the Gods)*, the concluding opera in Richard Wagner's epic Ring Cycle (*Der Ring des Niebelungen*), debuted at Bayreuth in 1876, comes the sublime "Immolation Scene." Following the death of Siegfried, iconic hero of Teutonic myth, Brünnhilde, his lover, rides on horseback into the flames. The fire billows fiercely and seems about to devour the entire stage and the chorus of terrified onlookers who crowd to the foreground. But the flames die down, and the Rhine surges up in a mighty flood, bearing the Rhinemaidens on its crest. On seeing them, Hagen, the villain of the opera, leaps into the river, like a madman, to capture the ring the maidens guard.

The ring—after which Wagner's entire four-opera cycle is named—symbolizes all that is good and righteous. *"Zurück vom Ring!"* ("Away from the ring!"), Hagen bellows—whereupon the Rhinemaidens drag him beneath the waves, then reappear, one of them holding up the ring in a gesture of joyous triumph.

The roiling Rhine subsides. In the distance a glow breaks through a dark band of clouds, revealing Valhalla—the paradise of German myth—and Wotan, the chief god, who faces his own fiery doom. The music storms to a great climax and then dies away as the theme of redemption through love soars high in the violins. The curtain falls.

No wonder Wagner was Hitler's favorite composer.

Led by Hitler, the people of Nazi Germany—or a majority of them—persuaded themselves that they were in pursuit of all that is good and righteous, only to see it snatched away by the "criminals" of Versailles. In the end, there was an immolation—many immolations, in fact. Typical was the firestorm of Dresden, treasured city of the Reich. And, day after day, there were the fires of the crematoria at Auschwitz and the other death camps. Had Hitler's orders been followed, even Paris would have been consumed in flame.

As for the Führer, holed up and cowering in his squalid bunker, Berlin in flames above him, he, too, rode toward his personal immolation, taking with him his beloved Alsatian dog, Blondi, and his mistress-turned-wife, Eva Braun. The question left in the smoke-choked air was: Would any redemption follow for Germany?

Reds over the Vistula

On January 17, 1945, not long before the destruction of Dresden, the Red Army crossed the Vistula, a river that flows through the middle of Poland. The Soviets had come into Poland from the southeast, a path that brought them close to the concentration camp at Auschwitz. Ten days later, Russian infantrymen pushed their way through the front entrance, under the iron gate-arch decorated with the supremely sadistic motto *Arbeit Macht Frei*, "Labor Makes You Free."

Inside, the Red Army troops discovered some 5,000 survivors, so feeble from hunger, privation, and disease that they could barely cheer. The Soviets almost immediately dynamited the gas chambers. Later, officials from the Red Cross went into the camp. Nazi authorities at Auschwitz had tried to cover up evidence of their crimes. They had burned all sorts of personal effects of their victims. The Red Cross nevertheless discovered almost 400,000 men's suits, more than 800,000 women's coats, seven tons (a remarkable but verified figure) of human hair, and mountains of eyeglasses, toothbrushes, and shoes. The National Holocaust Museum in Washington, D.C., has an exhibit of the shoes.

And then there were mass graves containing hundreds of thousands of corpses.

In Berlin, on the day the Soviets crossed the Vistula, several top German military officials, Generals Keitel, Jodl, and Guderian, and Marshal Hermann Göring, approached Hitler's office in the Chancellery, located in the center of the city. The building had been damaged by bombs, and the officers had to pick their way through back corridors where windows were covered with cardboard. At the door to the office, SS guards took the officers' side arms and searched their briefcases. Hitler's guards were extremely vigilant after the Wolf's Lair assassination attempt.

Hitler shuffled in at 4:20 P.M., late for what had been a four o'clock appointment. His shoulders were stooped, and his left arm hung limp. Whether this was the result of an injury sustained during the July 20 explosion, a neurological problem (most modern physicians who have seen late newsreel footage of Hitler believe he suffered from Parkinson's Disease), or perhaps a stroke is unknown. He had been injured in the explosion, that much is certain, and the use of his right hand was impaired. He could barely shake hands with his visitors. As he sank heavily into a chair, he looked at least a decade older than his 55 years.

The mood of the conference was grim. Objectively, it was clear that Nazi Germany could not survive for much longer. Even Hitler understood this—but he had an idea. He proposed putting Heinrich Himmler, head of the SS, in charge of a special unit that would march forward into the face of the Soviet advance. Guderian thought the notion was crazy and said so. The statement of that obvious truth—that a pointless suicide mission was, well, pointless—was the end of his influence in what was left of Hitler's court.

On the last day of January 1945, Soviet tanks crossed the Oder River, the traditional boundary between Poland and Germany. Now no natural barrier lay between the Red Army and Berlin. On January 16, Hitler moved his headquarters down into the *Führerbunker,* a subterranean bunker 28 feet beneath the walled garden of the Reich Chancellery and below the upper floor of the bunker complex, a space called the *Vorbunker* (forward bunker), about eight feet above the *Führerbunker.* In the reinforced spartan shelter underground, the supply of water and electricity was always uncertain, and the air itself was stuffy and malodorous. Hitler emerged from time to time, and even continued to use his office in the Chancellery.

Then, shortly before noon on February 3, nearly a thousand B-17s of Eighth U.S. Air Force, escorted by 575 P-51 fighter aircraft, conducted the largest U.S. raid on Berlin. The Chancellery was all but destroyed, and Hitler henceforth moved all operations into the bunker, only leaving it occasionally for short strolls with his Alsatian, Blondi. In April, his mistress Eva Braun moved in, as did Josef Goebbels. Goebbels's wife, Magda, and their 6 children moved into the Vorbunker, where about 24 staff personnel also sheltered, including Hitler's trusted secretary Traudl Junge, nurse Erna Flegel, Hitler's personal physician, Dr. Theodor Morell, and telephone switchboard operator, SS Sergeant Rochus Misch. From the recollections of Junge, Flegel, and Misch, comes what little we know firsthand about Hitler's final days.

On April 16, the Red Army began the Battle of Berlin, and on April 20, Hitler made his last foray to the surface, decorating a group of Hitler Youth boy soldiers with the Iron Cross—the medal he himself had won in World War I.

The ceremony concluded, the man who, until recently, controlled most of continental Europe now controlled no more than about 1,350 square feet of bunker space. Here, beneath the ruins of his capital, Hitler spent much of his time studying cardboard models of what had been intended as a new Munich and a new Linz. He had always wanted to be an artist—or an architect.

Yalta

While Hitler played with cardboard models in his bunker and contemplated sending bespectacled little Himmler into the teeth of the Red Army, the Allied "Big Three"—Franklin D. Roosevelt, Joseph Stalin, and Winston Churchill—met on February 12, 1945, at Yalta, a resort town replete with czarist palaces that overlooked the Black Sea. They agreed that their demand to Germany would be unconditional surrender and nothing less, and they publicly announced the same.

Roosevelt, Churchill, and Stalin jointly made clear that they also intended to dismember Germany and force it to pay reparations. Contrast this with the end of World War I, when President Woodrow Wilson had insisted on keeping Germany largely intact, except for the territory it had seized from France after the Franco-Prussian War of 1870-1871. Roosevelt did resist the demand of Secretary of the Treasury Henry Morgenthau, who was Jewish, to turn postwar Germany into an agrarian nation incapable of ever making war again, but the president was fervent in his wish to see Germany forever neutered as a great power.

For some years after the World War II, historians and others debated the wisdom of the "unconditional surrender" demand, which also applied to the Japanese. The argument against it held that it served only to heighten the Nazi nothing-to-lose determination to fight to the death. There is some validity to this argument, no doubt. But if you are going to fight to the bitter end, you must have something to fight with. By the time of the Yalta statement, the Nazi war machine was almost nonexistent.

After the bombing of Dresden, Goebbels proposed that captured Allied bomber crews be killed in retaliation. Down in the bunker, Hitler was tempted to go along with the idea, but his foreign minister, Joachim von Ribbentrop, and others persuaded him otherwise. Such executions would be *prima facie* war crimes, and most of the top Nazis realized they themselves would soon be prisoners.

Churchill, Roosevelt, and Stalin at Yalta.
(FDR Presidential Library)

Peace "Negotiations"

Throughout the second half of February 1945, newspapers in neutral Sweden reported that a certain high-ranking Nazi was suing for peace. The personage in question was none other than Heinrich Himmler, the sadist who headed the SS. The news stories exaggerated the facts, but it was true that Himmler had extended very feeble and very self-interested peace feelers. Count Folke Bernadotte, a Swedish nobleman, had been in Berlin and had spoken with Himmler at the SS chief's unofficial headquarters, a sanatorium some 75 miles north of the city. Bernadotte was surprised by Himmler's manner and appearance. He had expected to encounter a diabolical fire eater and found instead an affable individual, soft-spoken and polite to the point of being deferential. When the Swedish diplomat asked him what he wanted, the SS chief replied by raising the issue of a German surrender *with* one condition: His own personal safety guaranteed by a grant of asylum in Sweden.

Would Himmler, as a token of goodwill, grant any immediate concessions, such as releasing at least some Jews from the concentration camps? Bernadotte asked.

No, he would not. With this refusal, any deal was off.

Separately, Ribbentrop also made an approach to the Swedes. Through an agent named Hesse, he put out his own feelers to a Stockholm banker, Raoul Wallenberg. The banker's message back to Ribbentrop was blunt. The Big Three were determined to destroy Germany, period.

The Oder and the Rhine

A thousand years earlier, the borders of the German-speaking people had been the Oder, which flowed to the Baltic just a bit east of Berlin, and the Rhine. By the beginning of March 1945, the Reich that Hitler boasted would last a thousand years had been squeezed back between those same two rivers. And the compression was bound only to increase. From both east and west, Hitler's enemies were poised for advances they were certain would bring an end to Nazi Germany at last. Having crossed Poland into Germany, Marshal Zhukov's Red Army was encountering almost no resistance. On the west, where the British and the Americans had reached the Rhine, engineers threw a pontoon bridge across the river.

Leading the American armored units, General Patton—"Old Blood and Guts," his men called him—walked to the middle of the bridge, announced "I've been waiting a long time to do this!" and, as he himself noted in his diary, took "a piss and then picked up some dirt on the far side in emulation of William the Conqueror" (who picked up a clod of English soil when he landed at Pevensey, on the southeast coast of Britain, at the start of the Norman Conquest of 1066).

Back in the bunker, Hitler was falling to pieces both physically and mentally. He now walked in a profound, foot-dragging shuffle; his face was deathly white except for large red blotches; his hands trembled; and he was administered multiple daily doses of a remarkable array of narcotics, stimulants, and tranquilizers (including cocaine, adrenaline, bromide, atropine, belladonna, methamphetamine, morphine, sodium barbitone, and Eukodal [oxycodone], among other substances) by Dr. Theodor Morell, a noted specialist in the treatment of syphilis, from which the Führer may have also suffered.

Except for Dr. Morell, Goebbels, Eva Braun, and a handful of associates from the old days, Hitler was very much alone. Himmler was away, secretly negotiating with Bernadotte. Göring had ensconced himself in the villa at Berchtesgaden. He had proposed to Hitler by telegram that he turn over leadership of Germany to him. When Hitler refused, Göring decided that the southerly mountaintop location near Munich would put him in a better position to surrender to the Americans—rather than the Russians. Completely disgusted by the collapse of leadership around him, General Heinz Guderian took his leave of the Führer. In parting, he announced that he would look for a quiet place in the country that wouldn't be overrun for another weekend.

On Easter Sunday the Ruhr, that economic heart of the German economy, stopped beating. It was overrun by the Allied advance. A few days later, the Red Army entered Vienna, and hordes of Viennese, even the police, fled the onetime imperial capital.

Hitler's Last Hope

Across the Atlantic Ocean, in a cottage in the southwestern Georgia village of Warm Springs, a retreat that came to be known as the Little White House, President Franklin D. Roosevelt stayed in bed nearly all morning of April 12, 1945. An adult victim of polio (some modern physicians believe he actually suffered from Guillain-Barré Syndrome) contracted in the 1920s, FDR had built a cottage and bought a nearby hotel, an establishment that had access to a pool fed by the 90-degree spring waters. He had visited the place regularly ever since and had loved to frolic with the other "polios," as they called themselves, in the soothing waters.

By 1945, however, he was a very sick man, suffering from runaway hypertension, congestive heart failure, and the combined emotional weight of dealing with the Great Depression followed by World War II. The long airplane trip to Yalta and back had left him drained, and he hoped Warm Springs would work its usual restorative magic.

Not this time.

Only with the help of his valet was he able to rouse himself from bed, bathe, and dress. He dressed rather formally, in a blue suit and a red necktie, because he was to sit for a portrait by a Russian painter, Elizabeth Shoumatoff. With him in Warm Springs was also Lucy Mercer Rutherford, who had been the social secretary of his wife, Eleanor Roosevelt, and who, although married and living in South Carolina, had engaged in a romantic affair with FDR and remained close to him. In inviting her to Warm Springs, the president probably realized that it was likely the last time he would see her.

As he sat for the portrait by a card table, he shuffled through a few official papers. Suddenly he said, "I have a terrific headache." They were his last words. He fell into unconsciousness, and, two hours later, was dead of a massive cerebral hemorrhage. He was 63 years old.

Despite rumors of ill health—and everyone could see that the president appeared unwell—the news was shattering to the people of the United States. Roosevelt had recently been elected to an unprecedented fourth term following an unprecedented third. He was, in a word, adored. Almost equally shocked were the Allies, especially Winston Churchill, with whom the president had forged a deep bond.

Hitler and the others in the bunker were overjoyed by the news. With the archenemy gone, they believed, the Reich would surely experience a reversal of fortune. Hitler made a broadcast to the troops, exhorting them to have faith that now they could be saved.

The next day, April 13, all German troops in the valley of the Ruhr surrendered. Zhukov also crashed across the Oder and started along the road to Berlin. The bunker was only 45 miles away.

Bombs over Berlin

On April 20, Hitler and his remaining minions drank champagne toasts in celebration of the Führer's 56th birthday. The Americans celebrated it with that 1,000-bomber attack on the German capital. The same day, an advance Red Army unit moved up to within 20 miles of Berlin.

In the bunker, Hitler's top officers, Grand Admiral Karl Dönitz and Field Marshal Wilhelm Keitel, were frantic. Keitel had organized the search for the would-be Wolf's Lair assassins and later had engineered Hitler's return to Berlin. He had proven his loyalty. Now, however, he urged Hitler to send out peace feelers. When Hitler refused to do anything of the kind, Keitel and Dönitz both pleaded with him to at least leave Berlin. The road to Berchtesgaden was still clear, they said. Leave before it is too late!

Hitler ignored their advice.

Himmler, his own attempts at a peace accommodation having failed, visited the bunker to pay his birthday respects to the Führer and then risked the ongoing battle to drive several hours for a meeting some 44 miles (70 kilometers) north of Berlin with one Norbert Masur, neutral Sweden's representative to the World Jewish Congress (WJC). The encounter was as grotesque as it was desperate. After all the monstrous things he had done, Himmler apparently believed that by making a few last-minute concessions he could save his own hide. In the end, and with Bernadotte's help, the WJC was given custody of about 7,000 women from the women's Ravensbrück concentration camp. The meeting was a betrayal of Hitler, of course, but Himmler was well suited to the role of a rat leaving a sinking ship.

On April 21, 1945, the same day Himmler met with Masur, the Red Army came within artillery range of Berlin. Even down in the bunker, the impact of the Soviet shells was both audible and palpable.

Martin Bormann, a top Hitler aide, knew it was all over. Finding a telephone that was still working, he called his wife, who was at Berchtesgaden. He told her that he had located a hiding place for her and their children in the Tyrol. He himself would stay with Hitler in the bunker until the end.

On April 22, Eva Braun promised that she, too, would remain. With that promise, Hitler did something that no one around him had ever seen him do. He kissed Braun—on the lips.

On April 23, Göring at Berchtesgaden was told in a telephone call that Hitler had collapsed. What was the Reichsfuhrer Göring to do? To him, the answer was obvious. He prepared to run.

Death in Berlin

Holed up with his wife and butler at Berchtesgaden, Hermann Göring thought himself quite safe. Allied bombers on their way to Salzburg and other Austrian sites had passed overhead but had left the villa untouched. Göring, however, had been deluding himself. On the morning of April 25, at exactly 10 A.M., a wave of British Lancasters swept in from over the mountain, dropping explosives all around the perimeter of the villa. Göring apparently thought they were just trying to trap him. Later in the morning, however, another wave appeared, then another and another, unloading blockbusters directly on the estate.

How Göring managed to survive is unknown, but Hitler was furious with him for not remaining on station in Berlin. He could not fly into the arms of the Führer. Nor did the *Luftwaffe* chieftain want to wait until the Russians moved in. He had but one choice. With his wife, he fled Berchtesgaden, on foot, walking westward toward the American lines. Somewhere in his clothing he secreted a cyanide pill—just in case.

That same morning the Soviet pincers were about to close on Berlin. By dawn two days later the city was completely encircled.

Hitler Decides His Own Future

Down in the bunker, Hitler started to worry—in conferences at least—about his personal fate. With the end of the war nearing, he let it be known that he had no intention of allowing Stalin to exhibit him like a bear in a cage. Yet there was no longer any way he could leave Berlin—nor would he, if he could. He was still the Führer, he said. How could he ask others to die for Germany if he himself tried to flee?

By the morning of April 26, the Soviets had overrun the Berlin airports and were making their way toward the center of the city. The resistance, which had been fierce, was now disjointed, with some officers trying to sneak out of the capital so they could surrender to the Americans rather than the Russians. In her quarters in the *Vorbunker*, Frau Goebbels wrote to her son by a previous marriage, who was now an Allied prisoner of war. The "glorious ideals" of National Socialism were shattered, she wrote.

The next morning, April 27, an officer brought word to the bunker that all of Berlin's ammunition and supply dumps were now in Russian hands. In two days' time, with all supplies gone, the troops still in the city would be unable to resist any longer. He urged Hitler to risk a breakout.

Hitler had other plans.

Officially renouncing all his official titles, he signed two documents. The first made Admiral Dönitz president and head of state of the Reich and commander in chief of the armed forces; the second appointed Goebbels as chancellor, the equivalent of prime minister, the number two man in the government.

Next, seated at the main conference table in the bunker and surrounded by his loyal aides, Hitler dictated his rambling last will and testament. This completed, he launched into his last speech.

> Since I did not feel that I could accept the responsibility of marriage during the years of struggle, I have decided now, before the end of my earthly career, to take as my wife the girl who, after many years of loyal friendship, came of her own free will to this city, already almost besieged, in order to share my fate. Death will compensate us as for what we were both deprived of by my labors in the service of my people.

The next could have come straight out of Wagner:

> My wife and I choose to die in order to escape the shame of overthrow or capitulation. It is our wish that our bodies be burned immediately, here where I have performed the greater part of my daily work during the 12 years I served my people.

A Pre-Mortem Wedding

The wedding ceremony of Adolf Hitler and Eva Braun took place on the evening of April 28, like everything else, down in the bunker. Eight guests were present, including the Goebbelses, husband and wife. Someone found a lingering bureaucrat who had the authority to officiate. His name, appropriately enough, was Wagner. Eva Braun wore a dress of black silk, and Hitler was in uniform, swastika band on his left arm. After swearing to Herr Wagner that they were both of Aryan blood (a requirement under Nazi law), the newlyweds signed the marriage certificate. Martin Bormann and Frau and Herr Goebbels appended their signatures as witnesses. The hour was just before midnight, April 28.

The Final Days

By the middle of the next morning, April 29, Soviet troops had entered the *Tiergarten,* the zoo. Other units, coming in from the east, south, and north, were heading for the bunker. Just outside the bunker, Martin Bormann was picking his way through the rubble to the headquarters of Admiral Dönitz. Bormann needed to give him the signed document appointing him head of state. Down in the bunker, Frau Eva Hitler slept until noon.

Early evening brought the news of Mussolini's gruesome death. "I will not fall into the hands of the enemy dead or alive!" Hitler said in response. "After I die, my body shall be burned and so remain undiscovered forever!"

Shortly after midnight, Hitler entered the bunker's canteen. There he said goodbye to a group of about 20 office staff and officers.

After he left, descending the staircase to his bedroom, those remaining in the canteen erupted in celebration, albeit with absolutely nothing to celebrate. Dancing and drinking what was left of the champagne, they whooped and hollered so loudly that a sour-faced aide to Martin Bormann looked in at the door, admonishing them to quiet down. Bormann was in his office nearby, composing a telegram to Dönitz. Hitler, the message said, written already in the past tense, would have wanted the new head of state to execute all traitors.

Late in the morning of April 30, a Soviet advance guard arrived on the street adjacent to the bunker.

Knowing that Hitler wished to be cremated, an aide sent out for jerrycans of gasoline. The only ones available, he learned, were buried under the zoo, too far away to reach. He told an orderly to siphon gasoline out of nearby wrecked cars (or possibly from vehicles in the subterranean garage adjacent to the Chancellery).

In his bedroom suite, Hitler bade farewell to Hans Baur, for many years his personal pilot. He gave the man his beloved portrait of Frederick the Great. "He, too," Hitler remarked, "was the victim of his generals."

Afternoon came. Soviet soldiers had located the gate to the bunker.

Inside, in the *Vorbunker*, Traudl Junge was telling the Goebbels children a fairy story to keep them from wandering down to the *Führerbunker*, where chaos reigned.

It was 3:30 P.M., April 30, 1945. From below came the sound of a shot. Young Helmut Goebbels thought it was a bomb. It was not. Eva Hitler had crushed between her back molars the glass cyanide capsule her husband gave her. Adolf Hitler, who had earlier successfully tested one of his cyanide capsules on Blondi, the dog he loved, is believed to have put a capsule in his mouth, biting down on it as he shot himself in the temple.

As quickly as possible, guards retrieved the bodies, hauled them to the Chancellery garden above, doused them with the siphoned gasoline, and set them ablaze.

The next morning, May 1, as Soviet infantrymen were entering the Chancellery garden, Frau Goebbels administered to each of her children, who had been dosed with a sedative, a cyanide pill. On their way out of the bunker, she and her husband were shot to death, possibly by Red Army soldiers, although some accounts report that Josef Goebbels shot his wife and then himself.

Martin Bormann disappeared. Some thought he had escaped to Argentina, but he was also reported to have died in a hail of Soviet gunfire on the streets of Berlin. In 1972, his remains were discovered, with evidence (broken glass in the jaw) suggesting death by cyanide capsule.

Two weeks later, Heinrich Himmler fell into British hands. Before a doctor could examine him thoroughly, he, too, bit down on a cyanide capsule.

Surrender

With Hitler's death, the remaining German leaders harbored the hope that the Allies would now see Germany as a bulwark against further Soviet expansion into Europe. From the naval base at Kiel, Admiral Dönitz on May 4 sent an aide to Allied headquarters at Reims, the ancient cathedral town in northeastern France. Dönitz was hoping to make a separate peace directly with Ike.

Eisenhower would have nothing to do with it. Refusing to see any German officers, he sent word through his top aide, General Walter Bedell Smith, that there would be no bargaining whatsoever. Germany was to surrender unconditionally and to do so to the Western Allies and the Soviets at the same time.

Three days later, *Wehrmacht* Chief of Staff Alfred Jodl led a small German delegation up the front steps of the Reims schoolhouse that served as Eisenhower's command center. They were ushered into a former classroom, where the walls were covered with maps. The room was small and Allied officers bumped into one another as they made their way to their assigned chairs around a heavy oak table. Jodl stood before them, tall, erect, his uniform crisp, a monocle in his eye, the very model of a Prussian army general. He bowed stiffly from the waist, and then stood erect again.

Eisenhower pointedly refused to greet Jodl. Instead, he waited in his private office next door while the German signed the papers of surrender. Only then did he consent to acknowledge the enemy general. It was shortly after 2 A.M., May 8, 1945. As General Smith led Jodl into the inner chamber, Eisenhower remained seated behind his desk. Jodl bowed again, and stood at attention. Without rising, Eisenhower asked if he understood the terms.

Ja.

Was he ready to execute them?

Ja.

Did he realize that he would be held personally accountable if fighting erupted again?

Ja.

With that, Jodl was escorted out of the building. The two men had exchanged neither salute nor handshake nor any greeting at all. This concluded, Eisenhower entered the old classroom. All the British and American officers broke out into cheers. Flashbulbs exploded, and newsreel cameras whirred. Flashing his famous grin, Ike held up, in the form of a V for victory, the pens with which the surrender had been signed.

Dead tired, Ike went back into his office and dictated a remarkable cablegram to the War Department in Washington: "The mission of this Allied force was fulfilled at 0241, local time, May 7th, 1945."

The story of Nazi Germany was over, and as the war in Europe ended, thoughts of punishing those responsible for the atrocities began to be spoken. Back in April, just a few days after FDR's death,

Robert Jackson, an associate justice of the United States Supreme Court, received a visitor in his chambers. It was Samuel Rosenman, who had been a speechwriter and confidant to the late president. The president wanted to know, Rosenman said, meaning Truman but speaking as if FDR were still alive, if Justice Jackson would prosecute remaining Nazi leaders as war criminals. After some consideration, Jackson agreed to do so. Soon, he was off to Germany to serve as the chief American representative in the Nuremberg war crimes trials.

The Least You Need to Know

- With the Battle of the Bulge over and the Soviet forces crossing the Vistula River in Poland, Roosevelt, Stalin, and Churchill, the "Big Three," felt confident enough to issue their demand for Germany's unconditional surrender.

- As the borders of Germany contracted, Hitler and other top-ranking Germans harbored the wild hope that the Allies would accept Germany as a partner in stopping the Soviet advance.

- Hitler and Goebbels died in Berlin. Himmler committed suicide in the northern part of Germany. Terrified of a Russian revenge, the rest of the top Nazis fled to the American and British lines—or sought escape to distant nations, especially in Central and South America.

Judgment: 1945–1946

A question continues to hang over the Nuremberg war crimes trials (as well as over the somewhat later International Military Tribunal for the Far East, conducted in Tokyo): Can judicial proceedings imposed by the victors ever be fair or is the result inevitably "victors' justice"? No one denies that the Nazis started World War II in Europe and committed unspeakable atrocities. But did they violate previously created and widely accepted international laws? Or were the surviving top Nazis tried on an *ex post facto* basis—that is, on the basis of laws promulgated after the deeds had been committed?

Justice Robert Jackson and the Start of the Nuremberg Trials

A dignified man in his fifties, somewhat balding, who usually wore a blue pinstriped three-piece suit with a gold chain stretched across his slight paunch, Justice Robert Jackson conveyed the solid air one expected from an associate justice of the United States Supreme Court. Everything about his background suggested that same solidity. After law school in Albany, he had become a prosecuting attorney in rural upper New York State. In many ways, he was the classic conservative lawyer. But, a Democrat, he also had a populist streak that led him sometimes to defend the little guy against the forces of the big corporations. In 1932, he also publicly denounced corruption in the New York Democratic Party. His scathing attacks on political hacks brought him to the attention of Franklin D. Roosevelt, who, once in the White House, gave Jackson a job in the Justice Department. Jackson rose rapidly through the ranks and, in 1942, FDR appointed him to the Supreme Court.

Jackson became renowned for his sense of justice in Supreme Court cases. In a 1943 case involving a Jehovah's Witness family in West Virginia who had not let their children salute the flag at the start of school days, Jackson struck off one of the golden passages in the literature of the Supreme Court:

> If there is any fixed star in our constitutional constellation, it is that no official, high or petty, can prescribe what shall be orthodox in politics, nationalism, religion, or other matters of opinion or force citizens to confess by word or act their faith therein. If there are any circumstances which permit such an exception, they do not now occur to us.

Jackson's fairmindedness was exactly what recommended him to President Truman in the weeks after the death of FDR. The governments of the victorious powers, Great Britain, the Soviet Union, and the United States, had agreed quickly on the need to place all the surviving Nazis they could find on trial for war crimes. They also agreed to hold the hearings in Nuremberg (Nürnberg), the medieval city about 100 miles north of Munich where many of the Nazis' most dramatic rallies had taken place.

But lots of people, especially in Britain and America, raised a troubling question. Would such a trial represent justice or just revenge? There wasn't even an existing international court in which such a trial could take place. More important, there was no significant body of international law that defined crimes of war in clear distinction to standard and generally accepted military action. The U.S. Constitution had banned the passage of *ex post facto* laws, statutes designed to punish people for committing acts before those acts were deemed criminal. Were the Nazis then to be tried on an *ex post facto* basis—in violation of the lead Ally's own most basic law?

The question troubled President Harry S. Truman greatly. He hoped that the appointment of Justice Jackson as chief prosecutor would make the proceedings in Nuremberg both be and appear to be just.

After months of preparation, Justice Jackson, in early November 1945, flew to Germany and took a train to Nuremberg. After 11 Allied bombing raids, the city was almost wholly in ruins. He took a room in the only hotel still standing, and the trials opened on November 20, 1945.

The Nuremberg Trials

The Palace of Justice had been rapidly restored. It stands today as it stood then, a four-story building with three courtyards and lots of gables on its multiple pointed roofs. Behind it, in 1945, stood a long semicircular cement wall that held the Nazi prisoners.

Of the 22 prisoners to be tried, the most important ones were:

- **Albert Speer** was a handsome, slightly balding architect who had presided over German arms production for most of the war and now stood accused of exploiting slave labor.

- **Colonel General Alfred Jodl,** accused of war crimes and crimes against humanity, served as the chief of operations of the German armed forces and, subsequently, as commander in chief, surrendered to General Eisenhower. The Soviets insisted on his being put on trial.

- **Grand Admiral Karl Dönitz,** the head of the German navy and Hitler's chosen successor, had the deceptive air of a meek college professor. He was accused of war crimes, crimes against humanity, waging wars of aggression, and crimes against the laws of war.

- **Hans Frank,** Nazi governor general of Poland, was known as the "Butcher of Jews." He was accused of war crimes and crimes against humanity in executing the "Final Solution" in Poland and in terrorizing the Polish population generally.

- **Joachim von Ribbentrop** was a former champagne salesman who won Hitler's favor and became the Nazi foreign minister. He was convicted of crimes against peace, planning wars of aggression, war crimes, and crimes against humanity.

- **Rudolf Hess** was a dark-haired, heavy-browed man who had been with Hitler since the earliest days in Munich and had risen to the rank of third-highest Nazi. A pilot in World War I, Hess made a solo flight from Germany to Scotland in May 1941. Why he did this remains a mystery; the British, who incarcerated him for the duration of the war, have never released records of their many interviews with him. Possible motives for the flight range from insanity to acting as Hitler's envoy in an effort to persuade the British to ally with the Reich. Convinced that this second explanation was correct, the Soviet Union demanded that Hess be put on trial for conspiracy, crimes against peace, war crimes, and crimes against humanity.

- **Hermann Göring** was a World War I flying ace who became chief of the *Luftwaffe*. Believing that the Western Allies would treat him with respect, he crossed U.S. lines and was captured by elements of the 36th Infantry Division. Among other things, he was implicated in the Holocaust. Convicted of crimes against peace, planning wars of aggression, war crimes, and crimes against humanity, he never showed remorse.

- **Martin Bormann,** one of Hitler's top administrators, was tried *in absentia*—without being present. It was reported that he had been killed by Soviet forces in Berlin, but his skeletal remains were recovered in 1972, and glass fragments found in the jaw suggest that he had committed suicide by biting down on a cyanide capsule.

These and the other Nazi prisoners had been kept one to a cell. Their food was slop. Their only clothing consisted of shapeless gray prison uniforms. They were not allowed shoelaces, neckties, belts, razors, or even nail-clippers—anything that might be used to commit suicide. Each cell door had a peephole, so that guards from the United States, Great Britain, and the Soviet Union could keep watch on their prisoners 24 hours a day.

On November 29, 1945, the defendants were awakened by the banging of washbasins out in the corridor and the raucous chatter of their guards. Since none of the Germans had clothing appropriate to a courtroom, the civilians among them were provided with ill-fitting, cheaply made suits. Outside their cells, they were allowed to use shoelaces and to put on neckties. The military were given back their uniforms, with all insignia and decorations removed.

Each day of the trials, they were marched single-file through the prison corridors into the courtroom. There, the prisoners were ushered into an oblong wooden box furnished with two rows of straight-backed chairs. There they sat, surrounded by U.S. military police, who stood at ease, but were armed. There they heard the formal charges read against them.

The Proceedings

On the first day of the trial, the defendants pleaded "not guilty." Justice Jackson then introduced massive documentary evidence that was, in effect, a history of Nazi Germany presented in the form of four main charges:

- First: That the Nazis criminally conspired to seize power in Germany.
- Second: That Nazi Germany planned, prepared, initiated, and waged wars of aggression, in violation of foreign treaties.
- Third: That the Nazis committed war crimes in the countries and territories occupied by the German armed forces: abuse and murder of civilian populations, deportations for slave labor, killing of prisoners of war and hostages, wanton destruction of cities, towns, and villages, and the conscription of civilian labor.
- Fourth: That the Nazis committed crimes against humanity—murder, extermination, enslavement, deportation, and persecution on political, racial, and religious grounds.

Jackson followed these charges against the individual defendants with indictments against the organizations of Nazi Germany: the party, the cabinet, the SA, the SS, the Gestapo, and the high command of the German armed forces.

The justice based these charges not so much on eyewitness testimony as on hundreds of thousands of documents gathered from captured Nazi archives. German bureaucrats are famous for generating meticulous and voluminous documentation. Nazi bureaucrats were German bureaucrats, and they kept remarkably detailed records pointing directly to their nation's crimes. It must be remembered that Hitler had promised a thousand-year Reich, built, in part, on the enterprise of permanently purging all undesirables—Jews, in particular—from German society. The records the Nazi bureaucrats compiled were, as the Reich leadership saw it, a documentary history of a glorious enterprise.

Documents entered into evidence at Nuremberg fill 19 thick volumes, supplementing the 23-volume record of the trials themselves. Time and again, U.S. prosecutors shot down the claims of the defense by producing incriminating orders signed by the defendants themselves.

The Nazis in the dock were divided into those who had shown remorse and were even penitent (for instance, Hans Frank, chief overseer of the Polish Holocaust, had recently converted to Catholicism, and Albert Speer, czar of slave labor, was extraordinarily cooperative, especially in bearing witness against his former colleagues); those who, as military officers, claimed that they had only been following orders; and those who, such as Hermann Göring, were simply and utterly defiant.

Because of his former rank in the Nazi Party, Göring was the most challenging of the defendants to try. Although he denied prior knowledge of the death camps, he insisted on upholding the principles on which those camps were built, such as *Lebensraum*, the dream of "living space" spelled out in *Mein Kampf*. Lucid, entertaining, sometimes humorous, but always domineering, Göring displayed a remarkable memory for the details of Nazi history. "I am determined to go down in German history as a great man," he told an Allied psychiatrist. In the dock, he seemed to regard himself as an actor playing the greatest role of his life. Göring's interruptions were so frequent and his assertions so impertinent that, at one point, even the imperturbable Justice Jackson lost his temper, and the trial had to be recessed for several days.

The Nuremberg trials dragged on for month after month. The court had ruled out a *tu quoque* defense. Latin for "you also," this is also known as the "hypocrisy defense," meaning, in the case of the Nuremberg trials, a defense based on the allegation that the Allies committed the same acts as the Germans. The defense attorneys thus had no alternative to challenging the authenticity, sheet by sheet, of the evidentiary documents the prosecution had collected. The prosecution and defense of the 21 defendants took a long time. And then the judges—Soviet, British, and American—devoted a full month to pondering their verdicts.

SUPPORTING ACTORS

Hess provided plenty of dramatic moments. When the British turned him over for trial, he claimed that he suffered from amnesia. In the dock on November 30, 1945, however, he suddenly stood up and declared that his memory had returned. He accepted full responsibility for what he had done as a Nazi. But when he sat down again, he seemed to relapse into his earlier obliviousness.

The Verdicts and the Sentences

At last, on September 30, 1946, the judges delivered their verdicts and sentences.

Three of the defendants, including Franz von Papen, who had been forced to resign as chancellor during the machinations of Hitler's rise to power, were found not guilty.

Seven were found guilty and sentenced to prison terms of various lengths. Hess got life, Speer 20 years, and Dönitz, who had not been involved in the death camps, was sentenced to imprisonment for 10 years.

The remaining 11 defendants were found guilty as charged and were sentenced to death by hanging. Among these, Göring alone managed to avoid the noose. Playing out his macabre role to the end, he resorted to the cyanide capsule he had kept hidden for so long.

Nagging Questions

The phenomenon that was Nazi Germany was so horrific and so far beyond the bounds of ordinary, organized human behavior in the modern era of civilization that it raised many questions, including those that linger still. We have addressed them—and others—in the text of this book. But three of the most consequential and most persistent questions call for more concentrated discussion:

- ✪ Were the Nuremberg trials legally valid?
- ✪ What brought about Nazi Germany's defeat?
- ✪ How and why did Hitler and the Nazis rise to power in the first place?

The Justice of Nuremberg

"History," Winston Churchill observed, "is written by the victors." Can the equivalent—"Justice is decided by the victors"—be said? The Nuremberg prosecutor and his assistants as well as the judges were from the three victorious Allied nations: Great Britain, the Soviet Union, and the United States. The independence of the judges and the objectivity of their justice was—and doubtless among some, continues to be—subject to some doubt.

Like many issues of law, the question of independence and objectivity is not strictly philosophical. Often, the law itself addresses these issues. In the case of the fairness and authority of the Nuremberg tribunal, the Charter of the League of Nations, an organization Germany had joined, called for and authorized international sanctions against aggressors. Of course, effectively, the League of Nations was defunct by World War II. Moreover, Germany withdrew from the league in 1933, the Soviet Union was ejected from it on December 14, 1939, for its invasion of Finland, and the United States had never been a member. Still, there were other international agreements outside of the League of Nations that can be reasonably cited as the basis for the Nuremberg tribunal.

In 1925, at Locarno in Switzerland, the European powers signed a number of treaties pertaining to international relations and international law—including one in which Germany guaranteed the borders of Belgium and France unconditionally. At Locarno, by its own volition and not under compulsion by the Treaty of Versailles, Germany accepted its own borders, both east and west, and renounced unilateral military action even in the east. Three years later, in 1928, at Paris, French foreign minister Aristide Briand and the American secretary of state Frank B. Kellogg negotiated a treaty that condemned recourse to war as a solution to international problems. The document was signed by 65 nations, including Germany. In 1929, a new version of the Geneva Convention, which Germany signed, mandated the humane treatment of prisoners of war. There was reasonable legal basis for arguing that the Jews and others who died in the extermination camps were prisoners of war.

Despite this body of legal precedent, Senator Robert A. Taft, a conservative Ohio Republican, condemned the Nuremberg trials as a kangaroo court that handed down *ex post facto* verdicts. Considering the source, this criticism carried considerable weight. The judgment of history as it currently stands, however, leans toward the greater weight of legal precedent for the verdicts. Most historians consider the Nuremberg trials far better than simply instance of victors' justice.

Germany's Defeat

Yet why did Germany fail to emerge victorious? What, precisely, caused Germany not only to lose the war, but to lose it so decisively? For the defeat was much worse than it had been in World War I. After all, on the Western Front, the earlier war had been fought mostly on French territory. Though among the victors, it was France, not Germany, that had a landscape of ruins to show for its experience of 1914-1918. In 1945, it was much of Germany that was in ruins. Why so great a defeat? It is obvious and easy to pin the blame on Hitler's tactical mistakes:

- ⊙ The Soviet campaign was full of Hitler's bungling. Much to the anguish of his generals, Hitler diverted forces from Moscow to Stalingrad, a city which had less value to the Soviets than their capital. By taking Stalingrad, Hitler stretched Germany's supply lines to the breaking point.

- ⊙ Hitler allowed—indeed, effectively commanded—his troops to abuse and slaughter local populations, especially the Ukrainians, who, mostly anti-Stalinists, could have been natural allies of Germany against Russia. (As it was, Ukrainian collaboration with Nazi Germany was extensive. Although some 4.5 million Ukrainians joined the Red Army and a quarter-million served in pro-Soviet partisan guerrilla groups, significant numbers of Ukrainians joined pro-Nazi auxiliary police units, volunteered to serve in the German regular army, or joined an all-Ukrainian SS division—the "Galizien.")

- ⊙ Even in the face of inexorable pressure from the Soviets after Stalingrad, Hitler persisted in carrying out the extermination of the Jews, thereby diverting men and resources from the imperiled Eastern Front.

Yet even without these errors, Germany most likely could never have won. No matter what the Germans did, the Soviet Union had two resources against which even a rationally led German army would have eventually crumbled: space and people. Even superb German-built machinery wears out, and in the nearly 1,000 miles from Warsaw to Moscow, German tanks, armored cars, and other mechanized vehicles broke down at unprecedented rates. The farther the remaining units penetrated into the Soviet Union, the more vulnerable they became to guerrilla attacks from the flanks and rear.

And then there were the immutable facts of demographics. The Soviet population was much larger than the German: about 170.6 million in the USSR versus 70.7 million in Germany, Austria, Memeland, and the Sudetenland in 1939. The Soviets suffered tremendous casualties, but they could replace their losses. Soviet troops at Stalingrad came at the Germans in human waves. When they were shot down, more soon followed. Hitler's invasion of the Soviet Union was a classic example of military overextension. Without possibility of resupply and reinforcement, his forces were swallowed up both by massive attack and the vast, hostile landscape. It was Napoleon in 1812 writ even larger in 1941-1943.

Germany's Eastern Front was cataclysmic, but the campaign in the west, which had begun so brilliantly, also deteriorated in a case of overextension. Once France was knocked out of the war, Britain fought a valiant but largely desperate defense. Hitler had relatively little to fear from Britain alone, but when the United States joined the Allied cause, Germany was strategically doomed.

If Hitler and Göring had refrained from conducting massive air raids against Britain, the United States might not have entered the European war (but would have directed its military primarily against Japan, in response to the bombing of Pearl Harbor on December 7, 1941). A European stalemate might have ensued, allowing Germany to hold onto France for decades—barring the development of an effective and sustained French insurgency.

In June 1939, however, President Franklin Roosevelt promised King George VI that if London were ever bombed, the United States would intervene. Hitler could not have known about that conversation, but he did remember quite well the consequences of the U.S. entry into World War I. Long before Pearl Harbor forced American entry into World War II, Hitler ordered his submarine commanders at all costs to avoid attacking vessels carrying Americans. The last thing he wanted was another *Lusitania*. What Hitler did not understand was that the bombing of London and other British cities would have much the same effect as the sinking of the *Lusitania*. Winston Churchill's words of defiance reached American radio sets, and the authoritative baritone of CBS radio correspondent Edward R. Murrow, reporting live from London in the midst of the Blitz, stirred the wrath of the American people against Nazi Germany. For this reason, in the summer of 1941, Congress allowed President Roosevelt to wage what amounted to an undeclared naval war against Germany in the Atlantic.

Hitler, in the meantime, widened the air assault on England in an overextension of German power virtually guaranteed to bring America in. Hitler's first mistake was turning from the initial objective of the air campaign, the destruction of the RAF, to the terrorizing of civilian Britain. Once the war became a matter of personal vengeance, directed at killing civilians instead of killing the enemy military, Hitler lost the strategic initiative. Reaching beyond military objectives always risks over-stretching one's resources. Nations, after all, are bigger than armies.

The Rise of Nazi Germany

On the surface, at least, Nazi Germany remains difficult to explain. Yet while the rise of Nazism strikes us as unprecedented, bits and pieces of it have existed in other countries and other times.

Many countries—in recent times, the Soviet Union and Communist China are the most obvious examples—have endured government by cult of personality—Joseph Stalin and Mao Zedong, in the case of the Soviets and the Chinese. Other nations have succumbed to virulent, irrational racism. Think of Apartheid-era South Africa or the American South in the era of slavery (and for many years afterward). Anti-Semitism has existed elsewhere. The Middle Ages in Europe saw many acts of anti-Semitism, and the Renaissance was no better. In 1492, the year Columbus sailed for King Ferdinand and Queen Isabella, those monarchs expelled the Jews from Spain and started the Spanish Inquisition. From 1821 through the early twentieth century, anti-Jewish pogroms were common occurrences in Czarist Russia. Persecutions targeting other groups have also been common. From 1914 to 1923 the Ottoman Empire deported, starved, or slaughtered perhaps 1.5 million ethnic Armenians. In December 1937, the Japanese perpetrated what the Chinese to this day call the "Rape of Nanjing."

Other countries have also had—and some have still—their extreme political elements, replete with flags, banners, symbols, mystical ideologies, and a credo of violence. Other countries commit and have committed unprovoked acts of aggression: Japan, Iraq, the Soviet Union, and some would point to the actions of the United States in Vietnam.

Elements of the terror go on and on, but all of the disparate pieces of government by atrocity came together in *Nazi Germany*. Why?

Let us review Germany's circumstances following World War I. The nation was defeated—but most defeated countries do not respond by spawning aggressive extremist governments. In the case of Germany, the terms of peace were dictated by vengeful and aggrieved victors. The Treaty of Versailles, forced upon Germany, was relentlessly punitive. The defeated nation was like a wounded animal—injured, even partially dismembered, but still capable of attack. It is also true that other countries have been treated unfairly, ripped up, moved around, and distorted geographically, all without turning into Nazi-like war machines.

Other countries also have experienced the hyperinflation that devastated Germany in the early 1920s. France, Greece, Hungary, Poland, the Philippines are just a few of the nations that have undergone hyperinflation—and none of them responded by sprouting a Nazi-like movement or regime.

The Great Depression hit Germany hard, no question about it. But it also afflicted the rest of industrialized Europe and North America. In the Depression years the United States witnessed right-wing protest movements, such as that spearheaded by Huey Long of Louisiana. The heavily Roman Catholic population of Montreal flirted with Mussolini-like fascism. Yet, in the end, both the United States and Canada remained democratic. In neither place was there ever a serious possibility of extremist revolution.

Then, too, there was the matter of Hitler's dramatics. People spoke of Hitler's "hypnotic" powers of persuasion, as if they were supernatural. No question, Hitler was a good actor. He was an avid student of the Viennese theater—at least when he could scrape together the price of a cheap seat—and he practiced facial expressions and hand gestures in front of a mirror. In 1925, his personal photographer, Heinrich Hoffmann, created a series of photographs of Hitler orating and emoting. The Führer-to-be studied himself and chose the gestures and mannerisms that struck him as effective, while rejecting those even he thought "silly." He rehearsed. It was a matter of showmanship, not witchcraft. Indeed, Nazi rallies in Nuremberg and elsewhere were marvels of stagecraft. But talented politicians around the world have often taken pains to put on a good show. In 1907, Teddy Roosevelt sent the Great White Fleet around the world and it returned to coastal Virginia exactly one week before the end of his presidency. In politics as in the theater, timing is everything. Yet TR hardly overthrew the government of the United States as Hitler overthrew that of Germany.

So, we are still left to determine precisely what it was about the time and the place and the culture that gave rise to the phenomenon known as Nazi Germany. Perhaps the ancient Greeks, at the recorded beginnings of Western Civilization, had the answer. The dramas of the Greek tragedians, most notably those of Sophocles (497/496-406/405 B.C.), embody an element of character called *hubris,* unthinking pride, the pride that goes before a fall. Students of Greek tragedy call *hubris* the "fatal flaw."

The Fatal Flaw

Hubris is overweening pride, arrogance, and insolence. Hubris is found in the person who lives by his or her own rules in defiance of the prevailing mores and laws of a nation or a society or of what may be considered humanity itself. Hubris is a narcissistic belief in yourself and yourself alone. It is an overweening confidence that you are in control of your destiny—a delusion for which the gods of Greece mocked men. Most of all, hubris is the conviction that you can remake the world in your own image. *Hubris* is the fatal flaw.

There are mental diseases in which something like hubris dominates thought and behavior. Colloquially, we speak of megalomania. Psychiatrists diagnose narcissistic personality disorder (NPD), which is characterized by exaggerated feelings of self-importance, a craving for admiration, and an absence of empathy. Many people have believed that Adolf Hitler was "insane" or "crazy" or just plain "nuts." Modern psychologists and psychiatrists believe that NPD afflicts 1 percent of the general population. This makes it neither a very common nor a very rare disorder.

Perhaps Hitler was mentally ill. If so, he lived in a national culture that contained elements conducive to the development of NPD or, at least, a culture capable of reinforcing the expression of that disorder.

Hitler's musical idol, Richard Wagner, was absolutely convinced that his innovative approach to opera—opera as immersive "music drama"—would render obsolete all other forms not just of opera, but of art itself. Wagner not only wrote the scores for his operas, he also wrote the librettos (the scripts). They were huge works of tremendous intensity, scaling the heights of passion, the depths of pessimism, the uncontrollable drive of sensual fervor, and the tormented desire for fulfillment and redemption. He truly created his own worlds, built on Germanic mythology.

Richard Wagner was very specifically a *German* composer and dramatist. He regarded Germany as having fallen from a golden age, and he was determined to regain that greatness for his country and his people. He regarded himself and his work as instruments of national redemption. It was by no accident that Wagner drew his themes from German folklore. He exalted the German people, the *Volk*. And it followed from this exaltation that the enemy was the Jew.

"The Jew," Wagner wrote, "speaks the language of the nation in whose midst he dwells from generation to generation, but he speaks it always as an alien. … Judaism is the evil conscience of our modern civilization." For Wagner, the Jewish people were the villainous agents of Germany's decline. For him, it followed that Germany could find its redemption only by eliminating the Jewish people.

None of this is to say that Wagner caused Hitler. Rather, in a remarkable way, Wagner foretold the tragic story of Nazi Germany. It was not a tale that Wagner made up. He mined it from elements long present in German history, mythology, and culture. It made for great art—and also for potentially horrific politics, social policy, law, and national self-identity.

MODERN DAY PARALLELS

The history of drama and literature is full of the working out of the fatal flaw. The Greek tragedies revolved around the theme. So did much of Shakespeare. Macbeth's belief that he could murder the king and get away with it led to his own death; King Lear's refusal to heed the wisdom of his daughter Cordelia produced his ruin. Leo Tolstoy's Anna Karenina's defiance of the rules of society turned into her suicide. Gustave Flaubert's Emma Bovary suffered a similar fate. So did the Don Juan, or Don Giovanni, of legend. An extreme excess of self-assurance leads to doom.

Nationalism in Response to a Sense of Inferiority

Let us assume that 1 percent of the human population is indeed afflicted with NPD. It does not follow that this 1 percent inevitably become dictatorial leaders of cults of personality that visit catastrophe upon the world—even if elements of their cultural milieu nurture their delusions.

In the culture and politics of post-World War I Germany, there was another crucial ingredient. It was the counterpoint to hubris, namely a sense of collective national inferiority.

Let's review some German history. Let's go back to what Wagner himself might have considered the golden age of Germany.

On Christmas Day in the year 800, Pope Leo III placed the crown of the Roman Empire on the head of Karl, King of the Franks. We know him better as Charlemagne, but the Germans claimed him as their own, Karl der Grosse, Karl the Great. His coronation, symbolizing the union of the Roman and the Teuton, marked the creation of the Holy Roman Empire. Charlemagne initiated a golden age with conquests that ranged from the border of Spain down past Rome, into Moravia and Croatia, and over to Danzig. During the Middle Ages, the Holy Roman Empire degenerated from the era of Charlemagne to a time in which it could be described as the French philosopher Voltaire characterized it in his 1756 *Essay on Universal History, the Manners, and Spirit of Nations*, as "neither holy, nor Roman, nor an empire." Pass through the end of the Middle Ages, through the Renaissance, and into the Enlightenment. By the eighteenth century, Prussia—German remnant of the Holy Roman Empire—had become a poor country cousin of the great powers of Europe. A sense of national inferiority was created that carried into the nineteenth century, to be addressed at long last by Otto von Bismarck. He led the creation of a genuine German Empire; in the process, however, not so much winning the universal admiration of Europe as instilling fear into it—fear of a Germany unstoppable in its hunger for greater empire. The Europe Bismarck created was a complex web of treaty obligations, some public, some secret, and all fueled by mutual suspicion and distrust. The Europe of Bismarck was a hemisphere on a hair trigger, and all it took was an assassination in an obscure corner of the Balkans to start a European war that expanded into a world war.

Contrary to the Treaty of Versailles, Kaiser Wilhelm II was not the sole aggressor in World War I. But his unthinking lockstep loyalty to the irrational aggression of Austria-Hungary, allowing the Viennese tail to wag the Berliner dog, made the all-engulfing war inevitable. In his hopeful belief that he could keep Austria's conflict with Serbia localized in the Balkans, Kaiser Wilhelm II made himself, his nation, Europe, and part of the world (including the United States) the victim of his own delusion.

In the end, overextended, Germany lost World War I. Add to this obvious fact a less obvious point: It was *Germany* that lost. It was a nation with intense feelings of inferiority that had recently clawed its way back to a vaunted golden age through a combination of mythology, art, music, politics, warfare, and Bismarck's diplomacy—only to be cast down again by the humiliating terms of the Treaty of Versailles. Punishing Germany, proud Germany, humiliated Germany, and then forcing it to confess itself exclusively guilty of starting the war, this was, as Britain's Prime Minister David Lloyd George feared, a peace settlement that practically guaranteed another war.

Hitler's Promise of Redemption

It is important to recognize that Adolf Hitler made little political headway during the 1920s. What propelled him to power was the economic collapse brought by the Great Depression. To be sure, other countries suffered terribly from the economic collapse as well. But in Germany, the mixture of pride, grievance, and privation was potentially explosive. And Hitler possessed the matches to light the fuse.

He promised what Bismarck had promised—and delivered. He promised redemption in the form of a return to greatness. In fact, he promised far more than a return. The golden age was a fine thing. The German Empire of Wilhelm II was feared and respected. But these were in the past. What Hitler promised was *the future*—a future greater than gold and greater than anything Bismarck's diplomacy had accomplished. It was a future that would last a thousand years. And it was a future that Germany would own all to itself.

Redemption would be greater than all that had come before. It was Adolf Hitler's sublime Wagnerian theme. As in one of the master's operas, it would be total national and racial redemption.

Hitler was a highly effective orator, no doubt. He was a skilled politician, too. But he was also gifted with an extraordinarily receptive audience, a nation hungry for redemption. The hunger overcame doubt, and the German people conceived a great faith that the Führer could and should slay *all* the dragons—the Czechs and the Poles, who had deprived the ethnic Germans within their borders of their rights; the Allies who had imposed on Germany the horrible Treaty of Versailles (and this meant especially the French); the Communists, who had stood in the way of Hitler's rise; and the Jews, who had stood in the way of the resurgence of Germany itself. Hitler saw this as clearly as Wagner had seen it.

The Lack of Resources in Spite of the Pride

The people's intense hunger for redemption created a collective hubris, an overwhelming confidence in their ability to achieve redemption. Hubris is a fatal flaw. For a flaw to become a fissure, pressure must be applied. That pressure came in the form of reality itself. Ultimately, Nazi Germany lacked the resources to pull it all off. Redemption without limits, it turned out, required more than Germany had.

This is why Albert Speer was compelled to use slave labor in his arms factories. This is why Erwin Rommel's campaign collapsed in North Africa. This is why Germany lost—really, lost the war—at Stalingrad. This is why Hitler could not fend off Eisenhower's invasion on the beaches of Normandy. The reach of Nazi Germany exceeded its grasp—fatally.

The Jewish Holocaust Proves Aryan Superiority a Myth

And, in the end, there was the Holocaust—in many ways, the Nazis' supreme war aim. It is a tragedy all but incomprehensible. Far from being the enemies of the German nation, the Jews had contributed vitally to the economic and cultural life of the nation and its people. That they had done so, however, was a historical fact Hitler could not make fit into his guiding mythology. In their very successes, the Jews proved that the idea of Aryan racial superiority was without basis in reality. The presence of Jews in a Nazi Germany proclaimed Nazi Germany a fraud. That the Jews spoiled the Nazi delusion marked them for destruction.

The Least You Need to Know

- The Nuremberg Trials pronounced the verdicts of the victors upon the vanquished. But, in the end, the proceedings were genuine trials, an attempt to do justice based on evidence. The trials were the work of nations built on laws not the prejudices of men. The trials were intended to show future generations what fate would await those who ever attempted to follow the course laid out by Nazi Germany.

- Contrary to what some people have alleged, the Nuremberg verdicts were not based on *ex post facto* laws. They were founded on established legal, diplomatic, and moral precedent.

- Through its *hubris*, its overweening arrogance, Germany, once a great country, under the Nazis collapsed in ruin. As it did so, it took six million of the Jewish people down with it, committing the crime of the centuries.

Chronology

The following list gives important dates that define the context of the rise and fall of Nazi Germany.

1870–1871	Franco–Prussian War; victory over France brings the unification of Germany and founding of German Empire engineered by Otto von Bismarck.
1890	Dismissal of Bismarck by Kaiser Wilhelm II.
1914	Assassination of Franz Ferdinand, Archduke of the Austro–Hungarian Empire (June 28).
1914	Outbreak of World War I (July 28–August 4).
1918	Armistice (November 11); first phase (October 29-November 9) of the German Revolution of 1918-1919.
1919	Treaty of Versailles signed (June 28, 1919); second phase (November 3, 1918-August 11, 1919) of the German Revolution of 1918-1919.
1923	French occupation of the Ruhr; peak of the German hyperinflation and final stabilization of the German currency.
1929	Beginning of worldwide Great Depression; global unemployment hits Germany very hard.
1932	Nazi electoral victories.
1933	Hitler becomes chancellor of Germany.
1935	Remilitarization of Germany commences.
1936	German reoccupation of the Rhineland.
1938	*Anschluss:* German annexation of Austria.
1938	Munich agreement signed (September 30); German annexation of the Sudetenland (German-speaking parts of Czechoslovakia) and other concessions to Hitler.
1939	Seizure and occupation of the rest of Czechoslovakia (March); Nazi–Soviet Pact (August 23); invasion of Poland (September 1).

1940	Conquest of Denmark, Norway, Luxembourg, Belgium, Holland, and France.
1941	Invasion of the Soviet Union (Operation Barbarossa, June 22-December 5).
1943	Defeat at Stalingrad (January 31).
1944	Landing of Allied troops on the Normandy coast (D-Day, June 6)
1945	Collapse of Germany and Hitler's death (April 30).
1945	German surrender (V-E Day, May 7-8)

Additional Reading

I hope I've whetted your appetite for more. The following titles are informative and worth your time.

Brecher, Elinor J. *Schindler's Legacy: True Stories of the List Survivors*. New York: Plume, 1994.
Stories of persons featured in the movie *Schindler's List*.

Bullock, Alan. *Hitler: A Study in Tyranny*. New York: Harper & Row, 1964.
The first major biography of Hitler in English.

Craig, William. *Enemy at the Gates: The Battle for Stalingrad*. New York: Penguin, 1973.
Probably the best single work on the Battle of Stalingrad.

Dawidowicz, Lucy S. *The War Against the Jews, 1933–1945*. New York: Holt, Rinehart and Winston, 1975.
A powerful year-by-year, country-by-country account of the Holocaust.

Deathridge, John and Carl Dahlhaus. *Wagner*. New York: Norton, 1984.
A biography of the composer, so adored by the Nazis.

Erickson, John. *The Road to Berlin: Stalin's War with Germany*. London: Weidenfeld & Nicolson, 1983.
The story of the Red Army's epic struggle to drive the Germans out of Russia.

———. *The Road to Stalingrad; Stalin's War with Germany*. London: Weidenfeld & Nicolson, 1973.
Covers Hitler's invasion of the Soviet Union.

Frank, Anne. *The Diary of a Young Girl; The Definitive Edition*. Otto H. Frank and Mirjam Pressler, eds. Susan Massotty, trans. New York: Doubleday, 1995.
The classic story of the Holocaust told from the point of view of Anne Frank, a young Jewish girl whose family went into hiding during the Holocaust.

Fritzsche, Peter. *Life and Death in the Third Reich*. Cambridge, MA: Belknap Press, 2008.
The most thoroughly researched picture of day-to-day life in Nazi Germany.

Goldhagen, Daniel Jonah. *Hitler's Willing Executioners: Ordinary Germans and the Holocaust*. New York: Knopf, 1996.
A brilliant and controversial view of the support of the German citizenry for the Holocaust.

Hamann, Brigitte. *Hitler's Vienna: A Dictator's Apprenticeship.* New York: Oxford University Press, 1999.
> A vivid view of Hitler's days in Vienna.

Hamerow, Theodore S. *On the Road to the Wolf's Lair: German Resistance to Hitler.* Cambridge: Harvard University Press, 1997.
> The definitive story of the plot to kill Hitler.

Hitler, Adolf. *Mein Kampf.* Boston: Houghton Mifflin, 1971.
> This comes in lots of editions, but they're all his own words.

Kershaw, Ian. *The End: The Defiance and Destruction of Hitler's Germany, 1944-1945* (New York: Penguin, 2011).
> Addresses the reasons for the stubborn resilience of Nazi Germany in the final act of World War II.

Hitler: A Biography. New York: W. W. Norton, 2010.
> A truly magisterial biography of the dictator.

Hitler, the Germans, and the Final Solution. New Haven, CT: Yale University Press, 2009.
> Explores the role of the German people in the Holocaust.

Large, David Clay. *Where Ghosts Walked: Munich's Road to the Third Reich.* New York: Norton, 1997.
> An excellent biography of the city that gave birth to Nazism.

McKee, Alexander. *Dresden 1945: The Devil's Tinderbox.* New York: Dutton, 1984.
> The best picture of the bombing of Dresden.

Newman, Simon. *March 1939: The British Guarantee to Poland: A Study in the Continuity of British Foreign Policy.* Oxford: Clarendon, 1976.
> A dissent from the usual view of British appeasement of Hitler.

Persico, Joseph E. *Nuremberg: Infamy on Trial.* New York: Viking, 1994.
> The most vivid portrayal of the Nuremberg trials.

Rhodes, Richard. *Masters of Death: The SS Einsatzgruppen and the Invention of the Holocaust.* New York: Knopf, 2002.
> The immediate origins of the Holocaust.

Rosenbaum, Ron. *Explaining Hitler: The Search for the Origins of His Evil.* New York: Random House, 1998.
> A recent and fascinating survey of contending theories about Hitler's character.

Self, Robert, *Neville Chamberlain: A Biography.* London: Routledge, 2017.
> The only full-scale biography of the much-maligned architect of "appeasement."

Shirer, William L. *The Rise and Fall of the Third Reich: A History of Nazi Germany*. New York: Fawcett Crest, 1959.

An early view—massive and worthwhile—of Nazi Germany by a reporter who was there.

Toland, John. *Adolf Hitler*. 2 vols. Garden City: Doubleday, 1976.

Toland was a journalist who became a best-selling historian of the Second World War.

Waite, Robert G. L. *Kaiser and Führer: A Comparative Study of Personality and Politics*. Toronto: University of Toronto Press, 1998.

Despite their backgrounds, as this work shows, Hitler and Wilhelm II were very much alike.

Citations

The sources of the most important quotations are listed in this appendix.

Chapter 1

"Not by speeches … but by blood and iron!": quoted in "Excerpt from Bismarck's 'Blood and Iron Speech'" (1862), http://germanhistorydocs.ghi-dc.org/sub_document. cfm?document_id=250&language=english.

Chapter 2

"If he laughs … enjoyment of any joke …": quoted in Michael Balfour's *The Kaiser and His Times*. London: Cresset, 1969, p. 63.

"Our navy … if God helps us": quoted in Balfour, p. 206.

"What more can I do … holds a dagger …": Louis Snyder's *Basic History of Modern Germany*. Princeton: Van Nostrand, 1957, p. 74.

"… it will be some damn foolish thing …": quoted in William Whitaker, *Some Damn Fool Thing* (Bloomington, IN: iUniverse, 2017), epigraph.

Chapter 3

"It was a beautiful evening … starting a war.": Georg Alexander von Müller, *The Kaiser and His Court*. New York: Harcourt, Brace & World, 1961, p. 7.

The Page–Grey dialogue: John Milton Cooper's *Walter Hines Page*. Chapel Hill: University of North Carolina Press, 1977, p. 314.

Chapter 4

"… home before the leaves have fallen …" Quoted in NPR Staff, "WWI: The Battles That Split Europe, And Families," NPR Books (April 30, 2011), http://www.npr.org/2011/04/30/135803783/wwi-the-battle-that-split-europe-and-families.

"On the first day of February … Texas and Arizona …": quoted in Barbara Tuchman's *The Zimmermann Telegram*. New York: Ballantine, 1959, pp. 201–202.

Chapter 6

"I was a young … clear conscience …": quoted in Adolf Hitler's, *Mein Kampf*. Boston: Houghton Mifflin, 1971, p. 23.

"Now the first shrapnel … outside [the trenches]": quoted in Hitler, p. 159.

"I was eating … was killed": quoted in Hitler, p. 170.

Chapter 9

"The Horst Wessel Song": quoted in Snyder, p. 72.

Chapter 11

"… be prepared … against the wall": quoted in Giles MacDonough, *The Last Kaiser: The Life of Wilhelm II* (New York: St. Martin's, 2000), 452.

Chapter 12

"In one instant … Bayreuth Master knew no bounds": quoted in Frederic Spotts, *Bayreuth: A History of the Wagner Festival* (New Haven, CT: Yale University Press, 1994), 141.

"… helps explain the fantasies … the Nazis harbored": quoted from Peter Fritzsche, *Life and Death in the Third Reich* (Cambridge, MA: Belknap Press, 2008), 4.

Chapter 15

"demonstrations … are not to be hampered": quoted in Anna M. Wittmann, *Talking Conflict: The Loaded Language of Genocide, Political Violence, Terrorism, and Warfare* (Santa Barbara, CA: ABC-CLIO, 2017), 261.

"The bright faithfulness … know any better": quoted in David Irving's *The War Path: Hitler's Germany, 1933–1939*. New York: Viking, 1978, p. 171.

"I wonder if … did like about him": quoted in Irving, p. a73.

Chapter 16

"We are not gathered here today … but *when!*": quoted in Gene Smith, *The Dark Summer* (New York: Collier Books, 1989), 144.

"We in Poland … at any price.": Quoted in Lynne Olson and Stanley Cloud, *A Question of Honor: The Kosciusko Squadron* (New York: Knopf, 2007), 37.

Chapter 17

"Life here is still quite normal …": quoted in William L. Shirer, *Berlin Diary*. New York: Popular Library, 1940, pp. 153–156.

"No one in our class … were mentioned": quoted in Richard Bessel, *Life in the Third Reich*. Oxford: Oxford University Press, 1987, p. 27.

"… that if the Allies planned …": quoted in Simon & Schuster's *Encyclopedia of World War II,* p. 447.

Chapter 18

Einstein's Letter: quoted in Martin J. Sherwin, *A World Destroyed*. New York: Vintage, 1977, pp. 27–28.

Hitler's facial expression: Shirer, *Berlin Diary,* p. 307.

Chapter 19

Scene at Bordeaux airport: quoted in Edward Spears, *Assignment to Catastrophe*. London: Heinemann, 1954, p. 18.

"France has lost a battle! … Vive la France!": quoted in Charles de Gaulle, "The Flame of French Resistance," *The Guardian* (April 29, 2007), https://www.theguardian.com/theguardian/2007/apr/29/greatspeeches1.

Chapter 20

"I vegetated … war wore on": quoted in William Shirer, *The Rise and Fall of the Third Reich*. Greenwich, CT: Fawcett, 1959, p. 889.

"The Nazi blight …": Shirer, *The Rise and Fall of the Third Reich,* p. 890.

Chapter 23

"How can we expect … stirred to action?": quoted in Michael Ruse, *Atheism: What Everyone Needs to Know* (New York: Oxford University Press, 2015), 220.

Chapter 24

The Canadian soldier's recollection: Earl F. Ziemke, *The Soviet Juggernaut*. Alexandria: Time-Life, 1980, p. 126.

The McAuliffe "Nuts!" episode is documented in Kenneth J. McAuliffe Jr., "The story of the NUTS! Reply," from 101st Airborne Division official website (January 11, 2012), accessed at https://www.army.mil/article/92856.

Chapter 25

Wagner's attitude toward the Jews: Albert Goldman and Evert Sprinchorn, eds., and H. Ashton Ellis, trans. *Wagner on Music and Drama*. London: Victor Gollancz, 1977, pp. 51–59.

Adolf Hitler's will is quoted in "The Holocaust Documents," http://www.auschwitz.dk/Will.htm.

Index

C

D

G

H

I

J

Y-Z